EVINRUDE/JOHNSON
OUTBOARD SHOP MANUAL
2 - 40 HP · 1973 - 1986 (Includes Electric Motors)

By
KALTON C. LAHUE

ALAN AHLSTRAND
Editor

JEFF ROBINSON
Publisher

CLYMER PUBLICATIONS
World's largest publisher of books
devoted exclusively to do-it-yourself vehicle maintenance.

12860 MUSCATINE STREET · P.O. BOX 4520 · ARLETA, CALIFORNIA 91333-4520

FIRST EDITION
First Printing December, 1984

SECOND EDITION
*Updated by Kalton C. Lahue to include 1985-1986
models*
First Printing August, 1986
Second Printing January, 1987

Printed in U.S.A.

ISBN: 0-89287-404-X

Production Coordinator, Janet Long

*Tools shown in Chapter Two courtesy of Thorsen Tool, Dallas, TX. Test equipment shown in Chapter Two courtesy
of Dixson, Inc., Grand Junction, CO.*

COVER: Photographed by Michael Brown Photographic Productions, Los Angeles, CA. Assisted by Bill Masho.

•Boat courtesy of Dave Lawless. Driver—Dubie.
*•Photo boat courtesy of Cypress Gardens, FL and driven
  by Mike Monts de Oca.*
•Special thanks to Jerry Imber for all his assistance.

CONTENTS

Quick Reference Data

TIGHTENING TORQUES

Fastener	in.-lb.	ft.-lb.
Ignition coil screws	60-80	
Power pack screw	48-60	
Starter motor through bolts		
9.9 and 15 hp	30-40	
18-35 hp	60-84	
40 hp		50
Standard bolts and nuts		
No. 6	7-10	
No. 8	15-22	
No. 10	25-35	
No. 12	35-40	
1/4 in.		5-7
5/16 in.		10-12
3/8 in.		18-20
7/16 in.		28-30

TEST WHEEL RECOMMENDATIONS

Model	Year	Test wheel	Shaft dia. (in.)	Engine rpm
2	1973-on	316021	7/16	3,900
4 Weedless	1973	316021	7/16	3,800
4 Standard	1973	316960	1/2	4,100
4 Standard	1973-on	317738	11/16	4,550
4 Deluxe	all	390123	*	5,100
4.5	all	390123	*	5,100
5	all	390239	1/2	4,900
6	1973-1975	380757	9/16	4,000
6	1976-1979	379673	9/16	4,500
6	1982-on	390239	1/2	4,900
7.5	1980-1983	390239	1/2	4,900
8	1984-on	390239	1/2	4,900
9.5	1973	379673	9/16	4,400
9.9	1974-1984	386537	*	5,400
9.9	1985-on	386537	*	5,500
15	1974-on	386537	*	6,200
20	1973	376913	5/8	4,650
20	1980-1984	388880	*	4,650
20	1985-on	386891	*	4,550
25	1973-1976	376913	5/8	4,900
25	1977	388295	*	4,650
25	1978-1984	388880	*	5,200
25	1985-on	394145	*	4,800
30	1984	386891	*	5,300
30	1985-on	394145	*	5,400
35	1976-1984	386891	*	5,300
40	1973-1976	378566	*	4,500
40 Electric	1985-on	387635	*	4,900
40 Manual	1985-on	382861	*	5,200

* Information not available.

APPROXIMATE STATE OF CHARGE

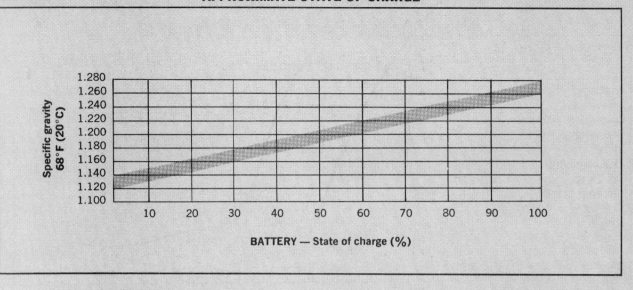

RECOMMENDED SPARK PLUGS

Model	hp/cyl.	Champion plug type	Gap (in.)
2	2/1	J6C	0.030
4 (1973-1976)	4/2	J6C	0.030
4 (1977-1980)	4/2	L77J4	0.040
4 (1981)	4/2	L7J	0.030
4 (1982-on)	4/2	L86	0.040
4 deluxe	4/2	QL77J4 *	0.040
4.5	4.5/2	QL77J4 *	0.040
5	5/2	QL77J4 *	0.040
6 (1973-1976	6/2	J6C	0.030
6 (1977-on)	6/2	QL77J4 *	0.040
7.5	7.5/2	QL77J4	0.040
8	8/2	QL77J4	0.040
9.5	9.5/2	J6C	0.030
9.9 (1974-1976)	9.9/2	UL81J	0.030
9.9 (1977-on)	9.9/2	QL77J4 *	0.040
15 (1974-1976)	15/2	UL81J	0.030
15 (1977-on)	15/2	QL77J4 *	0.040
18	18/2	UJ4J	0.030
20 (1973)	20/2	UJ4J	0.030
20 (1981-1982)	20/2	QL77J4	0.040
20 (1985-on)	20/2	QL77J4 *	0.040
25 (1973-1974)	25/2	UJ4J	0.030
25 (1975-1976)	25/2	J6C	0.030
25 (1977-on)	25/2	QL77J4 *	0.040
30	30/2	QL77J4 *	0.040
35 (1975-1976)	35/2	UL81J	0.030
35 (1977-1984)	35/2	QL77J4	0.040
40 (1973)	40/2	J6C	0.030
40 (1974)	40/2	UJ4J	0.030
40 (1975-1976)	40/2	UL81J	0.030
40 (1985-on)	40/2	QL77J4 *	0.040

* For sustained high speed operation, Champion QL78V or L78V (non-adjustable gap) is recommended for 1985 and later models.

GEARCASE CLEARANCE SPECIFICATIONS

Bearing housing bushing to drive shaft	
6 hp	
1973	0.0015-0.0030 in.
1974-1979	0.0015-0.0025 in.
Drive shaft and bushing in gear case	
2 hp	0.0010-0.0028 in.
4 hp weedless	0.001-0.003 in.
Front gear to gearcase bushing	
6 hp (1973-1979)	0.0010-0.0022 in.
Gearcase bushing to propeller shaft	
2 hp	0.0007-0.0022 in.
4 hp (1973-1980)	0.0005-0.0020 in.
Gearcase head and propeller shaft	
2 hp	0.0007-0.0022 in.
6 hp (1973-1979)	0.0010-0.0020 in.
Gear head and bushing assembly	
4 hp	
1973	0.0005-0.0020 in.
1974-1980	0.0007-0.0022 in.
4 hp weedless	0.0005-0.0015 in.
Pinion and bushing in gearcase	
4 hp (1973-1980)	0.0005-0.0018 in.
Propeller on shaft	
2 hp	
1973	0.0022-0.0057 in.
1974-on	0.0022-0.0067 in.
4 hp	0.0030-0.0055 in.
4 hp weedless	
1973	0.0020-0.0063 in.
1974-on	0.0020-0.0053 in.
6 hp (1973-1979)	0.007-0.009 in.
Propeller shaft in front gear bushing	
6 hp (1973-1979)	0.0005-0.0015 in.
9.9 and 15 hp	0.0002-0.0087 in.
20-40 hp	0.0010-0.0020 in.
Propeller shaft to reverse gear bushing	
6 hp (1973-1979)	0.0005-0.0015 in.
20-40 hp	0.0005-0.0015 in.
Rear reverse gear bushing	
6 hp	
1973	0.0005-0.0020 in.
1974-1979	0.0005-0.0025 in.
20-40 hp	0.0005-0.0020 in.

CARBURETOR ALTITUDE ORIFICE CHART

1973-1979

Model/Year	Sea level	3,000 to 6,000 ft.	6,000 to 10,000 ft.
4/1973-1977	Adj.	Adj.	Adj.
4/1978 Std. length	0.031	0.029	0.027
4/1978 Long shaft	0.029	0.027	0.025
4/1979	0.031	0.029	0.027
6/1973-1975	44	42D	39D
6/1976	52D	49D	45D
6/1977-1979	42D	39D	38D
9.5/1973	49	45D	43D
9.9/1974-1975	51N	49N	46N
9.9/1976	40N	38N	36N
9.9/1977-1978	38N	36N	34N
9.9/1979	40N	38N	36N
15/1974	60N	58N	56N
15/1975-1976	58N	56N	54N
15/1977-1979	54N	52N	50N
25/1973-1976	72	69D	67D
25/1977	55D	54D	52D
25/1978-1979	49D	45D	45D
35/1976-1979	59D	53D	47D
40/1973-1976	670	64D	63D

1980-1982

Model/Year	Sea level		3,000-6,000 ft.		6,000-10,000 ft.	
	Low Speed	High Speed	Low Speed	High Speed	Low Speed	High Speed
4/All	Adj.	0.031*	Adj.	0.029*	Adj.	0.027*
4.5/All	Adj.	0.033*	Adj.	0.030*	Adj.	0.027*
7.5/All	Adj.	35N	Adj.	32N	Adj.	29N
9.9/All	Adj.	38N	Adj.	36N	Adj.	34N
15/1980	Adj.	54N	Adj.	51N	Adj.	48N
15/1981-1982	Adj.	56N	Adj.	53N	Adj.	50N
20/All	Adj.	49D	Adj.	43D	Adj.	37D
25/1980	Adj.	49D	Adj.	43D	Adj.	37D
25/1981-1982	Adj.	59D	Adj.	53D	Adj.	47D
35/All	Adj.	59D	Adj.	53D	Adj.	47D

* Idle style.

EVINRUDE/JOHNSON
OUTBOARD SHOP MANUAL
2 - 40 HP · 1973 - 1986 (Includes Electric Motors)

INTRODUCTION

This Clymer shop manual covers service and repair of all Evinrude/Johnson 2-40 hp outboard models from 1973-1986. Step by step instructions and hundreds of illustrations guide you through jobs ranging from simple maintenance to complete overhaul.

This manual is written for use with engines designed and used for recreational purposes only. Racing and commercial engines are not included

Chapters One through Eleven contain general information on all models and specific information on 1973-1984 models. The supplement at the end of the book contains specific information on 1985-1986 models which differs from that in the main book.

This manual can be used by anyone from a first time owner/amateur to a professional mechanic. Easy to read type, detailed drawings and clear photographs give you all the information you need to do the work right.

Having a well-maintained engine will increase your enjoyment of your boat as well as assure your safety offshore. Keep this shop manual handy and use it often. It can save you hundreds of dollars in maintenance and repair bills and make yours a reliable, top-performing boat.

Chapter One

General Information

This detailed, comprehensive manual contains complete information on maintenance, tune-up, repair and overhaul. Hundreds of photos and drawings guide you through every step.

Troubleshooting, tune-up, maintenance and repair are not difficult if you know what tools and equipment to use and what to do. Anyone not afraid to get their hands dirty, of average intelligence and with some mechanical ability can perform most of the procedures in this book. See Chapter Two for more information on tools and techniques.

A shop manual is a reference. You want to be able to find information fast. Clymer books are designed with you in mind. All chapters are thumb tabbed. Important items are indexed at the end of the book. All procedures, tables, photos, etc., in this manual assume that the reader may be working on the machine or using this manual for the first time.

Keep this book handy in your tool box. It will help you to better understand how your machine runs, lower repair and maintenance costs and generally increase your enjoyment of your marine equipment.

MANUAL ORGANIZATION

This chapter provides general information useful to marine owners and mechanics.

Chapter Two discusses the tools and techniques for preventive maintenance, troubleshooting and repair.

Chapter Three describes typical equipment problems and provides logical troubleshooting procedures.

Following chapters describe specific systems, providing disassembly, repair, assembly and adjustment procedures in simple step-by-step form. Specifications concerning a specific system are included at the end of the appropriate chapter.

NOTES, CAUTIONS AND WARNINGS

The terms NOTE, CAUTION and WARNING have specific meanings in this manual. A NOTE provides additional information to make a step or procedure easier or clearer. Disregarding a NOTE could cause inconvenience, but would not cause damage or personal injury.

A CAUTION emphasizes areas where equipment damage could result. Disregarding a CAUTION could cause permanent mechanical damage; however, personal injury is unlikely.

A WARNING emphasizes areas where personal injury or even death could result from negligence. Mechanical damage may also occur. WARNINGS *are to be taken seriously*. In some cases, serious injury or death has resulted from disregarding similar warnings.

TORQUE SPECIFICATIONS

Torque specifications throughout this manual are given in foot-pounds (ft.-lb.) and either Newton meters (N•m) or meter-kilograms (mkg). Newton meters are being adopted in place of meter-kilograms in accordance with the International Modernized Metric System. Existing torque wrenches calibrated in meter-kilograms can be used by performing a simple conversion: move the decimal point one place to the right. For example, 4.7 mkg = 47 N•m. This conversion is accurate enough for mechanics' use even though the exact mathematical conversion is 3.5 mkg = 34.3 N•m.

ENGINE OPERATION

All marine engines, whether 2- or 4-stroke, gasoline or diesel, operate on the Otto cycle of intake, compression, power and exhaust phases.

4-stroke Cycle

A 4-stroke engine requires 2 crankshaft revolutions (4 strokes of the piston) to complete the Otto cycle. **Figure 1** shows gasoline 4-stroke engine operation. **Figure 2** shows diesel 4-stroke engine operation.

2-stroke Cycle

A 2-stroke engine requires only 1 crankshaft revolution (2 strokes of the piston) to complete the Otto cycle. **Figure 3** shows gasoline 2-stroke engine operation. While diesel 2-strokes exist, they are not commonly used in light marine applications.

FASTENERS

The material and design of the various fasteners used on marine equipment are not arrived at by chance or accident. Fastener design determines the type of tool required to work with the fastener. Fastener material is carefully selected to decrease the possibility of physical failure or corrosion. See *Galvanic Corrosion* in this chapter for more information on marine materials.

Threads

Nuts, bolts and screws are manufactured in a wide range of thread patterns. To join a nut and bolt, the diameter of the bolt and the diameter of the hole in the nut must be the same. It is just as important that the threads on both be properly matched.

The best way to tell if the threads on 2 fasteners are matched is to turn the nut on the bolt (or the bolt into the threaded hole in a piece of equipment) with fingers only. Be sure both pieces are clean. If much force is required, check the thread condition on each fastener. If the thread condition is good but the fasteners jam, the threads are not compatible.

Four important specifications describe every thread:

    a. Diameter.
    b. Threads per inch.
    c. Thread pattern.
    d. Thread direction.

Figure 4 shows the first 2 specifications. Thread pattern is more subtle. Italian and British standards exist, but the most commonly used by marine equipment manufacturers are American standard and

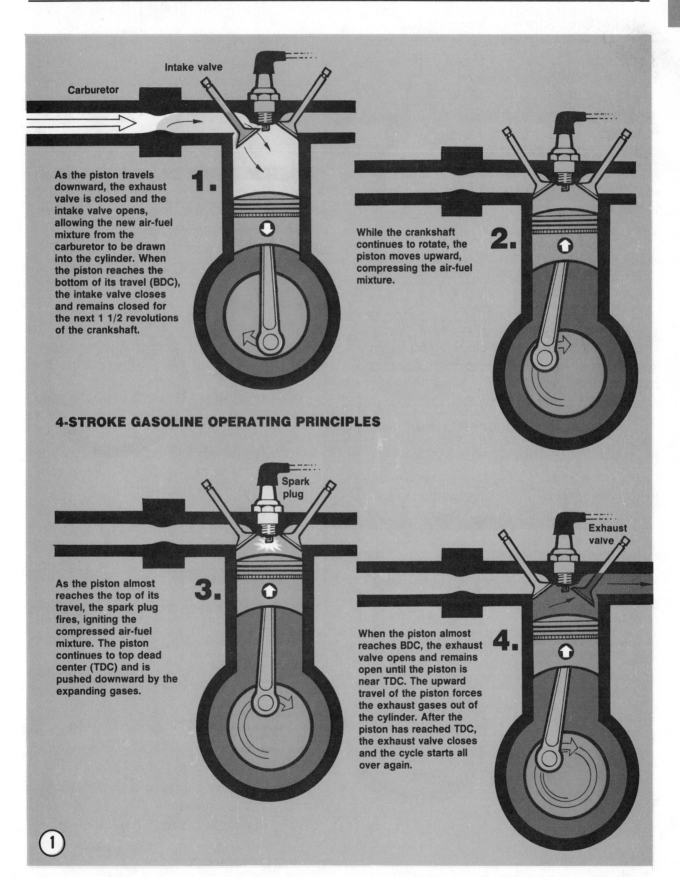

Intake valve

Carburetor

As the piston travels downward, the exhaust valve is closed and the intake valve opens, allowing the new air-fuel mixture from the carburetor to be drawn into the cylinder. When the piston reaches the bottom of its travel (BDC), the intake valve closes and remains closed for the next 1 1/2 revolutions of the crankshaft.

1.

While the crankshaft continues to rotate, the piston moves upward, compressing the air-fuel mixture.

2.

4-STROKE GASOLINE OPERATING PRINCIPLES

Spark plug

As the piston almost reaches the top of its travel, the spark plug fires, igniting the compressed air-fuel mixture. The piston continues to top dead center (TDC) and is pushed downward by the expanding gases.

3.

Exhaust valve

When the piston almost reaches BDC, the exhaust valve opens and remains open until the piston is near TDC. The upward travel of the piston forces the exhaust gases out of the cylinder. After the piston has reached TDC, the exhaust valve closes and the cycle starts all over again.

4.

① 1

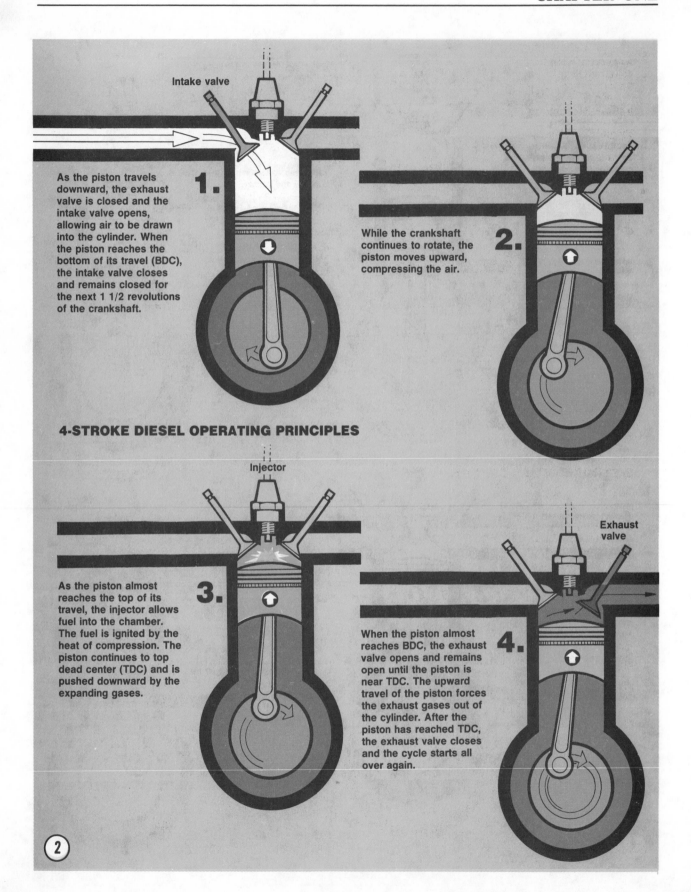

Intake valve

1.

As the piston travels downward, the exhaust valve is closed and the intake valve opens, allowing air to be drawn into the cylinder. When the piston reaches the bottom of its travel (BDC), the intake valve closes and remains closed for the next 1 1/2 revolutions of the crankshaft.

2.

While the crankshaft continues to rotate, the piston moves upward, compressing the air.

4-STROKE DIESEL OPERATING PRINCIPLES

Injector

3.

As the piston almost reaches the top of its travel, the injector allows fuel into the chamber. The fuel is ignited by the heat of compression. The piston continues to top dead center (TDC) and is pushed downward by the expanding gases.

Exhaust valve

4.

When the piston almost reaches BDC, the exhaust valve opens and remains open until the piston is near TDC. The upward travel of the piston forces the exhaust gases out of the cylinder. After the piston has reached TDC, the exhaust valve closes and the cycle starts all over again.

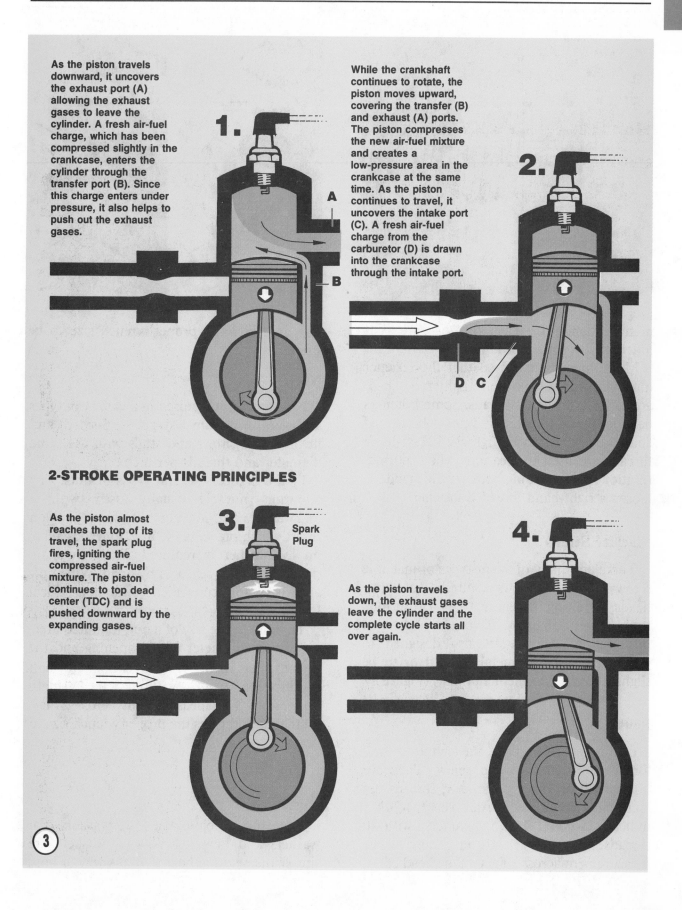

As the piston travels downward, it uncovers the exhaust port (A) allowing the exhaust gases to leave the cylinder. A fresh air-fuel charge, which has been compressed slightly in the crankcase, enters the cylinder through the transfer port (B). Since this charge enters under pressure, it also helps to push out the exhaust gases.

While the crankshaft continues to rotate, the piston moves upward, covering the transfer (B) and exhaust (A) ports. The piston compresses the new air-fuel mixture and creates a low-pressure area in the crankcase at the same time. As the piston continues to travel, it uncovers the intake port (C). A fresh air-fuel charge from the carburetor (D) is drawn into the crankcase through the intake port.

2-STROKE OPERATING PRINCIPLES

As the piston almost reaches the top of its travel, the spark plug fires, igniting the compressed air-fuel mixture. The piston continues to top dead center (TDC) and is pushed downward by the expanding gases.

Spark Plug

As the piston travels down, the exhaust gases leave the cylinder and the complete cycle starts all over again.

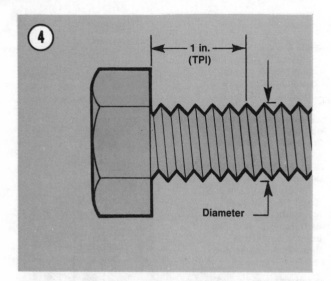

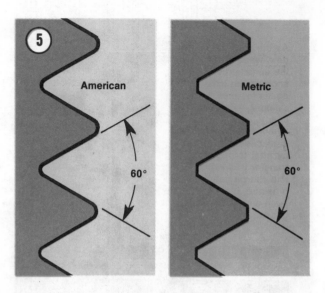

metric standard. The threads are cut differently as shown in **Figure 5**.

Most threads are cut so that the fastener must be turned clockwise to tighten it. These are called right-hand threads. Some fasteners have left-hand threads; they must be turned counterclockwise to be tightened. Left-hand threads are used in locations where normal rotation of the equipment would tend to loosen a right-hand threaded fastener.

Machine Screws

There are many different types of machine screws. **Figure 6** shows a number of screw heads requiring different types of turning tools (see Chapter Two for detailed information). Heads are also designed to protrude above the metal (round) or to be slightly recessed in the metal (flat) (**Figure 7**).

Bolts

Commonly called bolts, the technical name for these fasteners is cap screw. They are normally described by diameter, threads per inch and length. For example, 1/4-20×1 indicates a bolt 1/4 in. in diameter with 20 threads per inch, 1 in. long. The measurement across 2 flats on the head of the

bolt indicates the proper wrench size to be used.

Nuts

Nuts are manufactured in a variety of types and sizes. Most are hexagonal (6-sided) and fit on bolts, screws and studs with the same diameter and threads per inch.

Figure 8 shows several types of nuts. The common nut is usually used with a lockwasher. Self-locking nuts have a nylon insert which prevents the nut from loosening; no lockwasher is required. Wing nuts are designed for fast removal by hand. Wing nuts are used for convenience in non-critical locations.

To indicate the size of a nut, manufacturers specify the diameter of the opening and the threads per inch. This is similar to bolt specification, but without the length dimension. The measurement across 2 flats on the nut indicates the proper wrench size to be used.

Washers

There are 2 basic types of washers: flat washers and lockwashers. Flat washers are simple discs with a hole to fit a screw or bolt.

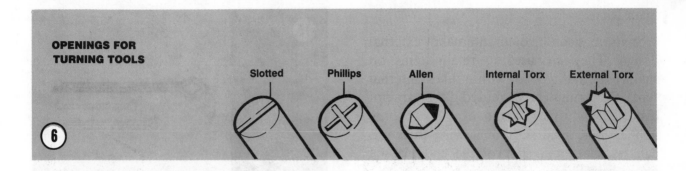

OPENINGS FOR TURNING TOOLS

⑥   Slotted   Phillips   Allen   Internal Torx   External Torx

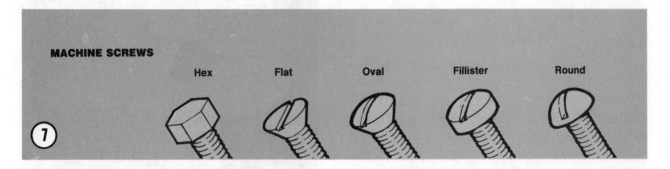

MACHINE SCREWS

⑦   Hex   Flat   Oval   Fillister   Round

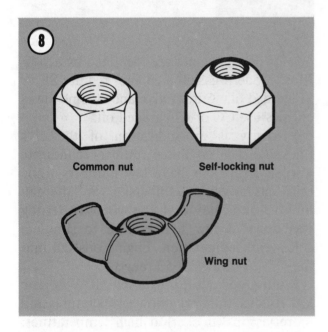

⑧

Common nut   Self-locking nut

Wing nut

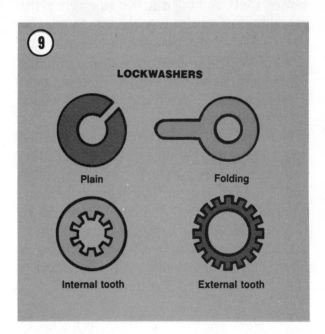

⑨

LOCKWASHERS

Plain   Folding

Internal tooth   External tooth

Lockwashers are designed to prevent a fastener from working loose due to vibration, expansion and contraction. **Figure 9** shows several washers. Note that flat washers are often used between a lockwasher and a fastener to provide a smooth bearing surface. This allows the fastener to be turned easily with a tool.

Cotter Pins

Cotter pins (**Figure 10**) are used to secure special kinds of fasteners. The threaded stud must have a hole in it; the nut or nut lock piece has projections which the cotter pin ends wrap around. Cotter pins should not be reused after removal.

Snap Rings

Snap rings can be of an internal or external design. They are used to retain items on shafts (external type) or within tubes (internal type). Snap rings can be reused if they are not distorted during removal. In some applications, snap rings of varying thickness can be selected to control the end play of parts assemblies.

LUBRICANTS

Periodic lubrication assures long service life for any type of equipment. It is especially important to marine equipment, which is exposed to salt or brackish water and other harsh environments. The *type* of lubricant used is just as important as the lubrication service itself, although in an emergency the wrong type of lubricant is better than none at all. The following paragraphs describe the types of lubricants most often used on marine equipment. Be sure to follow the equipment manufacturer's recommendations for lubricant types.

Generally, all liquid lubricants are called "oil." They may be mineral-based (including petroleum bases), natural-based (vegetable and animal bases), synthetic-based or emulsions (mixtures). "Grease" is an oil to which a thickening base has been added so that the end product is a semi-solid. Grease is often classified by the type of thickener added; lithium soap is commonly used.

4-stroke Engine Oil

Oil for 4-stroke engines is graded by the American Petroleum Institute (API) and the Society of Automotive Engineers (SAE) in several categories. Oil containers display these ratings on the top or label (**Figure 11**).

API oil grade is indicated by letters; oils for gasoline engines are identified by an "S" while

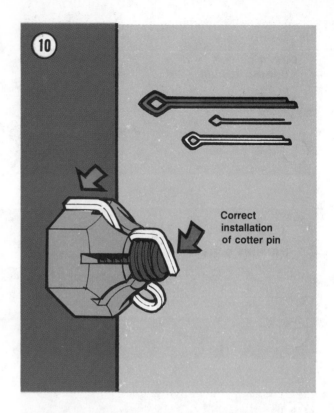

Correct installation of cotter pin

oils for diesel engines are identified by a "C." Most modern gasoline engines require SE or SF graded oil. Automotive and marine diesel engines use CC or CD graded oil.

Viscosity is an indication of the oil's thickness. The SAE uses numbers to indicate viscosity; thin oils have low numbers while thick oils have high numbers. A "W" after the number indicates that the viscosity testing was done at low temperature to simulate cold-weather operation. Engine oils fall into the 5W-20W and 20-50 range.

Multi-grade oils (for example, 10W-40) are less viscous (thinner) at low temperatures and more viscous (thicker) at high temperatures. This allows the oil to perform efficiently across a wide range of engine operating temperatures.

2-stroke Engine Oil

Lubrication for a 2-stroke engine is provided by oil mixed with the incoming

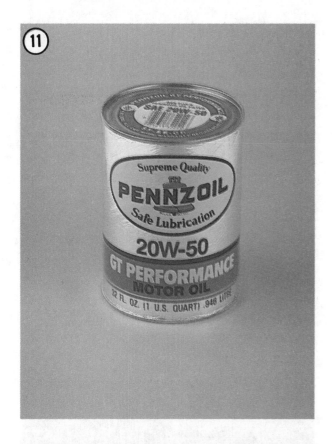

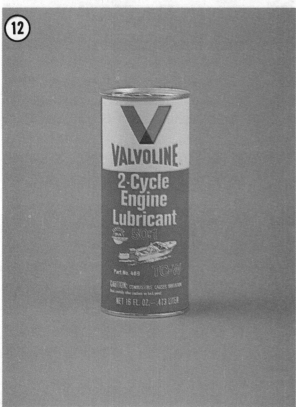

fuel-air mixture. Some of the oil mist settles out in the crankcase, lubricating the crankshaft and lower end of the connecting rods. The rest of the oil enters the combustion chamber to lubricate the piston rings and cylinder walls. This oil is burned during the combustion process.

Engine oil must have several special qualities to work well in a 2-stroke engine. It must mix easily and stay in suspension in gasoline. When burned, it can't leave behind excessive deposits. It must be appropriate for the high temperatures associated with 2-stroke engines.

The National Marine Manufacturer's Association (NMMA) and the Boating Industry Association (BIA) have set standards for oil for use in 2-stroke, water-cooled engines. This is the BIA TC-W (two-cycle, water-cooled) grade (**Figure 12**). The oil's performance in the following areas is evaluated:

    a. Lubrication (prevention of wear and scuffing).
    b. Spark plug fouling.
    c. Preignition.
    d. Piston ring sticking.
    e. Piston varnish.
    f. General engine condition (including deposits).
    g. Exhaust port blockage.
    h. Rust prevention.
    i. Mixing ability with gasoline.

In addition to oil grade, manufacturers specify the ratio of gasoline to oil required during break-in and normal engine operation.

Gear Oil

Gear lubricants are assigned SAE viscosity numbers under the same system as 4-stroke engine oil. Gear lubricant falls into the SAE 72-250 range (**Figure 13**). Some gear lubricants are multi-grade; for example, SAE 85W-90.

Various additives are put into gear oils to tailor them for specific uses; these additive packages are graded by the API and identified by the letters "GL" and a number. GL-4 and GL-5 are the most commonly used.

Grease

Greases are graded by the National Lubricating Grease Institute (NLGI). Greases are graded by number according to the consistency of the grease; these ratings range from No. 000 to No. 6, with No. 6 being the most solid. A typical multipurpose grease is NLGI No. 2 (**Figure 14**). For specific applications, equipment manufacturers may require grease with an additive such as molybdenum disulfide (MOS^2).

GASKET SEALANT

Gasket sealant is used instead of pre-formed gaskets between some engine mating surfaces. Two types of gasket sealant are commonly used: room temperature vulcanizing (RTV) and anaerobic. Since these 2 materials have different sealing properties, they cannot be used interchangeably.

RTV Sealant

This is a black silicone gel supplied in tubes (**Figure 15**). Moisture in the air causes RTV to cure. Always place the cap on the tube as soon as possible when using RTV. RTV has a shelf life of one year and will not cure properly when the shelf life has expired. Check the expiration date on RTV tubes before using and keep partially used tubes tightly sealed.

Applying RTV Sealant

Clean all gasket residue from mating surfaces. Surfaces should be clean and free of oil and dirt. Remove all RTV gasket material

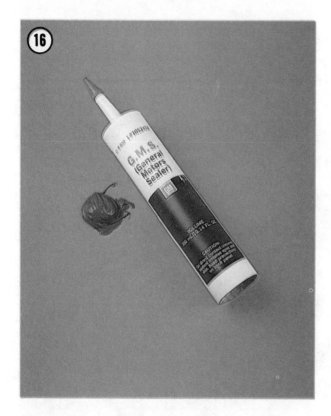

from blind attaching holes, as it can cause a "hydraulic" effect and affect bolt torque.

Apply RTV sealant in a continous bead 2-3 mm (0.08-0.12 in.) thick. Circle all mounting holes unless otherwise specified. Torque mating parts within 10 minutes after application.

Anaerobic Sealant

This is a red gel supplied in tubes (**Figure 16**). It cures only in the absence of air, as when squeezed tightly between 2 machined mating surfaces. For this reason, it will not spoil if the cap is left off the tube. It should not be used if one mating surface is flexible.

Applying Anaerobic Sealant

Clean all gasket residue from mating surfaces. Surfaces must be clean and free of oil and dirt. Remove all gasket material from blind attaching holes, as it can cause a "hydraulic" effect and affect bolt torque.

Apply anaerobic sealant in a 1 mm or less (0.04 in.) bead to one sealing surface. Circle all mounting holes. Torque mating parts within 15 minutes after application.

GALVANIC CORROSION

A chemical reaction occurs whenever 2 different types of metal are joined by an electrical conductor and immersed in an electrolyte. Electrons transfer from one metal to the other through the electrolyte and return through the conductor.

The hardware on a boat is made of many different types of metal. The boat hull acts as a conductor between the metals; even if the hull is wood or fiberglass, the slightest film of water within the hull provides conductivity. Water is an electrolyte. This combination creates a good environment for electron flow (**Figure 17**). Unfortunately, this electron flow results in galvanic corrosion of the metal involved. That is, one of the metals is corroded or eaten away by the process. The amount of electron flow (and therefore the amount of corrosion) depends on several factors:

   a. The types of metal involved.
   b. The efficiency of the conductor.
   c. The strength of the electrolyte.

Metals

The chemical composition of the metals used in marine equipment has a significant effect on the amount and speed of galvanic corrosion. Certain metals are more resistant to corrosion than others. These electrically negative metals are commonly called "noble"; they act as the cathode in any reaction. Metals which are more subject to corrosion are electrically positive; they act as the anode in a reaction. The more noble metals include titanium, 18-8 stainless steel

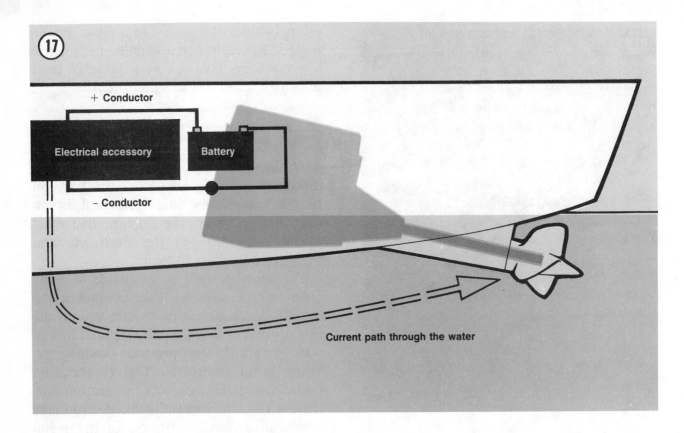

Current path through the water

and nickel. Less noble metals include zinc, aluminum and magnesium. Galvanic corrosion becomes more severe as the difference between the two metals increases.

In some cases, galvanic corrosion can occur within a single piece of metal. Common brass is a mixture of zinc and copper; when immersed in an electrolyte, the zinc portion of the mixture will corrode away as reaction occurs between the zinc and the copper particles.

Conductors

The hull of the boat often acts as the conductor between different types of metal. Marine equipment such as an outboard motor or stern drive unit can also act as the conductor. Large masses of metal, firmly connected together, are more efficient conductors than water. Rubber mountings and vinyl-based paint can act as insulators between pieces of metal.

Electrolyte

The water in which a boat operates acts as the electrolyte for the galvanic corrosion process. The better a conductor the electrolyte is, the more severe and rapid the corrosion.

Cold, clean fresh water is the poorest electrolyte. As water temperature increases, its conductivity increases. Pollutants will increase conductivity; brackish or salt water is also an efficient electrolyte. This is one of the reasons that most manufacturers recommend a fresh-water flush for marine equipment after operation in salt water.

PROTECTION FROM GALVANIC CORROSION

Because of the environment in which marine equipment must operate, it is practically impossible to totally prevent galvanic corrosion. There are several ways by which the process can be slowed; after taking these precautions, the next step is to "fool" the process into occuring only where *you* want it to occur. This is the role of galvanic anodes and impressed current systems.

Slowing Corrosion

Some simple precautions can help to reduce the amount of corrosion taking place outside the hull. These are *not* a substitute for the corrosion protection methods discussed under *Galvanic Anodes* and *Impressed Current Systems* in this chapter, but they can help these protection methods do their job.

Use fasteners of a metal more noble than the part they are fastening. If corrosion occurs, the larger equipment will suffer but the fastener will be protected. Because fasteners are usually very small in comparison to the equipment being fastened, the equipment can survive the loss of material. If the fastener were to corrode instead of the equipment, major problems could arise.

Keep all painted surfaces in good condition. If paint is scraped off and bare metal exposed, corrosion will rapidly increase. Use a vinyl- or plastic-based paint which acts as an electrical insulator.

Be careful when using metal-based anti-fouling paints. These should not be applied to metal parts of the boat or they will actually react with the equipment, causing corrosion between the equipment and the layer of paint. Organic-based paints are available for use on metal surfaces.

Where a corrosion protection device is used, remember that it must be immersed in the electrolyte along with the rest of the boat to have any effect. If you raise the power unit out of the water when the boat is docked, any anodes on the power unit will be removed from the corrosion cycle and will not protect

the rest of the equipment that is still immersed. Also, such corrosion protection devices must not be painted, as that would insulate them from the corrosion process.

Any change in the boat's equipment (such as the installation of a new stainless steel propellor) will change the corrosion process. Keep in mind that when you add new equipment or change materials, you should review your corrosion protection system to be sure it is up to the job.

Galvanic Anodes

Anodes are usually made of zinc, a far from noble metal. They are specially made lumps of metal designed to do nothing but corrode. Properly fastening such pieces to the boat will cause them to act as the anode in *any* galvanic reaction that occurs; any other metal present will act as the cathode and will not be damaged.

Anodes must be used properly to be effective. Simply fastening lumps of zinc to your boat in random locations won't do the job.

You must determine how much zinc surface area is required to adequately protect the equipment's surface area. A good starting point is provided by Military Specification MIL-A-818001, which states that one square inch of new zinc anode will protect either:

    a. 800 square inches of freshly painted steel.

    b. 250 square inches of bare steel or bare aluminum alloy.

    c. 100 square inches of copper or copper alloy.

This rule is for a boat at rest. When underway, more anode area is required to protect the same equipment surface area.

The zinc must be fastened so that it has good electrical contact with the metal to be protected. If possible, the zinc can be attached directly to the other metal. If that is not possible, the entire network of metal parts in the boat should be electrically tied together so that all pieces are protected.

Good quality anodes have inserts of some other metal around the fastener holes. Otherwise, the zinc could erode away around the fastener. The anode can then become loose or even fall off, removing all protection.

Another Military Specification (MIL-A-18001) defines the type of alloy preferred, which will corrode at a uniform rate without forming a crust which could reduce its efficiency after a time.

Impressed Current Systems

An impressed current system can be installed on any boat that has a battery. The system consists of an anode, a control box and a sensor. The anode in this system is coated with a very noble metal (such as platinum) so that it is almost corrosion-free and will last indefinitely. The sensor, under the boat's waterline, monitors the potential for corrosion. When it senses that corrosion could be occuring, it transmits this information to the control box.

The control box connects the boat's battery to the anode. When the sensor signals the need, the control box applies positive battery voltage to the anode. Current from the battery flows from the anode to all other metal parts of the boat, no matter how noble or non-noble these parts are. This battery current takes the place of any galvanic current flow.

Only a very small amount of battery current is needed to counteract galvanic corrosion. Manufacturers estimate that it would take 2 or 3 months of constant use to drain a typical marine battery, assuming the battery is never recharged.

An impressed current system is more expensive to install than simple zinc anodes but, considering its low maintenance

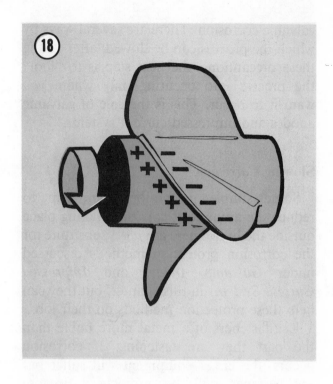

requirements and the excellent protection it provides, the long-term cost may actually be lower.

PROPELLORS

The propellor is the final link between the boat's drive system and the water. A perfectly maintained engine and hull are useless if the propellor is the wrong type or has been allowed to deteriorate. Although propellor selection for a specific situation is beyond the scope of this book, the following information on propellor construction and design will allow you to discuss the subject intelligently with your marine dealer.

How a Propellor Works

As the curved blades of a propellor rotate through the water, a high-pressure area is created on one side of the blade and a low-pressure area exists on the other side of the blade (**Figure 18**). The propellor moves toward the low-pressure area, carrying the boat with it.

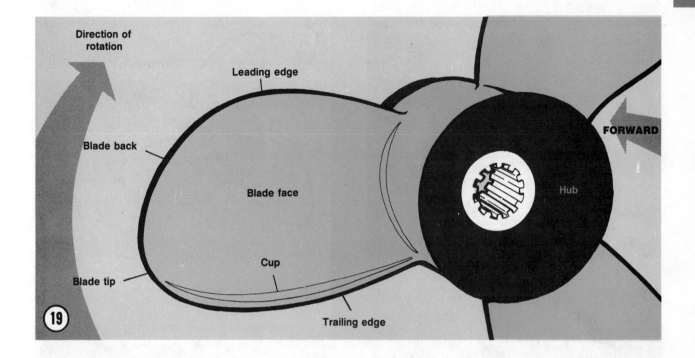

Propellor Parts

Although a propellor may be a 1-piece unit, it is made up of several different parts (**Figure 19**). Variations in the design of these parts make different propellors suitable for different jobs.

The blade tip is the point on the blade farthest from the center of the propellor hub. The blade tip separates the leading edge from the trailing edge.

The leading edge is the edge of the blade nearest to the boat. During normal rotation, this is the blade that first cuts through the water.

The trailing edge is the edge of the blade farthest from the boat.

The blade face is the surface of the blade that faces away from the boat. During normal rotation, high pressure exists on this side of the blade.

The blade back is the surface of the blade that faces toward the boat. During normal rotation, low pressure exists on this side of the blade.

The cup is a small curve or lip on the trailing edge of the blade.

The hub is the central portion of the propellor. It connects the blades to the propellor shaft (part of the boat's drive system). On some drive systems, engine exhaust is routed through the hub; in this case, the hub is made up of an outer and an inner portion, connected by ribs.

The diffuser ring is used on through-hub exhaust models to prevent exhaust gases from entering the blade area.

Propellor Design

Changes in length, angle, thickness and material of propellor parts make different propellors suitable for different situations.

Diameter

Propellor diameter is the distance from the center of the hub to the blade tip, multiplied

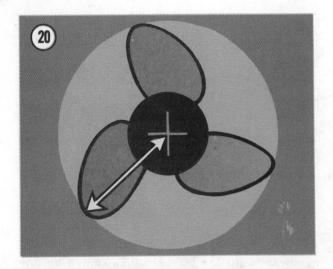

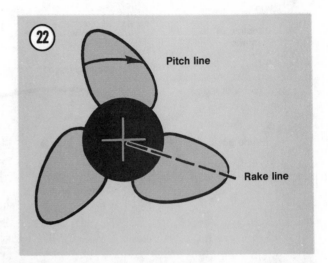

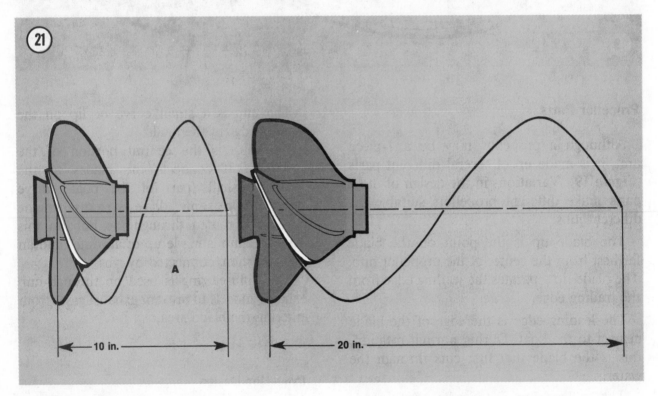

by 2. That is, it is the diameter of the circle formed by the blade tips during propellor rotation (**Figure 20**).

Pitch and rake

Propellor pitch and rake describe the placement of the blade in relation to the hub (**Figure 21**).

Pitch is expressed by the theoretical distance that the propellor would travel in one revolution. In A, **Figure 22**, the propellor would travel 10 inches in one revolution. In B, **Figure 22**, the propellor would travel 20 inches in one revolution. This distance is only theoretical; during actual operation, the propellor achieves about 80% of its rated travel.

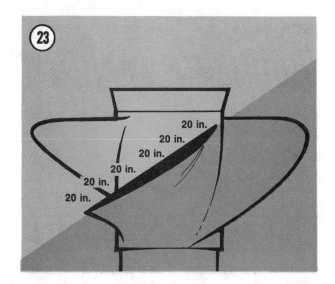

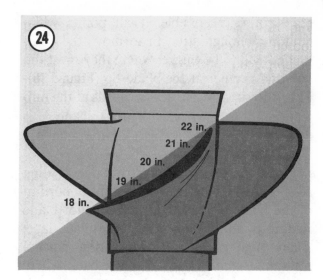

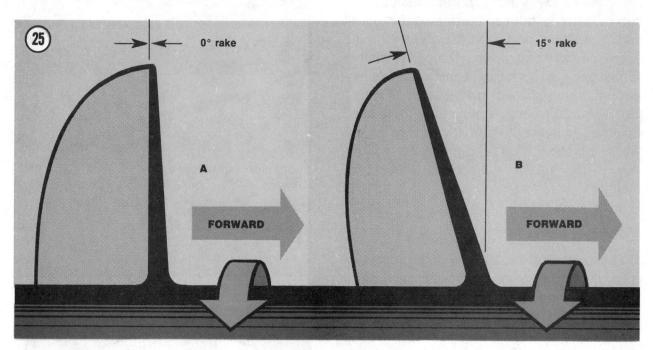

Propellor blades can be constructed with constant pitch (**Figure 23**) or progressive pitch (**Figure 24**). Progressive pitch starts low at the leading edge and increases toward the trailing edge. The propellor pitch specification is the average of the pitch across the entire blade.

Blade rake is specified in degrees and is measured along a line from the center of the hub to the blade tip. A blade that is perpendicular to the hub (A, **Figure 25**) has 0° of rake. A blade that is angled from perpendicular (B, **Figure 25**) has a rake expressed by its difference from perpendicular. Most propellors have rakes ranging from 0-20 degrees.

Blade thickness

Blade thickness is not uniform at all points along the blade. For efficiency, blades should be as thin as possible at all points while retaining enough strength to move the boat. Blades tend to be thicker where they meet the hub and thinner at the blade tip (**Figure 26**). This is to support the heavier loads at the hub section of the blade. This thickness is dependent on the strength of the material used.

When cut along a line from the leading edge to the trailing edge in the central portion of the blade (**Figure 27**), the propellor blade resembles an airplane wing. The blade face, where high pressure exists during normal rotation, is almost flat. The blade back, where low pressure exists during normal rotation, is curved, with the thinnest portions at the edges and the thickest portion at the center.

Propellors that run only partially submerged, as in racing applications, may have a wedge-shaped cross-section (**Figure 28**). The leading edge is very thin; the blade thickness increases toward the trailing edge, where it is the thickest. If a propellor such as this is run totally submerged, it is very inefficient.

Number of blades

The number of blades used on a propellor is a compromise between efficiency and vibration. A one-bladed propellor would be the most efficient, but it would also create high levels of vibration. As blades are added, efficiency decreases, but so do vibration levels. Most propellors have 3 blades, representing the most practical trade-off between efficiency and vibration.

Material

Propellor materials are chosen for strength, corrosion resistance and economy. Stainless steel, aluminum and bronze are the most commonly used materials. Bronze is quite strong but rather expensive. Stainless steel is

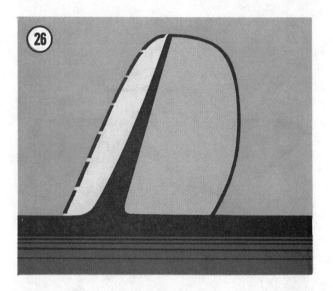

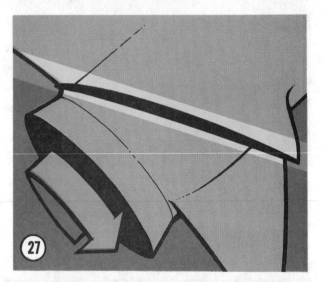

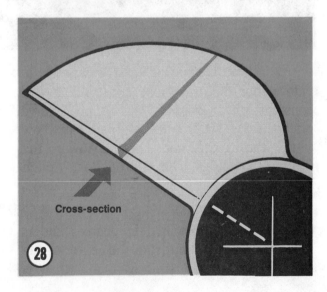

Cross-section

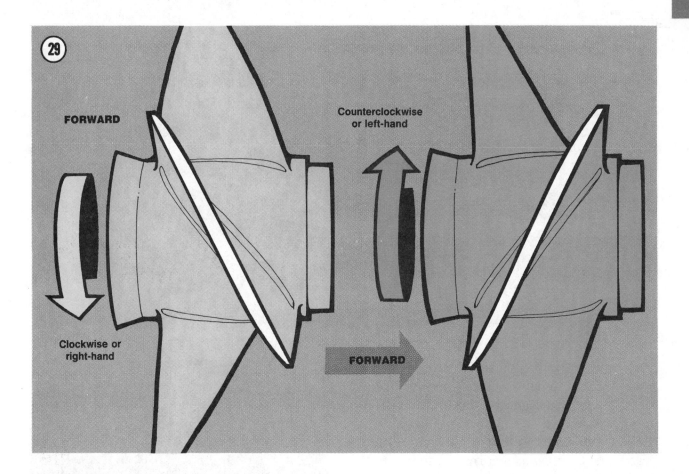

FORWARD

Clockwise or
right-hand

Counterclockwise
or left-hand

FORWARD

more common than bronze because of its combination of strength and lower cost. Aluminum alloys are the least expensive but usually lack the strength of steel. Plastic propellors may be used in very low horsepower applications.

Direction of rotation

Propellors are made for both right-hand and left-hand rotation, although right-hand is the most commonly used. When seen from behind the boat in forward motion, a right-hand propeller turns clockwise while a left-hand propellor turns counterclockwise. Off the boat, you can tell the difference by observing the angle of the blades (**Figure 29**) from the rear of the hub. A right-hand propellor's blades slant from the lower left to the upper right; a left-hand propellor's blades are the opposite.

Cavitation and Ventilation

Cavitation and ventilation are *not* interchangeable terms; they refer to 2 distinct problems encountered during propeller operation.

To understand cavitation, you must first understand the relationship between pressure and the boiling point of water. At sea level, water will boil at 212° F. As pressure increases, such as within an engine's closed cooling system, the boiling point of water increases—it will boil only at some temperature higher than 212° F. The opposite is also true; as pressure decreases, water will boil at a temperature lower than 212° F. If pressure drops low enough, water will boil at typical ambient temperatures of 50-60° F.

We have said that, during normal propeller operation, low pressure exists on the blade back. Normally, the pressure does not drop

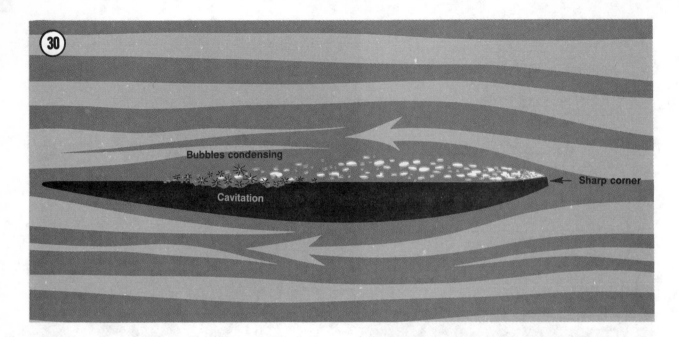

Bubbles condensing

Cavitation

Sharp corner

low enough for boiling to occur. However, poor blade design or selection or blade damage can cause an unusual pressure drop on a small area of the blade (**Figure 30**). Boiling can occur in this small area. As the water boils, air bubbles form. As the boiling water passes to a higher-pressure area of the blade, the boiling stops and the bubbles collapse. The collapsing bubbles release enough energy to erode the surface of the blade.

This entire process of pressure drop, boiling and bubble collapse is called "cavitation." The damage caused by the collapsing bubbles is called a "cavitation burn." It is important to remember that cavitation is caused by a decrease in pressure, *not* an increase in temperature.

Ventilation is not as complex a process as cavitation. Ventilation refers to air entering the blade area, either from above the surface of the water or from a through-hub exhaust system. As the blades meet the air, the propellor momentarily over-revs, losing most of its thrust. An added complication is that as the propeller over-revs, pressure on the blade back decreases and massive cavitation occurs.

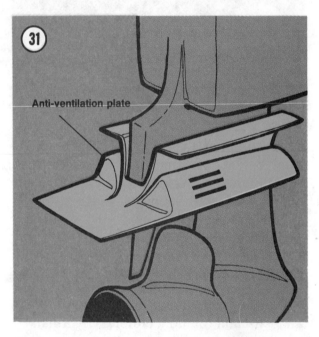

Anti-ventilation plate

Most pieces of marine equipment have a plate above the propellor area designed to keep surface air from entering the blades (**Figure 31**). This plate is correctly called an "anti-ventilation plate," although you will often see it called an "anti-cavitation plate." Through-hub exhaust systems also have specially designed hubs to keep exhaust gases from entering the blade area.

Chapter Two

Tools and Techniques

This chapter describes the common tools required for marine equipment repairs and troubleshooting. Techniques that will make your work easier and more effective are also described. Some of the procedures in this book require special skills or expertise; in some cases, you are better off entrusting the job to a dealer or qualified specialist.

SAFETY FIRST

Professional mechanics can work for years and never suffer a serious injury. If you follow a few rules of common sense and safety, you too can enjoy many safe hours servicing your marine equipment. You can hurt yourself or damage the equipment if you ignore these rules.

1. Never use gasoline as a cleaning solvent.
2. Never smoke or use a torch near flammable liquids such as cleaning solvent. If you are working in your home garage, remember that your home gas appliances have pilot lights.
3. Never smoke or use a torch in an area where batteries are being charged. Highly explosive hydrogen gas is formed during the charging process.

4. Use the proper size wrenches to avoid damage to fasteners and injury to yourself.
5. When loosening a tight or stuck fastener, think of what would happen if the wrench should slip. Protect yourself.
6. Keep your work area clean, uncluttered and well lighted.
7. Wear safety goggles during all operations involving drilling, grinding or the use of a cold chisel.
8. Never use worn tools.
9. Keep a Coast Guard approved fire extinguisher handy. Be sure it is rated for gasoline (Class B) and electrical (Class C) fires.

BASIC HAND TOOLS

A number of tools are required to maintain marine equipment. You may already have some of these tools for home or car repairs. There are also tools made especially for marine equipment repairs; these you will have to purchase. In any case, a wide variety of quality tools will make repairs easier and more effective.

Keep your tools clean and in a tool box. Keep them organized with the sockets and related drives together, the open end and box wrenches together, etc. After using a tool, wipe off dirt and grease with a clean cloth and place the tool in its correct place.

The following tools are required to perform virtually any repair job. Each tool is described and the recommended size given for starting a tool collection. Additional tools and some duplications may be added as you become more familiar with the equipment. You may need all English size tools, all metric size tools or a mixture of both.

Screwdrivers

The screwdriver is a very basic tool, but if used improperly it will do more damage than good. The slot on a screw has a definite dimension and shape. A screwdriver must be selected to conform with that shape. Use a small screwdriver for small screws and a large one for large screws or the screw head will be damaged.

Two types of screwdriver are required: a common (flat-blade) screwdriver (**Figure 1**) and Phillips screwdrivers (**Figure 2**).

Screwdrivers are available in sets which often include an assortment of common and Phillips blades. If you buy them individually, buy at least the following:

    a. Common screwdriver—5/16×6 in. blade.

    b. Common screwdriver—3/8×12 in. blade.

    c. Phillips screwdriver—size 2 tip, 6 in. blade.

Use screwdrivers only for driving screws. Never use a screwdriver for prying or chiseling. Do not try to remove a Phillips or Allen head screw with a common screwdriver; you can damage the head so that the proper tool will be unable to remove it.

Keep screwdrivers in the proper condition and they will last longer and perform better.

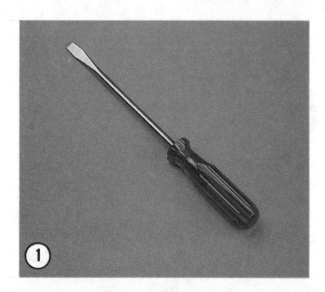

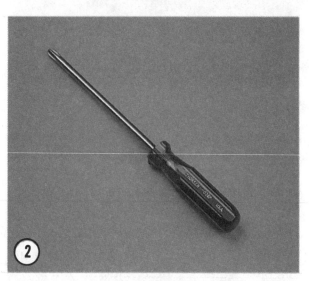

Always keep the tip of a common screwdriver in good condition. **Figure 3** shows how to grind the tip to the proper shape if it becomes damaged. Note the parallel sides of the tip.

Pliers

Pliers come in a wide range of types and sizes. Pliers are useful for cutting, bending and crimping. They should never be used to cut hardened objects or to turn bolts or nuts. **Figure 4** shows several types of pliers.

Each type of pliers has a specialized function. Gas pliers are general purpose pliers

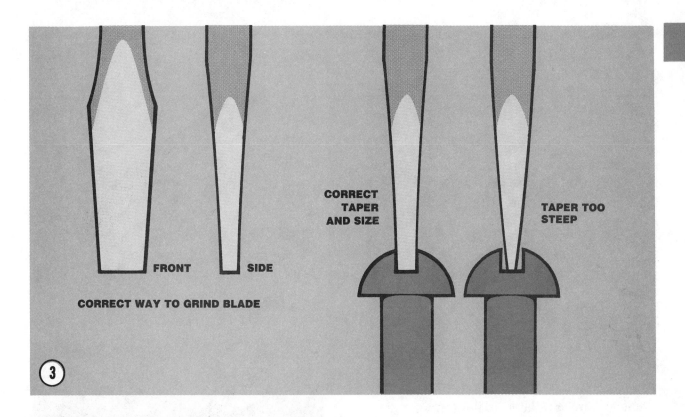

CORRECT
TAPER
AND SIZE

TAPER TOO
STEEP

FRONT   SIDE

CORRECT WAY TO GRIND BLADE

③

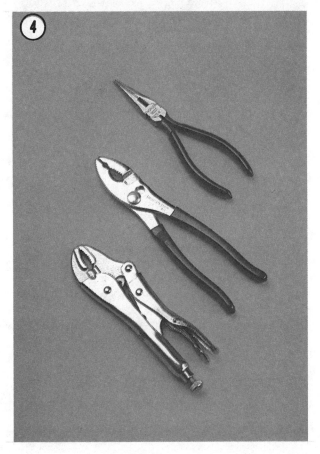

④

and are used mainly for holding things and for bending. Vise Grips are used as pliers or to hold objects very tight like a vise. Needlenose pliers are used to hold or bend small objects. Channel lock pliers can be adjusted to hold various sizes of objects; the jaws remain parallel to grip around objects such as pipe or tubing. There are many more types of pliers. The ones described here are the most commonly used.

Box and Open-end Wrenches

Box and open-end wrenches are available in sets or separately in a variety of sizes. See **Figure 5** and **Figure 6**. The number stamped near the end refers to the distance between 2 parallel flats on the hex head bolt or nut.

Box wrenches are usually superior to open-end wrenches. An open-end wrench grips the nut on only 2 flats. Unless it fits well, it may slip and round off the points on the nut. The box wrench grips all 6 flats. Both 6-point and 12-point openings on box

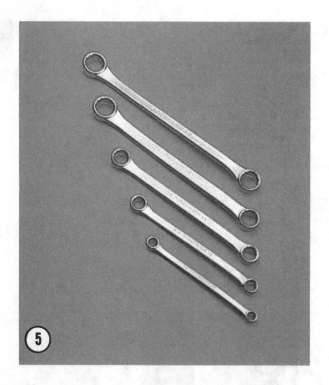

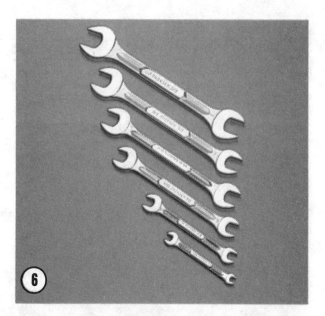

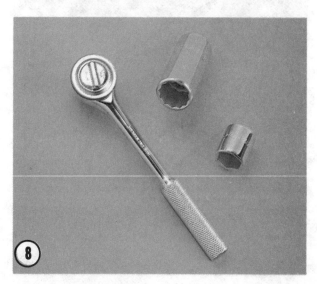

wrenches are available. The 6-point gives superior holding power; the 12-point allows a shorter swing.

Combination wrenches which are open on one side and boxed on the other are also available. Both ends are the same size.

Adjustable (Crescent) Wrenches

An adjustable wrench (also called crescent wrench) can be adjusted to fit nearly any nut or bolt head. See **Figure 7**. However, it can loosen and slip, causing damage to the nut and maybe to your knuckles. Use an adjustable wrench only when other wrenches are not available.

Crescent wrenches come in sizes ranging from 4-18 in. overall. A 6 or 8 in. wrench is recommended as an all-purpose wrench.

Socket Wrenches

This type is undoubtedly the fastest, safest and most convenient to use. See **Figure 8**. Sockets which attach to a ratchet handle are available with 6-point or 12-point openings

2

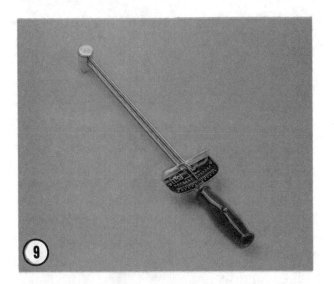

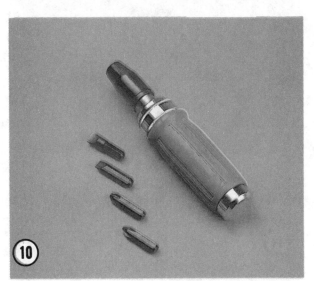

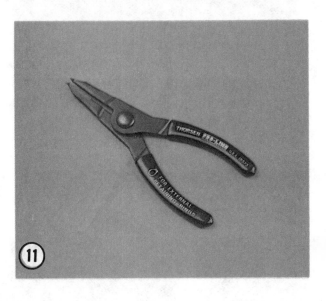

and 1/4, 3/8 and 3/4 inch drives. The drive size indicates the size of the square hole which mates with the ratchet handle.

Torque Wrench

A torque wrench (**Figure 9**) is used with a socket to measure how tight a nut or bolt is installed. They come in a wide price range and with either 3/8 or 1/2 in. square drive. The drive size indicates the size of the square drive which mates with the socket. Purchase one that measures 0-140 N•m (1-100 ft.-lb.).

Impact Driver

This tool (**Figure 10**) makes removal of tight fasteners easy and eliminates damage to bolts and screw slots. Impact drivers and interchangeable bits are available at most large hardware and auto parts stores.

Circlip Pliers

Circlip pliers (sometimes referred to as snap-ring pliers) are necessary to remove circlips. See **Figure 11**. Circlip pliers usually come with several different size tips; many designs can be switched from internal type to external type.

Hammers

The correct hammer is necessary for repairs. Use only a hammer with a face (or head) of rubber or plastic or the soft-faced type that is filled with buck shot (**Figure 12**). These are sometimes necessary in engine tear-downs. *Never* use a metal-faced hammer as severe damage will result in most cases. You can always produce the same amount of force with a soft-faced hammer.

Feeler Gauge

This tool has either flat or wire measuring gauges (**Figure 13**). Wire gauges are used to measure spark plug gap; flat gauges are used for all other measurements. A non-magnetic (brass) gauge may be specified when working around magnetized parts.

Other Special Tools

Some procedures require special tools; these are identified in the appropriate chapter. Unless otherwise specified, the part number used in this book to identify a special tool is the marine equipment manufacturer's part number.

Special tools can usually be purchased through your marine equipment dealer. Some can be made locally by a machinist, often at a much lower price. You may find certain special tools at tool rental dealers. Don't use makeshift tools if you can't locate the correct special tool; you will probably cause more damage than good.

TEST EQUIPMENT

Multimeter

This instrument (**Figure 14**) is invaluable for electrical system troubleshooting and service. It combines a voltmeter, an ohmmeter and an ammeter into one unit, so it is often called a VOM.

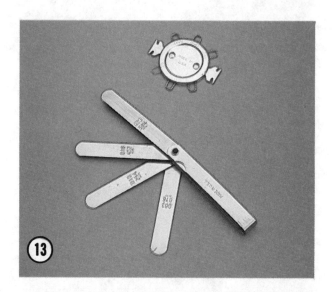

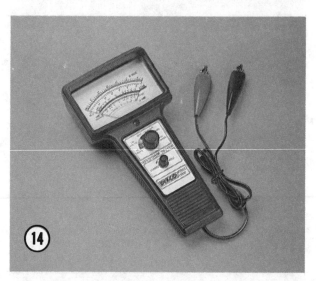

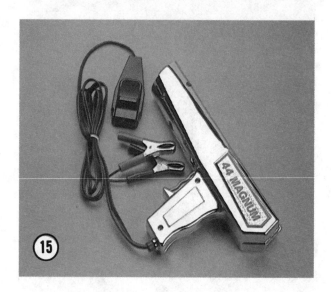

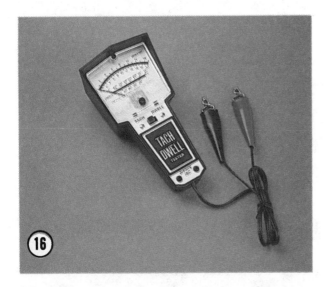

(16)

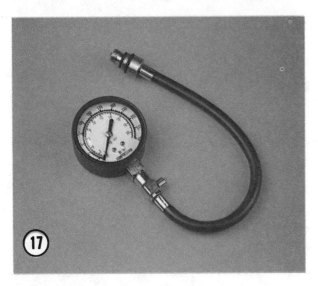

(17)

Strobe Timing Light

This instrument is necessary for dynamic tuning (setting ignition timing while the engine is running). By flashing a light at the precise instant the spark plug fires, the position of the timing mark can be seen. The flashing light makes a moving mark appear to stand still opposite a stationary mark.

Suitable lights range from inexpensive neon bulb types to powerful xenon strobe lights. See **Figure 15**. A light with an inductive pickup is best, as it eliminates any possible damage to ignition wiring.

Tachometer/Dwell Meter

A portable tachometer is necessary for tuning. See **Figure 16**. Ignition timing and carburetor adjustments must be performed at the specified idle speed. The best instrument for this purpose is one with a low range of 0-1,000 or 0-2,000 rpm and a high range of 0-4,000 rpm. Extended range (0-6,000 or 0-8,000 rpm) instruments lack accuracy at lower speeds. The instrument should be capable of detecting changes of 25 rpm on the low range.

A dwell meter is often combined with a tachometer. Dwell meters are used with breaker point ignition systems to measure the amount of time the points remain closed during engine operation.

Compression Gauge

This tool (**Figure 17**) measures the amount of pressure present in the engine's combustion chamber during the compression stroke. This indicates general engine condition. Compression readings can be interpreted along with vacuum gauge readings to pinpoint specific engine mechanical problems.

The easiest type to use has screw-in adaptors that fit into the spark plug holes. Press-in rubber-tipped types are also available.

Vacuum Gauge

The vacuum gauge (**Figure 18**) measures the intake manifold vacuum created by the engine's intake stroke. Manifold and valve problems can be identified by interpreting the readings; when combined with compression gauge readings, other engine problems can be diagnosed.

Some vacuum gauges can also be used as fuel pressure gauges to trace fuel system problems.

Hydrometer

Battery electrolyte specific gravity is measured with a hydrometer (**Figure 19**); this indicates the battery's state of charge. The best type has automatic temperature compensation; otherwise, you must calculate the compensation yourself.

Precision Measuring Tools

Various tools are needed to make precision measurements. A dial indicator (**Figure 20**), for example, is used to determine run-out of rotating parts and end play of parts assemblies. A dial indicator can also be used to precisely measure piston position in relation to top dead center; some engines require this measurement for ignition timing adjustment.

Vernier calipers (**Figure 21**) and micrometers (**Figure 22**) are other precision measuring tools used to determine the size of parts (such as piston diameter).

Precision measuring equipment must be stored, handled and used carefully or it will not remain accurate.

SERVICE HINTS

Most of the service procedures covered in this manual are straightforward and can be performed by anyone reasonably handy with tools. It is suggested, however, that you consider your own skills and toolbox carefully before attempting any operation involving major disassembly of the engine or gearcase.

Some operations, for example, require the use of a press. It would be wiser to have these performed by a shop equipped for such work,

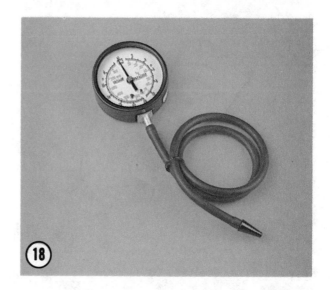

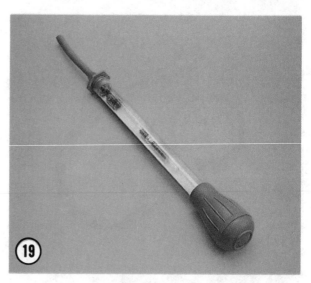

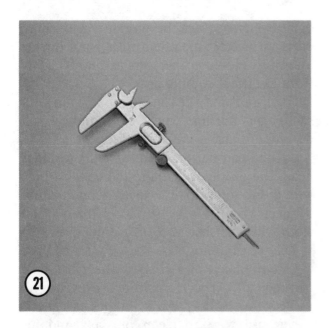

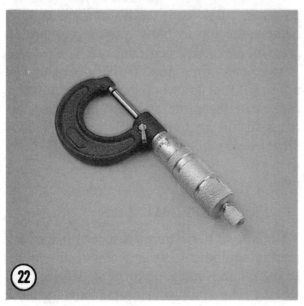

There are special cleaners, such as Gunk or Bel-Ray Degreaser, for washing the engine and related parts. Just spray or brush on the cleaning solution, let it stand, then rinse it away with a garden hose. Clean all oily or greasy parts with cleaning solvent as you remove them.

> *WARNING*
> *Never use gasoline as a cleaning agent. It presents an extreme fire hazard. Be sure to work in a well-ventilated area when using cleaning solvent. Keep a Coast Guard approved fire extinguisher, rated for gasoline fires, handy in any case.*

Much of the labor charged for repairs made by dealers is for the removal and disassembly of other parts to reach the defective unit. It is frequently possible to perform the preliminary operations yourself and then take the defective unit in to the dealer for repair.

Once you have decided to tackle the job yourself, read the entire section in this manual which pertains to it, making sure you have identified the proper one. Study the illustrations and text until you have a good idea of what is involved in completing the job satisfactorily. If special tools or replacement parts are required, make arrangements to get them before you start. It is frustrating and time-consuming to get partly into a job and then be unable to complete it.

rather than trying to do the job yourself with makeshift equipment. Other procedures require precise measurements. Unless you have the skills and equipment required, it would be better to have a qualified repair shop make the measurements for you.

Preparation for Disassembly

Repairs go much faster and easier if the equipment is clean before you begin work.

Disassembly Precautions

During disassembly of parts keep a few general precautions in mind. Force is rarely needed to get things apart. If parts are a tight fit, such as a bearing in a case, there is usually a tool designed to separate them. Never use a screwdriver to pry apart parts with machined surfaces (such as cylinder heads and crankcases). You will mar the surfaces and end up with leaks.

Make diagrams (or take an instant picture) wherever similar-appearing parts are found. For example, head and crankcase bolts are often not the same length. You may think you can remember where everything came from, but mistakes are costly. There is also the possibility you may be sidetracked and not return to work for days or even weeks, in which interval carefully laid out parts may have become disturbed.

Tag all similar internal parts for location and mark all mating parts for position. Record number and thickness of any shims as they are removed. Small parts such as bolts can be identified by placing them in plastic sandwich bags. Seal and label them with masking tape.

Wiring should be tagged with masking tape and marked as each wire is removed. Again, do not rely on memory alone.

Protect finished surfaces from physical damage or corrosion. Keep gasoline off painted surfaces.

Assembly Precautions

No parts, except those assembled with a press fit, require unusual force during assembly. If a part is hard to remove or install, find out why before proceeding.

Cover all openings after removing parts to keep dirt, small tools, etc., from falling in.

When assembling 2 parts, start all fasteners, then tighten evenly in an alternating or crisscross pattern if no specific tightening sequence is given.

When assembling parts, be sure all shims and washers are installed exactly as they came out.

Whenever a rotating part butts against a stationary part, look for a shim or washer. Use new gaskets if there is any doubt about the condition of the old ones. Unless otherwise specified, a thin coat of oil on gaskets may help them seal effectively.

Heavy grease can be used to hold small parts in place if they tend to fall out during assembly. However, keep grease and oil away from electrical components.

High spots may be sanded off a piston with sandpaper, but fine emery cloth and oil will do a much more professional job.

Carbon can be removed from the cylinder head, the piston crown and the exhaust port with a dull screwdriver. *Do not* scratch either surface. Wipe off the surface with a clean cloth when finished.

The carburetor is best cleaned by disassembling it and soaking the parts in a commercial carburetor cleaner. Never soak gaskets and rubber parts in these cleaners. Never use wire to clean out jets and air passages; they are easily damaged. Use compressed air to blow out the carburetor *after* the float has been removed.

Take your time and do the job right. Do not forget that a newly rebuilt engine must be broken in the same as a new one. Use the break-in oil recommendations and follow other instructions given in your owner's manual.

SPECIAL TIPS

Because of the extreme demands placed on marine equipment, several points should be kept in mind when performing service and repair. The following items are general suggestions that may improve the overall life of the machine and help avoid costly failures.

1. Unless otherwise specified, use a locking compound such as Loctite Lock N' Seal No. 2114 (blue Loctite) on all bolts and nuts, even if they are secured with lockwashers. This type of Loctite does not harden completely and allows easy removal of the bolt or nut. A screw or bolt lost from an engine cover or bearing retainer could easily cause serious and expensive damage before its loss is noticed.

When applying Loctite, use a small amount. If too much is used, it can work its way down the threads and stick parts together not meant to be stuck.

Keep a tube of Loctite in your tool box; when used properly it is cheap insurance.

2. Use a hammer-driven impact tool to remove and install screws and bolts. These tools help prevent the rounding off of bolt heads and screw slots and ensure a tight installation.

3. When straightening out the fold-over type lockwasher, use a wide-blade chisel such as an old and dull wood chisel. Such a tool provides a better purchase on the folded tab, making straightening out easier.

4. When installing the fold-over type lockwasher, always use a new washer if possible. If a new washer is not available, always fold over a part of the washer that has not been previously folded. Reusing the same fold may cause the washer to break, resulting in the loss of its locking ability and a loose piece of metal adrift in the engine.

When folding the washer over, start the fold with a screwdriver and finish it with a pair of pliers. If a punch is used to make the fold, the fold may be too sharp, thereby increasing the chances of the washer breaking under stress.

These washers are relatively inexpensive and it is suggested that you keep several of each size in your tool box for repairs.

5. When replacing missing or broken fasteners (bolts, nuts and screws), always use authorized replacement parts. They are specially hardened for each application. The wrong 50-cent bolt could easily cause serious and expensive damage.

6. When installing gaskets, always use authorized replacement gaskets *without* sealer, unless designated. Many gaskets are designed to swell when they come in contact with oil. Gasket sealer will prevent the gaskets from swelling as intended, which can result in oil leaks. Authorized replacement gaskets are cut from material of the precise thickness needed. Installation of a too thick or too thin gasket in a critical area could cause equipment damage.

MECHANIC'S TECHNIQUES

Removing Frozen Fasteners

When a fastener rusts and cannot be removed, several methods may be used to loosen it. First, apply penetrating oil such as Liquid Wrench or WD-40 (available at any hardware or auto supply store). Apply it liberally and let it penetrate for 10-15 minutes. Rap the fastener several times with a small hammer; do not hit it hard enough to cause damage. Reapply the penetrating oil if necessary.

For frozen screws, apply penetrating oil as described, then insert a screwdriver in the slot and rap the top of the screwdriver with a hammer. This loosens the rust so the screw can be removed in the normal way. If the screw head is too chewed up to use a screwdriver, grip the head with Vise Grip pliers and twist the screw out.

Avoid applying heat unless specifically instructed, as it may melt, warp or remove the temper from parts.

Remedying Stripped Threads

Occasionally, threads are stripped through carelessness or impact damage. Often the threads can be cleaned up by running a tap (for internal threads on nuts) or die (for external threads on bolts) through threads. See **Figure 23**.

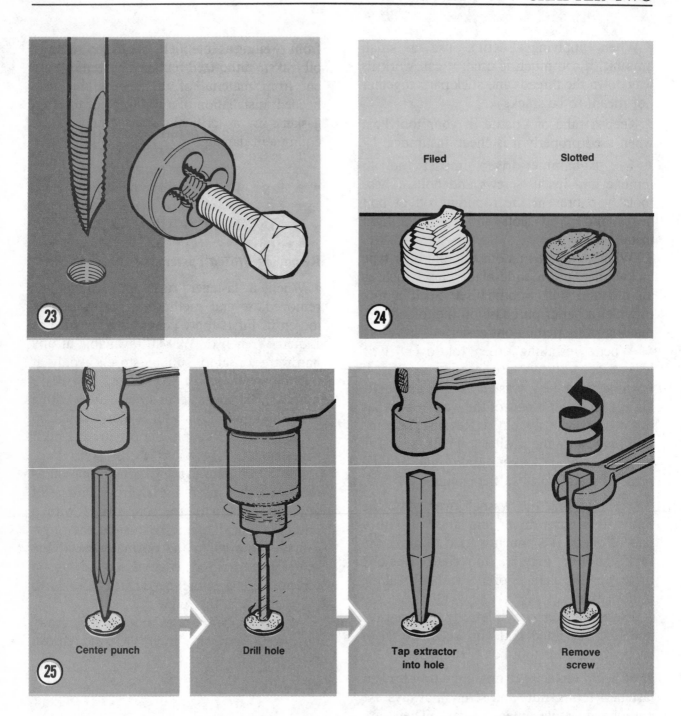

Removing Broken Screws or Bolts

When the head breaks off a screw or bolt, several methods are available for removing the remaining portion.

If a large portion of the remainder projects out, try gripping it with Vise Grips. If the projecting portion is too small, file it to fit a wrench or cut a slot in it to fit a screwdriver. See **Figure 24**.

If the head breaks off flush, use a screw extractor. To do this, centerpunch the remaining portion of the screw or bolt. Drill a small hole in the screw and tap the extractor into the hole. Back the screw out with a wrench on the extractor. See **Figure 25**.

Chapter Three

Troubleshooting

NOTE
Troubleshooting procedures for electric outboard motors are in Chapter Eleven.

Troubleshooting is a relatively simple matter when it is done logically. The first step in any troubleshooting procedure is to define the symptoms as fully as possible and then localize the problem. Subsequent steps involve testing and analyzing those areas which could cause the symptoms. A haphazard approach may eventually solve the problem, but it can be very costly in terms of wasted time and unnecessary parts replacement.

Never assume anything. Don't overlook the obvious. If the engine suddenly quits when running, check the easiest and most accessible spots first. Make sure there is gasoline in the tank, the fuel petcock is in the ON position, the spark plug wires are properly connected and the wiring harnesses are properly connected.

If a quick visual check of the obvious does not turn up the cause of the problem, look a

little further. Learning to recognize and describe symptoms accurately will make repairs easier for you or a mechanic at the shop. Saying that "it won't run" isn't the same as saying "it quit at high speed and wouldn't start."

Gather as many symptoms together as possible to aid in diagnosis. Note whether the engine lost power gradually or all at once, what color smoke (if any) came from the exhaust and so on. Remember—the more complicated an engine is, the easier it is to troubleshoot because symptoms point to specific problems.

After the symptoms are defined, areas which could cause the problems should be tested and analyzed. You don't need fancy or complicated test equipment to determine whether repairs can be attempted at home. A few simple checks can save a large repair bill and time lost while the engine sits in a shop's service department.

On the other hand, be realistic and don't attempt repairs beyond your abilities. Service departments tend to charge heavily for putting together a disassembled engine that may have been abused. Some won't even take on such a job—so use common sense and don't get in over your head.

Proper lubrication, maintenance and periodic tune-ups as described in Chapter Four will reduce the necessity for troubleshooting. Even with the best of care, however, an outboard motor is prone to problems which will eventually require troubleshooting.

This chapter contains brief descriptions of each operating system and troubleshooting procedures to be used. **Tables 1-3** at the end of the chapter present typical starting, ignition and fuel system problems with their probable causes and solutions.

OPERATING REQUIREMENTS

Every outboard motor requires 3 basic things to run properly: an uninterrupted supply of fuel and air in the correct proportions, proper ignition at the right time and adequate compression. If any of these are lacking, the motor will not run. The electrical system is the weakest link in the chain. More problems result from electrical malfunctions than from any other source. Keep this in mind before you blame the fuel system and start making unnecessary carburetor adjustments.

If a motor has been sitting for any length of time and refuses to start, check the condition of the battery first to make sure it has an adequate charge, then look to the fuel delivery system. This includes the gas tank, fuel pump, fuel lines and carburetor(s). Rust may have formed in the tank, obstructing fuel flow. Gasoline deposits may have gummed up carburetor jets and air passages. Gasoline tends to lose its potency after standing for long periods. Condensation may contaminate it with water. Drain the old gas and try starting with a fresh tankful. If the carburetor

is getting a satisfactory supply of good fuel, turn to the starting system.

STARTING SYSTEM

Description

Johnson/Evinrude 9.5 hp and larger outboard motors may be equipped with an electric starter motor (**Figure 1**). The motor is mounted vertically on the engine. When battery current is supplied to the starter motor, its pinion gear is thrust upward to engage the teeth on the engine flywheel. Once the engine starts, the pinion gear disengages from the flywheel. This is similar to the method used in cranking an automotive engine.

The starting system requires a fully charged battery to provide the large amount of electrical current required to operate the starter motor. The battery may be charged externally or by an alternator stator and rectifier system which keeps the battery charged while the engine is running.

Starting Circuit
(9.5, 9.9 and 15 hp)

The starting circuit on Johnson and Evinrude 9.5, 9.9 and 15 hp outboards equipped with an electric starting system consists of the battery, starter motor, ignition

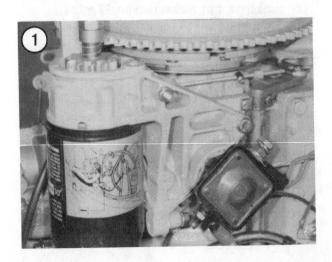

switch, neutral start switch and connecting wiring.

Turning the ignition switch to START completes the circuit between the battery and starter motor when the shift lever is in NEUTRAL. The neutral start switch prevents current flow if the shift control lever is not in NEUTRAL.

Starting Circuit
(18-40 hp)

The starting circuit on 18-40 hp models consists of the battery, starter motor, starter and choke switches, starter and choke solenoids, ignition switch, neutral start switch, a fuse (on some models) and connecting wiring.

Turning the ignition switch to START allows current to flow through the solenoid coil. The solenoid contacts close and allow current to flow from the battery through the solenoid to the starter motor. The neutral start switch prevents current flow through the solenoid coil if the shift control lever is not in NEUTRAL. The choke solenoid operates in a similar manner to move the choke valve linkage and open the choke for starting.

General troubleshooting procedures are provided in **Table 1**.

> *CAUTION*
> *Do not operate the starter motor continuously for more than 30 seconds. Allow the motor to cool for at least 2 minutes between attempts to start the engine.*

Troubleshooting Preparation
(All Models)

Before troubleshooting the starting circuit, make sure:

   a. The battery is fully charged.

   b. The control lever is in NEUTRAL.

   c. All electrical connections are clean and tight.

   d. The wiring harness is in good condition, with no worn or frayed insulation.

   e. Battery cables are the proper size and length. Replace undersize cables or relocate battery to shorten distance between battery and starter solenoid.

   f. The fuse installed in the red lead between ignition switch and solenoid is good, if so equipped.

   g. The fuel system is filled with an adequate supply of fresh gasoline that has been properly mixed with Johnson or Evinrude 50/1 Lubricant. See Chapter Four.

Starting Difficulties
With Older Engines

Many older 2-stroke engines are plagued by hard starting and generally poor running for which there seems to be no good cause. Carburetion and ignition are satisfactory and a compression test shows all is well in the engine's upper end.

What a compression test does not show is a lack of primary compression. The crankcase in a 2-stroke engine must be alternately under pressure and vacuum. After the piston closes the intake port, further downward movement of the piston causes the trapped mixture to be pressurized so it can rush quickly into the cylinder when the scavenging ports are opened. Upward piston movement creates a vacuum in the crankcase, enabling air-fuel mixture to be drawn in from the carburetor.

If the crankshaft seals or case gaskets leak, the crankcase cannot hold pressure or vacuum and proper engine operation becomes impossible. Any other source of leakage, such as defective cylinder base gaskets or porous or cracked crankcase castings, will result in the same conditions.

Older engines suffering from hard starting should be checked for pressure leaks with a small brush and soap suds solution. The

3

following is a list of possible leakage points in the engine:
- a. Crankshaft seals.
- b. Spark plug threads.
- c. Cylinder head joint.
- d. Cylinder base joint.
- e. Carburetor mounting flange(s).
- f. Crankcase joint.

Troubleshooting
(9.5-15 hp)

Refer to **Figure 2** for the following procedure.

1. Remove the fuel pump to permit access to the neutral start switch terminals. See Chapter Six.

2. Place the control box shift lever in NEUTRAL.

3. Connect the red voltmeter lead to point 1, **Figure 2**. Connect the black lead to a good engine ground. Depress the starter switch button. The voltmeter should indicate battery voltage (approximately 12 volts).

4. If no voltage is shown in Step 3, connect the red voltmeter lead to point 2. There should be no voltage reading. If there is, check the neutral start switch for continuity as described in this chapter.

5. Connect the red voltmeter lead to point 3 and depress the starter switch button. If voltage is indicated, the neutral start switch requires adjustment as described in this chapter. If no voltage is indicated, depress the neutral start switch manually. If voltage is now indicated, the neutral start switch requires adjustment as described in this chapter. If no voltage is indicated, replace the switch.

6. Connect the red voltmeter lead to point 4 and depress the starter switch button. There

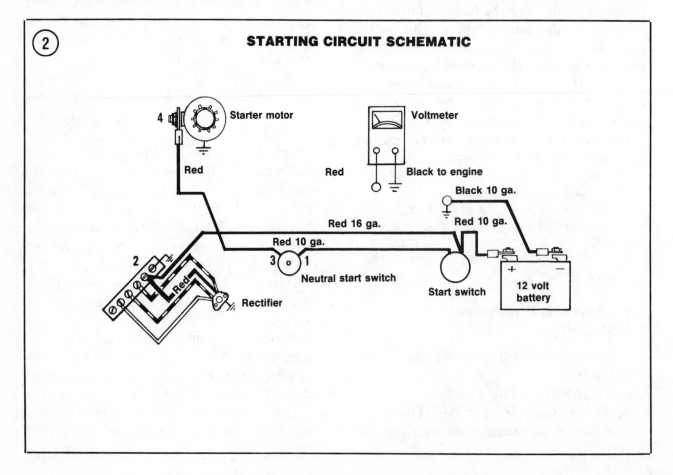

STARTING CIRCUIT SCHEMATIC

should be voltage. If not, there is an open in the wiring between point 3 and point 4.

7. If there is voltage in Step 6 but the starter motor will not turn over, replace the starter.

Troubleshooting
(18-40 hp with Remote Control)

Refer to **Figure 3** (1973-1982) or **Figure 4** (1983-on) for this procedure.

1A. 1973-1982—Locate the neutral start switch at point 1 (**Figure 3**) and remove the white wire. Connect a 12-volt test light between a good engine ground and the white wire.

1B. 1983-on—Disconnect the black ground lead at point 1 (**Figure 4**). Connect a 12-volt test light between the lead and a good engine ground.

2A. 1973-1982—Turn the ignition switch to START. If the light comes on, proceed with Step 3. If the light does not come on, proceed with Step 4.

2B. 1983-on—Turn the ignition switch to START. If the light comes on, proceed with Step 4. If the light does not come on, proceed with Step 9.

3. Connect the white wire to the switch with the test lamp still connected. Turn the switch to START. If the light does not come on,

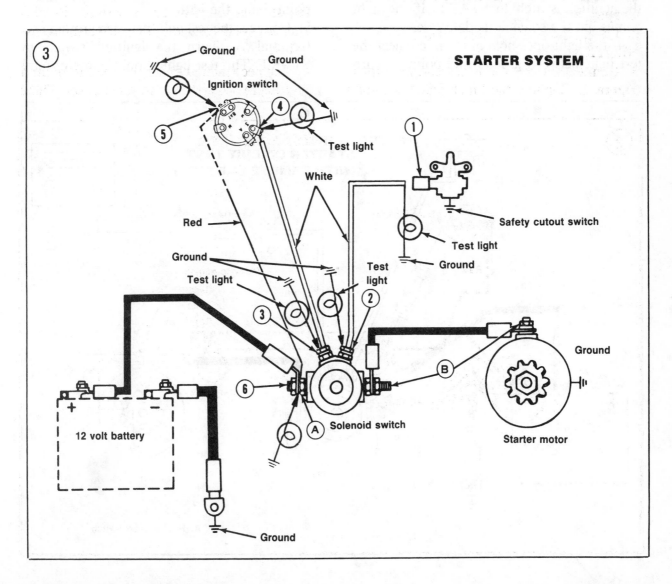

proceed with Step 9. If the light comes on, the switch is not properly connected or it is defective. The throttle may be advanced too far for it to function properly.

NOTE
Turn the key to OFF prior to connecting or disconnecting the light in the following steps. This will prevent the possibility of a shock.

4. Connect the test light between ground and point 2. If the light comes on, the wire is not making contact between point 1 and point 2.
5. If the light does not come on, connect the test light between ground and point 3. Turn the ignition switch to START. If the light comes on, the solenoid is defective.
6. If the light does not come on, connect the test light between ground and point 4. Turn

the ignition switch to START. If the light comes on, the lead between point 3 and point 4 is loose, corroded or disconnected. On 1983 and later models, the neutral start switch may also be open or improperly adjusted.
7. If the light does not come on, connect the test light between ground and point 5. Leave the ignition switch OFF. If the light comes on, the switch is defective.
8. If the light does not come on, check for an open or burned fuse between point 5 and 6 and correct as required. Connect the test light between ground and point 6. Leave the ignition switch OFF. The light should light. If it does not, check for an open circuit between point 6 and the battery.
9. Connect the test light between ground and terminal A. Turn the ignition switch to START. The test light should come on and

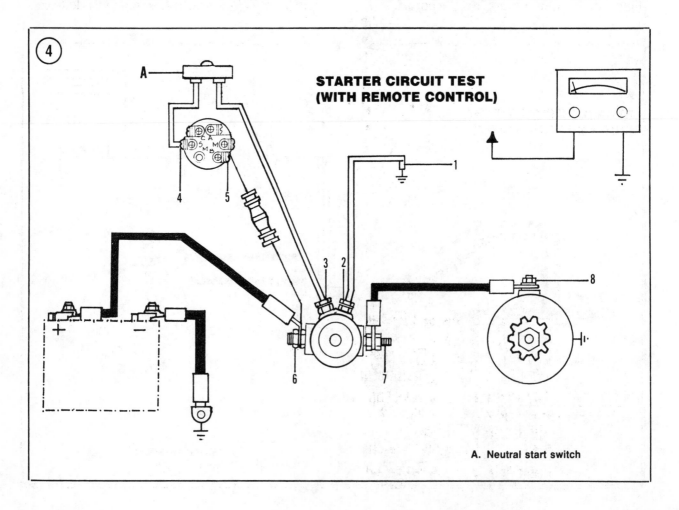

④

STARTER CIRCUIT TEST (WITH REMOTE CONTROL)

A

A. Neutral start switch

the solenoid should click. If the light does not come on, the solenoid is defective.

10. Connect the test light between ground and terminal B. Turn the ignition switch to START. If the light comes on but the starter motor will not turn over, replace the starter motor. If the light does not come on, check for a broken cable or a poor connection.

Troubleshooting
(18-40 hp with Push Button Start)

Refer to **Figure 5** for this procedure.

1. Locate the neutral start switch (A) at point 1 and remove the yellow/red lead. Connect a 12-volt test light between a good ground on the engine and the yellow/red lead.

2. Depress the push button (B). If the test light comes on, proceed to Step 3. If the test light does not come on, reconnect the yellow/red lead to the neutral start switch and proceed with Step 6.

3. Connect the test light between ground and point 2. Depress the push button (B). If the test light comes on, the lead is open between point 1 and point 2.

4. Connect the test light between ground and point 3. Depress the push button. If the test light comes on, the solenoid is defective.

5. Connect the test light between ground and point 4. If the test light comes on, check the push button. If the test light does not come on, look for an open between point 4 and the positive battery terminal.

6. Connect the test light between ground and point 5. Depress the push button. The test light should come on and the solenoid should click. If it does not, the solenoid is defective.

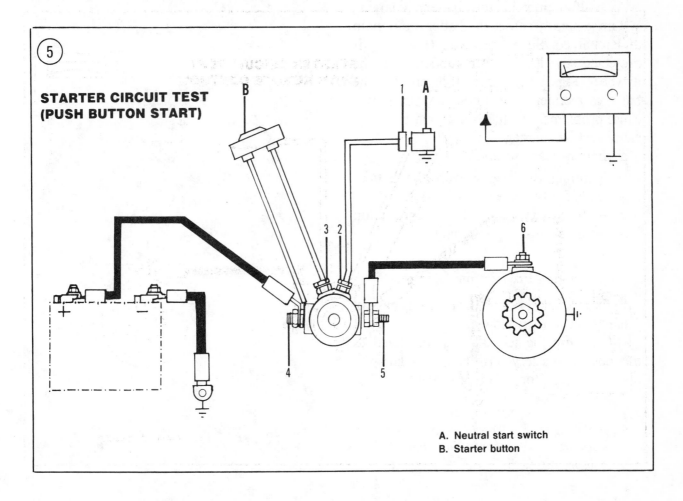

⑤

STARTER CIRCUIT TEST (PUSH BUTTON START)

A. Neutral start switch
B. Starter button

7. Connect the test light between ground and point 6. Depress the push button. If the light comes on but the starter motor will not turn over, replace the starter motor. If the light does not come on, check for a broken cable or a poor connection.

CHARGING SYSTEM

Description

The charging system on 7.5-40 hp models consists of permanent magnets cast in the flywheel (**Figure 6**), a stator assembly containing coils wound on a laminated iron core (**Figure 7**), a rectifier (**Figure 8**), the battery and connecting wiring. Flywheel rotation past the stator coils produces alternating current (AC), which is sent to the rectifier for conversion to direct current (DC).

A malfunction in the battery charging system generally causes the battery to remain undercharged. Since the stator (**Figure 7**) is protected by its location underneath the flywheel (**Figure 6**), it is more likely that the battery, rectifier or connecting wiring will cause problems. The following conditions will cause rectifier damage:

    a. Battery leads reversed.

    b. Running the engine with the battery leads disconnected.

    c. A broken wire or loose connection resulting in an open circuit.

Troubleshooting Preparation

Before troubleshooting the charging circuit, visually check the following.

1. Make sure the red cable is connected to the positive battery terminal. If polarity is reversed, check for a damaged rectifier.

> *NOTE*
> *A damaged rectifier will generally be discolored or have a burned appearance.*

2. Check for corroded or loose connections. Clean, tighten and insulate with OMC Black Neoprene Dip as required.

3. Check battery condition. Clean and recharge as required.

4. Check wiring harness between the armature plate and battery for damaged or deteriorated insulation and corroded, loose or

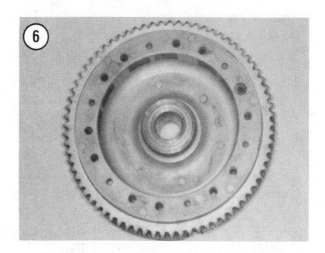

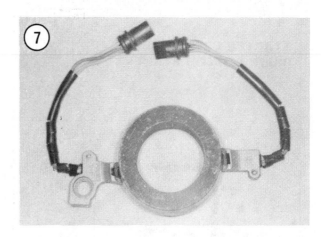

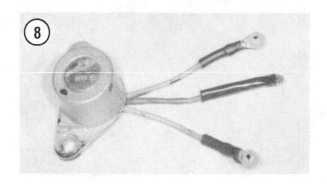

faulty connections. Repair or replace as required.

Alternator Output Quick Check

A quick check of the alternator output can be made with an induction ammeter (**Figure 9**). Fit the ammeter over the positive battery cable and run the motor at full throttle in a

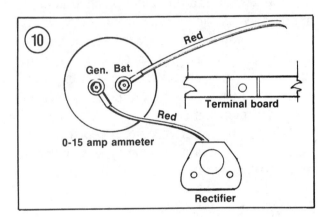

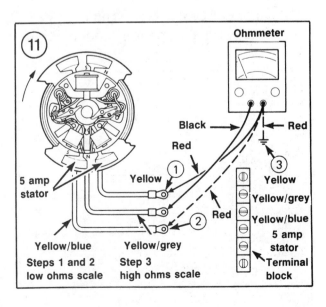

test tank or in the water. The induction ammeter will show the alternator output. The total electrical load on the system from the engine and accessories cannot exceed 5 amps (1973-1982) or 4 amps (1983-on).

Alternator Output Test

Perform this test for a more accurate reading of alternator output. Refer to **Figure 10** for this procedure.
1. Disconnect the red rectifier and starter motor leads at the terminal board.
2. Connect the rectifer lead to the negative terminal of a low-reading 15 amp ammeter. Connect the starter motor lead to the positive terminal on the ammeter.
3. With the engine in a test tank or in the water, start and run at full throttle. The ammeter should read approximately 5 amps (1973-1982) or 4 amps (1983-on).
4. If no charge is shown, test the stator and rectifier as described in this chapter.

Stator Test

Refer to **Figure 11** for this procedure.
1. Disconnect the yellow, yellow/grey and yellow/blue leads at the terminal block.
2. Set the ohmmeter on the low ohm scale.
3. Connect the black ohmmeter test lead to the yellow (1973-1982) or yellow/grey (1983-on) wire terminal.
4. Connect the red ohmmeter test lead to the yellow/grey (1973-1983) or yellow (1983-on) stator lead. The ohmmeter should read 0.25-0.45 ohms (1973-1982) or 0.22-0.32 ohms (1983-on).
5. Move the red ohmmeter test lead to the yellow/blue stator lead. The ohmmeter should read:
   a. 0.25-0.45 ohms (1973-1976).
   b. 0.45-0.65 ohms (1977-1982).
   c. 0.22-0.32 ohms (1983-on).
6. Move the red ohmmeter test lead to a good engine ground. It should read infinity,

indicating an open circuit. If any other reading is shown, the stator is shorted to ground.

Rectifier Test

Figure 12 is a schematic of the rectifier. Refer to **Figure 13** for typical location and test connections.

1. Ground one ohmmeter test lead at the rectifier case. Connect the other test lead to the yellow/grey rectifier lead. Note the ohmmeter reading.
2. Reverse the test leads and note the ohmmeter reading. The ohmmeter should read zero in one direction and infinity in the other. If the reading is the same in Step 1 and Step 2, the diode is defective and the rectifier should be replaced. High resistance indicates an open diode; low resistance indicates a shorted diode.
3. Repeat Step 1 and Step 2 to test the yellow and the yellow/blue rectifier leads.
4. Connect one ohmmeter test lead to the red rectifier lead. Connect the other test lead to the yellow/grey rectifier lead. Note the ohmmeter reading.
5. Reverse the test leads and note the ohmmeter reading. The ohmmeter should read zero in one direction and infinity in the other. If the reading is the same in Step 4 and Step 5, the rectifier is defective.
6. Repeat Step 4 and Step 5 to test the yellow rectifier lead, then the yellow/blue rectifier lead.
7. Replace the rectifier if the readings are not as specified.

AC Lighting Coil Test
(Electric Start Models)

Electric start models have an additional coil assembly mounted on the armature plate.

1. Disconnect the 3-wire connector at the armature plate.

2. With an ohmmeter on the low scale, insert the black probe in the connector yellow/grey lead socket and the red probe in the yellow lead socket. The ohmmeter should read 0.83-0.89 ohms.
3. Move the red probe to the yellow/blue lead socket. The ohmmeter should read 1.18-1.24 ohms.
4. Set the ohmmeter on the high scale and move the red lead to a good ground. If the ohmmeter shows a reading other than infinity, either the coil is defective or the wiring is shorted to ground. Replace the coil or correct the wiring as required.

IGNITION SYSTEM

The wiring harness used between the ignition switch and engine is adequate to handle the electrical needs of the outboard. It *will not* handle the electrical needs of accessories. Whenever an accessory is added, run new wiring between the battery and accessory, installing a separate fuse panel on the instrument panel.

If the ignition switch requires replacement, *never* install an automotive-type switch. A marine-type switch must always be used.

Description

Variations of two different ignition systems have been used on Johnson and Evinrude

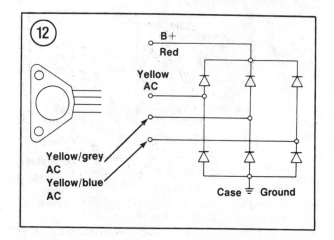

outboards since 1973. See Chapter Seven for a full description. For the purposes of troubleshooting, the ignition systems can be divided into 2 basic types:

    a. A flywheel magneto breaker-point ignition.

    b. A flywheel magneto capacitor discharge (CD 2) breakerless ignition.

General troubleshooting procedures are provided in **Table 2**.

Troubleshooting Precautions

Several precautions should be strictly observed to avoid damage to the ignition system.

1. Do not reverse the battery connections. This reverses polarity and can damage the rectifier or power pack unit on CD 2 ignitions.

2. Do not "spark" the battery terminals with the battery cable connections to check polarity.

3. Do not disconnect the battery cables with the engine running.

4. Do not crank engine if the power pack unit (CD 2 ignition) is not grounded to engine.

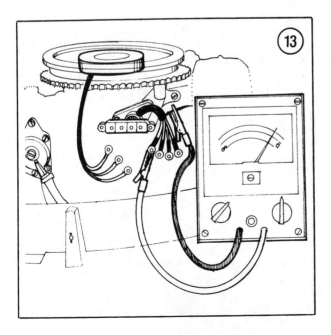

5. Do not touch or disconnect any ignition components when the engine is running, while the ignition switch is ON or while the battery cables are connected.

6. If you must run an engine with a CD 2 ignition system without the battery connected to the harness, disconnect the armature plate rectifier leads at the terminal board and tape them separately.

Troubleshooting Preparation (All Ignition Systems)

NOTE
To test the wiring harness for poor solder connections in Step 1, bend the molded rubber connector while checking each wire for resistance.

1. Check the wiring harness and all plug-in connections to make sure all terminals are free of corrosion, all connectors are tight and the wiring insulation is in good condition.

2. Check all electrical components that are grounded to the engine for a good ground.

3. Make sure that all ground wires are properly connected and the connections are clean and tight.

4. Check remainder of the wiring for disconnected wires and short or open circuits.

5. Make sure there is an adequate supply of fresh and properly mixed fuel available to the engine.

6. Check the battery condition on electric start models. Clean terminals and recharge battery, if necessary.

7. Check spark plug cable routing. Make sure the cables are properly connected to their spark plugs.

8. Remove all spark plugs, keeping them in order. Check the condition of each plug. See Chapter Four.

9. Install a spark tester (**Figure 14**) between the plug wire and a good ground to check for spark at each cylinder. See **Figure 15**. Set the spark tester air gap to 7/16-1/2 in. Crank the

engine over while watching the spark tester. If a spark jumps at each plug gap, the ignition system is good.

10. If a spark tester is not available, remove each spark plug and reconnect the proper plug cable to one plug. Lay the plug against the cylinder head so its base makes a good connection and turn the engine over. If there is no spark or only a weak one, check for loose connections at the coil and battery. Repeat the check with each remaining plug. If the connections are good, the problem is most likely in the ignition system.

BREAKER POINT IGNITION TROUBLESHOOTING

This procedure requires the use of a Stevens S-80 or Merc-O-Tronic M-80 neon test light. Refer to **Figure 16** (No. 1 ignition coil) and **Figure 17** (No. 2 ignition coil) for test connections.

1. Disconnect the No. 1 ignition coil-to-armature plate blue primary lead. Connect the neon tester blue lead to the armature plate end of the coil lead. Connect the neon tester black lead to a good engine ground. Set the tester switch to position No. 1.

2. Remove the spark plugs.

3. Crank the engine while watching the neon tester:

   a. If the tester light is bright and steady, remove the No. 1 ignition coil for further testing as described in this chapter.

   b. If the tester light is dim, the No. 1 condenser is open.

   c. If there is no tester light, check the breaker point gap(s) and condition. Regap or replace as required.

4. Disconnect the No. 2 ignition coil blue/white lead (**Figure 17**) and repeat Steps 1-3 on 2-cylinder engines.

Component Testing

An ignition analyzer must be used for accurate testing of the breaker points, condenser(s), driver and ignition coil(s). Johnson and Evinrude recommend the use of the Merc-O-Tronic, Stevens ST-75 or Stevens M.A.-75 or M.A.-80. These can be purchased through your local Johnson or Evinrude

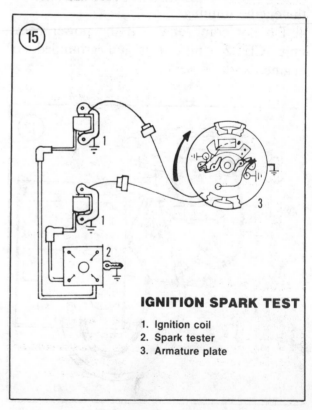

IGNITION SPARK TEST

1. Ignition coil
2. Spark tester
3. Armature plate

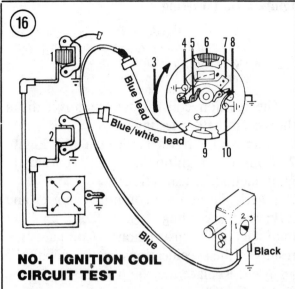

**NO. 1 IGNITION COIL
CIRCUIT TEST**

1. No. 1 coil	7. Driver coil
2. No. 2 coil	8. No. 2 breaker point set
3. Direction of rotation	9. No. 2 magnet
4. No. 1 condenser	10. No. 2 condenser
5. No. 1 breaker point set	
6. No. 1 magnet	

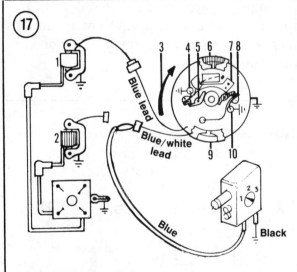

**NO. 2 IGNITION COIL
CIRCUIT TEST**

1. No. 1 coil	6. No. 2 magnet
2. No. 2 coil	7. Driver coil
3. Direction of rotation	8. No. 2 breaker point set
4. No. 1 condenser	9. No. 1 magnet
5. No. 1 breaker point set	10. No. 2 condenser

dealer. Each analyzer includes detailed instructions for component testing as well as complete component specifications according to engine model and year of manufacture. The procedures given here are general in nature to acquaint you with component testing. Refer to the instructions provided with the particular analyzer to be used for the exact procedure.

Breaker Point Testing

1. Remove the flywheel. See Chapter Eight.
2. Disconnect the breaker point leads from the armature plate.
3. Connect one analyzer test lead to the breaker arm. Connect the other test lead to the breaker point screw terminal.
4. Set the analyzer controls according to manufacturer's instructions.
5. If the breaker points are good, the analyzer needle will rest in the "OK" segment (Merc-O-Tronic) or green segment (Stevens).
6. If the analyzer needle does not fall within the specified segment on the scale, clean the points with electrical contact cleaner and recheck the analyzer leads to make sure the connections are tight before discarding the points. The low current used in this test makes clean points and proper connections very important.

Condenser Testing

1. Remove the flywheel. See Chapter Eight.
2. Disconnect the condenser lead from the breaker point set.
3. Connect one analyzer test lead to the condenser lead. Connect the other test lead to the breaker plate.

WARNING
High voltage is involved in a condenser leakage test. Handle the analyzer leads carefully and turn the analyzer switch to DISCHARGE before disconnecting it from the condenser.

4. Set the analyzer controls according to manufacturer's instructions and check the condenser for leakage, resistance and capacity.

5. Compare the results in Step 4 with the specifications provided by the analyzer manufacturer. Replace the condenser if it fails any of the 3 tests.

Driver Coil Testing

1. Remove the flywheel. See Chapter Eight.
2. Disconnect the driver coil leads at the breaker points.
3. Connect an ohmmeter between the driver coil leads. Set the ohmmeter on the low ohms scale:
   a. Manual start models should show a resistance of 1.05-1.85 ohms (40 hp) 0.75-0.85 ohms (all others).
   b. Electric start models should show a resistance of 2.2-3.2 ohms.
4. Connect the ohmmeter between either driver coil lead and a good engine ground. Set the ohmmeter on the high ohms scale. If the ohmmeter does not read infinity, the driver coil or its leads are shorted to ground. Replace the driver coil. See Chapter Seven.

Ignition Coil Testing

WARNING
All coil tests should be performed on a wooden or insulated bench top to prevent shock hazards or leakage.

The ignition coil must be removed from the system before testing.
1. Remove the flywheel. See Chapter Eight.
2. Connect an ignition analyzer according to manufacturer's instructions.
3. Check the coil for continuity, power and leakage according to the analyzer manufacturer's instructions. Compare the results to the specifications provided with the analyzer. Replace the coil if it fails any of the 3 tests. See Chapter Seven.

CD 2 IGNITION TROUBLESHOOTING

The 4-wire connector plugs connect the charge and sensor coil leads to the power pack. The 3-wire connector plugs connect the power pack and ignition coils. No timing adjustments are required with a CD 2 ignition. Correct timing will be maintained as long as the wires are properly positioned in the connectors.

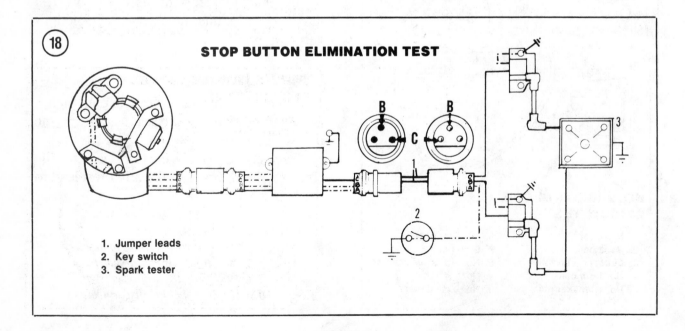

(18) STOP BUTTON ELIMINATION TEST

1. Jumper leads
2. Key switch
3. Spark tester

If the ignition system produces a satisfactory spark and the engine backfires but will not start, the ignition timing may be 180° off. Check to make sure the black/white wire in the 4-wire connector is positioned in connector terminal B. Also check to make sure the No. 1 coil (orange) wire is in the 3-wire connector B terminal and that it connects with the power pack (orange/blue) wire in the other connector B terminal.

Jumper leads are required for troubleshooting. Fabricate 4 leads using 8 in. lengths of 16-gauge wire. Connect a pin (OMC part NO. 511469) at one end and a socket (OMC part No. 581656) with one inch of tubing (OMC part No. 519628) at the other. Ohmmeter readings should be made when the engine is cold. Readings taken on a hot engine will show increased resistance caused by heat and result in unnecessary parts replacement without solving the basic problem.

OMC states that output tests should be made with a Stevens CD-77 or Electro-Specialties PRV-1 voltmeter.

Stop Button Elimination Test

Refer to **Figure 18** for this procedure.
1. Connect a spark tester as shown in **Figure 18**. Set the tester air gap to 1/2 in.

2. Separate the power pack-to-ignition coil 3-wire connector. Insert a jumper wire between the connector B terminals. Insert a jumper wire between the connector C terminals.
3. Crank the engine with a starter rope while watching the spark tester. If there is no spark or a spark at only one gap, remove the jumper wires and reconnect the connector plugs. Perform the *Sensor Coil Resistance Test* as described in this chapter.
4. If a spark jumps both gaps alternately, the problem is in the stop button circuit or the emergency ignition cutoff switch.

Sensor Coil Resistance Test

1. Separate the power pack-to-armature plate 4-wire connector. Insert jumper wires in terminals B and C of the armature plate end of the connector.
2. Connect an ohmmeter between the 2 jumper wires (**Figure 19**) and note the reading. If it is not 30-50 ohms, replace the sensor coil.
3. Set the ohmmeter on the high scale. Ground the black test lead at the armature plate and connect the red test lead to the C terminal jumper wire (**Figure 20**). The ohmmeter needle should not move. If it does, the sensor coil is grounded. Check for a

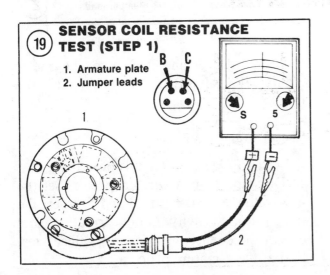

SENSOR COIL RESISTANCE TEST (STEP 1)
1. Armature plate
2. Jumper leads

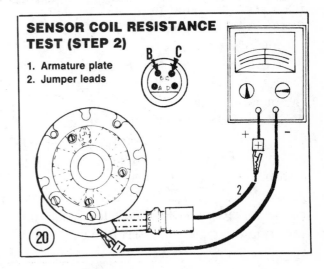

SENSOR COIL RESISTANCE TEST (STEP 2)
1. Armature plate
2. Jumper leads

grounded sensor coil lead before replacing the coil.

4. Remove the jumper wires and perform the *Charge Coil Resistance Test.*

Charge Coil Resistance Test

1. With the 4-terminal connector plug disconnected, insert jumper wires in terminals A and D of the armature plate end of the connector.

2. Connect an ohmmeter between the jumper wires (**Figure 21**) and note the reading. If it is not 500-650 ohms (400-550 ohms for 1973-1982 electric start models), replace the charge coil.

3. Set the ohmmeter on the high scale. Ground the black test lead at the armature plate and connect the red test lead to the A terminal jumper wire (**Figure 22**). The ohmmeter needle should not move. If it does, the charge coil is grounded. Check for a grounded charge coil lead before replacing the coil.

Charge Coil Output Test

Refer to **Figure 23** for this procedure.

1. Disconnect the 4-wire connector. Set the CD voltmeter switches to NEGATIVE and 500. Insert the red test lead in cavity A of the armature plate end of the connector. Ground the black test lead at the armature plate.

2. Crank the engine and note the meter reading.

3. Move the red test lead to cavity D of the connector and crank the engine again. Note the meter reading.

4. There should be no meter reading in Step 2 or Step 3. If there is, the charge coil is grounded. Check for a grounded charge coil lead before replacing the coil.

5. Leave the red test lead in cavity D of the connector. Remove the black test lead from the armature plate and insert it in cavity A of the connector.

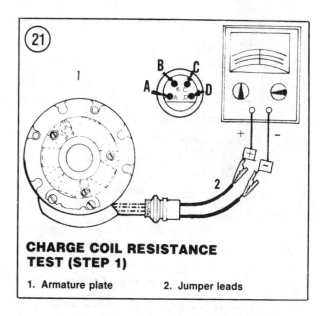

CHARGE COIL RESISTANCE TEST (STEP 1)

1. Armature plate   2. Jumper leads

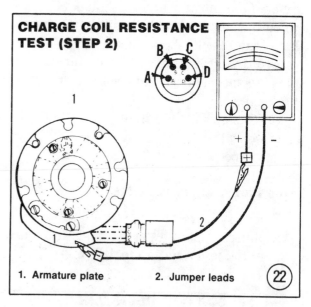

CHARGE COIL RESISTANCE TEST (STEP 2)

1. Armature plate   2. Jumper leads

6. Crank the engine and note the meter reading. If it is less than 230 volts, replace the charge coil.

Sensor Coil Output Test

Refer to **Figure 24** for this procedure.

1. Disconnect the 4-wire connector. Set the CD voltmeter switches to S and 5. Insert the red test lead in cavity C of the armature plate end of the connector. Ground the black test lead at the armature plate.

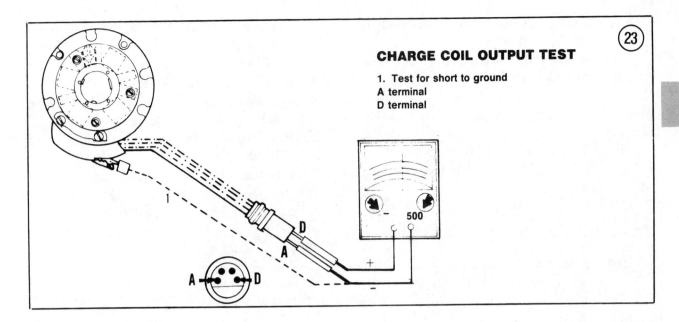

CHARGE COIL OUTPUT TEST

1. Test for short to ground
A terminal
D terminal

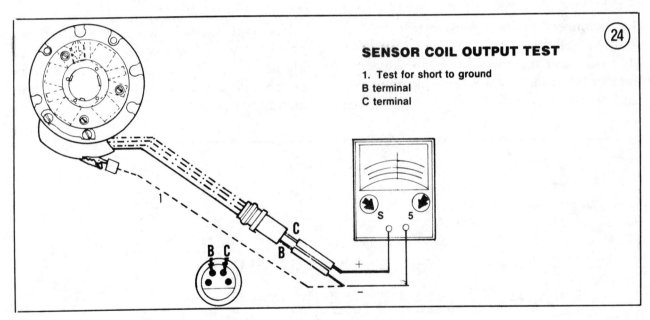

SENSOR COIL OUTPUT TEST

1. Test for short to ground
B terminal
C terminal

2. Crank the engine and note the meter reading.

3. Move the red test lead to cavity B of the connector and crank the engine again. Note the meter reading.

4. There should be no meter reading in Step 2 or Step 3. If there is, the sensor coil is grounded. Check for a grounded sensor coil lead before replacing the coil.

5. Leave the red test lead in cavity B of the connector. Remove the black test lead from the armature plate and insert it in cavity C of the connector.

6. Crank the engine and note the meter reading. If it is less than 0.3 volts, replace the sensor coil.

Power Pack Output Test

Refer to **Figure 25** for this procedure.

1. Disconnect the 3-wire connector. Set the CD voltmeter switches to NEGATIVE and

500. Insert jumper wires between terminals B and C of the connector.

2. Connect the red test lead to the jumper lead at terminal B and ground the black test lead.

3. Crank the engine and note the meter reading.

4. Move the red test lead to the jumper lead at terminal C. Crank the engine and note the meter reading.

5. If the meter reading is 180 volts or more in Step 3 or Step 4, check the ignition coil(s). If there is no reading, the power pack is probably defective. Substitute a known-good power pack and repeat the procedure.

Ignition Coil Resistance Test

1. Disconnect the high tension lead at the ignition coil.

2. Disconnect the 3-wire connector. Insert a jumper lead in terminal B of the ignition coil end of the connector.

3. Connect the ohmmeter red test lead to the B terminal jumper lead. Connect the black test lead to a good engine ground. The meter should read 0.1 ± 0.05 ohms.

4. Set the ohmmeter on the high scale. Move the black test lead to the ignition coil high tension terminal. The meter should read 225-325 ohms.

5. If the readings are not as specified in Step 3 or Step 4, replace the No. 1 ignition coil.

6. Move the jumper lead from terminal B to terminal C and repeat the procedure to test the No. 2 ignition coil.

IGNITION AND NEUTRAL START SWITCH

The ignition and neutral start switches can be tested with a self-powered test lamp or ohmmeter. If defective, replace the ignition switch with a marine switch. Do not use an automotive ignition switch.

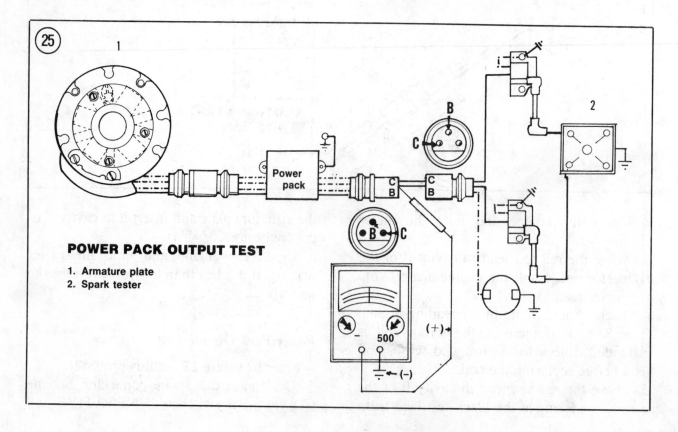

POWER PACK OUTPUT TEST

1. Armature plate
2. Spark tester

Ignition Switch Test

Refer to **Figure 26** for this procedure.

1. Disconnect the negative battery lead. Disconnect the positive battery lead.

2. Connect a test lamp or ohmmeter leads between the BATT and A switch terminals. With the switch in the OFF position, there should be no continuity.

3. Turn the switch to the ON position. The test lamp should light or the meter show continuity.

4. Turn the switch to the START position. The test lamp should light or the meter show continuity.

5. Hold the switch key in the START position and move the test lead from terminal A to terminal S. The test lamp should light or the meter show continuity.

6. Turn the switch off. Move the test leads to the 2 terminals marked M. The test lamp should light or the meter show continuity.

7. Turn the switch first to the START, then to the ON position. There should be no continuity in either position.

8. Turn the switch OFF. Move the test leads to terminal B and terminal C. Turn the switch ON. There should be no continuity. If equipped with a choke primer system, push inward on the key and the test lamp should light or the meter show continuity.

9. Repeat Step 8 with the switch in the START position. The results should be the same.

> *NOTE*
> *It is possible the switch may pass this test but still have an internal short. If the switch passes but does not function properly, have it leak-tested by a dealer.*

10. Replace the switch if it fails any of the steps in this procedure.

Neutral Start Switch Test and Adjustment (9.9 and 15 hp)

Switch adjustment is possible only when the manual interlock cam and lockout lever/hub adjustments have not been disturbed. See *Shift Lever Adjustment*, Chapter Nine. Refer to **Figure 27** for this procedure.

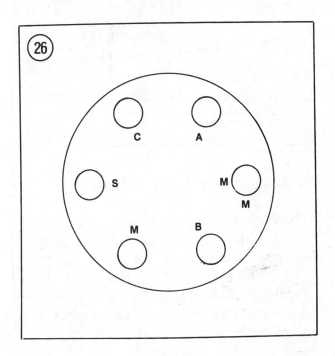

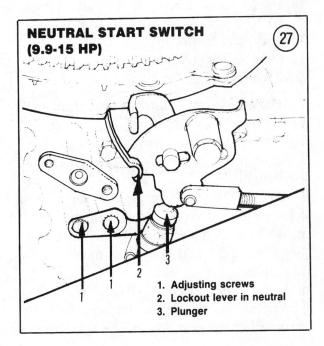

NEUTRAL START SWITCH (9.9-15 HP)

1. Adjusting screws
2. Lockout lever in neutral
3. Plunger

1. Disconnect the negative battery cable.
2. Remove the engine cover.
3. Shift into NEUTRAL.
4. Disconnect the starter motor cable.
5. Connect one ohmmeter test lead to the starter motor cable. Connect the other test lead to a good engine ground.
6. Depress the starter button. The test lamp should light or the ohmmeter show continuity.
7. Shift into FORWARD. Depress the starter button. There should be no continuity. Repeat this step after shifting into REVERSE.
8. If continuity is shown in Step 7:
   a. Remove the fuel pump and move it out of the way. See Chapter Six.
   b. Loosen the neutral start switch screws.
   c. With the shift lever in NEUTRAL, center the plunger switch with its lobe on the lockout lever, then raise the switch to depress its plunger 3/32-5/32 in.
   d. Repeat Step 6 and Step 7 to check adjustment.
9. Reinstall fuel pump. Install engine cover. Connect the negative battery cable.

Neutral Start Switch
Test and Adjustment
(18-35 hp)

Refer to **Figure 28** for this procedure.
1. Disconnect the negative battery cable.
2. Remove the engine cover.
3. Disconnect the switch-to-solenoid lead at the switch.
4. Connect an ohmmeter or test lamp between the switch and ground (**Figure 28**).
5. With the shift lever in NEUTRAL, the test lamp should light or the meter show continuity.
6. Shift into FORWARD and then REVERSE. There should be no continuity shown in either gear.

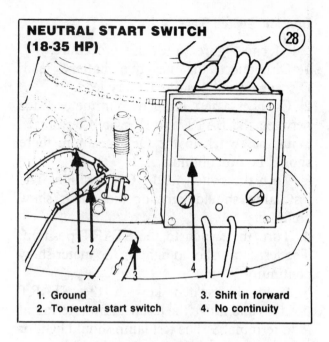

NEUTRAL START SWITCH (18-35 HP)

1. Ground
2. To neutral start switch
3. Shift in forward
4. No continuity

28

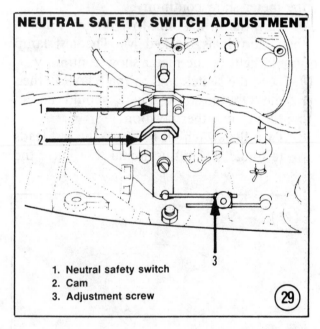

NEUTRAL SAFETY SWITCH ADJUSTMENT

1. Neutral safety switch
2. Cam
3. Adjustment screw

29

7. If continuity is shown in Step 6:
   a. Shift into NEUTRAL.
   b. Loosen the switch locknut and turn the adjustment screw until the test light or meter shows continuity.
   c. Shift into FORWARD and then REVERSE. If the light or meter shows continuity in either gear, replace the switch.

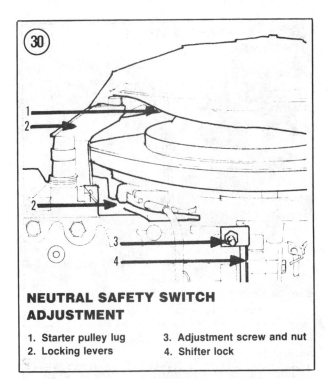

NEUTRAL SAFETY SWITCH ADJUSTMENT

1. Starter pulley lug
2. Locking levers
3. Adjustment screw and nut
4. Shifter lock

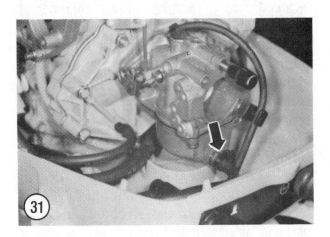

Neutral Start Switch Test and Adjustment (40 hp Electric Start)

Refer to **Figure 29** for this procedure.
1. Remove the engine cover.
2. Place shift lever in NEUTRAL.
3. Check the lockout lever cam. It should be centered under the neutral switch plunger.
4. If adjustment is required, loosen the linkage screw and position the cam lever, then tighten the screw.

Neutral Start Switch Test and Adjustment (40 hp Manual Start)

Refer to **Figure 30** for this procedure.
1. Remove the engine cover.
2. Place shift lever in NEUTRAL.
3. Check clearance between lockout lever and starter pulley lugs.
4. If clearance is not 0.030-0.060 in., loosen the shifter locknut and adjust the screw to bring it within specifications, then tighten the locknut.

FUEL SYSTEM

Many outboard owners automatically assume the carburetor is at fault when the engine does not run properly. While fuel system problems are not uncommon, carburetor adjustment is seldom the answer. In many cases, adjusting the carburetor only compounds the problem by making the engine run worse.

Fuel system troubleshooting should start at the gas tank and work through the system, reserving the carburetor(s) as the final point. The majority of fuel system problems result from an empty fuel tank, sour fuel, a plugged fuel filter or a malfunctioning fuel pump. **Table 3** provides a series of symptoms and causes that can be useful in localizing fuel system problems.

Troubleshooting

As a first step, check the fuel flow. Remove the fuel tank cap and look into the tank. If there is fuel present, disconnect and ground the spark plug lead(s) as a safety precaution. Disconnect the fuel line at the carburetor (**Figure 31**, typical) and place it in a suitable container to catch any discharged fuel. See if gas flows freely from the line when the primer bulb is squeezed.

If there is no fuel flow from the line, the fuel petcock may be shut off or blocked by rust or foreign matter, the fuel line may be stopped up or kinked or a primer bulb check valve may be defective. If a good fuel flow is present, crank the engine 10-12 times to check fuel pump operation. A pump that is operating satisfactorily will deliver a good, constant flow of fuel from the line. If the amount of flow varies from pulse to pulse, the fuel pump is probably failing.

Carburetor chokes can also present problems. A choke that sticks open will show up as a hard starting problem; one that sticks closed will result in a flooding condition.

During a hot engine shut-down, the fuel bowl temperature can rise above 200°, causing the fuel inside to boil. While marine carburetors are vented to atmosphere to prevent this problem, there is a possibility some fuel will percolate over the high-speed nozzle.

A leaking inlet needle and seat or a defective float will allow an excessive amount of fuel into the intake manifold. Pressure in the fuel line after the engine is shut down forces fuel past the leaking needle and seat. This raises the fuel bowl level, allowing fuel to overflow into the manifold.

Excessive fuel consumption may not necessarily mean an engine or fuel system problem. Marine growth on the boat's hull, a bent or otherwise damaged propeller or a fuel line leak can cause an increase in fuel consumption. These areas should all be checked *before* blaming the carburetor.

Electric Primer System

A primer solenoid is used on 1984 20-35 hp electric models instead of a choke solenoid. See **Figure 32**. When the key is inserted in the ignition switch and depressed, the solenoid opens electrically and allows fuel to pass from the fuel pump into the

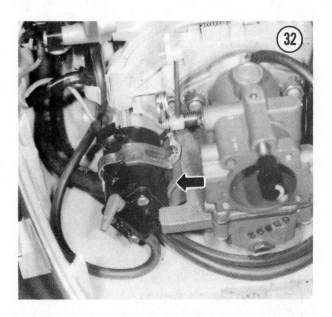

carburetor in sufficient quantity to start the engine.

The primer solenoid operation can be checked by running the engine at approximately 2,000 rpm and depressing the ignition key. If the solenoid is functioning properly, the engine will run rich and drop about 1,000 rpm until the key is released. If the solenoid is suspected of not operating properly, shut the engines off and disconnect the purple/white wire at the terminal board. Connect an ohmmeter between the purple/white wire and the black primer solenoid ground lead. The ohmmeter should read 4-6 ohms. If the solenoid does not perform as described, remove and repair or replace it. See Chapter Six.

ENGINE TEMPERATURE AND OVERHEATING

Proper engine temperature is critical to good engine operation. An engine that runs too hot will be damaged internally. One that operates too cool will not run smoothly or efficiently.

A variety of problems can cause engine overheating. Some of the most commonly encountered are a defective thermostat, low

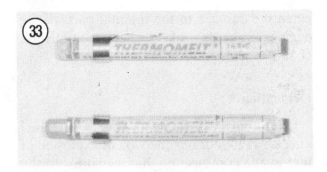

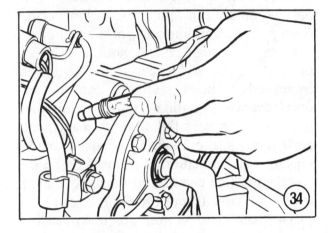

output or defective water pump, damaged or mispositioned water passage restrictors or even engine flashing in the cylinder head casting water discharge passage that was not removed during manufacture.

The flashing problem is most common in 1976 and later 25-35 hp engines. It can be easily diagnosed by running the engine at 3,000 rpm in a test tank. If the water discharged by the pump indicator hose indicates that the water pump is satisfactory, check the water spray from the exhaust relief on the back of the exhaust housing. If there is little or none, remove the cylinder head water cover (see Chapter Eight) and check the water discharge passage at the bottom of the head for flashing. If found, it can be removed with a small punch or sharp knife.

Troubleshooting

Engine temperature can be checked with the use of Markal Thermomelt Stiks available

at your Johnson or Evinrude dealer. This heat-sensitive stick looks like a large crayon (**Figure 33**) and will melt on contact with a metal surface at a specific temperature.

Three thermomelt sticks are required to properly check a Johnson or Evinrude outboard according to model: a 100° F (37° C) stick, a 125° F (52° C) stick and a 163° F (73° C) stick. The stick should not be applied to the center of the cylinder head, as this area is normally hotter than 163° F.

NOTE
Use the 100° F and 163° F stick(s) with 1984 5, 6 and 8 hp models. Use the 125° F and 163° F stick(s) with all others.

The test is most efficient when carried out on a motor operating on a boat in the water. If necessary to perform the test using a test tank, run the engine at 3,000 rpm for a minimum of 5 minutes to bring it to operating temperature. Make sure inlet water temperature is below 80° F (26° C) and perform the test as follows.

1. Mark the cylinder water jacket with each stick (**Figure 34**). The mark will appear similar to a chalk mark. Make sure sufficient material is applied to the metal surface.
2. With the engine at operating temperature and running at idle in FORWARD gear, the 100° F (1984 5, 6 and 8 hp) or 125° F (all others) stick mark should melt. If it does not melt on thermostat-equipped models (6-35 hp), the thermostat is stuck open and the engine is running cold.
3. With the engine at operating temperature and running at full throttle in FORWARD gear, the 163 degree F stick mark should not melt. If it does, the power head is overheating. Look for a defective water pump or clogged or leaking cooling system. On thermostat-equipped models, the thermostat may be stuck closed.

ENGINE

Engine problems are generally symptoms of something wrong in another system, such as ignition, fuel or starting. If properly maintained and serviced, the engine should experience no problems other than those caused by age and wear.

Overheating and Lack of Lubrication

Overheating and lack of lubrication cause the majority of engine mechanical problems. Outboard motors create a great deal of heat and are not designed to operate at a standstill for any length of time. Using a spark plug of the wrong heat range can burn a piston. Incorrect ignition timing, a defective water pump or thermostat, a propeller that is too large (over-propping) or an excessively lean fuel mixture can also cause the engine to overheat.

Preignition

Preignition is the premature burning of fuel and is caused by hot spots in the combustion chamber (**Figure 35**). The fuel actually ignites before it is supposed to. Glowing deposits in the combustion chamber, inadequate cooling or overheated spark plugs can all cause preignition. This is first noticed in the form of a power loss but will eventually result in

extensive damage to the internal parts of the engine because of higher combustion chamber temperatures.

Detonation

Commonly called "spark knock" or "fuel knock," detonation is the violent explosion of fuel in the combustion chamber prior to the proper time of combustion (**Figure 36**). Severe damage can result. Use of low octane gasoline is a common cause of detonation.

Even when high octane gasoline is used, detonation can still occur if the engine is improperly timed. Other causes are over-advanced ignition timing, lean fuel mixture at or near full throttle, inadequate engine cooling, cross-firing of spark plugs, excessive accumulation of deposits on piston and combustion chamber or the use of a prop that is too large (over-propping).

Since outboard motors are noisy, engine knock or detonation is likely to go unnoticed by owners, especially at high engine rpm when wind noise is also present. Such inaudible detonation, as it is called, is usually the cause when engine damage occurs for no apparent reason.

Poor Idling

A poor idle can be caused by improper carburetor adjustment, incorrect timing or

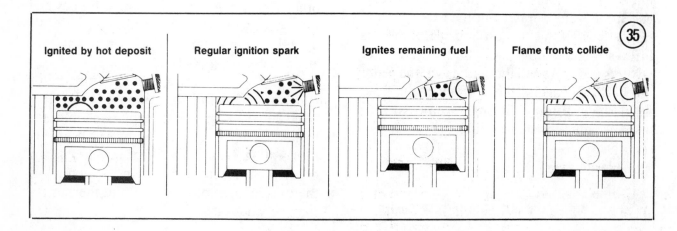

| Ignited by hot deposit | Regular ignition spark | Ignites remaining fuel | Flame fronts collide |

ignition system malfunctions. Check the gas cap vent for an obstruction.

Misfiring

Misfiring can result from a weak spark or a dirty spark plug. Check for fuel contamination. If misfiring occurs only under heavy load, as when accelerating, it is usually caused by a defective spark plug. Run the motor at night to check for spark leaks along the plug wire and under spark plug cap or use a spark leak tester.

WARNING
Do not run engine in a dark garage to check for spark leak. There is considerable danger of carbon monoxide poisoning.

Water Leakage in Cylinder

The fastest and easiest way to check for water leakage in a cylinder is to check the spark plugs. Water will clean a spark plug. If one of the 2 plugs on a multi-cylinder engine is clean and the other is dirty, there is most likely a water leak in the cylinder with the clean plug.

To remove all doubt, install a dirty plug in each cylinder. Run the engine in a test tank or on the boat in water for 5-10 minutes. Shut the engine off and remove the plugs. If one plug is clean and the other dirty (or if both plugs are clean), a water leak in the cylinder(s) is the problem.

Flat Spots

If the engine seems to die momentarily when the throttle is opened and then recovers, check for a dirty main jet in the carburetor, water in the fuel or an excessively lean mixture.

Power Loss

Several factors can cause a lack of power and speed. Look for air leaks in the fuel line or fuel pump, a clogged fuel filter or a choke/throttle valve that does not operate properly. Check ignition timing.

A piston or cylinder that is galling, incorrect piston clearance or a worn/sticky piston ring may be responsible. Look for loose bolts, defective gaskets or leaking machined mating surfaces on the cylinder head, cylinder or crankcase. Also check the crankcase oil seal; if worn, it can allow gas to leak between cylinders.

Piston Seizure

This is caused by one or more pistons with incorrect bore clearances, piston rings with an

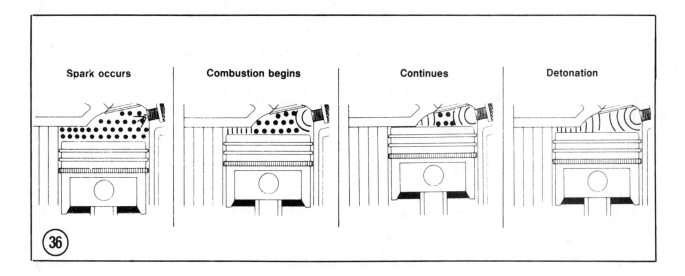

| Spark occurs | Combustion begins | Continues | Detonation |

36

improper end gap, the use of an oil-fuel mixture containing less than 1 part oil to 50 parts of gasoline or an oil of poor quality, a spark plug of the wrong heat range or incorrect ignition timing. Overheating from any cause may result in piston seizure.

Excessive Vibration

Excessive vibration may be caused by loose motor mounts, worn bearings or a generally poor running motor.

Engine Noises

Experience is needed to diagnose accurately in this area. Noises are difficult to differentiate and even harder to describe. Deep knocking noises usually mean main bearing failure. A slapping noise generally comes from a loose piston. A light knocking noise during acceleration may be a bad connecting rod bearing. Pinging should be corrected immediately or damage to the piston will result. A compression leak at the head-to-cylinder joint will sound like a rapid on-off squeal.

Table 1 STARTER TROUBLESHOOTING

Trouble	Cause	Remedy
Pinion does not move when starter is turned on	Blown fuse	Replace fuse.
	Pinion rusted to armature shaft	Remove, clean or replace as required.
	Series coil or shunt broken or shorted	Replace coil or shunt.
	Loose switch connections	Tighten connections.
	Rusted or dirty plunger	Clean plunger.
Pinion meshes with ring gear but starter does not run	Worn brushes or brush springs touching armature	Replace brushes or brush springs.
	Dirty or burned commutator	Clean or replace as required.
	Defective armature field coil	Replace armature.
	Worn or rusted armature shaft bearing	Replace bearing.
Starter motor runs at full speed before pinion meshes with ring gear	Worn pinion sleeve	Replace sleeve.
	Pinion does not stop in correct position	Replace pinion.
Pinion meshes with gear and motor starts but engine does not crank	Defective overrunning clutch	Replace overrunning clutch.

(continued)

Table 1 STARTER TROUBLESHOOTING (continued)

Trouble	Cause	Remedy
Starter motor does not stop when turned off after engine has started	Rusted or dirty plunger	Clean or replace plunger.
Starter motor speed low and high-current draw	Armature may be dragging on pole shoes from bent shaft, worn bearings or loose pole shoes	Replace shaft or bearings and/or tighten pole shoes.
	Tight or dirty bearings	Loosen or clean bearings.
High current draw with no armature rotation	A direct ground switch, at terminal or at brushes or field connections	Replace defective parts.
	Frozen shaft bearings which prevent armature from rotating	Loosen, clean or replace bearings.
Starter motor has grounded armature or field winding	Field and/or armature is burned or lead is thrown out of commutator due to excess leakage	Raise grounded brushes from commutator and insulate them with cardboard. Use an ignition analyzer and test points to check between insulated terminal or starter motor and starter motor frame (remove ground connection of shunt coils on motors with this feature). If analyzer shows resistance (meter needle moves to right), there is a ground. Raise other brushes from armature and check armature and fields separately to locate ground.
Starter motor has grounded armature or field winding	Current passes through armature first, then to ground field windings	Disconnect grounded leads, then locate any abnormal grounds in starter motor.
Starter motor fails to operate and draws no current and/or high resistance	Open circuit in fields or armature, at connections or brushes or between brushes and commutator	Repair or adjust broken or weak brush springs, worn brushes, high insulation between commutator bars or a dirty, gummy or oily commutator.

3

(continued)

Table 1 STARTER TROUBLESHOOTING (continued)

Trouble	Cause	Remedy
High resistance in starter motor	Low no-load speed and a low current draw and low developed torque	Closed "open" field winding on unit which has 2 or 3 circuits in starter motor (unit in which current divides as it enters, taking 2 or 3 parallel paths).
High free speed and high current draw	Shorted fields in starter motor	Install new fields and check for improved performance. (Fields normally have very low resistance, thus it is difficult to detect shorted fields, since difference in current draw between normal starter motor field windings would not be very great.)
Excessive voltage drop	Cables too small	Install larger cables to accomodate high current draw.
High circuit resistance	Dirty connections	Clean connections.
Starter does not operate	Run-down battery	Check battery with hydrometer. If reading is below 1.230, recharge or replace battery.
	Poor contact at terminals	Remove terminal clamps. Scrape terminals and clamps clean and tighten bolts securely.
	Wiring or key switch corroded	Install new switch or wiring. Coat with sealer to protect against further corrosion.
	Starter solenoid	Check for resistance between: (a) positive ($+$) terminal of battery and large input terminal of starter solenoid, (b) large wire at top of starter motor and negative ($-$) terminal of battery, and (c) small terminal of starter solenoid and positive battery terminal. Key switch must be in START position. Repair all defective parts.
	Starter motor	With a fully charged battery, connect a negative ($-$) jumper wire to upper terminal on side of starter motor and a positive jumper to large lower terminal of starter motor. If motor still does not operate, remove for overhaul or replacement.

(continued)

Table 1 STARTER TROUBLESHOOTING (continued)

Trouble	Cause	Remedy
Starter turns over too slowly	Low battery or poor contact at battery terminal	See "Starter does not operate".
	Poor contact at starter solenoid or starter motor	Check all terminals for looseness and tighten all nuts securely.
	Starter mechanism	Disconnect positive (+) battery terminal. Rotate pinion gear in disengaged position. Pinion gear and motor should run freely by hand. If motor does not turn over easily, clean starter and replace all defective parts.
Starter spins freely but does not engage engine	Low battery or poor contact at battery terminal	See "Starter does not operate."
	Poor contact at starter solenoid or or starter motor	See "Starter does not operate."
	Dirty or corroded pinion drive	Clean thoroughly and lubricate the spline underneath the pinion with Lubriplate 777
Starter does not engage freely	Pinion or flywheel gear	Inspect mating gears for excessive wear. Replace all defective parts.
	Small anti-drift spring	If drive pinion interferes with flywheel gear after engine has started, inspect anti-drift spring located under pinion gear. Replace all defective parts. NOTE: If drive pinion tends to stay engaged in flywheel gear when starter motor is in idle position, start motor @ 1/4 throttle to allow starter pinion gear to release flywheel ring gear instantly.
Starter keeps on spinning after key is turned ON	Key not fully returned	Check that key has returned to normal ON position from START position. Replace switch if key constantly stays in START position.
	Starter solenoid	Inspect starter solenoid to see if contacts have become stuck in closed position. If starter does not stop running with small yellow lead disconnected from starter solenoid, replace starter solenoid.

(continued)

Table 1 STARTER TROUBLESHOOTING (continued)

Trouble	Cause	Remedy
Wiring or key switch	Inspect all wires for defects	Open remote control box and inspect wiring @ switches. Repair or replace all defective parts.
Wires overheat	Battery terminals improperly connected	Check that negative marking on harness matches that of battery. If battery is connected improperly, red wire to rectifier will overheat.
	Short circuit in system	Inspect all wiring connections and wires for looseness or defects. Open remote control box and inspect wiring @ switches.
	Short circuit in choke solenoid	Repair or replace all defective parts. Check for high resistance. If blue choke wire heats rapidly when choke is used, choke solenoid may have internal short. Replace if defective.
	Short circuit in starter solenoid	If yellow starter solenoid lead overheats, there may be internal short (resistance) in starter solenoid. Replace if defective.
	Low battery voltage	Battery voltage is checked with an ampere-volt tester when battery is under a starting load. Battery must be recharged if it registers under 9.5 volts. If battery is below specified hydrometer reading of 1.230, it will not turn engine fast enough to start it.

Table 2 IGNITION TROUBLESHOOTING

Symptom	Probable cause
Engine won't start, but fuel and spark are good	Defective or dirty spark plugs. Spark plug gap set too wide. Improper spark timing. Shorted stop button. Air leaks into fuel pump. Broken piston ring(s). Cylinder head, crankcase or cylinder sealing faulty. Worn crankcase oil seal.

(continued)

Table 2 IGNITION TROUBLESHOOTING (continued)

Symptom	Probable cause
Engine misfires @ idle	Incorrect spark plug gap. Defective, dirty or loose spark plugs. Spark plugs of incorrect heat range. Leaking or broken high tension wires. Weak armature magnets. Defective coil or condenser. Defective ignition switch. Spark timing out of adjustment.
Engine misfires @ high speed	See "Engine misfires @ idle." Coil breaks down. Coil shorts through insulation. Spark plug gap too wide. Wrong type spark plugs. Too much spark advance.
Engine backfires	Cracked spark plug insulator. Improper timing. Crossed spark plug wires. Improper ignition timing.
Engine preignition	Spark advanced too far. Incorrect type spark plug. Burned spark plug electrodes.
Engine noises (knocking at power head)	Spark advanced too far.
Ignition coil fails	Extremely high voltage. Moisture formation. Excessive heat from engine.
Spark plugs burn and foul	Incorrect type plug. Fuel mixture too rich. Inferior grade of gasoline. Overheated engine. Excessive carbon in combustion chambers.
Ignition causing high fuel consumption	Incorrect spark timing. Leaking high tension wires. Incorrect spark plug gap. Fouled spark plugs. Incorrect spark advance. Weak ignition coil. Preignition.

Table 3 FUEL SYSTEM TROUBLESHOOTING

Symptom	Probable cause
No fuel @ carburetor	No gas in tank. Air vent in gas cap not open. Air vent in gas cap clogged. Fuel tank sitting on fuel line. Fuel line fittings not properly connected to engine or fuel tank.

(continued)

Table 3 FUEL SYSTEM TROUBLESHOOTING (continued)

Symptom	Probable cause
No fuel at carburetor (continued)	Air leak @ fuel connection. Fuel pickup clogged. Defective fuel pump.
Flooding @ carburetor	Choke out of adjustment. High float level. Float stuck. Excessive fuel pump pressure. Float saturated beyond buoyancy.
Rough operation	Dirt or water in fuel. Reed valve open or broken. Incorrect fuel level in carburetor bowl. Carburetor loose @ mounting flange. Throttle shutter not closing completely. Throttle shutter valve installed incorrectly.
Carburetor spit-back at idle	Chipped or broken reed valve(s).
Engine misfires @ high speed	Dirty carburetor. Lean carburetor adjustment. Restriction in fuel system. Low fuel pump pressure.
Engine backfires	Poor quality fuel. Air-fuel mixture too rich or too lean. Improperly adjusted carburetor.
Engine preignition	Excessive oil in fuel. Inferior grade of gasoline. Lean carburetor mixture.
Spark plugs burn and foul	Fuel mixture too rich. Inferior grade of gasoline.
High gas consumption: Flooding or leaking	Cracked carburetor casting. Leaks @ line connections. Defective carburetor bowl gasket. High float level. Plugged vent hole in cover. Loose needle and seat. Defective needle valve seat gasket. Worn needle valve and seat. Foreign matter clogging needle valve. Worn float pin or bracket. Float binding in bowl. High fuel pump pressure.
Overrich mixture	Choke lever stuck. High float level. High fuel pump pressure.
Abnormal speeds	Carburetor out of adjustment. Too much oil in fuel.

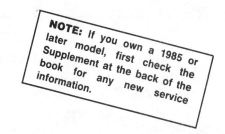
NOTE: If you own a 1985 or later model, first check the Supplement at the back of the book for any new service information.

Chapter Four

Lubrication, Maintenance and Tune-up

The modern outboard motor delivers more power and performance than ever before, with higher compression ratios, new and improved electrical systems and other design advances. Proper lubrication, maintenance and tune-ups have thus become increasingly important as ways in which you can maintain a high level of performance, extend engine life and extract the maximum economy of operation.

You can do your own lubrication, maintenance and tune-ups if you follow the correct procedures and use common sense. The following information is based on recommendations from Johnson and Evinrude that will help you keep your outboard motor operating at its peak performance level.

Tables 1-4 are at the end of the chapter.

LUBRICATION

Proper Fuel Selection

Two-stroke engines are lubricated by mixing oil with the fuel. The various components of the engine are thus lubricated as the fuel-oil mixture passes through the crankcase and cylinders. Since two-stroke fuel serves the dual function of producing ignition and distributing the lubrication, the use of low octane marine white gasolines should be avoided. Such gasolines also have a tendency to cause ring sticking and port plugging.

Johnson and Evinrude have recommended the use of regular unleaded gasoline with a minimum posted pump octane rating of 86 in all 1973-1981 2-35 hp outboards. However, obtaining regular unleaded gasoline with an octane rating that high is becoming extremely difficult. Accordingly, factory engineering issued new fuel recommendations in March 1983 for 1977 and later models, dropping the octane rating to 67. No mention of a change was made for 1973-1976 models. While leaded regular or leaded premium can be used when necessary, lead-free or low lead regular gasolines are preferable, as they offer longer spark plug life.

Sour Fuel

Fuel should not be stored for more than 60 days (under ideal conditions). Gasoline forms gum and varnish deposits as it ages. Such fuel will cause starting problems. A fuel additive such as OMC 2+4 Fuel Conditioner should be used to prevent gum and varnish formation during storage or prolonged periods of non-use but it is always better to drain the tank in such cases. Always use fresh gasoline when mixing fuel for your outboard.

Gasohol

Some gasolines sold for marine use now contain alcohol, although this fact may not be advertised. A mixture of 10 percent ethyl alcohol and 90 percent unleaded gasoline is called gasohol. This is considered suitable for use in Johnson and Evinrude outboards. Some gasolines, however, contain methyl alcohol or methanol. This is *not* recommended for use.

Fuels with an alcohol content tend to slowly absorb moisture from the air. When the moisture content of the fuel reaches approximately one percent, it combines with the alcohol and separates from the fuel. This separation does not normally occur when gasohol is used in an automobile, as the tank is generally emptied within a few days after filling it.

The problem does occur in marine use, however, because boats often remain idle between start-ups for days or even weeks. This length of time permits separation to take place. The alcohol-water mixture settles at the bottom of the fuel tank. Since outboard motors will not run on this mixture, it is necessary to drain the fuel tank, flush out the fuel system with clean gasoline and then remove, clean and reinstall the spark plugs before the engine can be started.

Continued use of fuels containing methanol can cause deterioration of fuel system components. The major danger of using gasohol in an outboard motor is that a shot of the water-alcohol mix may be picked

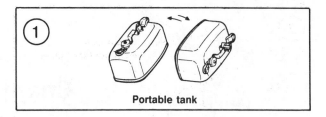

Portable tank

up and sent to one of the carburetors of a multicylinder engine. Since this mixture contains no oil, it will wash oil off the bore of any cylinder it enters. The other carburetor receiving good fuel-oil mixture will keep the engine running while the cylinder receiving the water-alcohol mixture can suffer internal damage.

The problem of unlabeled gasohol has become so prevalent around the United States that Miller Tools (32615 Park Lane, Garden City, MI 48135) now offers an Alcohol Detection Kit (part No. C-4846) so owners and mechanics can determine the quality of fuel being used.

The kit cannot differentiate between types of alcohol (ethanol, methanol, etc.) nor is it considered to be absolutely accurate from a scientific standpoint, but it is accurate enough to determine whether or not there is sufficient alcohol in the fuel that the user to should take precautions.

Recommended Fuel Mixture

Use the specified gasoline for your Johnson or Evinrude outboard and mix with Johnson or Evinrude 50/1 Lubricant in the following ratios:

> *CAUTION*
> *Do not, under any circumstances, use multigrade or other high detergent automotive oils or oils containing metallic additives. Such oils are harmful to 2-stroke engines. Since they do not mix properly with gasoline, do not burn as 2-cycle oils do and leave an ash residue, their use may result in piston scoring, bearing failure or other engine damage.*

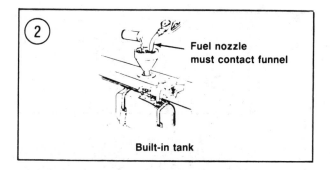

② Fuel nozzle
    must contact funnel

Built-in tank

a. Thoroughly mix one pint of Johnson or Evinrude 50/1 Lubricant with each 6 gallons of gasoline in your remote fuel tank. This provides a 50:1 mixture.

b. Operation in Canada requires mixing one U.S. pint of Johnson or Evinrude 50/1 Lubricant to each 5 Imperial gallons of gasoline in the remote fuel tank.

> *CAUTION*
> *There are a number of oil products on the market which specify use at 100:1. They are **not** BIA TC-W approved and should **not** be used.*

c. If Johnson or Evinrude 50/1 Lubricant is not available, any high-quality 2-stroke oil intended for outboard use may be substituted provided the oil meets BIA rating TC-W and specifies so on the container. Follow the manufacturer's mixing instructions on the container but do not exceed a 50:1 ratio.

Correct Fuel Mixing

> *WARNING*
> *Gasoline is an extreme fire hazard. Never use gasoline near heat, sparks or flame. Do not smoke while mixing fuel.*

Mix the fuel and oil outdoors or in a well-ventilated indoor location. Using less than the specified amount of oil can result in insufficient lubrication and serious engine damage. Using more oil than specified causes spark plug fouling, erratic carburetion, excessive smoking and rapid carbon accumulation.

Cleanliness is of prime importance. Even a very small particle of dirt can cause carburetion problems. Always use fresh gasoline. Gum and varnish deposits tend to form in gasoline stored in a tank for any length of time. Use of sour fuel can result in carburetor problems and spark plug fouling.

Above 32° F (0° C)

Measure the required amounts of gasoline and oil accurately. Pour the 50/1 Lubricant into the portable tank and add the fuel. Install the tank filler cap and mix the fuel by tipping the tank on its side and back to an upright position several times. See **Figure 1**.

If a built-in tank is used, insert a large metal filter funnel in the tank filler neck. Slowly pour the 50/1 Lubricant into the funnel at the same time the tank is being filled with gasoline. See **Figure 2**.

Below 32° F (0° C)

Measure the required amounts of gasoline and oil accurately. Pour about one gallon of gasoline in the tank and add the required amount of 50/1 Lubricant. Install the tank filler cap and shake the tank to thoroughly mix the fuel and oil. Remove the cap and add the balance of the gasoline.

If a built-in tank is used, insert a large metal filter funnel in the tank filler neck. Mix the required amount of 50/1 Lubricant with one gallon of gasoline in a separate container. Slowly pour the mixture into the funnel at the same time the tank is being filled with gasoline.

Consistent Fuel Mixtures

The carburetor idle adjustment is sensitive to fuel mixture variations which result from the use of different oils and gasolines or from inaccurate measuring and mixing. This may require readjustment of the idle needle. To prevent the necessity for constant readjustment of the carburetor from one batch of fuel to the next, always be consistent. Prepare each batch of fuel exactly the same as previous ones.

Pre-mixed fuels sold at some marinas are not recommended for use in Johnson or Evinrude outboards, since the quality and consistency of pre-mixed fuels can vary greatly. The possibility of engine damage resulting from use of an incorrect fuel mixture outweighs the convenience offered by pre-mixed fuel.

Lower Drive Unit Lubrication

Replace the lower drive unit lubricant after the first 20 hours of operation. Check every 50 hours of operation and top up if necessary. Drain and refill every 100 hours of operation or at least once a season. Use OMC HI-VIS gearcase lubricant.

> *CAUTION*
> *Do not use regular automotive grease in the lower drive unit. Its expansion and foam characteristics are not suitable for marine use.*

2 and 4 hp models

1. Place a suitable container under the gearcase.
2. Remove the drain/fill plug from the starboard side of the gearcase.
3. Position the gearcase with the starboard side facing down and let the lubricant drain completely.
4. Reposition gearcase with drain/fill hole facing up. Slowly fill with OMC HI-VIS gearcase lubricant until it appears at the hole.
5. Install the drain/fill plug and tighten to 60-80 in.-lb. (7-9 N•m).

4.5-40 hp models

1. Place a suitable container under the gearcase.

> *CAUTION*
> *Never lubricate the gearcase without first removing the oil level screw, as the injected lubricant displaces air which must be allowed to escape. The gearcase cannot be completely filled otherwise.*

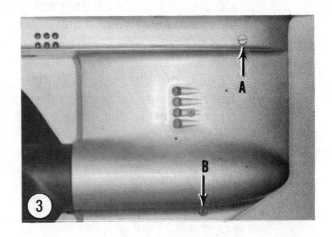

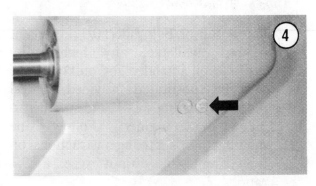

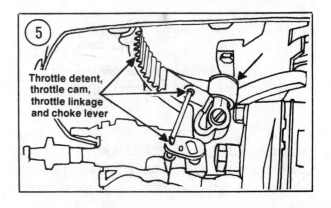

Throttle detent, throttle cam, throttle linkage and choke lever

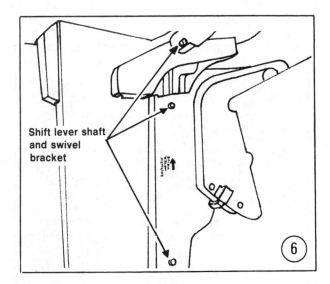

Shift lever shaft and swivel bracket

⑥

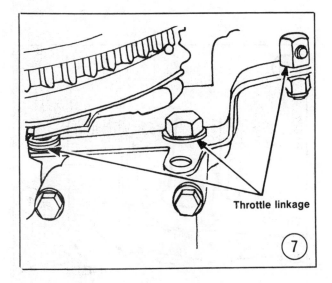

Throttle linkage

⑦

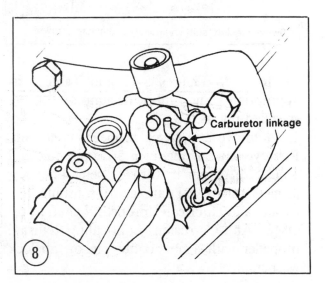

Carburetor linkage

⑧

4

2. Locate and remove the oil level plug and washer (A, **Figure 3**, typical).

> *NOTE*
> *The gearcase on some models will have a Phillips head screw located beside the slotted drain/fill plug (**Figure 4**). The Phillips head screw secures the shift rod in place—do not remove it by mistake.*

3. Locate and remove the drain/fill plug and washer (B, **Figure 3**, typical).
4. Allow the lubricant to completely drain.
5. Inject OMC HI-VIS lubricant into the drain/fill plug hole until excess fluid flows out the oil level plug hole.
6. Drain about one fluid ounce of fluid to allow for lubricant expansion.
7. Install the oil level plug. Remove the lubricant tube or nozzle from drain/fill hole and install the drain/fill plug. Be sure the washers are in place under the head of each, so water will not leak past the threads into the housing. Tighten both plugs to 60-80 in.-lb. (7-9 N•m).

Other Lubrication Points

Refer to **Figures 5-12** (typical) and **Table 1** for other lubricant points, frequency of lubrication and lubricant to be used.

> *CAUTION*
> *When lubricating the steering cable on models so equipped, make sure its core is fully retracted into the cable housing. Lubricating the cable while extended can cause a hydraulic lock to occur.*

Salt Water Corrosion of Gear Housing Bearing Carrier/Nut

Salt water corrosion that is allowed to build up unchecked can eventually split the gear housing and destroy the lower unit. If the motor is used in salt water, remove the propeller assembly and bearing housing at least once a year after the initial 20-hour inspection. Clean all corrosive deposits and dried-up lubricant from each end of the housing (**Figure 13**). Lubricate the bearing housing, O-ring and screw threads with OMC Gasket Sealing Compound. Install bearing housing and tighten screws to specifications (Chapter Nine).

STORAGE

The major consideration in preparing an outboard motor for storage is to protect it from rust, corrosion and dirt. Johnson and Evinrude recommend the following procedure.

1. Remove the engine cover. Remove the air silencer front cover, if so equipped.

2. Operate the motor in a test tank with the proper test wheel or on the boat in the water. Start the engine and let it warm up.

3. Disconnect the fuel line and let engine run at low rpm while pouring OMC Rust Preventive Oil or OMC Storage Fogging Oil into the carburetor throat(s) until the engine smokes excessively.

4. Shut the engine off. Reinstall air silencer front cover, if so equipped.

5. Remove the spark plugs as described in this chapter. Clean and regap or replace plugs. Leave spark plug leads disconnected.

6. Retard throttle and rotate flywheel several times to drain any water from the water pump.

7. Clean and lubricate starter motor drive mechanism, if so equipped.

8. Drain carburetor float chamber. Remove and replace fuel filter.

9. Drain and clean fuel tank. Disconnect fuel line from tank and wrap it around the tank ears. Store tank in a well-ventilated area away from heat or open flame.

10. Drain and refill gearcase as described in this chapter. Check condition of level and drain/fill plug gaskets. Replace as required.

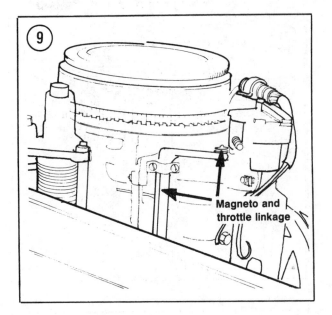

Magneto and throttle linkage

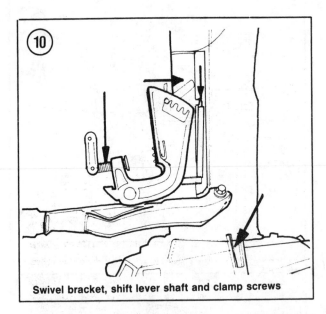

Swivel bracket, shift lever shaft and clamp screws

11. Refer to **Figures 5-12** and **Table 1** as appropriate and lubricate motor at all specified points.

12. Remove and check propeller condition. Remove any burring from drive pin hole and replace drive pin if worn or bent. Look for propeller shaft seal damage from fishing line. Clean and lubricate propeller shaft with OMC Anti-Corrosion Lubricant. Reinstall propeller with a new cotter pin or tab lock washer.

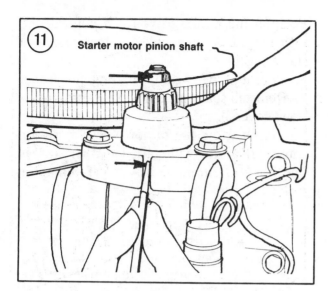

Starter motor pinion shaft

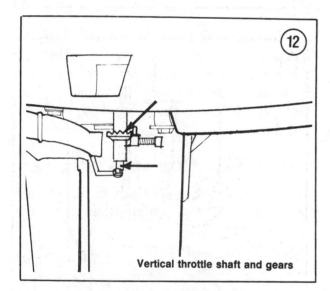

Vertical throttle shaft and gears

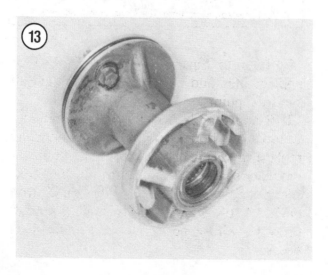

13. Clean all external parts of the motor with OMC All-Purpose Marine Cleaner and apply OMC Boat Polish.

14. Store the motor in an upright position in a dry and well-ventilated area.

15. Service the battery as follows:

a. Disconnect the negative battery cable, then the positive battery cable.

b. Remove all grease, corrosion and dirt from the battery surface.

c. Check the electrolyte level in each battery cell and top up with distilled water, if necessary. Fluid level in each cell should not be higher than 3/16 in. above the perforated baffles.

d. Lubricate the terminal bolts with grease or petroleum jelly.

CAUTION
A discharged battery can be damaged by freezing.

e. With the battery in a fully-charged condition (specific gravity 1.260-1.275), store in a dry place where the temperature will not drop below freezing. Do not store on a concrete surface.

f. Recharge the battery every 45 days or whenever the specific gravity drops below 1.230. Before charging, cover the plates with distilled water, but not more than 3/16 in. above the perforated baffles. The charge rate should not exceed 6 amps. Discontinue charging when the specific gravity reaches 1.260 at 80° F (27° C).

g. Before placing the battery back into service after winter storage, remove the excess grease from the terminals, leaving a small amount on. Install battery in a fully-charged state.

COMPLETE SUBMERSION

An outboard motor which has been lost overboard should be recovered as quickly as possible. If lost in salt water or fresh water containing sand or silt, disassemble and clean it immediately—any delay will result in rust and corrosion of internal components once it has been removed from the water. If the motor was running when it was lost, do not attempt to start it until it has been disassembled and checked. Internal components may be out of alignment and running the motor may cause permanent damage.

The following emergency steps should be accomplished immediately if the motor was lost in fresh water.

1. Remove the engine cover.
2. Remove the spark plug(s) as described in this chapter.
3. Remove the carburetor float bowl cover(s). See Chapter Six.
4. Disconnect the charge coil connectors.
5. Wash the outside of the motor with clean water to remove weeds, mud and other debris.

CAUTION
If there is a possibility sand or silt may have entered the power head or gearcase, do not try to start the motor or severe internal damage may occur.

CAUTION
Do not force the motor if it does not turn over freely when the rewind starter is operated in Step 6. This may be an indication of internal damage such as a bent connecting rod or broken piston.

6. Drain as much water as possible from the power head by placing the motor in a horizontal position. Use the starter rope to rotate the flywheel with the spark plug hole(s) facing downward.
7. Pour alcohol into the carburetor throat(s) to displace water. Operate rewind starter.

Position the motor so you can pour alcohol into the spark plug hole(s). Operate rewind starter again.
8. Repeat Step 7 with OMC Engine Cleaner.
9. Reinstall spark plug(s) and carburetor float bowl cover(s).
10. Try starting the motor with a fresh fuel source. If motor will start, let it run at least one hour to eliminate any water remaining inside.

CAUTION
If it is not possible to disassemble and clean the motor immediately, resubmerge it in water to prevent rust and corrosion formation until such time as it can be properly serviced.

11. If motor will not start in Step 10, try to diagnose the cause as fuel, electrical or mechanical, then correct. If the engine cannot be started within 2 hours, disassemble, clean and oil all parts thoroughly as soon as possible.

ANTI-CORROSION MAINTENANCE

1. Flush the cooling system with fresh water as described in this chapter after each time

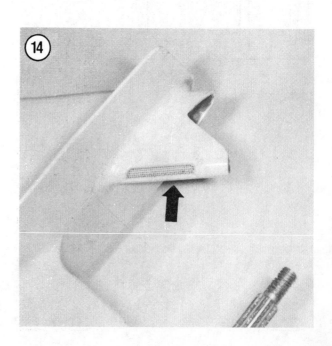

motor is used in salt water. Wash exterior with fresh water.

2. Dry exterior of motor and apply primer over any paint nicks and scratches. Use only tin anti-fouling paint; do not use paints containing mercury or copper. Do not paint sacrifical anodes or trim tab.

3. Lubricate power head with OMC Anti-Corrosion Lubricant. Apply OMC Black Neoprene Dip to all electrical connections as required.

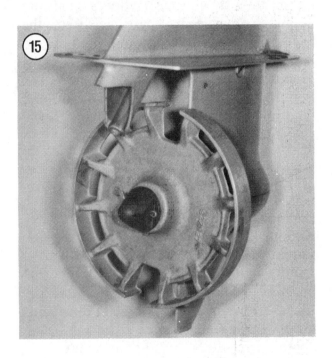

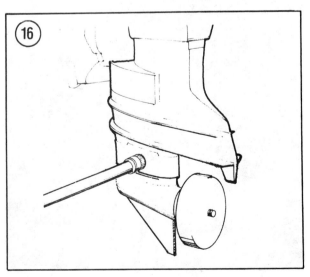

4. Check sacrifical anodes and replace any that are less than half their original size.

5. Lubricate more frequently than specified in **Table 1**. If used consistenly in salt water, reduce lubrication intervals by one-half.

ENGINE FLUSHING

Periodic engine flushing will prevent salt or silt deposits from accumulating in the water passageways. This procedure should also be performed whenever an outboard motor is operated in salt water or polluted water.

Keep the motor in an upright position during and after flushing. This prevents water from passing into the power head through the drive shaft housing and exhaust ports during the flushing procedure. It also eliminates the possibility of residual water being trapped in the drive shaft housing or other passageways.

Some Johnson and Evinrude outboards have the water intake located on the exhaust port (**Figure 14**). These models require the use of flushing devices other than a flush-test unit. See your Johnson or Evinrude dealer for the proper flushing device. Johnson and Evinrude recommend the outboard be run with a test wheel instead of the propeller when operated in a test tank or with a flush-test device. See **Figure 15** (typical). Test wheel recommendations are given in **Table 2**.

1. Remove the propeller and install the correct test wheel.

2. Attach the flushing device according to manufacturer's instructions. See **Figure 16** (typical).

3. Connect a garden hose between a water tap and the flushing device.

4. Open the water tap partially—do not use full pressure.

5. Shift into NEUTRAL, then start motor. Keep engine speed below 1,000 rpm (2-10 hp) or 1,200 rpm (25-40 hp).

6. Adjust water flow so that there is a slight loss of water around the rubber cups of the flushing device.

7. Check the motor to make sure that water is being discharged from the "tell-tale" nozzle. If it is not, stop the motor immediately and determine the cause of the problem.

CAUTION
Flush the motor for at least 5 minutes if used in salt water.

8. Flush motor until discharged water is clear. Stop motor.

9. Close water tap and remove flushing device from lower unit.

10. Remove test wheel and reinstall propeller.

TUNE-UP

A tune-up consists of a series of inspections, adjustments and parts replacements to compensate for normal wear and deterioration of outboard motor components. Regular tune-ups are important for power, performance and economy. Johnson and Evinrude recommend their outboards be serviced every 6 months or 50 hours of operation. If subjected to limited use, the engine should be tuned at least once a year.

Since proper outboard motor operation depends upon a number of interrelated system functions, a tune-up consisting of only one or two corrections will seldom give lasting results. For best results, a thorough and systematic procedure of analysis and correction is necessary.

Prior to performing a tune-up, it is a good idea to flush the motor as described in this chapter and check for satisfactory water pump operation.

The tune-up sequence recommended by Johnson and Evinrude includes the following:

a. Compression check.
b. Spark plug service.
c. Lower unit and water pump check.
d. Fuel system service.
e. Ignition system service.
f. Battery, starter motor and solenoid check (if so equipped).
g. Internal wiring harness check.
h. Engine synchronization and adjustment (Chapter Five).
i. Performance test (on boat).

Any time the fuel or ignition systems are adjusted or defective parts replaced, the engine timing, synchronization and adjustment *must* be checked. These procedures are described in Chapter Five. Perform the timing, synchronization and adjustment procedure for your engine *before* running the performance test.

Compression Check

An accurate cylinder compression check gives a good idea of the condition of the basic working parts of the engine. It is also an important first step in any tune-up, as a motor with low or unequal compression between cylinders *cannot* be satisfactorily tuned. Any compression problem discovered during this check must be corrected before continuing with the tune-up procedure.

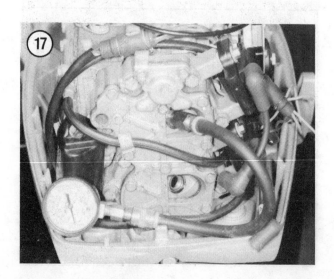

1. With the engine warm, disconnect the spark plug wire(s) and remove the plug(s) as described in this chapter.

2. Ground the spark plug wire(s) to the engine to disable the ignition system.

3. Connect the compression tester to the top spark plug hole according to manufacturer's instructions (**Figure 17**).

4. Make sure the throttle is held wide open and crank the engine through at least 4 compression strokes. Record the gauge reading.

5. Repeat Step 3 and Step 4 on 2-cylinder engines to test the other cylinder.

While minimum cylinder compression should not be less than 100 psi, the actual readings are not as important as the differences in readings when interpreting the results. A variation of more than 15 psi between 2 cylinders indicates a problem with the lower reading cylinder, such as worn or sticking piston rings and/or scored pistons or cylinders. In such cases, pour a tablespoon of engine oil into the suspect cylinder and repeat Step 3 and Step 4. If the compression is raised significantly (by 10 psi in an old engine), the rings are worn and should be replaced.

If the power head shows signs of overheating (discolored or scorched paint)

but the compression test turns up nothing abnormal, check the cylinder(s) visually through the transfer ports for possible scoring. A cylinder can be slightly scored and still deliver a relatively good compression reading. In such a case, it is also a good idea to double-check the water pump operation as a possible cause for overheating.

Spark Plugs

Johnson and Evinrude outboards are equipped with Champion, AC or NGK spark plugs selected for average use conditions. Under adverse use conditions, the recommended spark plug may foul or overheat. In such cases, check the ignition and carburetion systems to make sure they are operating correctly. If no defect is found, replace the spark plug with one of a hotter or colder heat range as required. **Table 3** gives the recommended spark plugs for all models covered in this book. **Table 4** contains a cross-reference for Champion, NGK, AC, Motorcraft and Autolite spark plugs.

Spark Plug Removal

CAUTION
Whenever the spark plugs are removed, dirt around them can fall into the plug holes. This can cause engine damage that is expensive to repair.

1. Blow out any foreign matter from around the spark plugs with compressed air. Use a compressor if you have one. If you do not, use a can of compressed inert gas, available from photo stores.

2. Disconnect the spark plug wires (**Figure 18**, typical) by twisting the wire boot back and forth on the plug insulator while pulling outward. Pulling on the wire instead of the boot may cause internal damage to the wire.

3. Remove the plugs with an appropriate size spark plug socket. Keep the plugs in order so you know which cylinder each came from.

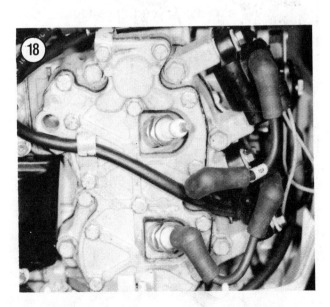

4. Examine each spark plug. See **Figure 19**. Compare its condition with **Figure 20**. Spark plug condition indicates engine condition and can warn of developing trouble.

5. Check each plug for make and heat range. All should be of the same make and number or heat range.

6. Discard the plugs. Although they could be cleaned and reused if in good condition, they seldom last very long. New plugs are inexpensive and far more reliable.

Spark Plug Gapping

New plugs should be carefully gapped to ensure a reliable, consistent spark. Use a special spark plug tool with a wire gauge. See **Figure 21** for one common type.

1. Remove the plugs and gaskets from the boxes. Install the gaskets.

> *NOTE*
> *Some plug brands may have small end pieces that must be screwed on (**Figure 22**) before the plugs can be used.*

2. Insert an appropriate wire gauge (see **Table 3**) between the electrodes. If the gap is correct, there will be a slight drag as the wire is pulled through. If there is no drag or if the wire will not pull through, bend the side electrode with the gapping tool (**Figure 23**) to change the gap. Remeasure with the wire gauge.

> *CAUTION*
> *Never try to close the electrode gap by tapping the spark plug on a solid surface. This can damage the plug internally. Always use the gapping and adjusting tool to open or close the gap.*

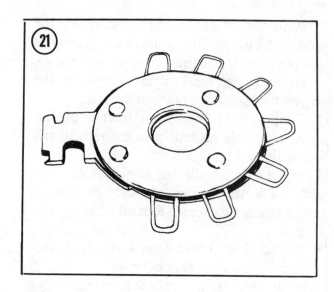

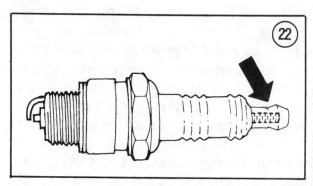

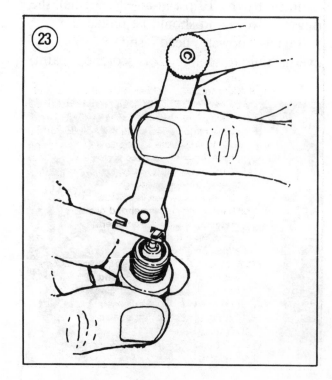

SPARK PLUG ANALYSIS
(CONVENTIONAL GAP SPARK PLUGS)

A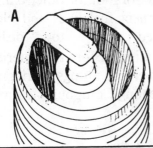

B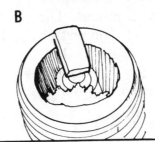

C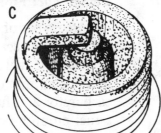

D

E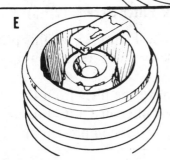

F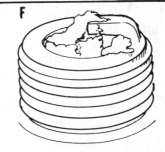

A. **Normal**—Light tan to gray color of insulator indicates correct heat range. Few deposits are present and the electrodes are not burned.

B. **Core bridging**—These defects are caused by excessive combustion chamber deposits striking and adhering to the firing end of the plug. In this case, they wedge or fuse between the electrode and core nose. They originate from the piston and cylinder head surfaces. Deposits are formed by one or more of the following:
  a. Excessive carbon in cylinder.
  b. Use of non-recommended oils.
  c. Immediate high-speed operation after prolonged trolling.
  d. Improper fuel-oil ratio.

C. **Wet fouling**—Damp or wet, black carbon coating over entire firing end of plug. Forms sludge in some engines. Caused by one or more of the following:
  a. Spark plug heat range too cold.
  b. Prolonged trolling.
  c. Low-speed carburetor adjustment too rich.
  d. Improper fuel-oil ratio.
  e. Induction manifold bleed-off passage obstructed.
  f. Worn or defective breaker points.

D. **Gap bridging**—Similar to core bridging, except the combustion particles are wedged or fused between the electrodes. Causes are the same.

E. **Overheating**—Badly worn electrodes and premature gap wear are indicative of this problem, along with a gray or white "blistered" appearance on the insulator. Caused by one or more of the following:
  a. Spark plug heat range too hot.
  b. Incorrect propeller usage, causing engine to lug.
  c. Worn or defective water pump.
  d. Restricted water intake or restriction somewhere in the cooling system.

F. **Ash deposits or lead fouling**—Ash deposits are light brown to white in color and result from use of fuel or oil additives. Lead fouling produces a yellowish brown discoloration and can be avoided by using unleaded fuels.

Spark Plug Installation

Improper installation of spark plugs is one of the most common causes of poor spark plug performance in outboard motors. The gasket on the plug must be fully compressed against a clean plug seat in order for heat transfer to take place effectively. This requires close attention to proper tightening during installation.

1. Inspect the spark plug hole threads and clean them with a thread chaser (**Figure 24**). Wipe the cylinder head seats clean before installing the new plugs.
2. Screw each plug in by hand until it seats. Very little effort is required. If force is necessary, the plug is cross-threaded. Unscrew it and try again.
3. Tighten the spark plugs. If you have a torque wrench, tighten to 17-20 ft.-lb. (24-27 N•m). If not, seat the plug finger-tight on the gasket, then tighten an additional 1/4 turn with a wrench.
4. Inspect each spark plug wire before reconnecting it to its cylinder. If insulation is damaged or deteriorated, install a new plug wire. Push wire boot onto plug terminal and make sure it seats fully.

Lower Unit and Water Pump Check

A faulty water pump or one that performs below specifications can result in extensive engine damage. Thus, it is a good idea to replace the water pump impeller, seals and gaskets once a year or whenever the lower unit is removed for service. See Chapter Nine.

Fuel System Service

The clearance between the carburetor and choke shutter should not be greater than 0.015 in. when the choke is closed or a hard starting condition will result. When changing from one brand of gasoline to another, it may be necessary to readjust the carburetor idle mixture needle slightly (1/4 turn) to accomodate the variations in volatility.

Fuel Lines

1. Visually check all fuel lines for kinks, leaks, deterioration or other damage.
2. Disconnect fuel lines and blow out with compressed air to dislodge any contamination or foreign material.
3. Coat fuel line fittings sparingly with OMC Gasket Sealing Compound and reconnect the lines.

Engine Fuel Filter

Three types of engine fuel filters are used: a petcock filter screen installed in the petcock between the fuel tank and carburetor on 2 hp models, an inline filter installed between the carburetor and fuel pump on 4 hp models or a fuel pump filter screen (all others).

Petcock Filter Screen (2 hp)

Refer to **Figure 25** for this procedure.
1. Unscrew and remove the fuel shut-off valve.
2. Remove the filter from the filter cup.
3. Clean filter in OMC Engine Cleaner and blow dry with compressed air.

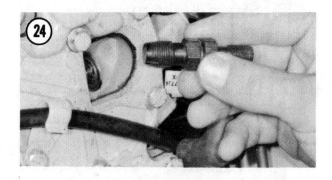

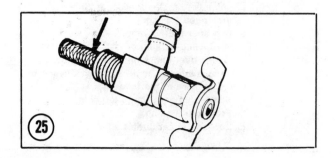

4. Installation is the reverse of removal. Use a drop of OMC Gasoila on the shut-off valve threads before installing valve in fuel tank.

Inline Filter (4 hp)

1. Remove the engine cover.
2. Compress the clamps holding the fuel lines to the filter with pliers and slide each clamp back on the hose about 1/2 inch.
3. Pull the filter from the lines. Discard the filter.
4. Connect the fuel lines to the new filter's nipples. Make sure the arrow embossed on the filter faces in the direction of fuel flow.
5. Compress each clamp with pliers and slide over the line until it touches the filter housing.
6. Check filter installation for leakage by priming fuel system with fuel line primer bulb.

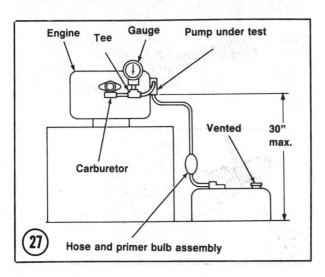

Fuel Pump Filter (4.5-40 hp)

Refer to **Figure 26** for this procedure.
1. Remove the screw holding the filter cover to the fuel pump.
2. Remove the filter screen from the pump housing or filter cover.
3. Clean the screen in OMC Engine Cleaner. If screen is excessively dirty or plugged, discard it and install a new one.
4. Install the filter screen in the filter cover.
5. Reinstall the filter cover to the fuel pump and tighten the screw securely.
6. Check filter assembly for leakage by priming fuel system with fuel line primer bulb.

Fuel Pump

The fuel pump does not generally require service during a tune-up.

Fuel pump diaphragms are fragile and a defective one often produces symptoms which appear to be an ignition system problem. A common malfunction results from a tiny pinhole or crack in the diaphragm caused by an engine backfire. This defect allows gasoline to enter the crankcase and wet-foul the spark plug at idle speed, causing hard starting and engine stall at low rpm. The problem disappears at higher speeds, as fuel quantity is limited. Since the plug is not fouled by excess fuel at higher speeds, it fires normally.

Fuel Pump Pressure Test

Check fuel pump pressure by installing a pressure gauge at the end of the fuel line leading to the upper carburetor. See **Figure 27**. With the engine running in a test tank or on the boat in the water, fuel pump pressure must be at least 1 psi at 600 rpm, 1.5 psi at 2,500-3,000 rpm and 2.5 psi at 4,500 rpm. If not, rebuild the fuel pump with a new diaphragm, check valves and gaskets. See Chapter Six.

Breaker Point Ignition System Service

An ignition analyzer must be used for an accurate check of the breaker points. Johnson and Evinrude recommend the use of the Merc-O-Tronic, Stevens ST-75 or Stevens M.A.-75 or M.A.-80. These can be purchased through your local Johnson or Evinrude dealer.

Check the breaker points as described in *Breaker Point Testing*, Chapter Three. If they fail to perform as specified, clean the points with electrical contact cleaner—do not file. If they still do not deliver a satisfactory reading, replace the points as described in this chapter.

Breaker Point Replacement (1-cylinder Models)

1. Move the armature plate to the full advance position.
2. Disconnect the breaker point and condenser leads.
3. Remove the hairpin clip at the top of the breaker point pivot post.
4. Remove the adjusting and locking screws. Remove the breaker point set.
5. Remove the condenser attaching screw. Remove the condenser.
6. Assemble the movable side of a new breaker point set to the non-movable side by slipping it over the breaker point pivot post.
7. Install assembled point set to the armature plate. Install the adjusting and locking screws finger-tight.

8. Install the hairpin clip in the breaker point pivot post groove.

> *CAUTION*
> *Do not rotate the crankshaft counterclockwise in Step 9 or the water pump impeller may be damaged.*

9. Rotate the crankshaft clockwise to position the breaker arm rubbing block on the high point of the cam.
10. Turn the adjusting screw to obtain a gap of 0.022 in. Measure gap with a flat feeler gauge.
11. Tighten the locking screw and recheck the point gap.
12. Install the new condenser and tighten the attaching screw securely.
13. Connect the breaker point and condenser leads.

Breaker Point Replacement (2-cylinder Models)

1. Move the armature plate to the full advance position.
2. Disconnect all breaker point and condenser leads.
3. Remove the hairpin clip at the top of each breaker point pivot post.

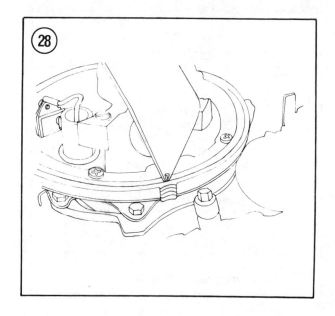

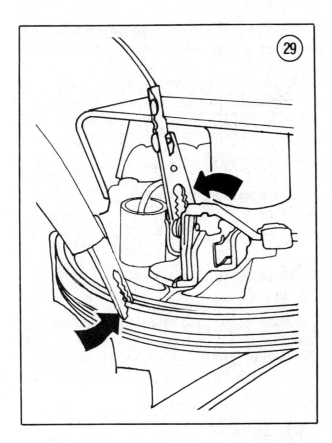

4. Remove the adjusting and locking screws. Remove the breaker point sets.

5. Remove the condenser attaching screws. Remove the condensers.

6. Assemble the movable side of a new breaker point set to the non-movable side by slipping it over the breaker point pivot post.

7. Install each assembled point set to the armature plate. Install the adjusting and locking screws finger-tight.

8. Install the hairpin clip in each breaker point pivot post groove.

9. Install the correct timing fixture (**Figure 28**) on the crankshaft. Use part No. 383602 (6 and 25 hp), part No. 383603 (4 hp), part No. 386635 (35 and 40 hp) or part No. 386636 (9.5, 9.9 and 15 hp).

10. Connect an ohmmeter between the breaker plate and front breaker point set screw terminal. See **Figure 29**.

CAUTION
Do not rotate the crankshaft counterclockwise in Step 11 or the water pump impeller may be damaged.

11. Rotate the crankshaft clockwise until the side of the timing fixture marked "T" or "TOP" aligns with the front timing mark projection on the armature plate. See **Figure 28**.

12. Slowly move the timing fixture clockwise until the meter needle deflects (points open). This should happen when the timing plate aligns with the timing mark as in Step 11. If it does not, rotate the timing fixture another full turn and align the fixture with the marks, then adjust the point set (**Figure 30**) until the meter needle deflects. Tighten the locking screw.

13. Rotate the crankshaft 180° and repeat Steps 9-12 to adjust the rear breaker point set. Use the rear timing mark projection on the armature plate.

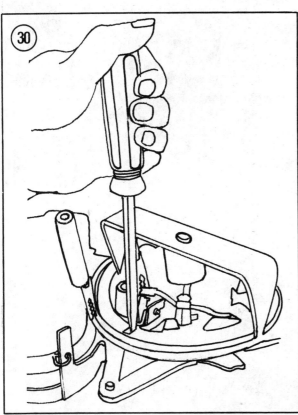

Battery and Starter Motor Check
(Electric Start Models Only)

1. Check the battery's state of charge. See Chapter Seven.

2. Connect a voltmeter between the starter motor positive terminal (**Figure 31**) and ground.

3. Turn ignition switch to START and check voltmeter scale:

   a. If voltage exceeds 9.5 volts and the starter motor does not operate, replace the motor.

   b. If voltage is less than 9.5 volts, recheck battery and connections. Charge battery, if necessary, and repeat procedure.

Solenoid Check
(Electric Start Models Only)

Any good volt-ohm-ammeter (VOA) can be used for this test.

1. Disconnect all leads from the starter solenoid. See **Figure 32**.

2. Connect the VOA meter leads to the soldered solenoid leads (1 and 2, **Figure 33**).

3. Set the meter to the R×1 scale. The meter should indicate continuity.

4. Set the meter to the R×1K scale. Connect the meter leads between the threaded terminals (3 and 4, **Figure 33**).

5. Connect a 12-volt battery between the soldered solenoid leads (1 and 2, **Figure 33**). The solenoid should click and the VOA meter should read zero ohms. If not, replace the solenoid.

Internal Wiring Harness Check

1. Check the wiring harness for signs of frayed or chafed insulation.

2. Check for loose connections between the wires and terminal ends.

3. Check the harness connector for bent electrical pins.

4. Check the harness connector and pin sockets for signs of corrosion and clean as required.

5. If the harness is suspected of contributing to electrical malfunctions, check all wires for continuity and resistance between harness connection and terminal end. Repair or replace as required.

Engine Synchronization and Adjustment

See Chapter Five.

Performance Test
(On Boat)

Before performance testing the engine, make sure that the boat bottom is cleaned of all marine growth and that there is no evidence of a "hook" or "rocker" (**Figure 34**)

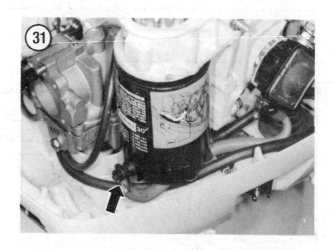

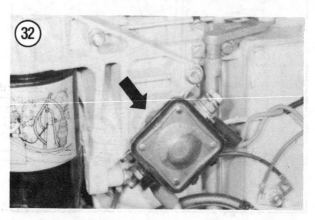

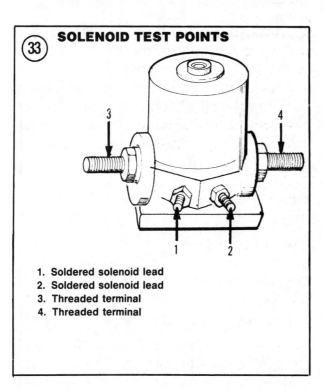

SOLENOID TEST POINTS

33

1. Soldered solenoid lead
2. Soldered solenoid lead
3. Threaded terminal
4. Threaded terminal

in the bottom. Any of these conditions will reduce performance considerably. The boat should be performance tested with an average load and with the motor tilted at an angle that will allow the boat to ride on an even keel. If equipped with an adjustable trim tab, it should be properly adjusted to allow the boat to steer in either direction with equal ease.

Check engine rpm at full throttle. If not within the maximum rpm range for the motor as specified in Chapter Five, check the propeller pitch. A high pitch propeller will reduce rpm while a lower pitch prop will increase it.

Readjust the idle mixture and speed under actual operating conditions as required to obtain the best low-speed engine performance.

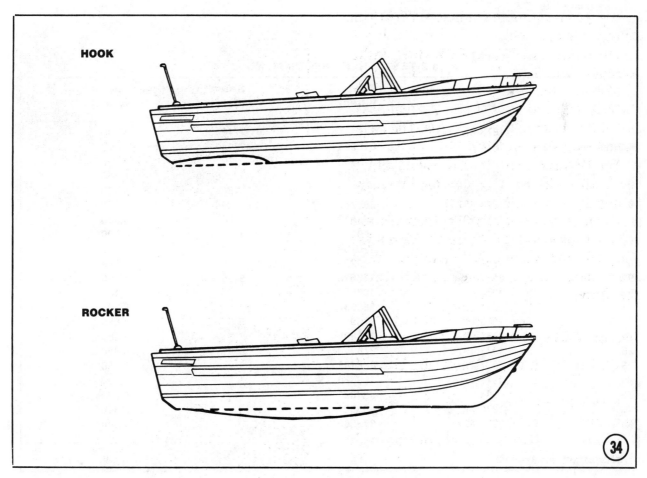

HOOK

ROCKER

34

Table 1 LUBRICATION & MAINTENANCE[1]

Lubrication points	Figure
Clamp screws, steering handle pivot and tilt/run lever	10
Throttle detent, cam, linkage and choke lever	5
Magneto and throttle linkage	7, 9
Shift lever fitting, reverse lock and swivel bracket	—
Fuel shut-off/choke shaft (integral tank)	—
Choke shaft (remote tank)	—
Choke linkage	8
Rear motor cover latch	—
Starter motor pinion shaft[2]	11
Vertical throttle shaft and gears	12

1. Complete list does not apply to all models. Perform only those tasks which apply to your model. Lubricate with OMC Triple-Guard Grease every 60 days (fresh water) or 30 days (salt water) as required.
2. Use Lubriplate 777.

Table 2 TEST WHEEL RECOMMENDATIONS

Model	Year	Test wheel	Shaft dia. (in.)	Engine rpm
2	1973-on	316021	7/16	3,900
4 Weedless	1973	316021	7/16	3,800
4 Standard	1973	316960	1/2	4,100
4 Standard	1973-on	317738	11/16	4,550
4.5	1980-1983	390123	1/2	5,100
6	1973-1975	380757	9/16	4,000
6	1976-1979	379673	9/16	4,500
6	1982-on	390239	1/2	4,900
7.5	1980-1983	390239	1/2	4,900
8	1984	390239	1/2	4,900
9.5	1973	379673	9/16	4,400
9.9	1974-on	386537	*	5,400
15	1974-on	386537	*	6,200
20	1973	376913	5/8	4,650
20	1980-on	388880	*	4,650
25	1973-1976	376913	5/8	4,900
25	1977	388295	*	4,650
25	1978-on	388880	*	5,200
30	1984	386891	*	5,300
35	1976-on	386891	*	5,300
40	1973-1976	378566	*	4,500

* Information not available.

Table 3 RECOMMENDED SPARK PLUGS

Model	hp/cyl.	Champion plug type	Gap (in.)
2	2/1	J6J[1]	0.030
4 (1973-1976)	4/2	J6J[1]	0.030
4 (1977-1980)	4/2	L77J4	0.040
4 (1981)	4/2	L7J	0.030
4 (1982-on)	4/2	L86	0.040
6 (1973-1976	6/2	J6J[1]	0.030
6 (1977-on	6/2	L77J4	0.040
7.5	7.5/2	L77J4	0.040
8	8/2	L77J4	0.040
9.5	9.5/2	J4J[1,2]	0.030
9.9 (1974-1976)	9.9/2	UL81J	0.030
9.9 (1977-on)	9.9/2	L77J4	0.040
15 (1974-1976)	15/2	UL81J	0.030
15 (1977-on)	15/2	L77J4	0.040
18	18/2	UJ4J	0.030
20 (1973)	20/2	UJ4J	0.030
20 (1981-1982)	20/2	L77J4	0.040
25 (1973-1974)	25/2	UJ4J	0.030
25 (1975-1976)	25/2	J4J[1]	0.030
25 (1977-on)	25/2	L77J4	0.040
30	30/2	L77J4	0.040
35 (1975-1976)	35/2	UL81J	0.030
35 (1977-on)	35/2	L77J4	0.040
40 (1973)	40/2	J4J	0.030
40 (1974)	40/2	UL4J	0.030
40 (1975-1976)	40/2	UL81J	0.030

1. Champion J4J and J6J plugs are superceded by J6C.
2. Use Champion J6J or AC M44C to prevent wet fouling if used primarily @ low speeds.

Table 4 SPARK PLUG CROSS-REFERENCE CHART

NGK	Champion	AC	Autolite
B6S	J6J*	M44C	354
B6HS	L7J	44F	355
B6HS	L86	44F	415
B7HS	UL81J	M42FF	—
B8S	J4J*	M42K	353
B9HS10	L77J4	M40FFX	2634

* Champion J4J and J6J plugs are superceded by J6C; no cross-reference is available for J6C at this time.

NOTE: If you own a 1985 or later model, first check the Supplement at the back of the book for any new service information.

Chapter Five

Engine Synchronization and Linkage Adjustments

If an engine is to deliver its maximum efficiency and peak performance, the ignition must be timed and the carburetor operation synchronized with the ignition. This procedure is the final step of a tune-up. It must also be performed whenever the fuel or ignition systems are serviced or adjusted.

Procedures for engine synchronization and linkage adjustment on Johnson and Evinrude outboards differ according to model and ignition system. This chapter is divided into self-contained sections dealing with particular models/ignition systems for fast and easy reference. Each section specifies the appropriate procedure and sequence to be followed and provides the necessary tune-up data. Read the general information at the beginning of the chapter and then select the section pertaining to your outboard.

ENGINE TIMING

As engine rpm increases, the ignition system must fire the spark plug(s) more rapidly. Proper ignition timing synchronizes the spark plug firing with engine speed.

Timing is not adjustable on engines with a breaker point ignition. Ignition timing with this system depends upon correct initial setting of the breaker point gap. Timing can be checked with a timing light (**Figure 1**). If the timing marks on the flywheel and armature plate or timing pointer do not align properly, the breaker point gap must be reset.

On 4.5-15 hp Johnson and Evinrude outboards with a CD ignition, timing

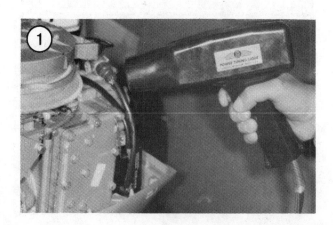

adjustments are not required. If the wires are correctly positioned in the 3-wire and 4-wire connectors, proper ignition timing will be maintained, provided the linkage adjustments have been made correctly.

Ignition timing is adjustable on 20-40 hp models; a timing light is required to set the timing properly. The engine must be run at full throttle in forward gear. This requires the use of a test tank and test wheel, as timing an engine while speeding across open water is neither easy nor safe.

SYNCHRONIZING

As engine speed increases, the carburetor must provide an increased amount of fuel for combustion. Synchronizing is the process of timing the carburetor operation to the ignition (and thereby the engine speed).

Required Equipment

Static timing of an engine with a breaker point ignition requires the use of a test lamp or ohmmeter and a timing fixture to set the breaker point gap. A timing light is used to check timing mark alignment.

Dynamic engine timing uses a stroboscopic timing light connected to the No. 1 spark plug wire. See **Figure 1**. As the engine is cranked or operated, the light flashes each time the spark plug fires. When the light is pointed at the moving flywheel, the mark on the

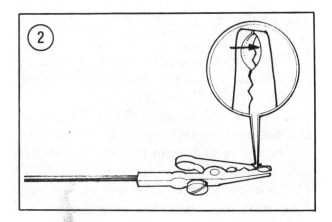

flywheel appears to stand still. The flywheel mark should align with the stationary timing pointer on the engine.

A simple tool called a throttle shaft amplifier can be made with an alligator clip and a length of stiff wire (a paper clip will do). This tool will exaggerate the movement of the carburetor throttle shaft and tell you that it's moving. The tool is especially useful on engines where the throttle cam and cam follower are partially hidden by the flywheel. To make the tool, enlarge the alligator clip's gripping surface by grinding out the front teeth on one side and secure the wire to the end of the clip. See **Figure 2**.

A tachometer connected to the engine is used to determine engine speed during idle and high-speed adjustments.

> *CAUTION*
> *Never operate the engine without water circulating through the gearcase to the engine. This will damage the water pump and the gearcase and can cause engine damage.*

Some form of water supply is required whenever the engine is operated during the procedure. Using a test tank is the most convenient method, although the procedures may be carried out with the boat in the water.

> *CAUTION*
> *Do not use a flushing device to provide water during synchronization and linkage adjustment. Without the exhaust backpressure of a submerged gearcase, the engine will run lean. The proper test wheel must be used to put a load on the propeller shaft or engine damage can result from excessive rpm.*

JOHNSON/EVINRUDE 2 (BREAKER POINT IGNITION)

The breaker points are mounted on a fixed base. Ignition timing on this model is non-adjustable. Correctly adjusted breaker points will align the flywheel timing mark between the 2 armature plate index marks when the engine is run at 1,000 rpm. See **Figure 3**. If the point gap is too large, timing will be retarded; a gap that is too small will advance timing.

Throttle Cam Adjustment

1. Remove the engine cover.
2. Remove the rewind starter.
3. Remove the fuel tank support bracket.
4. Move the armature lever slowly until the cam follower starts to open the throttle. The center of the cam follower roller should be between the 2 marks on the throttle cam (**Figure 4**).
5. If the roller and throttle cam marks do not align in Step 4, loosen the throttle cam mounting screws. Adjust the cam position until the throttle valve is closed and there is no play in the linkage. The throttle cam mark should align with the flat edge of the cam follower as the two make contact. Retighten the cam screws.

Needle Valve Adjustment

1. Install the engine in a test tank with the proper test wheel or on the boat in the water with the correct propeller.
2. Turn the carburetor high- and low-speed needles inward until they barely seat.
3. Back the high-speed needle out 3/4 turn; back the low-speed needle out 1 1/2 turns.
4. Remove the knob from each needle.
5. Start the engine and run at half throttle until the engine reaches operating temperature.
6. Connect a tachometer according to manufacturer's instructions. Run engine at full throttle and adjust the high-speed needle until the best high speed setting is obtained.

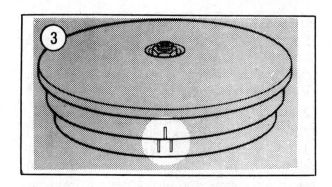

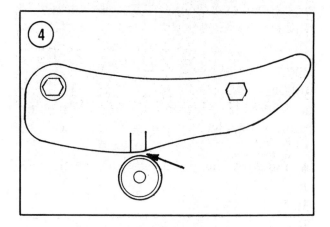

NOTE
The engine requires approximately 15 seconds to respond to adjustment in Step 7.

7. Bring engine speed back to 700-750 rpm and adjust low-speed needle to produce the highest rpm and smoothest operation.
8. Repeat Step 6 after the final low-speed adjustment has been made in Step 7.

NOTE
Do not disturb needle valve setting when reinstalling knob in Step 9.

9. Install the high-speed needle knob with its pointer facing down. Install the low-speed needle with its pointer facing up.
10. Run the engine in FORWARD gear at idle and note the tachometer. If throttle cam and needle valve adjustments are correct, the engine will idle at 650 rpm in gear.
11. Shut the engine off, remove the test equipment and install the engine cover.

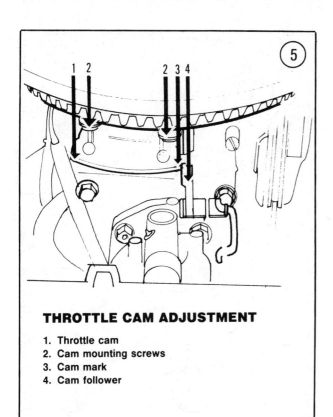

THROTTLE CAM ADJUSTMENT

1. Throttle cam
2. Cam mounting screws
3. Cam mark
4. Cam follower

Ignition Timing Check

1. Connect a tachometer and timing light according to manufacturer's instructions.
2. Start the engine and run at 1,000 rpm.
3. Point the timing light at the armature plate index marks. If the flywheel timing mark does not align between the armature plate index marks, adjust the breaker point gap. See Chapter Four.

JOHNSON/EVINRUDE 4 (BREAKER POINT IGNITION)

The breaker points are mounted on a fixed base. Ignition timing on this model is non-adjustable. Correctly adjusted breaker points will align the flywheel timing mark between the 2 armature plate index marks when the engine is run at 1,000 rpm. See **Figure 3**. If the point gap is too large, timing will be retarded; a gap that is too small will advance timing.

Throttle Cam Adjustment

1. Remove the engine cover.
2. Set the throttle grip to the STOP position.
3. Slowly rotate the throttle grip toward the ADVANCE position until the cam follower starts to open the throttle. The timing mark on the throttle cam should align with the starboard edge of the cam follower. See **Figure 5**.
4. If the roller and throttle cam marks do not align in Step 3, loosen the throttle cam mounting screws. Adjust the cam position until the throttle valve is closed and there is no play in the linkage. The throttle cam mark must be directly behind the round starboard edge of the cam follower as the two make contact. Retighten the cam screws.

Needle Valve Adjustment

1. Install the engine in a test tank with the proper test wheel or on the boat in the water with the correct propeller.
2. Turn the carburetor high- and low-speed needles inward until they barely seat.
3. Back the high-speed needle out 3/4 turn; back the low-speed needle out 1 3/4 turns.
4. Remove the knob from each needle.
5. Start the engine and run at half throttle until the engine reaches operating temperature.
6. Connect a tachometer according to manufacturer's instructions. Run engine at full throttle and adjust the high-speed needle until the best high speed setting is obtained.

NOTE
The engine requires approximately 15 seconds to respond to adjustment in Step 7.

7. Bring engine speed back to 700-750 rpm and adjust low-speed needle to produce the highest rpm and smoothest operation.
8. Repeat Step 6 after the final low-speed adjustment has been made in Step 7.

NOTE
Do not disturb needle valve setting when reinstalling knobs in Step 9.

9. Install the high-speed needle knob with its pointer facing straight up. Install the low-speed needle with its pointer facing straight down.

10. Run the engine in FORWARD gear at idle and note the tachometer. If throttle cam and needle valve adjustments are correct, the engine will idle at 600 rpm in gear.

11. Shut the engine off, remove the test equipment and install the engine cover.

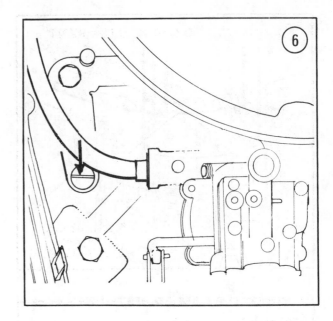

Throttle Tension Adjustment

If the throttle tension is correctly adjusted, engine speed will remain constant and the throttle lever will remain in position. If tension is incorrect, adjust by tightening the throttle tension screw (**Figure 6**) as required.

Ignition Timing Check

1. Connect a tachometer and timing light according to manufacturer's instructions.

2. Start the engine and run at 1,000 rpm.

3. Point the timing light at the armature plate index marks. If the flywheel timing mark does not align between the armature plate index marks, adjust the breaker point gap. See Chapter Four.

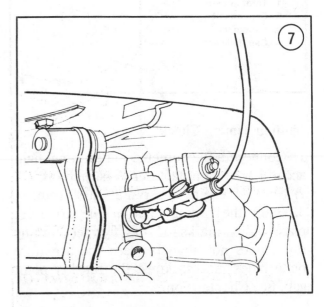

JOHNSON/EVINRUDE 4, 4.5 AND 7.5 (CD 2 IGNITION)

Timing adjustments are not required on these models. If the wires are correctly positioned in the 3-wire and 4-wire connectors, proper ignition timing will be maintained, provided the following adjustments are made correctly.

Throttle Cam Adjustment

1. Remove the engine cover.

2. Set the throttle grip to the STOP position.

3. Install the tool shown in **Figure 2** to the end of the throttle shaft opposite the cam follower linkage. Bend the tool wire 90° upward for easier viewing. See **Figure 7**.

4. Slowly rotate the throttle grip toward the ADVANCE position until the tool starts to move, indicating the cam follower is starting to open the throttle. The timing mark on the

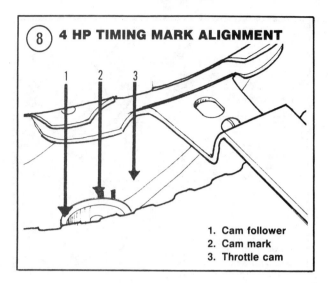

4 HP TIMING MARK ALIGNMENT

1. Cam follower
2. Cam mark
3. Throttle cam

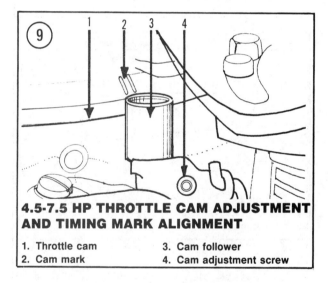

4.5-7.5 HP THROTTLE CAM ADJUSTMENT AND TIMING MARK ALIGNMENT

1. Throttle cam	3. Cam follower
2. Cam mark	4. Cam adjustment screw

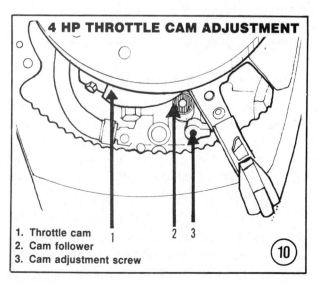

4 HP THROTTLE CAM ADJUSTMENT

1. Throttle cam
2. Cam follower
3. Cam adjustment screw

throttle cam should be centered under the cam follower roller. See **Figure 8** (Model 4) or **Figure 9** (Model 4.5 and 7.5).

5. Slowly back the cam adjusting screw out until the throttle valve has closed completely, then turn the screw in until the throttle shaft just starts to rotate. See **Figure 10** (Model 4) or **Figure 9** (Model 4.5 and 7.5) for adjusting screw location.

Needle Valve Adjustment

1. Install the engine in a test tank with the proper test wheel or on the boat in the water with the correct propeller.
2. Remove the knob from the low-speed needle.
3. Start the engine and run at half throttle until the engine reaches operating temperature.
4. Connect a tachometer according to manufacturer's instructions.

NOTE
The engine requires approximately 30 seconds to respond to adjustment in Step 5.

5. Bring engine speed back to 700-750 rpm and adjust low-speed needle to produce the highest rpm and smoothest operation.

NOTE
Do not disturb needle valve setting when reinstalling knob in Step 6.

6. Install the low-speed needle knob with its pointer facing down.
7. Run the engine in FORWARD gear at idle and note the tachometer. If throttle cam and needle valve adjustments are correct, the engine will idle at 600 rpm (Model 4) or 650 rpm (Model 4.5 and 7.5) in gear.
8. Shut the engine off, remove the test equipment and install the engine cover.

JOHNSON/EVINRUDE 6 (BREAKER POINT IGNITION)

The breaker points are mounted on a fixed base. Ignition timing on this model is non-adjustable. Correctly adjusted breaker points will align the flywheel timing mark between the 2 armature plate index marks when the engine is run at 1,000 rpm. See **Figure 3**. If the point gap is too large, timing will be retarded; a gap that is too small will advance timing.

Throttle Cam Adjustment

1. Remove the engine cover.
2. Set the throttle grip to the STOP position.
3. Slowly rotate the throttle grip toward the ADVANCE position until the starboard side of the cam follower roller is between the 2 index marks on the throttle cam. See **Figure 11**.
4. If the throttle valve is not closed when the cam roller and throttle cam marks align in Step 3, rotate the throttle grip until the throttle cam marks are directly behind the starboard edge of the roller. See **Figure 12**.
5. Loosen the throttle cam mounting screws. Make sure the choke knob is pushed completely in and move the cam toward the rear of the motor, then pull it forward until it just touches the cam follower. Tighten the screws and recheck the throttle valve to make sure it is closed and there is no play in the linkage.
6. If the throttle valve is not closed after the adjustment, check for a weak return spring or binding linkage.

Needle Valve Adjustment

1. Install the engine in a test tank with the proper test wheel or on the boat in the water with the correct propeller.

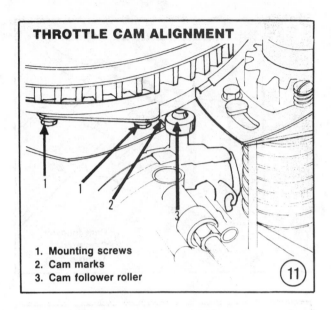

THROTTLE CAM ALIGNMENT

1. Mounting screws
2. Cam marks
3. Cam follower roller

11

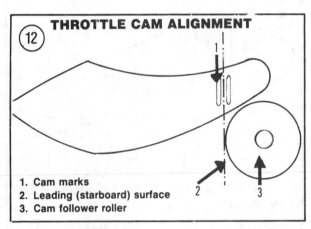

THROTTLE CAM ALIGNMENT

12

1. Cam marks
2. Leading (starboard) surface
3. Cam follower roller

2. Lightly seat the low-speed needle and back it out 1 1/2 turns. Remove the knob from the low-speed needle.
3. Start the engine and run at half throttle until the engine reaches operating temperature.
4. Connect a tachometer according to manufacturer's instructions.

NOTE
The engine requires approximately 15 seconds to respond to adjustment in Step 5.

5. Bring engine speed back to 700-750 rpm and adjust low-speed needle to produce the highest rpm and smoothest operation.

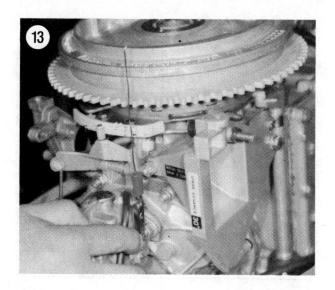

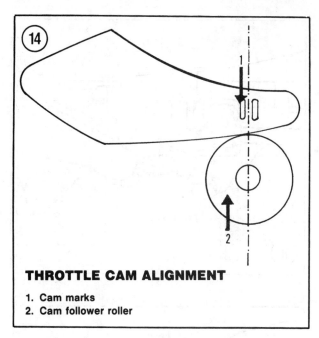

THROTTLE CAM ALIGNMENT

1. Cam marks
2. Cam follower roller

NOTE
Do not disturb needle valve setting when reinstalling knob in Step 6.

6. Install the low-speed needle knob with its pointer facing down.
7. Run the engine in FORWARD gear at idle and note the tachometer. If throttle cam and needle valve adjustments are correct, the engine will idle at 550 rpm in gear.
8. Shut the engine off, remove the test equipment and install the engine cover.

Ignition Timing Check

1. Connect a tachometer and timing light according to manufacturer's instructions.
2. Start the engine and run at 1,000 rpm.
3. Point the timing light at the armature plate index marks. If the flywheel timing mark does not align between the armature plate index marks, adjust the breaker point gap. See Chapter Four.

JOHNSON/EVINRUDE 5, 6 AND 8 (CD 2 IGNITION)

Timing adjustments are not required on these models. If the wires are correctly positioned in the 3-wire and 4-wire connectors, proper ignition timing will be maintained, provided the following adjustments are made correctly.

Throttle Cam Adjustment

1. Remove the engine cover.
2. Set the throttle grip to the STOP position.
3. Install the tool shown in **Figure 2** to the end of the throttle shaft opposite the cam follower linkage. See **Figure 13**.
4. Slowly rotate the throttle grip toward the ADVANCE position until the cam follower roller is centered between the throttle cam marks. See **Figure 14**. At this point, the tool installed in Step 3 should just start to move, indicating the throttle is starting to open.
5. If the roller and marks are not properly aligned when the tool starts to move, slowly back the cam follower adjustment screw (**Figure 15**) out until the throttle valve has closed completely, then turn the screw in until the throttle shaft just starts to rotate.

Needle Valve Adjustment

1. Install the engine in a test tank with the proper test wheel or on the boat in the water with the correct propeller.

5

2. Lightly seat the low-speed needle, then back it out 1 1/2 turns. Remove the knob from the low-speed needle.

3. Start the engine and run at half throttle until the engine reaches operating temperature.

4. Connect a tachometer according to manufacturer's instructions.

NOTE
The engine requires approximately 15 seconds to respond to adjustment in Step 5.

5. Bring engine speed back to 700-750 rpm and adjust low-speed needle to produce the highest rpm and smoothest operation.

NOTE
Do not disturb needle valve setting when reinstalling knob in Step 6.

6. Install the low-speed needle knob in its normal running position.

7. Run the engine in FORWARD gear at idle and note the tachometer. If throttle cam and needle valve adjustments are correct, the engine will idle at 550 rpm in gear.

8. If engine does not idle at 550 rpm in gear with the throttle lever in the SLOW position, turn the idle speed adjustment needle clockwise (increase) or counterclockwise (decrease) as required to bring engine speed to specifications. See **Figure 16**.

9. Shut the engine off, remove the test equipment and install the engine cover.

JOHNSON/EVINRUDE 9.5 (BREAKER POINT IGNITION)

The breaker points are mounted on a fixed base. Ignition timing on this model is non-adjustable. Correctly adjusted breaker points will align the flywheel timing mark between the 2 armature plate index marks when the engine is run at 1,000 rpm. See **Figure 3**. If the point gap is too large, timing

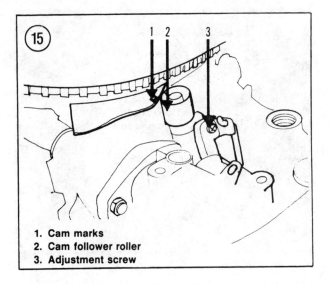

1. Cam marks
2. Cam follower roller
3. Adjustment screw

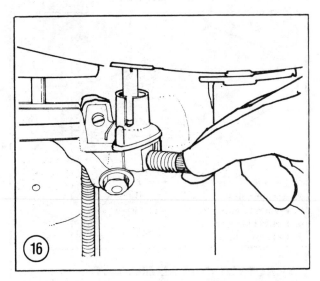

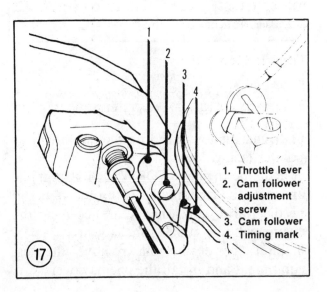

1. Throttle lever
2. Cam follower adjustment screw
3. Cam follower
4. Timing mark

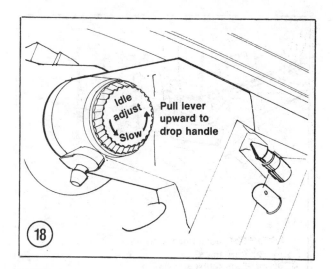

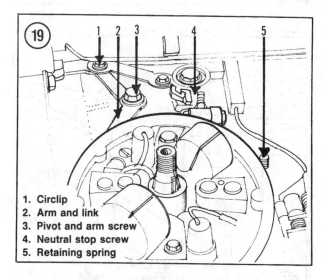

1. Circlip
2. Arm and link
3. Pivot and arm screw
4. Neutral stop screw
5. Retaining spring

will be retarded; a gap that is too small will advance timing.

Throttle Cam Adjustment

1. Remove the engine cover.
2. Loosen the cam follower adjustment screw (**Figure 17**).
3. Move the cam follower until it just touches the throttle cam.
4. Slowly rotate the throttle grip until the cam follower aligns with the timing mark on the throttle cam. See **Figure 17**.
5. Make sure the throttle valve is completely closed. Hold the throttle shaft in that position and position the throttle lever roller against the cam follower. Tighten adjustment screw securely.

Needle Valve Adjustment

1. Install the engine in a test tank with the proper test wheel or on the boat in the water with the correct propeller.
2. Lightly seat the low-speed needle and back it out 3/4 turns. Remove the knob from the low-speed needle.
3. Start the engine and run at half throttle until the engine reaches operating temperature.
4. Connect a tachometer according to manufacturer's instructions.

NOTE
The engine requires approximately 15 seconds to respond to adjustment in Step 5.

5. Briefly run the engine at full throttle to clear it out, then bring the engine speed back to 700-750 rpm (in gear).
6. Turn low-speed needle clockwise until the engine hesitates, then turn it counterclockwise until it reaches the fastest and smoothest running position.

NOTE
Do not disturb needle valve setting when reinstalling knob in Step 7.

7. Install the low-speed needle knob set mid-way between rich and lean.
8. Run the engine in FORWARD gear at idle and adjust the idle speed adjustment knob (**Figure 18**) until the engine idles at 550 rpm in gear.
9. Shift the engine into NEUTRAL and adjust the neutral stop screw to obtain an idle of 2,700-3,200 rpm. See **Figure 19** for neutral stop screw location (flywheel shown removed).
10. Shut the engine off, remove the test equipment and install the engine cover.

JOHNSON/EVINRUDE 9.9 AND 15 (BREAKER POINT IGNITION)

The breaker points are mounted on a fixed base. Ignition timing on these models is non-adjustable. Correctly adjusted breaker points will align the flywheel timing mark between the 2 armature plate index marks when the engine is run at 1,000 rpm. See **Figure 3**. If the point gap is too large, timing will be retarded; a gap that is too small will advance timing.

Throttle Cam Adjustment

1. Remove the engine cover.
2. Remove the air silencer cover and base.
3. Set the throttle grip to the STOP position.
4. Slowly rotate the throttle grip toward the ADVANCE position until the throttle cam timing mark intersects the cam follower roller. See **Figure 20**.
5. If the throttle valve is not closed when the cam roller and throttle cam mark align in Step 3, loosen the cam adjustment screws. Adjust cam back or forth as required and tighten screws.
6. Recheck adjustment by rotating the throttle grip while watching the throttle valve. The valve should start to open as the V-shaped cam mark passes the center of the roller.
7. Install the air silencer base and cover.

Needle Valve Adjustment

1. Install the engine in a test tank with the proper test wheel or on the boat in the water with the correct propeller.
2. Remove the knob from the low-speed needle.
3. Start the engine and run at half throttle until the engine reaches operating temperature.
4. Connect a tachometer according to manufacturer's instructions.

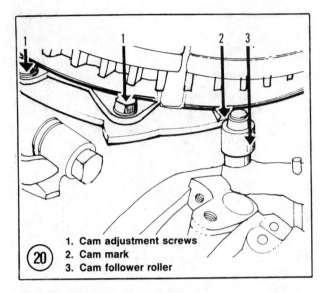

20
1. Cam adjustment screws
2. Cam mark
3. Cam follower roller

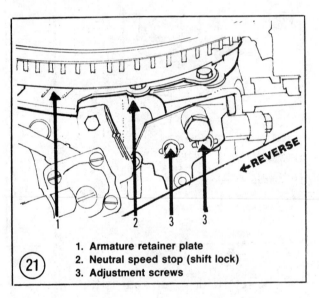

21
1. Armature retainer plate
2. Neutral speed stop (shift lock)
3. Adjustment screws

NOTE
The engine requires approximately 15 seconds to respond to adjustment in Step 5.

5. Bring engine speed back to 700-750 rpm and adjust low-speed needle to produce the highest rpm and smoothest operation.

NOTE
Do not disturb needle valve setting when reinstalling knob in Step 6.

6. Install the low-speed needle knob with its pointer facing down.

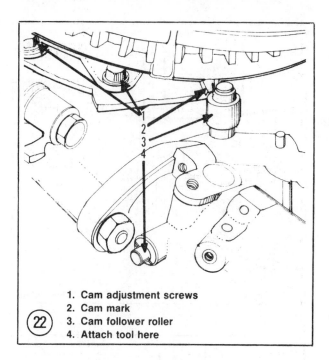

1. Cam adjustment screws
2. Cam mark
3. Cam follower roller
4. Attach tool here

⑳

7. Run the engine in FORWARD gear at idle and note the tachometer. If throttle cam and needle valve adjustments are correct, the engine will idle at 600 rpm in gear.

8. Shift the engine into NEUTRAL and loosen the shift lock stop adjustment screws. Adjust shift lock stop to obtain an idle of 3,000-4,000 rpm, then tighten screws. See **Figure 21** for neutral speed stop location.

9. Shut the engine off, remove the test equipment and install the engine cover.

JOHNSON/EVINRUDE 9.9 AND 15 (CD 2 IGNITION)

Timing adjustments are not required on these models. If the wires are correctly positioned in the 3-wire and 4-wire connectors, proper ignition timing will be maintained, provided the following adjustments are made correctly.

Throttle Cam Adjustment

1. Remove the engine cover.
2. Remove the air silencer cover and base.
3. Set the throttle grip to the STOP position.

4. Install the tool shown in **Figure 2** to the end of the throttle shaft opposite the cam follower linkage. See **Figure 22**.

5. Slowly rotate the throttle grip toward the ADVANCE position until the cam follower roller is centered between the raised marked area on the throttle cam. See **Figure 22**. At this point, the tool installed in Step 3 should just start to move, indicating the throttle is starting to open.

6. If the roller and marked area do not align properly when the tool starts to move, loosen the 2 cam adjustment screws (**Figure 22**) and adjust the cam position as required. Tighten screws and recheck alignment.

7. Install air silencer base and cover.

Needle Valve Adjustment

1. Install the engine in a test tank with the proper test wheel or on the boat in the water with the correct propeller.

2. Remove the knob from the low-speed needle.

3. Start the engine and run at half throttle until the engine reaches operating temperature.

4. Connect a tachometer according to manufacturer's instructions.

NOTE
The engine requires approximately 15 seconds to respond to adjustment in Step 5.

5. Bring engine speed back to 700-750 rpm in gear and adjust the low-speed needle to produce the highest rpm and smoothest operation.

NOTE
Do not disturb needle valve setting when reinstalling knob in Step 6.

6. Install the low-speed needle knob with its pointer facing down.

7. Run the engine in FORWARD gear at idle and note the tachometer. If throttle cam and

5

needle valve adjustments are correct, the engine will idle at 600 rpm in gear.

8. Shift the engine into NEUTRAL and loosen the shift lock stop adjustment screws. Adjust shift lock stop to obtain an idle of 3,000-4,000 rpm, then tighten screws. See **Figure 21** for neutral speed stop location.

9. Shut the engine off, remove the test equipment and install the engine cover.

JOHNSON/EVINRUDE 18, 20 AND 25 (BREAKER POINT IGNITION)

The breaker points are mounted on a fixed base. Ignition timing on these models is non-adjustable. Correctly adjusted breaker points will align the flywheel timing mark between the 2 armature plate index marks when the engine is run at 1,000 rpm. See **Figure 3**. If the point gap is too large, timing will be retarded; a gap that is too small will advance timing.

Throttle Cam Adjustment

1. Remove the engine cover.
2. Set the throttle grip to the STOP position.
3. Slowly rotate the throttle grip toward the ADVANCE position until the cam follower roller is centered between the 2 index marks on the throttle cam. See **Figure 23** (flywheel shown removed).
4. If the throttle valve is not closed when the cam roller and throttle cam marks align in Step 3, rotate the throttle grip until the cam follower roller and throttle cam index marks are positioned properly (Step 3).
5. Loosen the throttle shaft linkage screw (**Figure 24**). Hold the cam follower tightly against the cam and tighten the linkage screw.
6. Rotate the throttle grip from the STOP position toward ADVANCE. The throttle valve should start to open after the roller edge passes the second cam mark.

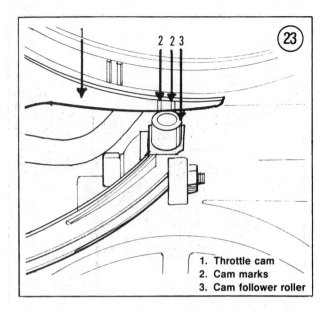

1. Throttle cam
2. Cam marks
3. Cam follower roller

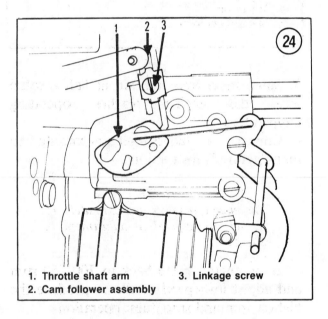

1. Throttle shaft arm   3. Linkage screw
2. Cam follower assembly

7. If the throttle valve is not closed after the adjustment, check for a weak return spring or binding linkage.

Needle Valve Adjustment

1. Install the engine in a test tank with the proper test wheel or on the boat in the water with the correct propeller.
2. Lightly seat the low-speed needle and back it out one full turn. Remove the low-speed needle valve arm.

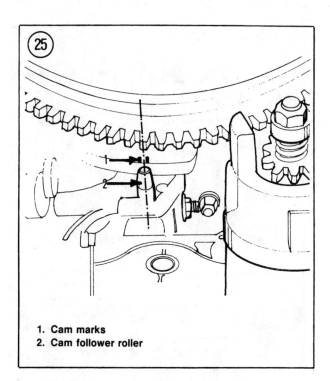

1. Cam marks
2. Cam follower roller

3. Start the engine and run at half throttle until the engine reaches operating temperature.

4. Connect a tachometer according to manufacturer's instructions.

NOTE
The engine requires approximately 15 seconds to respond to adjustment in Step 5.

5. Bring engine speed back to 700-750 rpm and adjust low-speed needle to produce the highest rpm and smoothest operation.

NOTE
Do not disturb needle valve setting when reinstalling the valve arm in Step 6.

6. Install the low-speed needle valve arm in the normal running position.

7. Run the engine in FORWARD gear at idle and adjust idle screw (if necessary) to bring the engine speed to 650 rpm in gear.

8. Shut the engine off, remove the test equipment and install the engine cover.

Ignition Timing Check

1. Connect a tachometer and timing light according to manufacturer's instructions.
2. Start the engine and run at 1,000 rpm.
3. Point the timing light at the armature plate index marks. If the flywheel timing mark does not align between the armature plate index marks, adjust the breaker point gap. See Chapter Four.

**JOHNSON/EVINRUDE 25 AND 30
(CD 2 IGNITION)
JOHNSON/EVINRUDE 35
(ALL IGNITIONS)**

Timing adjustments are not required on models with a CD 2 ignition. If the wires are correctly positioned in the 3-wire and 4-wire connectors, proper ignition timing will be maintained, provided the following adjustments are made correctly.

On Johnson/Evinrude models with a breaker point ignition, the breaker points are mounted on a fixed base. Ignition timing is non-adjustable. Correctly adjusted breaker points will align the flywheel timing mark between the 2 armature plate index marks when the engine is run at 1,000 rpm. See **Figure 3**. If the point gap is too large, timing will be retarded; a gap that is too small will advance timing.

Throttle Cam Adjustment

1. Remove the engine cover.
2. Set the throttle grip to the STOP position.
3. Slowly rotate the throttle grip toward the ADVANCE position until the throttle cam timing marks align with the cam follower roller. On 1980 and later 25 hp models, the roller should align with the second cam mark; on all other models, the roller should be centered between the marks. See **Figure 25**.
4. If the throttle valve is not closed when the cam roller and throttle cam marks align in

5

Step 3, loosen the cam adjustment screw (**Figure 26**). Adjust the cam up or down as required to align the marks and tighten the screw.

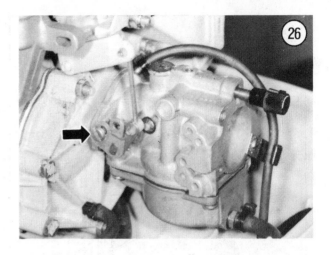

Throttle Control Rod Adjustment

1. With the shift lever in FORWARD gear, the throttle lever should touch its stop.
2. If it does not, loosen the adjustment collar screw (A, **Figure 27**).
3. Push the throttle control rod to a full open position. Position collar in contact with the nylon pivot block (B, **Figure 27**) and tighten the collar screw.

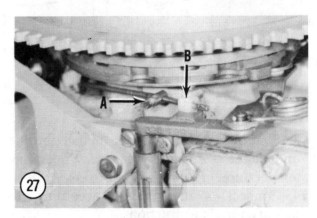

Needle Valve Adjustment

1. Install the engine in a test tank with the proper test wheel or on the boat in the water with the correct propeller.
2. Start the engine and run at half throttle until the engine reaches operating temperature.
3. Connect a tachometer according to manufacturer's instructions.

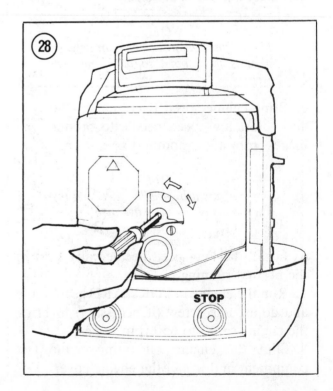

> *NOTE*
> *The engine requires approximately 15 seconds to respond to adjustment in Step 4.*

4. Bring engine speed back to 700-750 rpm and adjust low-speed needle to produce the highest rpm and smoothest operation. See **Figure 28**.
5. Run the engine in FORWARD gear at idle and note the tachometer. If idle speed is not 650 rpm, turn the idle speed needle (**Figure 29**) clockwise to increase or counterclockwise to decrease rpm.
6. Shut the engine off, remove the test equipment and install the engine cover.

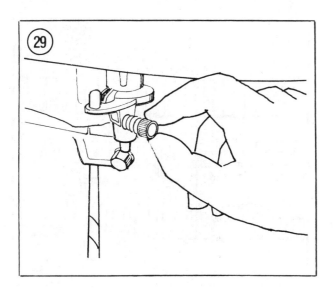

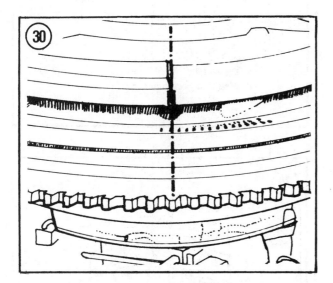

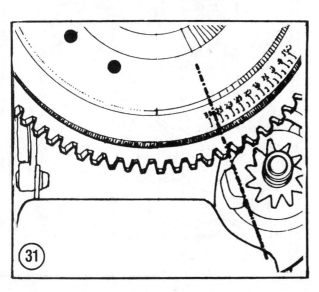

Full Throttle Stop Adjustment

1. Install the engine in a test tank with the proper test wheel or on the boat in the water with the correct propeller.

2. Remove the engine cover.

3. Connect a tachometer and timing light according to manufacturer's instructions.

4. Start the engine and run at full throttle.

5. Point the timing light at the flywheel to align the flywheel and stationary marks as shown in **Figure 30** (manual start) or **Figure 31** (electric start).

The stationary mark must align with the 34 degree mark (± 1 degree) on 1977-1981 25 hp and 1976 35 hp models. It must align with the 30 degree mark (± 1 degree) on 1982 and later 25 hp and 1977 and later 35 hp models. Due to increasing variations in fuel quality, there may be some changes in 1983 and later specifications. Follow the timing specification on the engine decal if it differs from those given here.

WARNING
Do not attempt to make the adjustment in Step 6 with the engine running. The adjustment screw is close to the moving flywheel and serious personal injury could result.

6. If the timing is not correct, shut the engine off. Loosen the timing stop adjustment screw locknut (**Figure 32**) and turn the screw in or

out as required to bring the timing within specifications.

7. Tighten the screw and start the engine. Recheck the timing.

8. Repeat Steps 5-7 until the timing is within specifications.

JOHNSON/EVINRUDE 40 (BREAKER POINT IGNITION)

The breaker points are mounted on a fixed base. Ignition timing is non-adjustable. Correctly adjusted breaker points will align the flywheel timing mark between the 2 armature plate index marks when the engine is run at 1,000 rpm. See **Figure 3**. If the point gap is too large, timing will be retarded; a gap that is too small will advance timing.

Throttle Cam Adjustment

1. Remove the engine cover.

2. Remove ring gear guard on electric start models.

3. Move the throttle control until the intake manifold projection is centered between the 2 throttle cam marks. See **Figure 33**.

4. If the throttle valve is not closed with the cam follower roller touching the cam, loosen the throttle arm clamp screw (**Figure 34**). Make sure the intake manifold projection intersects the throttle cam marks, the throttle valve is closed and the cam roller touches the cam, then tighten the clamp screw.

5. Close the throttle with the throttle control, then slowly reopen it. The throttle valve should start to open after the first cam mark passes the intake manifold projection. If it does not, repeat Step 4.

6. Manually rotate armature base to full advance position. Adjust control rod collar to provide 1/32 in. clearance at the pivot pin. See **Figure 35**.

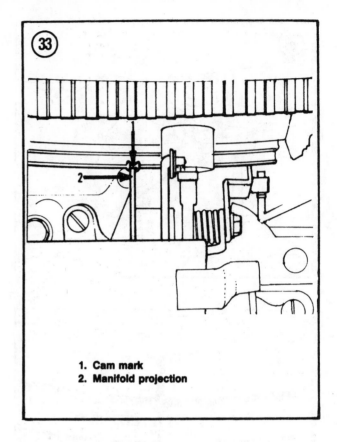

1. Cam mark
2. Manifold projection

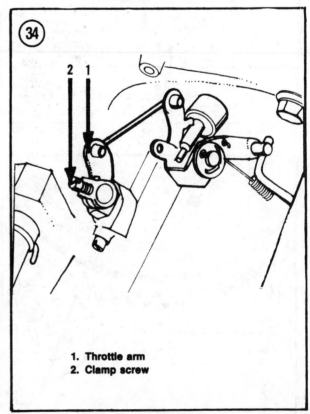

1. Throttle arm
2. Clamp screw

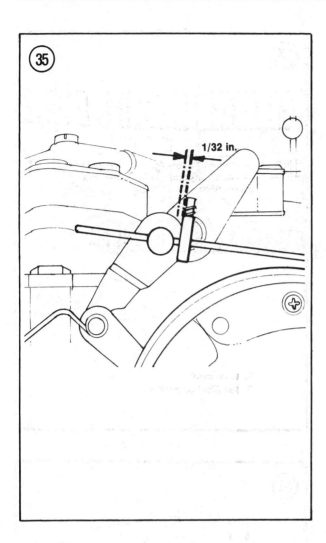

Needle Valve Adjustment

1. Install the engine in a test tank with the proper test wheel or on the boat in the water with the correct propeller.

2. Start the engine and run at half throttle until the engine reaches operating temperature.

3. Connect a tachometer according to manufacturer's instructions.

NOTE
The engine requires approximately 15 seconds to respond to adjustment in Step 4.

4. Bring engine speed back to 700-750 rpm and carefully remove the low-speed arm from the needle valve. Adjust the low-speed needle valve to produce the highest rpm and smoothest operation, then reinstall the low-speed arm without changing the needle valve position.

5. Run the engine in FORWARD gear at idle and note the tachometer. If idle speed is not 650 rpm, turn the idle adjustment screw on the throttle handle clockwise to increase or counterclockwise to decrease rpm.

5

NOTE: If you own a 1985 or later model, first check the Supplement at the back of the book for any new service information.

Chapter Six

Fuel System

This chapter contains removal, overhaul, installation and adjustment procedures for fuel pumps, carburetors, fuel tanks and connecting lines used with the Johnson and Evinrude outboards covered in this book. **Table 1** is at the end of the chapter.

FUEL PUMP

Johnson and Evinrude outboards equipped with an integral fuel tank use a gravity flow fuel system and require no fuel pump.

The diaphragm-type fuel pump used on models with a remote fuel tank operates by crankcase pressure. Since this type of fuel pump cannot create sufficient pressure to draw fuel from the tank during cranking, fuel is transferred to the carburetor for starting by operating the primer bulb installed in the fuel line.

Pressure pulsations created by movement of the pistons reach the fuel pump through a passageway between the crankcase and pump.

Upward piston motion creates a low pressure on the pump diaphragm. This low pressure opens the inlet check valve in the pump, drawing fuel from the line into the pump. At the same time, the low pressure draws the air-fuel mixture from the carburetor into the crankcase.

Downward piston motion creates a high pressure on the pump diaphragm. This pressure closes the inlet check valve and opens the outlet check valve, forcing the fuel into the carburetor and drawing the air-fuel mixture from the crankcase into the cylinder for combustion. **Figure 1** shows the operational sequence of a typical Johnson and Evinrude outboard fuel pump.

Johnson and Evinrude fuel pumps are self-contained, remote assemblies. Fuel pump shape and size differs according to engine size. The square pump shown in **Figure 2** is used on 4-15 hp engines. **Figure 3** shows the one used on 18 hp and larger models. The design of both pump styles is extremely simple and reliable in operation. Diaphragm

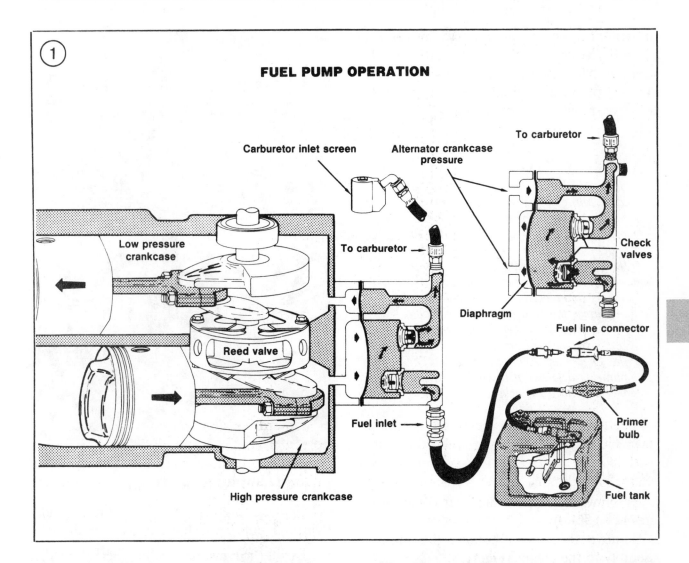

FUEL PUMP OPERATION

Carburetor inlet screen

Alternator crankcase pressure

To carburetor

Low pressure crankcase

To carburetor

Check valves

Diaphragm

Reed valve

Fuel line connector

Fuel inlet

Primer bulb

High pressure crankcase

Fuel tank

6

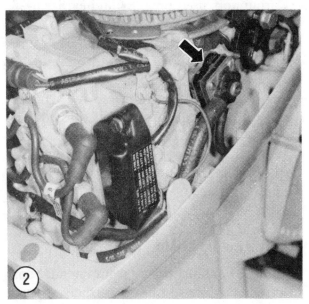

failures are the most common problem, although the use of dirty or improper fuel-oil mixtures can cause check valve problems. The fuel pump is serviced as an assembly; if defective, replace the entire unit.

NOTE
Some 1983 4-15 hp engines may stall after idling for a brief time but run satisfactorily at speeds above idle. The most likely cause is a fuel pump in which valve seat imperfections prevent the valves from seating. These pumps were installed on new motors at the factory and placed in replacement parts inventory. To test, position a portable fuel tank 24 inches below the pump and connected with a transparent hose. Run the engine at 700 rpm in gear. The pump is defective if it will not lift the fuel the entire 24 inches.

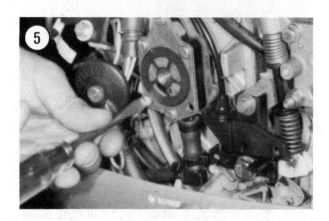

Removal/Installation

1. Unscrew and remove the filter cover and screen (**Figure 4**).
2. Remove the screws holding the pump assembly to the engine (**Figure 5**).
3. Remove and discard any straps holding the fuel lines to the fuel pump. Disconnect the lines at the pump.
4. Remove the pump and gasket from the engine. Discard the gasket.
5. Clean all gasket residue from the engine mounting pad. Work carefully to avoid gouging or damaging the mounting surface.
6. Clean the filter screen in OMC Engine Cleaner and blow dry with compressed air. If extremely dirty or damaged, install a new screen in Step 7.
7. Installation is the reverse of removal. Use new mounting and filter screen gaskets. Install new straps on the fuel line connections.

CARBURETORS

Many carburetors used on Johnson and Evinrude outboards have a fixed main jet orifice and require no high-speed adjustment.

Carburetors used on 1983 and earlier 6-35 hp models have a white Delrin needle valve retainer. Age and engine vibration can cause the retainer to lose its ability to prevent the low-speed needle from moving while the engine is running. An improved red retainer (part No. 315232) can be installed to correct the problem.

When removing and installing a carburetor, make sure the mounting nuts are securely tightened. A loose carburetor will cause a lean-running condition.

High Elevation Modifications

Table 1 contains orifice recommendations suggested by Johnson and Evinrude when a

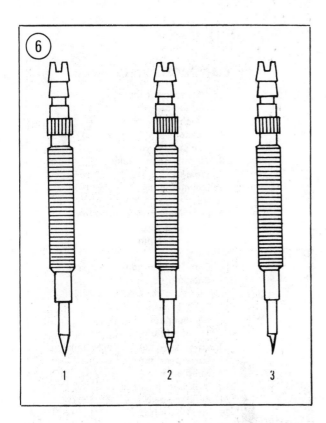

1973-1982 engine is used primarily at high elevation areas. Rejetting for high elevation operation will recover only that engine power lost due to the improper air-fuel ratio caused by the reduction in air density.

The propeller used must allow the engine to run within the recommended engine speed operating range. The correct propeller should place full throttle engine rpm in the middle of the recommended operating range. Changing the prop for high elevation operation will recover only that engine power lost by not operating within the proper rpm range.

Always rejet and prop the engine for the lowest elevation at which the boat will be operated to prevent the possibility of power head damage from a lean fuel mixture. If the boat is to be used extensively at both high and low elevations, you should have 2 sets of jets, 2 props and a fixed jet screwdriver (part No. 317002) for installation as required.

Your Johnson or Evinrude dealer can supply elevation modification stickers (part No. 393533) for application on the motor as a reminder of the original and elevation jet/prop sizes. Their use will assure that the correct information is always readily available.

Cleaning and Inspection

Before removing and disassembling any carburetor, be sure you have the proper overhaul kit, the proper tools and a sufficient quantity of fresh cleaning solvent. Work slowly and carefully, follow the disassembly procedures, refer to the exploded drawing of your carburetor when necessary and do not apply excessive force at any time.

It is not necessary to disassemble the carburetor linkage or remove the throttle cam or other external components. Wipe the carburetor casting and linkage with a cloth moistened in solvent to remove any contamination and operating film. Clean the carburetor castings with an aerosol type solvent and a brush. Do not submerge them in a hot tank or carburetor cleaner. A sealing compound is used around the metering tubes and on the casting to eliminate porosity problems. A hot tank or submersion in carburetor cleaner will remove this sealing compound.

Spray the cleaner on the casting and scrub off any gum or varnish with a small bristle brush. Spray the cleaner through the casting metering passages. Never clean passages with a wire or drill as you may enlarge the passage and change the carburetor calibration.

Blow castings dry with low-pressure (25 psi or less) compressed air. The use of higher pressures can damage the sealing compound.

Check the float for fuel absorption. Check the float arm for wear in the hinge pin and needle valve contact areas. Replace as required.

Check the needle valve tip for grooving, nicks or scratches. **Figure 6** shows a good

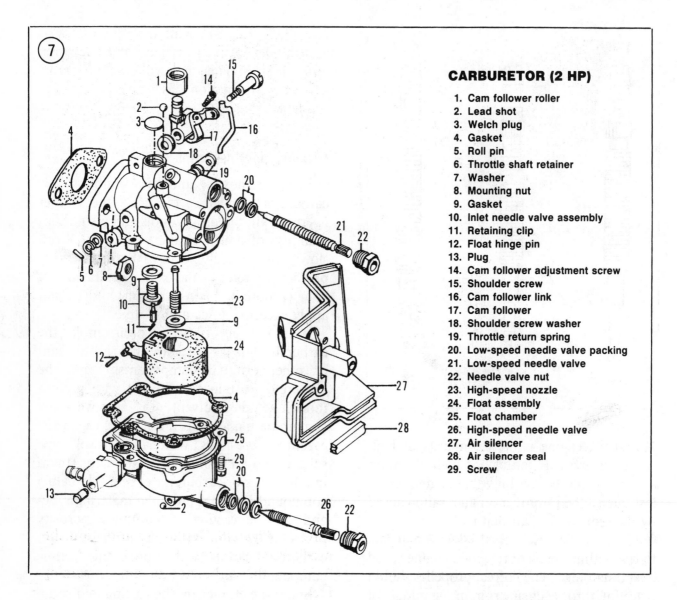

⑦

CARBURETOR (2 HP)

1. Cam follower roller
2. Lead shot
3. Welch plug
4. Gasket
5. Roll pin
6. Throttle shaft retainer
7. Washer
8. Mounting nut
9. Gasket
10. Inlet needle valve assembly
11. Retaining clip
12. Float hinge pin
13. Plug
14. Cam follower adjustment screw
15. Shoulder screw
16. Cam follower link
17. Cam follower
18. Shoulder screw washer
19. Throttle return spring
20. Low-speed needle valve packing
21. Low-speed needle valve
22. Needle valve nut
23. High-speed nozzle
24. Float assembly
25. Float chamber
26. High-speed needle valve
27. Air silencer
28. Air silencer seal
29. Screw

valve tip (1), a valve tip damaged from excessive pressure when seating (2) and one with wear on one side caused by vibration resulting from the use of a damaged propeller (3).

Check the throttle and choke shafts for excessive wear or play. The throttle and choke valves must move freely without binding. Replace the carburetor if any of these defects are noted.

Clean all gasket residue from mating surfaces and remove any nicks, scratches or slight distortion with a surface plate and emery cloth.

JOHNSON/EVINRUDE 2 (ALL) AND 4 (1973-1977)

Removal/Installation

1. Remove the engine cover.
2. Shut the fuel supply valve off.
3. Remove the low-speed knob from the needle valve.
4. Remove the rewind starter.
5. Disconnect the fuel line at the carburetor.
6. Pull out the 2 support bracket retainers and remove the fuel tank.
7. Align the speed control with the support bracket slot. Remove the support bracket

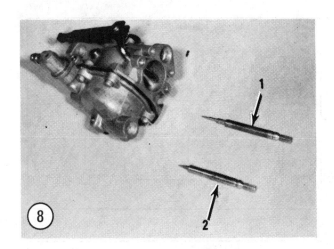

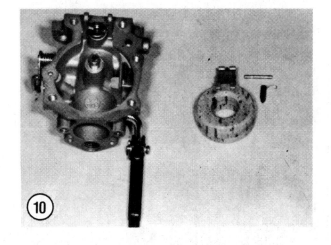

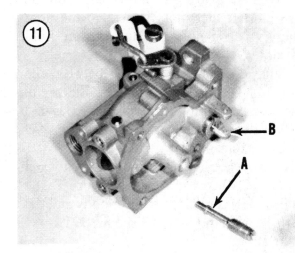

6

screws. Remove the support bracket and air silencer.

8. Remove the carburetor mounting nuts. Remove the carburetor.

9. Remove and discard the gasket.

10. Clean all gasket residue from the manifold mounting surface.

11. Installation is the reverse of removal. Use a new gasket. Adjust throttle cam (Chapter Five) before reinstalling support bracket and air silencer. Adjust carburetor (Chapter Five).

Disassembly/Assembly

Refer to **Figure 7** for this procedure.

1. Remove the high- and low-speed needle nuts. Remove the high-speed needle valve (1, **Figure 8**). Remove the low-speed needle valve (2, **Figure 8**). Remove and discard the needle valve packings.

2. Drain the carburetor of any remaining fuel.

3. Remove the float chamber screws. Separate the float chamber from the main body (**Figure 9**). Discard the float chamber gasket.

4. Remove the float assembly hinge pin. Lift the float and needle valve from the float chamber. See **Figure 10**.

5. Remove the high-speed nozzle (A, **Figure 11**). Remove and discard the nozzle gasket.

6. Remove the needle valve seat (B, **Figure 11**) with a wide-blade screwdriver. Discard the seat gasket.

7. Assembly is the reverse of disassembly. Compare new gaskets to the old ones to make

sure all holes are properly punched. Remove any loose gasket fibers or stamping crumbs adhering to the new gaskets. Adjust the float as described in this chapter. Lightly seat needle valves. Back high-speed needle out one full turn. Back low-speed needle out 1 1/4 turns. Install on engine and adjust carburetor (Chapter Five).

Float Adjustment

1. Invert the carburetor body with its gasket surface horizontal.

2. Place float gauge (part No. 324891) on the gasket surface and hold it next to the float (**Figure 12**). Do not let gauge pressure hold float down.

3. If the top of the float is not between the gauge notches (**Figure 12**), bend the metal float arm carefully (to avoid forcing the needle valve into its seat) and bring the level within specifications.

4. Return the carburetor body to its normal running position and check float drop. The distance between the carburetor body and the float as shown in **Figure 13** should be 1 1/8-1 1/2 in.

5. If the float drop is incorrect, carefully bend the tang (**Figure 13**) until it comes within specifications.

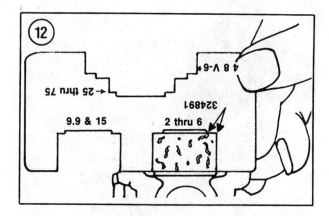

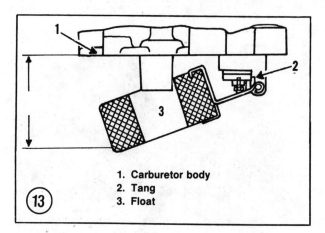

1. Carburetor body
2. Tang
3. Float

JOHNSON/EVINRUDE 4 (1978-ON) AND 4.5-8 (ALL)

Johnson/Evinrude 4 (1978-on) Removal/Installation

1. Remove the choke and low-speed adjustment knobs.

2. Remove the screws holding the lower motor cover at the front and rear.

3. Separate the motor cover in half and remove from the engine.

4. Disconnect the fuel line at the carburetor. Plug the line to prevent leakage.

5. Remove the 2 carburetor mounting nuts. Remove the carburetor and gasket. Discard the gasket.

6. Clean all gasket residue from the manifold mounting surface.

7. Installation is the reverse of removal. Use a new gasket. Adjust the carburetor (Chapter Five).

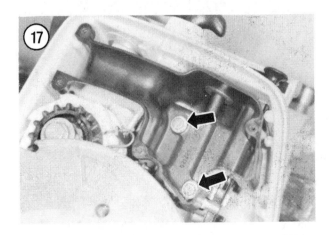

Johnson/Evinrude 4.5 Removal/Installation

1. Remove the engine cover.
2. Remove the low-speed knob (A, **Figure 14**).
3. Remove the choke knob retaining ring (B, **Figure 14**). Disconnect the knob at the

carburetor (C, **Figure 14**) and pull it out through the hole in the lower cover.

4. Remove the screw holding the cam follower and link (D, **Figure 14**). Move the cam follower out of the way to provide access to the mounting nut behind it.

5. Disconnect the fuel line at the carburetor. Plug the line to prevent leakage.

6. Remove the 2 carburetor mounting nuts. Remove the carburetor and gasket. Discard the gasket.

7. Clean all gasket residue from the manifold mounting surface.

8. Installation is the reverse of removal. Use a new gasket. Adjust the carburetor (Chapter Five).

Johnson/Evinrude 5-8 Removal/Installation

1. Remove the engine cover.
2. Remove the low-speed knob.
3. Remove the air silencer cover screws (**Figure 15**). Remove the cover.
4. Remove the manual starter. **Figure 16** shows one mounting screw; the second is located on the other side of the unit.
5. Remove the air silencer base screws (**Figure 17**). Remove the base.
6. Disconnect the choke lever at the carburetor and remove it from the engine.
7. Remove the screw holding the cam follower and link (D, **Figure 14**). Move the cam follower out of the way to provide access to the mounting nut behind it.
8. Disconnect the fuel line at the carburetor. Plug the line to prevent leakage.
9. Remove the 2 carburetor mounting nuts. Remove the carburetor and gasket. Discard the gasket.
10. Clean all gasket residue from the manifold mounting surface.
11. Installation is the reverse of removal. Use a new gasket. Adjust the carburetor (Chapter Five).

6

**Disassembly/Assembly
(All Models)**

Refer to **Figure 18** (4 hp), **Figure 19** (4.5 hp), **Figure 20** (5, 6 and 8 hp) or **Figure 21** (7.5 hp) for this procedure.

1. Remove the float chamber screws. Separate the float chamber from the main body. Discard the float chamber gasket.

2. On 4 and 4.5 hp models equipped with an integral fuel tank, unscrew and remove the fuel pump nipple, filter, roll pin and fuel shut-off valve from the float chamber. Discard the shut-off valve O-rings.

3A. 4 and 4.5 hp—Remove the low-speed needle nut. Remove the low-speed needle valve. Remove and discard the needle valve packings.

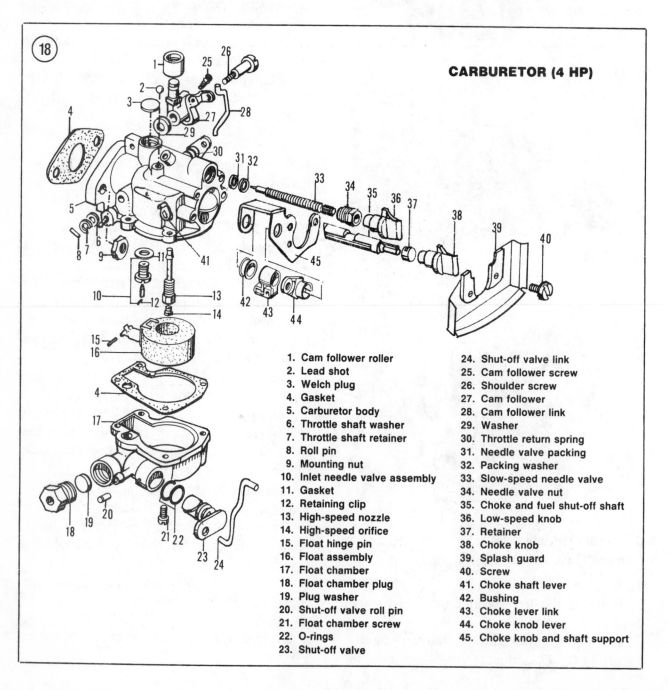

CARBURETOR (4 HP)

1. Cam follower roller	24. Shut-off valve link
2. Lead shot	25. Cam follower screw
3. Welch plug	26. Shoulder screw
4. Gasket	27. Cam follower
5. Carburetor body	28. Cam follower link
6. Throttle shaft washer	29. Washer
7. Throttle shaft retainer	30. Throttle return spring
8. Roll pin	31. Needle valve packing
9. Mounting nut	32. Packing washer
10. Inlet needle valve assembly	33. Slow-speed needle valve
11. Gasket	34. Needle valve nut
12. Retaining clip	35. Choke and fuel shut-off shaft
13. High-speed nozzle	36. Low-speed knob
14. High-speed orifice	37. Retainer
15. Float hinge pin	38. Choke knob
16. Float assembly	39. Splash guard
17. Float chamber	40. Screw
18. Float chamber plug	41. Choke shaft lever
19. Plug washer	42. Bushing
20. Shut-off valve roll pin	43. Choke lever link
21. Float chamber screw	44. Choke knob lever
22. O-rings	45. Choke knob and shaft support
23. Shut-off valve	

3B. 5-8 hp—Remove the low-speed needle valve. Insert a length of wire with a hooked end in the needle valve keyhole slot and remove the needle retainer.

4. Remove the float assembly hinge pin. Lift the float and needle valve from the float chamber.

5. Remove the needle valve seat with a wide-blade screwdriver. Discard the seat gasket.

6A. 4 and 4.5 hp—Remove the high speed nozzle. Remove and discard the nozzle gasket.

6B. 5-8 hp—Remove the high-speed orifice (if so equipped) from the carburetor body.

7. Assembly is the reverse of disassembly. Compare new gaskets to the old ones to make sure all holes are properly punched. Remove any loose gasket fibers or stamping crumbs adhering to the new gaskets. Install needle

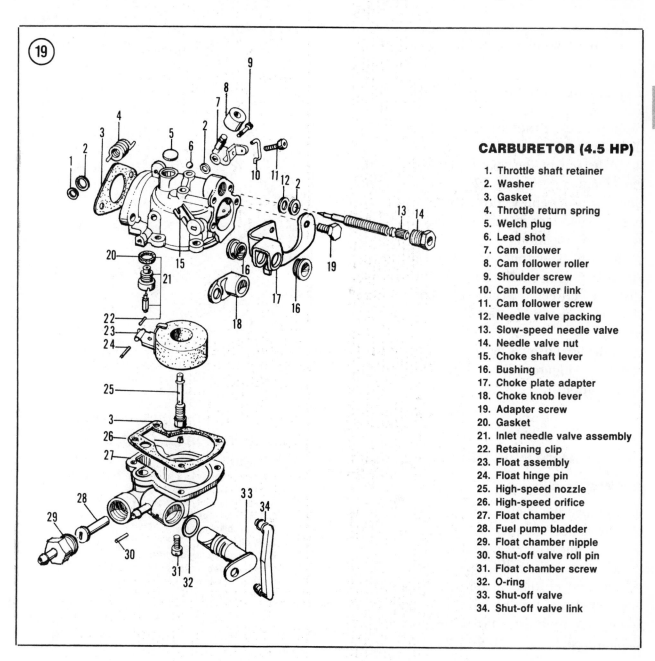

19

CARBURETOR (4.5 HP)

1. Throttle shaft retainer
2. Washer
3. Gasket
4. Throttle return spring
5. Welch plug
6. Lead shot
7. Cam follower
8. Cam follower roller
9. Shoulder screw
10. Cam follower link
11. Cam follower screw
12. Needle valve packing
13. Slow-speed needle valve
14. Needle valve nut
15. Choke shaft lever
16. Bushing
17. Choke plate adapter
18. Choke knob lever
19. Adapter screw
20. Gasket
21. Inlet needle valve assembly
22. Retaining clip
23. Float assembly
24. Float hinge pin
25. High-speed nozzle
26. High-speed orifice
27. Float chamber
28. Fuel pump bladder
29. Float chamber nipple
30. Shut-off valve roll pin
31. Float chamber screw
32. O-ring
33. Shut-off valve
34. Shut-off valve link

valve retainer with a flat punch on models so equipped. Adjust the float as described in this chapter. Lightly seat needle valve. Back low speed needle out one full turn. Install on engine and adjust carburetor (Chapter Five).

Float Adjustment

1. Invert the carburetor body with its gasket surface horizontal.

NOTE
Use the float gauge cutout marked "2 thru 6" for setting the 7.5 and 8 hp float in Step 2.

2. Place float gauge (part No. 324891) on the gasket surface and hold it next to the float (**Figure 12**). Do not let gauge pressure hold float down.

3. If the top of the float is not between the gauge notches (**Figure 12**), bend the metal float arm carefully (to avoid forcing the needle valve into its seat) and bring the level within specifications.

4. Return the carburetor body to its normal running position and check float drop. The distance between the carburetor body and the float as shown in **Figure 13** should be 1 1/8-1 1/2 in.

5. If the float drop is incorrect, carefully bend the tang (**Figure 13**) until it comes within specifications.

JOHNSON/EVINRUDE 9.5

Removal/Installation

1. Remove the engine cover.
2. Disconnect the fuel line at the carburetor. Plug the line to prevent leakage.
3. Lift the choke rod from the bellcrank.
4. Disconnect the cable-to-cover spring at the low-speed needle valve cable. Pull the low-speed knob from the cable and feed the cable through the control panel.

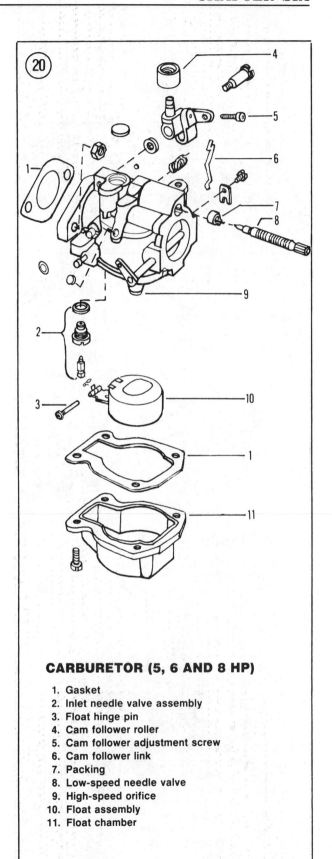

CARBURETOR (5, 6 AND 8 HP)

1. Gasket
2. Inlet needle valve assembly
3. Float hinge pin
4. Cam follower roller
5. Cam follower adjustment screw
6. Cam follower link
7. Packing
8. Low-speed needle valve
9. High-speed orifice
10. Float assembly
11. Float chamber

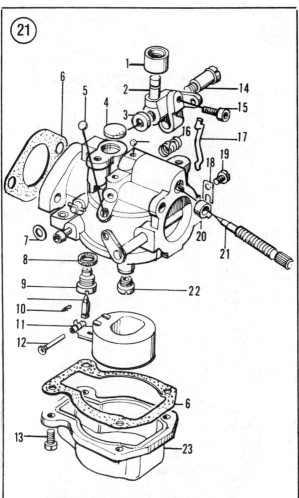

CARBURETOR (7.5 HP)

1. Cam follower roller
2. Cam follower
3. Washer
4. Welch plug
5. Lead shot
6. Gasket
7. Throttle shaft washer
8. Gasket
9. Inlet needle valve and needle assembly
10. Retaining clip
11. Float assembly
12. Float hinge pin
13. Float chamber screw
14. Shoulder screw
15. Cam follower adjustment screw
16. Throttle return spring
17. Cam follower link
18. Retaining clip
19. Screw
20. Needle valve retainer
21. Slow-speed needle valve
22. High-speed orifice plug
23. Float chamber

5. Remove the 5 screws holding the carburetor to the intake manifold. Swing the stabilizer bar to one side and remove the carburetor.

6. Clean all gasket residue from the manifold mounting surface.

7. Installation is the reverse of removal. Use a new gasket. Tighten flat head screw first to prevent carburetor distortion. Adjust the carburetor (Chapter Five).

Disassembly/Assembly

Refer to **Figure 22** for this procedure.

1. Remove the screw plug at the base of the float chamber and drain the fuel in the chamber into a container.

2. Remove the 4 screws holding the carburetor body to the float chamber.

3. Note the positioning of the washers and spring on the low-speed needle valve. Remove the needle valve, washers and spring.

4. Remove the float assembly hinge pin. Lift the float and needle valve from the float chamber.

5. Remove the needle valve seat with a wide-blade screwdriver. Discard the seat gasket.

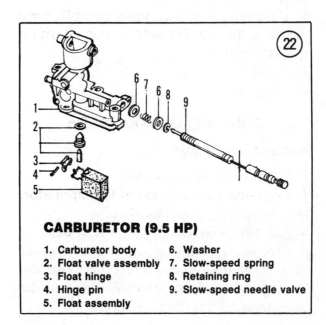

CARBURETOR (9.5 HP)

1. Carburetor body
2. Float valve assembly
3. Float hinge
4. Hinge pin
5. Float assembly
6. Washer
7. Slow-speed spring
8. Retaining ring
9. Slow-speed needle valve

6. Remove the high-speed jet from the float chamber with fixed jet screwdriver part No. 317002. See **Figure 23**.

7. Assembly is the reverse of disassembly. Compare new gaskets to the old ones to make sure all holes are properly punched. Remove any loose gasket fibers or stamping crumbs adhering to the new gaskets. Adjust the float as described in this chapter. Lightly seat needle valve. Back low-speed needle out 3/4 turn. Install on engine and adjust carburetor (Chapter Five).

Float Adjustment

1. Invert the carburetor body with its gasket surface horizontal, allowing the float weight to close the needle valve.

2. The float should be parallel with the casting face. Measure the distance between the casting and the top of the float. See **Figure 24**.

3. If the distance measured in Step 2 is not 13/16 in., bend the metal float arm carefully (to avoid forcing the needle valve into its seat) and bring the float within specifications.

4. Return the carburetor body to its normal running position and check float drop. The distance between the carburetor body and the float as shown in **Figure 25** should be 1 7/16 in. ±1/16 in.

5. If the float drop is incorrect, carefully bend the float tang until the drop is within specifications.

JOHNSON/EVINRUDE 9.9 AND 15

Removal/Installation

1. Remove the engine cover.

2. Remove the low-speed knob.

3. Remove the air silencer cover screws (**Figure 15**). Remove the cover.

4. Remove the air silencer base screws (**Figure 17**). Remove the base.

5. Remove the choke knob detent plate. Disconnect the choke lever from the choke

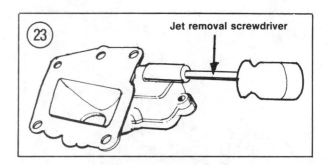

Jet removal screwdriver

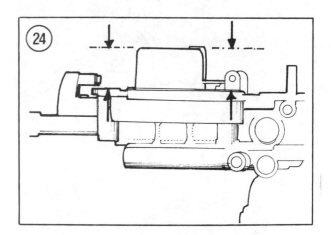

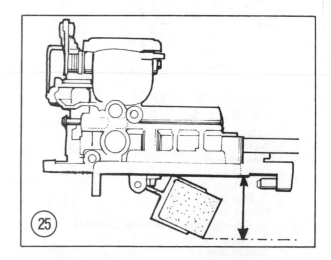

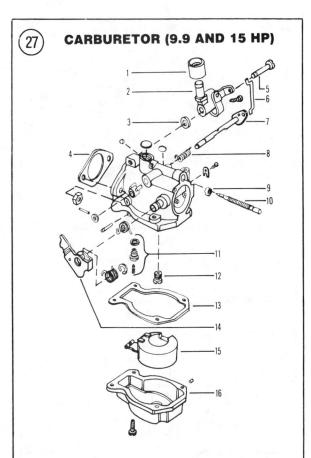

CARBURETOR (9.9 AND 15 HP)

1. Cam follower roller
2. Cam follower
3. Washer
4. Gasket
5. Shoulder screw
6. Cam follower link
7. Throttle shaft and lever
8. Throttle return spring
9. Retainer
10. Low-speed needle valve
11. Inlet needle valve assembly
12. High-speed orifice plug
13. Gasket
14. Choke lever
15. Float assembly
16. Float chamber

shaft. Pull choke knob and shaft out of the lower motor cover.

6. Remove the manual starter (**Figure 26**).

7. Remove the cam follower shoulder screw and washer (D, **Figure 14**). Disconnect lever from link and starter lockout pawl spring. Note position of link in cam follower.

8. Remove the 2 carburetor mounting nuts. Remove the carburetor, gasket and link. Note position of link on the throttle lever. Discard the gasket.

9. Disconnect the fuel line at the carburetor. Plug the line to prevent leakage.

10. Clean all gasket residue from the manifold mounting surface.

11. Installation is the reverse of removal. Use a new gasket. Connect link to throttle lever before mounting carburetor on intake manifold. Adjust the carburetor (Chapter Five).

Disassembly/Reassembly

Refer to **Figure 27** for this procedure.

1. Remove the float chamber screws. Separate the float chamber from the main body (**Figure 28**). Discard the float chamber gasket.

2. Remove the float assembly hinge pin. Remove the float. See A, **Figure 29**.

3. Remove the needle valve from the valve seat (B, **Figure 29**).

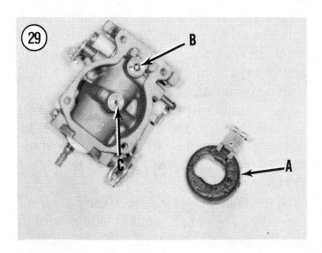

4. Remove the needle valve seat with a wide-blade screwdriver. Discard the seat gasket.

5. Remove the high-speed orifice plug (C, **Figure 29**).

6. Remove the low-speed needle valve (**Figure 30**). Insert a length of wire with a hooked end in the needle valve keyhole slot and remove the needle retainer.

7. Assembly is the reverse of disassembly. Compare new gaskets to the old ones to make sure all holes are properly punched. Remove any loose gasket fibers or stamping crumbs adhering to the new gaskets. Install needle valve retainer with a flat punch. Adjust the float as described in this chapter. Lightly seat needle valve. Back low-speed needle out one full turn (9.9 hp) or 7/8 turn (15 hp). Install on engine and adjust carburetor (Chapter Five).

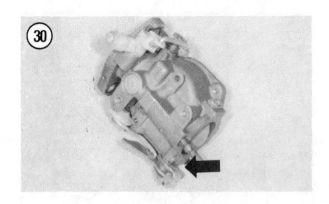

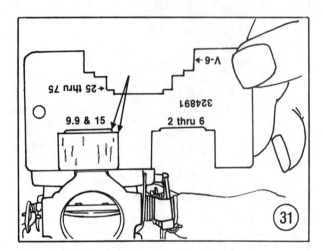

Float Adjustment

1. Invert the carburetor body with its gasket surface horizontal.

2. Place float gauge (part No. 324891) on the gasket surface and hold it next to the float (**Figure 31**). Do not let gauge pressure hold float down.

3. If the top of the float is not between the gauge notches (**Figure 31**), bend the metal float arm carefully (to avoid forcing the needle valve into its seat) and bring the level within specifications.

4. Return the carburetor body to its normal running position and check float drop. The distance between the carburetor body and the float as shown in **Figure 32** should be 1 1/8-1 1/2 in.

5. If the float drop is incorrect, carefully bend the tang (**Figure 32**) until it comes within specifications.

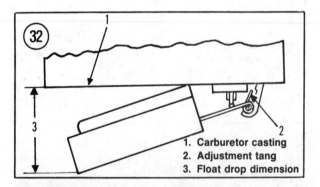

1. Carburetor casting
2. Adjustment tang
3. Float drop dimension

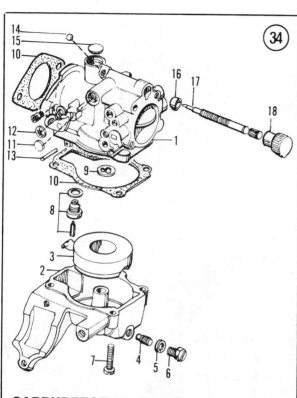

CARBURETOR (20-40 HP)

1. Carburetor body	10. Gasket
2. Float chamber	11. Welch plug
3. Float assembly	12. Retainer
4. Orifice plug	13. Float hinge pin
5. Screw plug washer	14. Lead shot
6. Screw plug	15. Welch plug
7. Float chamber screw	16. Needle valve retainer
8. Inlet needle valve	17. Slow-speed needle valve
assembly	18. Slow-speed
9. Nozzle gasket	adjustment knob

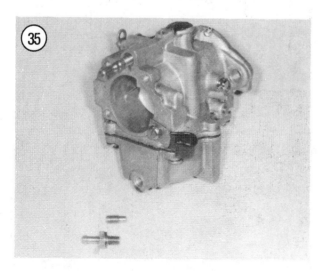

JOHNSON/EVINRUDE
20, 25, 30, 35 AND 40

Removal/Installation

1. Disconnect the carburetor fuel line at the fuel pump.

2A. 20-35 hp—Remove the screw holding the choke lever to the carburetor. Remove the wave washer and spacer, then disconnect the choke lever at the choke knob. Pull assembly from air silencer retainer.

2B. 40 hp—Disconnect low-speed arm and link from low-speed needle.

3. Remove the air silencer assembly.

4A. If equipped with a choke solenoid, remove the screw holding the solenoid and ground lead to the carburetor (A, **Figure 33**).

4B. If equipped with a primer solenoid, remove the solenoid screws and solenoid.

5. Disconnect the link between the throttle arm and cam follower (B, **Figure 33**).

6. Disconnect the oil recirculation line (C, **Figure 33**), if so equipped.

7. Remove the starter on electric start models if it interferes with carburetor removal. See Chapter Seven.

8. Remove the carburetor mounting nuts. Remove the carburetor and gasket. Discard the gasket.

9. Installation is the reverse of removal. Use a new gasket. Adjust the carburetor (Chapter Five).

Disassembly/Assembly

Refer to **Figure 34** typical for this procedure.

1. Remove the float bowl plug. Drain the carburetor and remove the high speed orifice with fixed jet screwdriver part No. 317002. See **Figure 35**.

2A. 20-35 hp—Remove the low speed needle valve (**Figure 36**). Insert a length of wire with a hooked end in the needle valve keyhole slot and remove the needle retainer.

6

2B. 40 hp—Remove the air intake screen, low-speed needle valve, packing nut, packings and washers.

3. Remove the screws holding the float chamber to the main body. Remove the float chamber. Remove and discard the gasket. See **Figure 37**.

4. Remove the float assembly hinge pin. Lift the float and needle valve from the float chamber. See **Figure 38**.

5. Remove the needle valve seat (**Figure 39**) with a wide blade screwdriver. Discard the seat gasket.

6. 40 hp—Remove the high-speed nozzle and gasket. Discard the gasket.

7. Assembly is the reverse of disassembly. Compare new gaskets to the old ones to make sure all holes are properly punched. Remove any loose gasket fibers or stamping crumbs adhering to the new gaskets. Install needle valve retainer with a flat punch. Adjust the float as described in this chapter. Lightly seat needle valve. Back low speed needle out 3/4 turn (20 and 25 hp) or 1 1/4 turn (35 hp). Reinstall on engine and adjust carburetor (Chapter Five).

Float Adjustment (20-35 hp)

1. Invert the carburetor body with its gasket surface horizontal.

2. Place float gauge (part No. 324891) on the gasket surface and hold it next to the float (**Figure 40**). Do not let gauge pressure hold float down.

3. If the top of the float is not between the gauge notches (**Figure 40**), bend the metal float arm carefully (to avoid forcing the needle valve into its seat) and bring the level within specifications.

4. Return the carburetor body to its normal running position and check float drop. The distance between the carburetor body and the

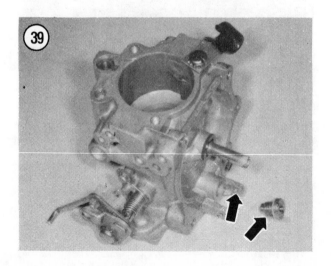

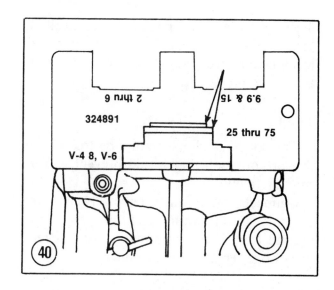

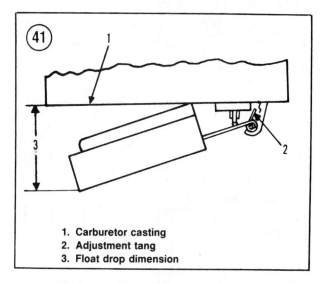

1. Carburetor casting
2. Adjustment tang
3. Float drop dimension

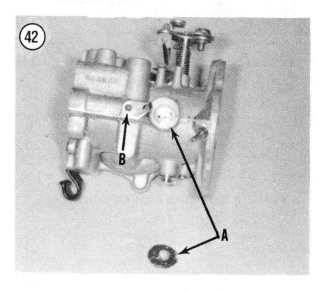

float as shown in **Figure 41** should be 1 1/8-1 5/8 in.

5. If the float drop is incorrect, carefully bend the tang (**Figure 41**) until it comes within specifications.

Float Adjustment (40 hp)

1. Invert the carburetor body with its gasket surface horizontal.

2. If the top of the float is not even with the gasket surface, bend the metal float arm carefully (to avoid forcing the needle valve into its seat) and bring the level within specifications.

CARBURETOR CORE PLUGS AND LEAD SHOT

Certain openings in the carburetor casting are covered with a core plug or have a lead shot installed. These usually require service only if the openings are leaking. **Figure 42** shows a carburetor with the core plug over the low-speed orifices removed (A) and a typical lead shot installed (B).

Core Plug Service

1. If leakage is noted, secure the carburetor in a vise with protective jaws.

2. Hold a flat end punch in the center of the core plug and tap sharply with a hammer to flatten the plug. Cover the plug area with OMC Adhesive M.

CAUTION
Do not drill more than 1/16 in. below the core plug in Step 3 or the casting will be damaged.

3. If this does not solve the leakage problem or if the low-speed orifices are completely plugged, carefully drill a 1/8 in. hole through the center of the plug and pry it from the casting with a punch.

4A. Clean all residue from the core plug hole in the casting. If the hole is out-of-round, replace the casting.

4B. If the low-speed orifices are plugged, clean with a brush and carburetor cleaner.

5. Coat the outer edge of a new core plug with OMC Adhesive M and position it in the casting opening with its convex side facing up.

6. Hold a flat end punch in the center of the core plug and tap sharply with a hammer to flatten the plug.

7. Coat the core plug with engine oil and blow compressed air (25 psi or less) through the casting passages to check for leakage.

8. Wipe the oil from the core plug and coat with OMC Adhesive M.

Lead Shot Service

1. If leakage is noted, secure the carburetor in a vise with protective jaws.

2. Tap the center of the lead shot sharply with a small hammer and appropriate size punch.

3. If leakage remains, carefully pry the lead shot from its opening with a suitable knife, awl or other sharp instrument.

4. Clean any residue from the lead shot opening in the casting.

5. Install a new lead shot in the opening and flatten out with a hammer and appropriate size punch.

6. Coat the core plug with engine oil and blow compressed air (25 psi or less) through the casting passages to check for leakage.

7. Clean the oil from the casting after pressure testing.

Carburetor Primer Solenoid
Removal/Installation

1. Disconnect the solenoid purple/white lead at the terminal board.

2. Remove the 2 screws and clamp holding the solenoid. Remove the solenoid.

3. Installation is the reverse of removal. Be sure to reinstall the ground lead under the lower clamp screw. Coat the screw with OMC Black Neoprene Dip.

Testing

The solenoid plunger must be free of any dirt or corrosion that would prevent it from moving freely.

Connect an ohmmeter between the solenoid purple/white lead and the black ground lead. If the ohmmeter does not read 4-7 ohms, replace the solenoid.

Disassembly/Assembly

1. Remove the cover screws (**Figure 43**). Remove the cover and gasket. Discard the gasket.

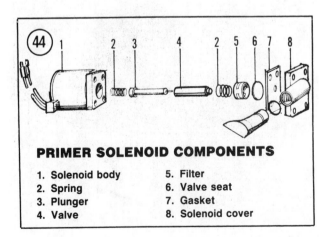

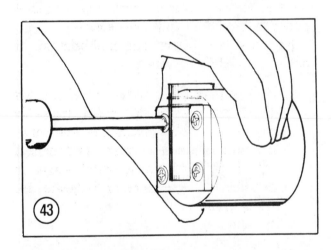

PRIMER SOLENOID COMPONENTS

1. Solenoid body
2. Spring
3. Plunger
4. Valve
5. Filter
6. Valve seat
7. Gasket
8. Solenoid cover

2. Remove the valve seat, filter, valve, plunger and both springs. See **Figure 44**.

3. Clean or replace the filter as required.

4. Clean the plunger to remove any contamination or corrosion.

5. Assembly is the reverse of disassembly. Install a new valve seat and use a new cover gasket.

ANTI-SIPHON DEVICES

In accordance with industry safety standards, late-model boats equipped with a built-in fuel tank will have some form of anti-siphon device installed between the fuel tank outlet and the outboard fuel inlet. This device is designed to shut the fuel supply off in case the boat capsizes or is involved in an accident. Quite often, the malfunction of such devices leads the owner to replace a fuel pump in the belief that it is defective.

Anti-siphon devices can malfunction in one of the following ways:

a. Anti-siphon valve: orifice in valve is too small or clogs easily; valve sticks in closed or partially closed position; valve fluctuates between open and closed position; thread sealer, metal filings or dirt/debris clogs orifice or lodges in the relief spring.

b. Solenoid-operated fuel shut-off valve: solenoid fails with valve in closed position; solenoid malfunctions, leaving valve in partially closed position.

c. Manually-operated fuel shut-off valve: valve is left in completely closed position; valve is not fully opened.

The easiest way to determine if an anti-siphon valve is defective is to bypass it by operating the engine with a remote fuel supply. If a fuel system problem is suspected, check the fuel filter first. If the filter is not clogged or dirty, bypass the anti-siphon device. If the engine runs properly with the anti-siphon device bypassed, contact the boat manufacturer for replacement of the anti-siphon device.

FUEL TANK

Integral Fuel Tank

All Johnson and Evinrude 2 hp models and some 4 and 4.5 hp models are fitted with an integral fuel tank. The integral tank on 4 hp engines so equipped is located in the engine cover. The integral tank on 2 and 4.5 hp models is located at the rear of the crankcase. The 2 hp tank is attached to a support bracket by 2 retainers; the 4.5 hp tank is held in place by a clamp strap. Integral fuel tanks are equipped with a fuel shut-off valve and filter assembly in the tank inlet fitting. **Figure 45** shows the 2 hp tank and valve.

Portable Fuel Tank

Figure 46 shows the components of the portable fuel tank, including the primer bulb assembly.

When some oils are mixed with gasoline and stored in a warm place, a bacterial substance will form. This substance is clear in color and covers the fuel pickup, restricting flow through the fuel system. Bacterial formation can be prevented by using OMC 2+4 Fuel Conditioner on a regular basis. If present, it can be removed with OMC Engine Cleaner.

To remove any dirt or water that may have entered the tank during refilling, clean the inside of the tank once each season by flushing with clean lead-free gasoline or kerosene.

Check the inside and outside of the tank for signs of rust, leakage or corrosion. Replace as required. Do not attempt to patch the tank with automotive fuel tank repair materials. Portable marine fuel tanks are subject to much greater pressure and vacuum conditions.

To check the fuel tank filter for possible restrictions, unscrew the fuel pickup nipple and withdraw the pickup tube and filter assembly from the tank. The filter on the end of the pickup tube can be cleaned with OMC Engine Cleaner.

Alcohol blended with gasoline may cause a gradual deteroriation of the indicator lens in portable fuel tanks. The use of a tank with an alcohol-resistant indicator lens is recommended if blended fuels are used with any frequency.

FUEL LINE AND PRIMER BULB

When priming the engine, the primer bulb should gradually become firm. If it does not become firm or if it stays firm even when disconnected, a check valve inside the primer bulb is malfunctioning.

The line should be checked periodically for cracks, breaks, restrictions and chafing. The bulb should be checked periodically for proper operation. Make sure all fuel line connections are tight and securely clamped.

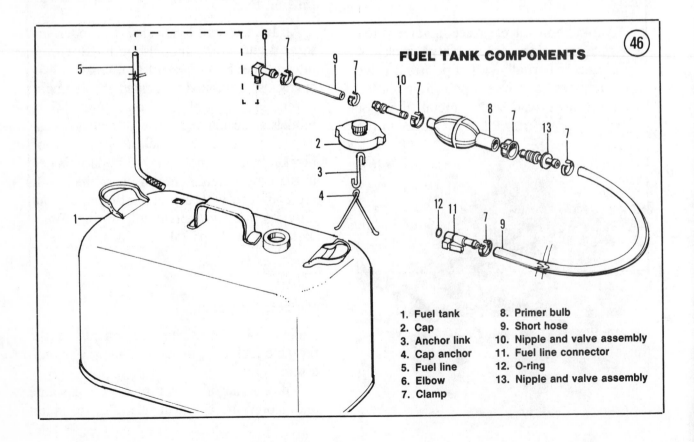

FUEL TANK COMPONENTS ㊻

1. Fuel tank
2. Cap
3. Anchor link
4. Cap anchor
5. Fuel line
6. Elbow
7. Clamp
8. Primer bulb
9. Short hose
10. Nipple and valve assembly
11. Fuel line connector
12. O-ring
13. Nipple and valve assembly

Table 1 CARBURETOR ALTITUDE ORIFICE CHART

1973-1979			
Model/Year	Sea level	3,000 to 6,000 ft.	6,000 to 10,000 ft.
4/1973-1977	Adj.	Adj.	Adj.
4/1978 Std. length	0.031	0.029	0.027
4/1978 Long shaft	0.029	0.027	0.025
4/1979	0.031	0.029	0.027
6/1973-1975	44	42D	39D
6/1976	52D	49D	45D
6/1977-1979	42D	39D	38D
9.5/1973	49	45D	43D
9.9/1974-1975	51N	49N	46N
9.9/1976	40N	38N	36N
9.9/1977-1978	38N	36N	34N
9.9/1979	40N	38N	36N
15/1974	60N	58N	56N
15/1975-1976	58N	56N	54N
15/1977-1979	54N	52N	50N
25/1973-1976	72	69D	67D
25/1977	55D	54D	52D
25/1978-1979	49D	45D	45D
35/1976-1979	59D	53D	47D
40/1973-1976	670	64D	63D

1980-1982						
Model/ Year	Sea level		3,000-6,000 ft.		6,000-10,000 ft.	
	Low Speed	High Speed	Low Speed	High Speed	Low Speed	High Speed
4/All	Adj.	0.031*	Adj.	0.029*	Adj.	0.027*
4.5/All	Adj.	0.033*	Adj.	0.030*	Adj.	0.027*
7.5/All	Adj.	35N	Adj.	32N	Adj.	29N
9.9/All	Adj.	38N	Adj.	36N	Adj.	34N
15/1980	Adj.	54N	Adj.	51N	Adj.	48N
15/1981-1982	Adj.	56N	Adj.	53N	Adj.	50N
20/All	Adj.	49D	Adj.	43D	Adj.	37D
25/1980	Adj.	49D	Adj.	43D	Adj.	37D
25/1981-1982	Adj.	59D	Adj.	53D	Adj.	47D
35/All	Adj.	59D	Adj.	53D	Adj.	47D

* Idle style.

NOTE: If you own a 1985 or later model, first check the Supplement at the back of the book for any new service information.

Chapter Seven

Electrical System

This chapter provides service procedures for the battery, starter motor (electric start models) and each ignition system used on Johnson and Evinrude outboard motors during the years covered by this manual. Wiring diagrams are included at the end of the book. **Tables 1-3** are at the end of the chapter.

BATTERY

Since batteries used in marine applications endure far more rigorous treatment than those used in an automotive charging system, they are constructed differently. Marine batteries have a thicker exterior case to cushion the plates inside during tight turns and rough weather. Thicker plates are also used, with each one individually fastened within the case to prevent premature failure. Spill-proof caps on the battery cells prevent electrolyte from spilling into the bilges. Automotive batteries are not designed to be run down and recharged repeatedly. For this reason, they should *only* be used in an emergency situation when a suitable marine battery is not available.

Johnson and Evinrude recommend that any battery used to crank an outboard motor have a cold cranking amperage of 350 amps and a reserve capacity of at least 100 minutes.

CAUTION
*Sealed or maintenance-free batteries are **not** recommended for use with the unregulated charging systems used on Johnson and Evinrude outboards. Excessive charging during continued high-speed operation will cause the electrolyte to boil, resulting in its loss. Since water cannot be added to such batteries, such overcharging will ruin the battery.*

Separate batteries may be used to provide power for any accessories such as lighting, fish finders, depth finder, etc. To determine the required capacity of such batteries, calculate the average discharge rate of the accessories and refer to **Table 1**. Batteries may be wired in parallel to double the ampere hour

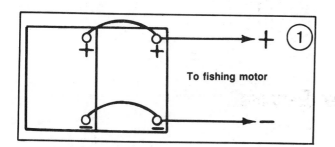

To fishing motor

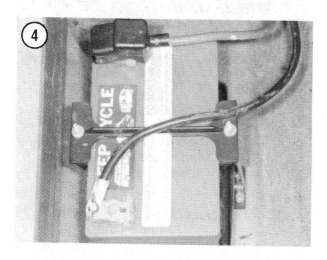

To fishing motor

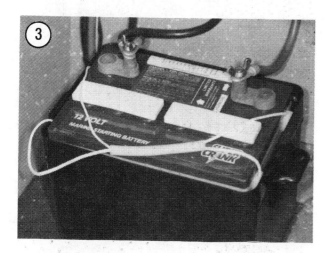

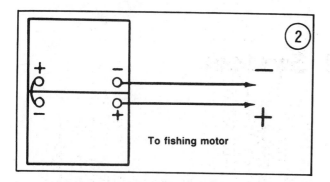

capacity while maintaining a 12-volt system. See **Figure 1**. For accessories which require 24 volts, batteries may be wired in series (**Figure 2**) but only accessories specifically requiring 24 volts should be connected into the system. Whether wired in parallel or in series, charge the batteries individually.

Battery Installation in Aluminum Boats

If a battery is not properly secured and grounded when installed in an aluminum boat, it may contact the hull and short to ground. This will burn out remote control cables, tiller handle cables or wiring harnesses.

Johnson and Evinrude recommend the following preventive steps be taken when installing a battery in a metal boat.

1. Choose a location as far as practical from the fuel tank while providing access for maintenance.
2. Install the battery in a plastic battery box with cover and tie-down strap (**Figure 3**).
3. If a covered container is not used, cover the positive battery terminal with a non-conductive shield or boot (**Figure 4**).
4. Make sure the battery is secured inside the battery box and the box is fastened in position with the tie-down strap.

Care and Inspection

1. Remove the battery container cover (**Figure 3**) or hold-down (**Figure 4**).
2. Disconnect the negative battery cable. Disconnect the positive battery cable.

NOTE
*Some batteries have a built-in carry strap (**Figure 5**) for use in Step 3.*

3. Attach a battery carry strap to the terminal posts. Remove the battery from the battery tray or container.
4. Check the entire battery case for cracks.

5. Inspect the battery tray or container for corrosion and clean if necessary with a solution of baking soda and water.

> *NOTE*
> *Keep cleaning solution out of the battery cells in Step 6 or the electrolyte will be seriously weakened.*

6. Clean the top of the battery with a stiff bristle brush using the baking soda and water solution (**Figure 6**). Rinse the battery case with clear water and wipe dry with a clean cloth or paper towel.

7. Position the battery in the battery tray or container.

8. Clean the battery cable clamps with a stiff wire brush or one of the many tools made for this purpose (**Figure 7**). The same tool is used for cleaning the battery posts. See **Figure 8**.

9. Reconnect the positive battery cable, then the negative cable.

> *CAUTION*
> *Be sure the battery cables are connected to their proper terminals. Connecting the battery backwards will reverse the polarity and damage the rectifier.*

10. Tighten the battery connections and coat with a petroleum jelly such as Vaseline or a light mineral grease.

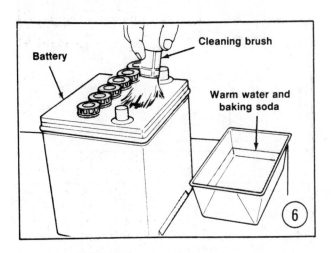

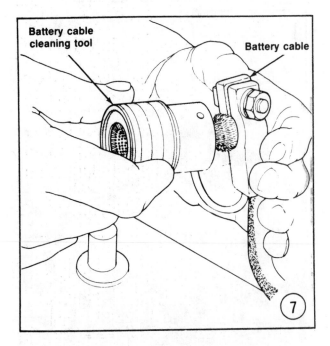

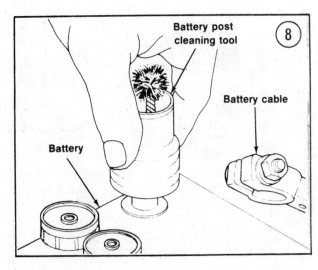

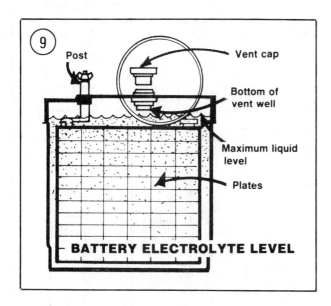

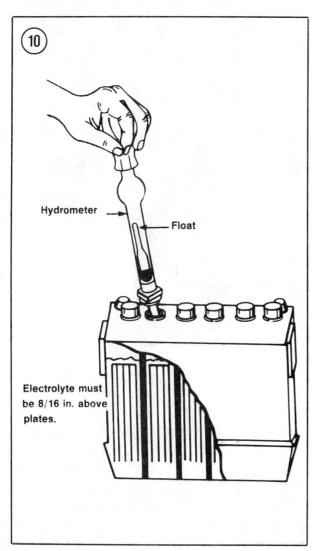

7

NOTE
Do not overfill the battery cells in Step 11. The electrolyte expands due to heat from charging and will overflow if the level is more than 3/16 in. above the battery plates.

11. Remove the filler caps and check the electrolyte level. Add distilled water, if necessary, to bring the level up to 3/16 in. above the plates in the battery case. See **Figure 9**.

Testing

Hydrometer testing is the best way to check battery condition. Use a hydrometer with numbered graduations from 1.100-1.300 rather than one with just color-coded bands. To use the hydrometer, squeeze the rubber ball, insert the tip in a cell and release the ball (**Figure 10**).

NOTE
Do not attempt to test a battery with a hydrometer immediately after adding water to the cells. Charge the battery for 15-20 minutes at a rate high enough to cause vigorous gassing and allow the water and electrolyte to mix thoroughly.

Draw enough electrolyte to float the weighted float inside the hydrometer. When using a temperature-compensated hydrometer, release the electrolyte and repeat this process several times to make sure the thermometer has adjusted to the electrolyte temperature before taking the reading.

Hold the hydrometer vertically and note the number in line with the surface of the electrolyte (**Figure 11**). This is the specific gravity for the cell. Return the electrolyte to the cell from which it came.

The specific gravity of the electrolyte in each battery cell is an excellent indicator of that cell's condition. A fully charged cell will read 1.260 or more at 68° F (20° C). A cell that is 75 percent charged will read from 1.220-1.230 while one with a 50 percent charge reads from 1.170-1.180. If the cell tests below 1.120, the battery must be recharged and one that reads 1.100 or below is dead. Charging is also necessary if the specific gravity varies more than 0.050 from cell to cell.

NOTE
If a temperature-compensated hydro-meter is not used, add 0.004 to the specific gravity reading for every 10° above 80° F (25° C). For every 10° below 80° F (25° C), subtract 0.004.

Charging

A good state of charge should be maintained in batteries used for starting. Check the battery with a voltmeter as shown in **Figure 12**. Any battery that cannot deliver at least 9.6 volts under a starting load should be recharged. If recharging does not bring it up to strength or if it does not hold the charge, replace the battery.

The battery does not have to be removed from the boat for charging, but it is a recommended safety procedure since a charging battery gives off highly explosive hydrogen gas. In many boats, the area around the battery is not well ventilated and the gas may remain in the area for hours after the charging process has been completed. Sparks or flames occuring near the battery can cause it to explode, spraying battery acid over a wide area.

For this reason, it is important you observe the following precautions:

    a. Do not smoke around batteries that are charging or have been recently charged.

    b. Do not break a live circuit at the battery terminals and cause an electrical arc that can ignite the hydrogen gas.

Disconnect the negative battery cable first, then the positive cable. Make sure the electrolyte is fully topped up.

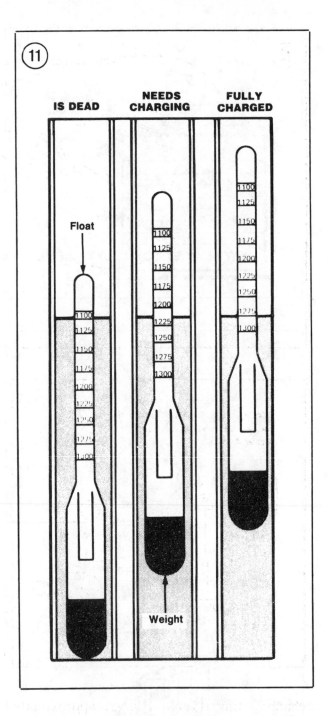

Connect the charger to the battery—negative to negative, positive to positive. If the charger output is variable, select a 4 amp setting. Set the voltage regulator to 12 volts and plug the charger in. If the battery is severely discharged, allow it to charge for at least 8 hours. Batteries that are not as badly discharged require less

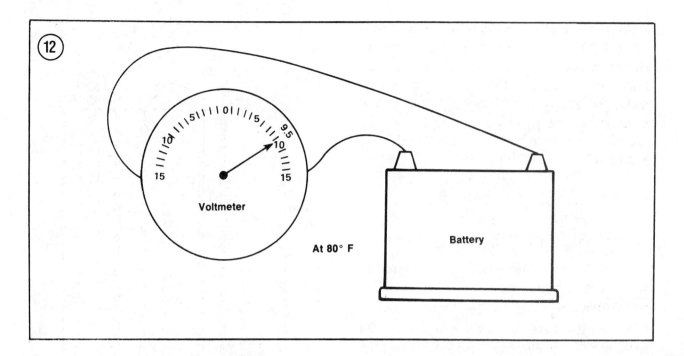

Voltmeter

At 80° F

Battery

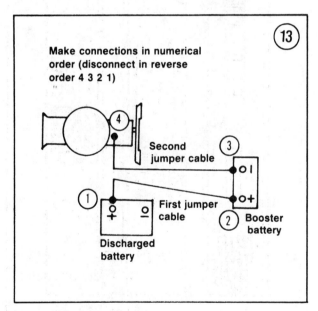

Make connections in numerical order (disconnect in reverse order 4 3 2 1)

Second jumper cable

First jumper cable

Booster battery

Discharged battery

7

jump starting it from another battery. If the proper procedure is not followed, however, jump starting can be dangerous. Check the electrolyte level before jump starting any battery. If it is not visible or if it appears to be frozen, do not attempt to jump start the battery.

WARNING
Use extreme caution when connecting a booster battery to one that is discharged to avoid personal injury or damage to the system.

1. Connect the jumper cables in the order and sequence shown in **Figure 13**.

WARNING
An electrical arc may occur when the final connection is made. This could cause an explosion if it occurs near the battery. For this reason, the final connection should be made to a good ground away from the battery and not to the battery itself.

charging time. **Table 2** gives approximate charge rates for batteries used primarily for cranking. Check the charging progress with the hydrometer.

Jump Starting

If the battery becomes severely discharged, it is possible to start and run an engine by

2. Check that all jumper cables are out of the way of moving engine parts.

3. Start the engine. Once it starts, run it at a moderate speed.

> *CAUTION*
> *Running the engine at wide-open throttle may cause damage to the electrical system.*

4. Remove the jumper cables in the exact reverse order shown in **Figure 13**. Remove the cables at point 4, then 3, 2 and 1.

BATTERY CHARGING SYSTEM

A battery charging system is standard on all electric start models.

The battery charging system on Johnson and Evinrude outboards consists of a flywheel with cast-in magnets, 2 stator coils on the armature plate, a rectifier and the battery.

Magneto breaker point and CD 2 ignition systems both use a flywheel containing magnets (**Figure 14**). Standard manual start flywheels use 2 magnets for the ignition system. Electric start flywheels use an additional 2 magnets for the charging system. Rotation of the flywheel stator magnets past the armature plate stator coils (**Figure 15**) creates alternating current. This current is sent to the rectifier (A, **Figure 16**, typical) where it is converted into direct current to charge the battery or power accessories.

A malfunction in the battery charging system will result in an undercharged battery. Perform the following visual inspection to determine the cause of the problem. If the visual inspection proves satisfactory, test the stator coils and rectifier. See Chapter Three.

1. Make sure that the battery cables are connected properly. The red cable must be connected to the positive battery terminal. If polarity is reversed, check for a damaged rectifier.
2. Inspect the battery terminals for loose or corroded connections. Tighten or clean as required.

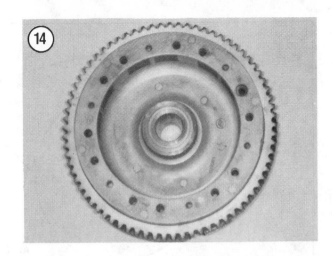

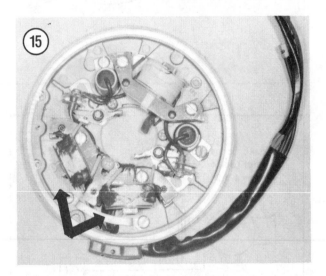

3. Inspect the physical condition of the battery. Look for bulges or cracks in the case, leaking electrolyte or corrosion build-up.
4. Carefully check the wiring between the stator coils and battery for signs of chafing, deterioration or other damage.
5. Check the circuit wiring for corroded, loose or open connections. Clean, tighten or connect as required.
6. Determine if the electrical load on the battery from accessories is greater than the battery capacity.

Stator Coil Replacement

See *Armature Plate Disassembly/Assembly* in this chapter.

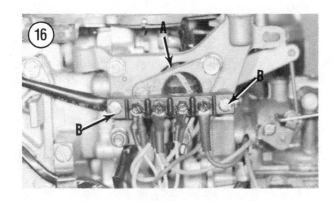

Rectifier Removal/Installation

1. Disconnect the red, yellow, yellow/grey and yellow/blue rectifier leads at the terminal board. See **Figure 16**.
2. Remove the 2 terminal board mounting screws (B, **Figure 16**) and move terminal board out of the way.
3. Remove the 2 rectifier mounting screws. Remove the rectifier.
4. Installation is the reverse of removal. Coat terminal board mounting screw threads with OMC Screw Lock. Coat rectifier lead connections with OMC Black Neoprene Dip.

ELECTRIC STARTING SYSTEM

Johnson and Evinrude outboards covered in this manual may use a rope-operated mechanical (rewind) starting system or an electric (starter motor) starting system. The electric starting system consists of the battery, starter solenoid, starter motor, neutral start switch, ignition switch and connecting wiring.

NOTE
The 9.5, 9.9 and 15 hp models have no separate starter solenoid. A heavy-duty start switch serves the solenoid function.

The starting system operation and troubleshooting is described in Chapter Three.

Marine starter motors are very similar in design and operation to those found on automotive engines. All Johnson and Evinrude starters use an inertia-type drive in which external spiral splines on the armature shaft mate with internal splines on the drive assembly.

The starter motor produces a very high torque but only for a brief period of time, due to heat buildup. Never operate the starter motor continuously for more than 30 seconds. Let the motor cool for at least 2 minutes before operating it again. If the starter motor does not turn over, check the battery and all connecting wiring for loose or corroded connections. If this does not solve the problem, refer to Chapter Three. Except for brush replacement, service to the starter motor by the amateur mechanic is limited to replacement with a new or rebuilt unit.

Starter Motor Removal/Installation (9.9 and 15 hp)

1. Disconnect the negative battery cable.
2. Remove the engine cover.
3. Remove the 2 screws holding the starter to the by-pass cover. Remove the starter.
4. Disconnect the starter lead at the bottom of the starter.
5. Installation is the reverse of removal. Tighten screws to 10-12 ft.-lb.

Starter Motor Removal/Installation (18-25 and 40 hp)

1. Disconnect the negative battery cable.
2. Remove the engine cover.
3. Disconnect the starter cables.
4. 40 hp—Remove the flywheel guard.
5. Remove the 4 cap screws holding the starter and mounting brackets to the motor.
6. Remove the starter and brackets from the bracket studs.
7. Remove the 2 starter motor through bolts. Separate the starter motor from the bracket.

7

8. Installation is the reverse of removal. Wipe the through bolt threads with engine oil. Tighten fasteners to specifications (**Table 3**). Coat the starter cable connections with OMC Black Neoprene Dip.

Starter Motor
Removal/Installation
(35 hp)

1. Disconnect the negative battery cable.
2. Remove the engine cover.
3. Disconnect all leads at the solenoid (**Figure 17**).
4. Remove the vertical throttle shaft clamp screws. Remove the clamp. See **Figure 18**.
5. Remove the air silencer assembly.
6. Remove the starter bracket front fastener (**Figure 19**).
7. Remove the upper and lower capscrews holding the starter bracket to the power head. Note that the lower capscrew is installed from the rear of the power head and has the starter ground lead attached.
8. Remove the starter motor with mounting bracket and solenoid attached.
9. Loosen the 2 solenoid clamp screws on the underside of the starter mounting bracket. Remove the solenoid.
10. Secure the mounting bracket in a vise with protective jaws.
11. Note alignment marks on starter case and bracket for reassembly reference. Remove the starter through-bolts. Separate the starter motor from its bracket.
12. Installation is the reverse of removal. Align starter and bracket marks. Wipe the through-bolt threads with engine oil. Install and tighten through-bolts to 60-84 in.-lb. Apply OMC Black Neoprene Dip to all electrical connections. Tighten bracket fasteners to specifications (**Table 3**).

Brush Replacement
(9.5, 9.9 and 15 hp)

Always replace brushes in complete sets. Refer to **Figure 20** (typical) for this procedure.
1. Remove the starter as described in this chapter.
2. Remove the 2 through-bolts and brush end cap from the starter.

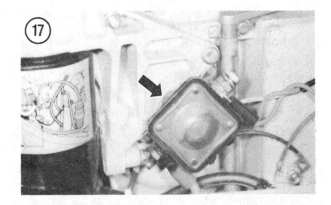

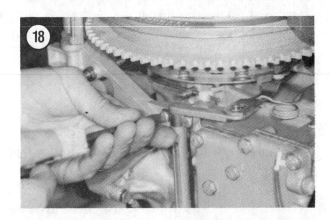

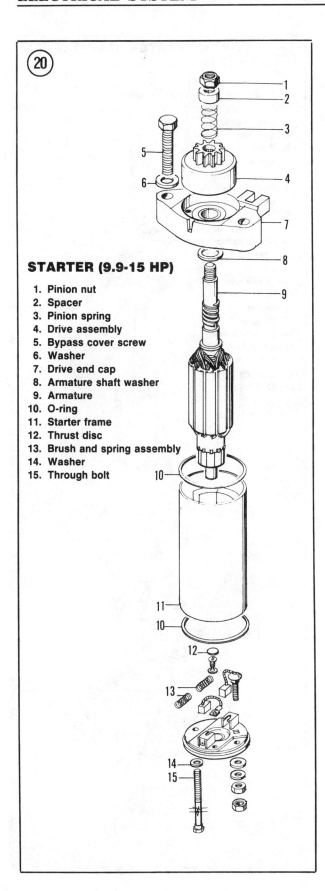

⓪

STARTER (9.9-15 HP)

1. Pinion nut
2. Spacer
3. Pinion spring
4. Drive assembly
5. Bypass cover screw
6. Washer
7. Drive end cap
8. Armature shaft washer
9. Armature
10. O-ring
11. Starter frame
12. Thrust disc
13. Brush and spring assembly
14. Washer
15. Through bolt

3. Inspect the brushes. Replace them both if either are oil-soaked, pitted or worn to 3/8 in. or less.

4. Remove screw holding each old brush. Remove brush from end cap holder.

5. Insert new brush in end cap holder and attach terminal to cap with screw.

6. Align brush end cap and frame marks. Keep brushes recessed in the brush holder and install end cap to starter frame.

7. Wipe the through-bolt threads with engine oil. Install and tighten through-bolts to 30-40 in.-lb. Apply OMC Black Neoprene Dip around the end cap and frame joint.

Brush Replacement (18-40 hp)

Always replace brushes in complete sets. Refer to **Figure 21** for this procedure.

1. Remove the starter and separate it from the mounting bracket as described in this chapter.

2. Carefully tap the commutator end cap from the starter frame.

3. Inspect the brushes in the brush holder on the commutator end of the armature. Replace all brushes if any are pitted, oil-soaked or worn to 3/8 in. or less.

4. Remove brushes and springs from brush holder. Remove brush holder from commutator end.

5. Check brush holder straightness. If brushes do not show full-face contact with commutator, holder is probably bent.

6. Install the insulated brush and terminal set in the commutator end cap as shown in **Figure 22**.

7. Install the brush holder in the commutator end cap. Install the brush springs in the holder. Insert the brushes and tighten the brush lead screws to the holder.

8. Fit the insulated brushes in the holder slots. **Figure 23** shows the reassembled brush holder and commutator end cap assembly.

7

9. Align the commutator end cap and starter frame marks. Hold the brushes in place and assemble the end cap to the frame. A putty knife with a 1×1/2 in. slot cut in its end makes a suitable tool for keeping the brushes in place during this step.

10. Secure the starter mounting bracket in a vise with protective jaws. Align starter and bracket marks.

11. Wipe the through-bolt threads with engine oil. Install and tighten through-bolts to 60-84 in.-lb. Apply OMC Black Neoprene Dip around the end cap and frame joint.

MAGNETO BREAKER POINT IGNITION SERVICE

NOTE
See Chapter Three for troubleshooting and test procedures.

The 2 hp model uses a magneto ignition with a combined primary/secondary ignition coil, a condenser and one set of breaker points mounted on an armature plate. The 1973 40 hp model is similar, with 2 combined ignition coils, 2 condensers and 2 sets of breaker points. The primary section of the coil connects to the stationary breaker point and is grounded to the armature plate. The secondary section of the coil connects to the spark plug and is also grounded to the armature plate.

All other models use a magneto ignition with 1 driver coil, 2 condensers and 2 sets of breaker points mounted on an armature plate. Electric start models also have 2 stator coils for the charging system. A combined primary/secondary ignition coil for each cylinder is mounted on the power head. The primary section of each ignition coil connects to the stationary breaker point set for its cylinder and is grounded to the armature plate. The secondary section of each ignition coil connects to the spark plug it fires and is also grounded to the armature plate.

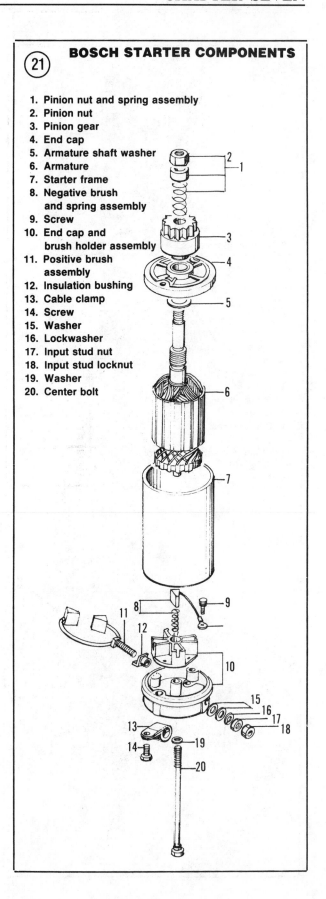

BOSCH STARTER COMPONENTS

21

1. Pinion nut and spring assembly
2. Pinion nut
3. Pinion gear
4. End cap
5. Armature shaft washer
6. Armature
7. Starter frame
8. Negative brush and spring assembly
9. Screw
10. End cap and brush holder assembly
11. Positive brush assembly
12. Insulation bushing
13. Cable clamp
14. Screw
15. Washer
16. Lockwasher
17. Input stud nut
18. Input stud locknut
19. Washer
20. Center bolt

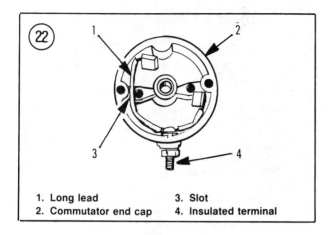

1. Long lead
2. Commutator end cap
3. Slot
4. Insulated terminal

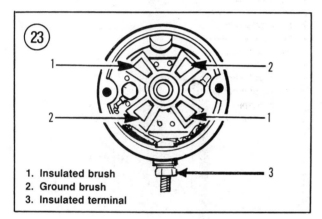

1. Insulated brush
2. Ground brush
3. Insulated terminal

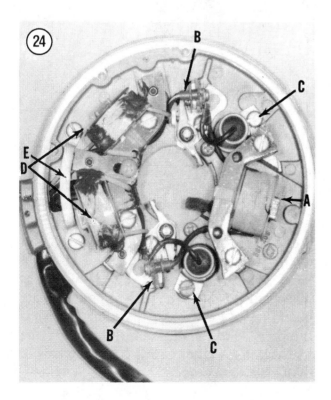

Figure 24 shows the location of the driver coil (A), breaker point sets (B), condensers (C) and stator coils (D) on the armature plate. The ignition coil on 2 hp models is identical in appearance and location to the driver coil shown in **Figure 24**. The ignition coils on 4-35 hp and 1974-1976 40 hp models are shown in **Figure 25**.

Operation

As the flywheel rotates, magnets around its inner diameter create current through the closed breaker points and back to the driver coil. When the cam opens the No. 1 point set, voltage rises quickly across the No. 1 ignition coil primary and the condenser absorbs excess current. The No. 1 ignition coil steps up the voltage to the secondary side and fires the No. 1 spark plug. The breaker points close and the flywheel continues to rotate, duplicating the sequence for the No. 2 point set and ignition coil to fire the No. 2 spark plug.

Armature Plate Removal/Installation

1. Remove the rewind starter, if so equipped. See Chapter Ten.
2. Remove the flywheel. See Chapter Eight.
3. On 2 hp models:
   a. Disconnect the high tension lead at the spark plug.

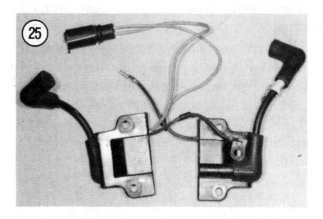

7

b. Disconnect the armature plate ground lead and plate screw located under the armature plate base.

c. Remove the plate from the power head.

4. On all other models:

a. Disconnect the spark plug leads.

b. Disconnect the armature plate lead connectors.

c. Remove the ignition coils from the power head.

d. Disconnect the stop switch connector.

e. On 18-40 hp models, disconnect armature link at throttle shaft arm.

f. On electric start models, disconnect the yellow, yellow/gray, yellow/blue and armature plate ground lead at the terminal board.

g. Remove the armature plate retaining screws. Remove armature plate and cable assembly from the power head. It is not necessary to remove the retainer and support plates from models so equipped.

5. Installation is the reverse of removal. Coat all electrical connections with OMC Black Neoprene Dip.

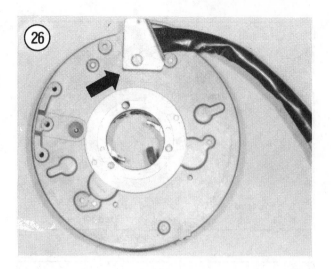

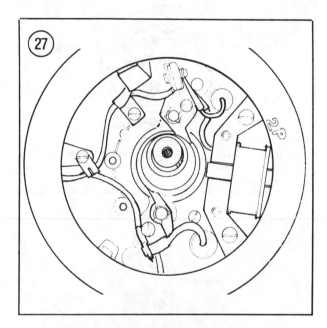

Armature Plate Disassembly/Assembly (Manual Start)

This procedure is used to replace the ignition coil (2 hp and 1973 40 hp), driver coil (4-35 hp and 1974-76 40 hp) or stator coils.

1. Turn the armature plate over and remove the cover plate. See **Figure 26** (typical).

2. Remove the 2 screws holding the wiring lead strap in place (E, **Figure 24**).

3. Refer to **Figure 24** and remove the screws holding the defective component(s) to the armature plate.

4. Pull the lead(s) of the defective component(s) from the insulation sleeve.

5. Remove the defective component(s) and lead(s) from the armature plate.

6. Assembly is the reverse of disassembly. If the driver coil is removed, replace the oiler wick underneath it and make sure the coil is properly aligned when reinstalled. Johnson and Evinrude recommend the use of a coil locating ring (part No. 317001) which is machined to fit over the armature plate bosses. See **Figure 27**. Position all leads carefully so they will not rub against the flywheel. Coat all electrical connections with OMC Black Neoprene Dip.

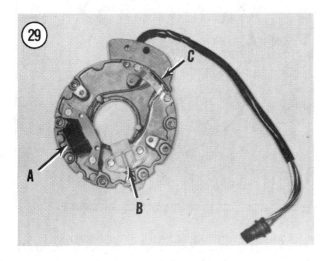

Armature Plate
Disassembly/Assembly
(Electric Start)

1. Turn the armature plate over and remove the cover plate. See **Figure 26** (typical).
2. Remove the wiring lead clamp on the top of the armature plate.
3. Remove the stator retaining screws. Remove the stator from the armature plate.
4. Assembly is the reverse of disassembly.

Secondary Ignition Coil Replacement
(Except 2 hp and 1973 40 Models)

1. Remove the engine cover.
2. Disconnect the spark plug lead of the coil to be replaced.
3. Disconnect the blue (No. 1 coil) or blue/white (No. 2 coil) primary lead from the armature plate connector.
4. Disconnect the coil ground lead (A, **Figure 28**).
5. Remove the attaching bolts and washers (B, **Figure 28**). Remove the coil from the power head.
6. Installation is the reverse of removal.

Secondary Ignition Coil Replacement
(2 hp Model)

The secondary coil is combined with the primary coil on these models. To replace the coil, refer to *Armature Plate Disassembly/ Assembly* in this chapter.

CD 2 IGNITION SYSTEM

NOTE
See Chapter Three for troubleshooting and test procedures.

The major components of the CD 2 ignition system on all models include the flywheel, charge coil, sensor coil, power pack, ignition coils, spark plugs and connecting wiring. The charge coil is located under the flywheel on the armature plate (A, **Figure 29**). The flywheel is fitted with permanent magnets inside its outer rim. As the crankshaft and flywheel rotate, the flywheel magnets pass the stationary charge coil. This creates an alternating current that is sent to the power pack where it is stored in a capacitor for release.

A sensor coil is also mounted under the flywheel on the armature plate (B, **Figure 29**). As the flywheel magnets pass the stationary sensor coil, an alternating current is created

7

and sent to the No. 1 SCR (switch) in the power pack. The power pack contains the electronic circuitry required to produce ignition at the proper time. The No. 1 SCR discharges the capacitor into the No. 1 ignition coil at the proper time. While this is happening, the capacitor is recharging in preparation for discharge through the No. 2 SCR.

Armature Plate Removal/Installation

The CD 2 ignition armature plate can be removed using the same procedure as described for magneto ignitions in this chapter.

Charge Coil, Sensor Coil or Stator Coil Replacement

The charge and sensor coils can be replaced individually on manual start models and 1984 electric start models. On all earlier electric start models, the charge, sensor and stator coils are enclosed in a potted ring and are replaced as an assembly. See **Figure 30**.

1. Turn the armature plate over and remove the cover plate. See **Figure 31** (typical).
2. Remove the 2 screws holding the wiring lead strap in place (C, **Figure 29**).
3. Refer to **Figure 29** or **Figure 30** and remove the screws holding the defective component(s) to the armature plate.
4A. Charge coil—Remove the A and D wire terminals from the 4-wire connector. See *Connector Terminal Removal/Installation* in this chapter.
4B. Sensor coil—Remove the B and C wire terminals from the 4-wire connector. See *Connector Terminal Removal/Installation* in this chapter.
4C. 1973-1983 electric start models— Remove all 4 wire terminals from the 4-wire connector. See *Connector Terminal*

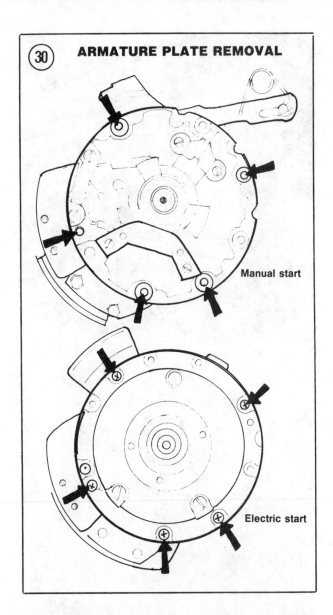

30 **ARMATURE PLATE REMOVAL**

Manual start

Electric start

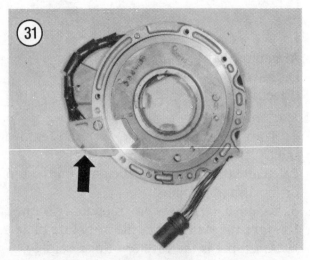

31

Removal/Installation in this chapter.

5. Pull the lead(s) of the defective component(s) from the insulation sleeve.

6. Remove the defective component(s) and lead(s) from the armature plate.

7. Assembly is the reverse of disassembly. Each coil must be properly aligned when reinstalled to prevent contact with the

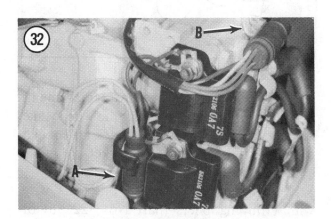

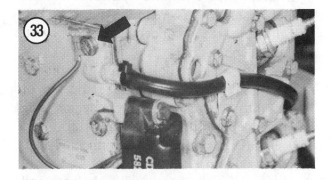

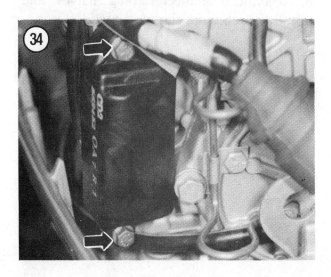

flywheel magnets and to produce maximum output. Johnson and Evinrude recommend the use of a coil locating ring (part No. 317001) which is machined to fit over the armature plate bosses. See **Figure 27**. Position all leads carefully so they will not rub against the flywheel. Coat all electrical connections (except connector plugs) with OMC Black Neoprene Dip.

Power Pack Replacement

The power pack electrical circuits are encased in a potting material and can be serviced only by replacement.

1. Disconnect the negative battery cable.

2. Remove the engine cowling.

3. Separate the 3-wire and 4-wire connectors between the power pack and the ignition coils/armature plate. See **Figure 32** (typical).

NOTE
On some engines, the ground lead is attached to one of the power pack mounting screws and is removed in Step 5.

4. Remove the screw holding the power pack ground lead (**Figure 33**).

5. Remove the power pack mounting bolts. See **Figure 34** (typical). Remove the power pack.

6. Installation is the reverse of removal. Position the lockwasher on the engine side of the ground wire connector to assure a good ground. Make sure there is sufficient slack in the ground wire; if too tight, it can cause an ignition failure. Tighten the mounting bolts to 48-60 in.-lb.

Secondary Ignition Coil Replacement

See *Secondary Ignition Coil Replacement (Except 2 hp and 1973 40 hp Model)* in this chapter.

7

Connector Terminal
Removal/Installation

Water-proof plug-in connectors are used in the CD 2 ignition system (**Figure 32**). If the connector halves are secured by a retaining clamp, it must be removed before they can be separated.

Whenever a component is replaced in the CD 2 system, the wires and their plug terminals must be removed from the connector. A set of 3 special tools is available for quick and easy terminal removal/ installation: insert tool part No. 32697, pin remover tool part No. 322698 and socket remover tool part No. 322699. Each tool has the appropriate tip for its intended use.

Connector terminals should be removed and installed according to this procedure. Use of tools or lubricant other than specified can result in high resistance connections, short circuits between terminals or connector material damage.

1. Lubricate the terminal pin or socket to be removed with rubbing alcohol at both ends of the connector cavity.

2. Hold the connector against the edge of a flat surface, allowing sufficient clearance for terminal/socket removal.

3. Insert the proper removal tool in the connector end of the plug and carefully push the terminal or socket from the plug. See **Figure 35**.

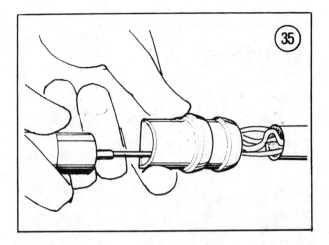

4. If the pin or socket requires replacement, install a new one on the end of the wire. Make sure the insulation is stripped back far enough to allow the new pin or socket to make complete contact with the wire.

5. Crimp the new terminal onto the wire with crimping pliers (part No. 322696) or equivalent. If crimping pliers are not available, solder the wire in the pin or socket.

6. Lubricate the connector cavity with rubbing alcohol.

7. Place the insert tool against the pin or socket shoulder. Carefully guide the pin or socket into the rear of the connector plug cavity and press it in place until the insert tool shoulder rests against the connector plug. Withdraw the insert tool.

8. Reconnect connector plug halves and install the retaining clamp, if used.

Table 1 BATTERY CAPACITY (HOURS)

Accessory draw	80 Amp-hour battery provides continuous power for	Approximate recharge time
5 amps	13.5 hours	16 hours
15 amps	3.5 hours	13 hours
25 amps	1.8 hours	12 hours
Accessory draw	105 Amp-hour battery provides continuous power for	Approximate recharge time
5 amps	15.8 hours	16 hours
15 amps	4.2 hours	13 hours
25 amps	2.4 hours	12 hours

Table 2 APPROXIMATE CHARGE RATE

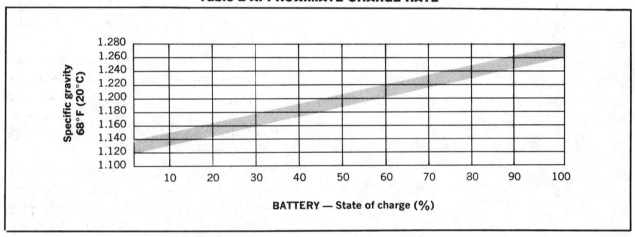

Table 3 TIGHTENING TORQUES

Fastener	in.-lb.	ft.-lb.
Ignition coil screws	60-80	
Power pack screw	48-60	
Starter motor through bolts		
9.9 and 15 hp	30-40	
18-35 hp	60-84	
40 hp		50
Standard bolts and nuts		
No. 6	7-10	
No. 8	15-22	
No. 10	25-35	
No. 12	35-40	
1/4 in.		5-7
5/16 in.		10-12
3/8 in.		18-20
7/16 in.		28-30

7

NOTE: If you own a 1985 or later model, first check the Supplement at the back of the book for any new service information.

Chapter Eight

Power Head

Basic repair of Johnson and Evinrude outboard power heads is similar from model to model, with minor differences. Some procedures require the use of special tools, which can be purchased from a dealer. Certain tools may be fabricated by a machinist, often at substantial savings. Power head stands are available from specialty shops such as Bob Kerr's Marine Tool Co. (P.O. Box 1135, Winter Garden, FL 32787).

Work on the power head requires considerable mechanical ability. You should carefully consider your own capabilities before attempting any operation involving major disassembly of the engine.

Much of the labor charge for dealer repairs involves the removal and disassembly of other parts to reach the defective component. Even if you decide not to tackle the entire power head overhaul after studying the text and illustrations in this chapter, it can be cheaper to perform the preliminary operations yourself and then take the power head to your dealer. Since many marine dealers have lengthy waiting lists for service (especially during the spring and summer season), this practice can reduce the time your unit is in the shop. If you have done much of the preliminary work, your repairs can be scheduled and performed much quicker.

Repairs go much faster and easier if your motor is clean before you begin work. There are special cleaners for washing the motor and related parts. Just spray or brush on the cleaning solution, let it stand, then rinse it away with a garden hose. Clean all oily or greasy parts with fresh solvent as you remove them.

WARNING
Never use gasoline as a cleaning agent. It presents an extreme fire hazard. Be sure to work in a well-ventilated area when using cleaning solvents. Keep a fire extinguisher rated for gasoline and oil fires nearby in case of emergency.

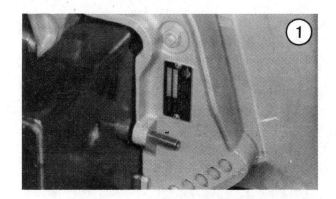

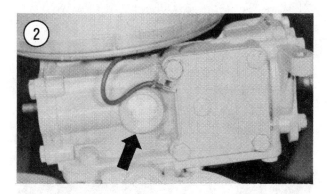

Once you have decided to do the job yourself, read this chapter thoroughly until you have a good idea of what is involved in completing the overhaul satisfactorily. Make arrangements to buy or rent any special tools necessary and obtain replacement parts before you start. It is frustrating and time-consuming to start an overhaul and then be unable to complete it because the necessary tools or parts are not at hand.

A limited number of new motors are assembled every year with cylinders that have been bored larger than standard. Such motors are identified by the letters "OS" stamped on the power head serial number welch plug. Cylinder reboring on these motors is not possible; a new cylinder and crankcase is required. If you have one of these engines, contact your Johnson or Evinrude dealer of cylinder repair becomes necessary. OMC has established a policy of absorbing certain costs for repair of these motors even if the motor is out of warranty.

Before beginning the job, re-read Chapter Two of this manual. You will do a better job with this information fresh in your mind.

Since this chapter covers a large range of models over a lengthy time period, the procedures are somewhat generalized to accommodate all models. Where individual differences occur, they are specifically pointed out. The power heads shown in the accompanying pictures are current designs. While it is possible that the components shown in the pictures may not be identical with those being serviced, the step-by-step procedures may be used with all models covered in this manual.

CAUTION
Whenever a power head is rebuilt, it should be treated as a new engine. Use a 25:1 mixture (non-VRO models) or a 50:1 mixture (VRO models) of gasoline and Johnson or Evinrude 50/l lubricant during the 10 hour break-in period and keep maximum engine speed under 3/4 throttle during this time.

Tables 1-3 are at the end of the chapter.

8

ENGINE SERIAL NUMBER

Johnson and Evinrude outboards are identified by engine serial number. This number is stamped on a plate riveted to the transom clamp (**Figure 1**). It is also stamped on a welch plug installed on the power head (**Figure 2**). Exact location of the transom clamp plate and welch plug varies according to model.

This information identifies the outboard and indicates if there are unique parts or if internal changes have been made during the model run. The serial number should be used when ordering any replacement parts for your outboard.

Starting with the 1980 model year, the model year designation is coded. The last 2 letters of the model code indicate the model year. To determine the year of a given model

(1980-on), write the word INTRODUCES. Below the word, number the letters 1-0. Match these numbers to the last 2 letters of the model code. As an example, J25TELCT is a 1983 model. The "C" represents 8 and the "T" represents 3.

FASTENERS AND TORQUE

Always replace a worn or damaged fastener with one of the same size, type and torque requirement.

Power head tightening torques are given in **Table 1**. Where a specification is not provided for a given bolt, use the standard bolt and nut torque according to fastener size.

Where specified, clean fastener threads with OMC Locquic Primer and then apply OMC Nut Lock or Screw Lock as required.

Power head fasteners should be tightened in 2 steps. Tighten to 50 percent of the torque value in the first step, then to 100 percent in the second step.

Retighten the cylinder head bolts after the engine has been run and warmed up.

To retighten the power head mounting fasteners properly, back them out one turn and then tighten to specifications.

When spark plugs are reinstalled after an overhaul, tighten to the specified torque. Warm the engine to normal operating temperature, let it cool down and retorque the plugs.

GASKETS AND SEALANTS

Three types of sealant materials are recommended: OMC Gasket Sealing Compound, Adhesive M and OMC Gel Seal II. Unless otherwise specified, OMC Gasket Sealing Compound is used with gaskets on older engines. Adhesive M is used primarily with crankcase spaghetti seals (gasket strips). Gel Seal II replaces the original Gel Seal and is used instead of a crankcase gasket with newer engines. Be sure to use the appropriate sealant specified for your engine.

FLYWHEEL

Removal/Installation

A strap wrench is used to hold the flywheel on manual start models. Use a flywheel holding tool on electric start models. The OMC universal puller kit (special part No. 378103) or equivalent is recommended for flywheel removal.

1. Remove the rewind starter assembly on 18-40 hp engines (**Figure 3**).
2. Remove the flywheel nut with an appropriate size socket and flywheel holding tool (**Figure 4**).

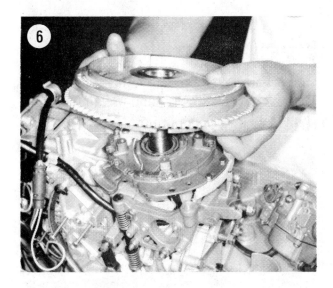

3. Install puller on flywheel with its flat side facing up.

4. Hold puller body with puller handle and tighten center screw. See **Figure 5**. If flywheel does not pop from the crankshaft taper, pry up on the rim of the flywheel with a large screwdriver while tapping the puller center screw with a brass hammer.

5. Remove puller from flywheel. Remove flywheel from crankshaft (**Figure 6**).

6. Remove the Woodruff key from the crankshaft key slot.

7. Remove the cam. On 2 hp models, remove cam drive pin.

8. Clean the crankshaft and flywheel tapers with OMC Cleaning Solvent.

NOTE
If the Woodruff key is installed incorrectly, cam position and ignition timing will be affected on magneto ignition models.

9. Install Woodruff key with its outer edge parallel to the crankshaft centerline. On 4.5-40 hp models, the single upset mark on the side of the key must face downward. See **Figure 7**.

10. Install cam with side marked "TOP" facing up, if removed. On 2 hp models, reinstall cam drive pin.

11. Install the flywheel and flywheel nut (**Figure 8**). Hold flywheel with the holding tool and tighten flywheel nut to specifications (**Table 2**).

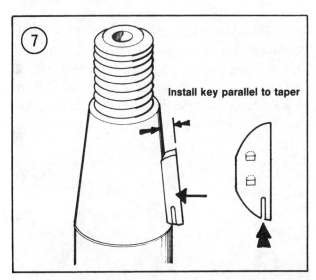

Install key parallel to taper

MAGNETO ARMATURE PLATE

Removal/Installation

1. Remove the flywheel as described in this chapter.

2. Disconnect armature link and control lever.

3. Disconnect the magneto armature plate leads. Disconnect the ground lead and stop switch connector.

8

4. On electric start models, disconnect the yellow, yellow/blue and yellow/grey leads at the terminal board.

5. Remove the screws holding the magneto armature plate to the retainer plate.

6. Remove the magneto armature plate and cable assembly from power head.

7. Remove the armature plate bearing (Delrin ring).

8. Disconnect any support plate linkage (varies with model). Note exact sequence of washers and bushings used for reassembly reference.

9. Remove the screws holding the armature support and retaining ring to the power head. Remove the support and retaining ring.

10. Installation is the reverse of removal. Coat crankcase boss with OMC Moly Lube and Delrin ring with Johnson/Evinrude 50/1 outboard lubricant. Squeeze ends of Delrin ring together with needlenose pliers and make sure it fits properly into armature plate boss. Complete engine synchronization and linkage adjustments. See Chapter Five.

CD 2 ARMATURE PLATE

Removal/Installation

1. Remove the flywheel as described in this chapter.

2. Remove all J-clamps holding armature plate leads in position.

3. Disconnect the 3-wire and 4-wire connectors.

4. On electric start models, disconnect the armature plate stator leads at the terminal board (**Figure 9**).

5. Remove the screws holding the armature plate to the retainer plate. Remove the armature plate from the power head (**Figure 10**).

6. Remove the armature plate bearing (Delrin ring).

7. Disconnect any support plate linkage (varies with model). Note exact sequence of washers and bushings used for reassembly reference.

8. Remove the screws holding the armature support and retainer plate to the power head. Remove the support and retaining ring (**Figure 11**).

NOTE
A replacement armature plate and pilot kit is available for 1977-on 9.9-35 hp motors with an excessively worn crankcase pilot bearing (Delrin ring) or armature plate. Use of this kit (part No. 392610) can eliminate the need for cylinder/crankcase replacement.

9. Installation is the reverse of removal. Coat crankcase boss with OMC Moly Lube and Delrin ring with Johnson/Evinrude 50/1 outboard lubricant. Squeeze ends of Delrin ring together with needlenose pliers and make sure it fits properly into armature plate boss

(**Figure 12**). Complete engine synchronization and linkage adjustments. See Chapter Five.

POWER HEAD

When removing any power head, it is a good idea to make a sketch or take an instant picture of the location, routing and positioning of wires and J-clamps for reassembly reference. Take notes as you remove wires, washers and engine grounds so they may be reinstalled in their correct position. Unless specified otherwise, install lockwashers on the engine side of the electrical lead to assure a good ground.

Removal/Installation (2 hp)

1. Disconnect the spark plug lead and remove the spark plug.

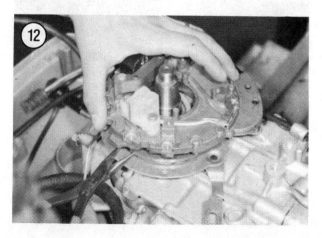

2. Remove the fuel tank filler cap. Remove the 4 engine cover mounting screws. Lift engine cover with starter assembly from power head. Note position of throttle detent spring under front port side screw. Reinstall filler cap.

3. Make sure the fuel supply valve is off. Disconnect the fuel line at the valve. Remove the 2 retainers holding the tank to its mounting bracket. Remove the tank.

4. Remove the choke lever and low-speed adjustment knob.

5. Remove the 2 front screws holding the mounting bracket to the carburetor. Remove the 2 rear screws holding the bracket to the power head. Align the speed control lever with the mounting bracket slot and remove the bracket and air silencer assembly.

6. Remove the 6 bolts holding the power head to the exhaust housing. Remove the power head and discard the gasket.

7. Installation is the reverse of removal. Lubricate drive shaft splines with OMC Moly Lube. Coat a new power head-to-exhaust housing gasket with OMC Gasket Sealing Compound. Tighten fasteners to specifications (**Table 1**). Connect fuel line, open fuel valve and check for leakage. Complete engine synchronization and linkage adjustments. See Chapter Five.

Removal/Installation (4 hp)

1. Remove the choke knob. Remove the low speed adjustment knob, if so equipped.

2. Loosen the front and rear lower motor cover screws. Disengage and spread cover open sufficiently to remove from the power head.

3. Disconnect the spark plug leads. Remove the spark plugs.

4. Remove the 5 screws holding the power head to the exhaust housing. Lift the power

8

head straight up and off the drive shaft. Remove and discard the power head gasket.

5. Install power head on holding fixture part No. 303605 if further service is necessary.

6. Installation is the reverse of removal. Lubricate drive shaft splines with OMC Moly Lube. Coat both sides of a new power head-to-exhaust housing gasket with OMC Gasket Sealing Compound. Tighten fasteners to specifications (**Table 1**). Complete engine synchronization and linkage adjustments. See Chapter Five.

Removal/Installation
(4 Deluxe and 4.5 hp)

1. Remove the engine cover.

2. Remove the fuel tank.

3. Disconnect the throttle linkage and remove the carburetor. See Chapter Six.

4. Remove the intake manifold and reed valve assembly.

5. Disconnect the 3-wire and 4-wire connectors.

6. Disconnect the spark plug leads and remove the spark plugs.

7. Remove the flywheel as described in this chapter.

8. Remove the armature plate as described in this chapter.

9. Remove the power pack.

10. Leave starter on crankcase unless it requires service. Tie a knot in the starter rope inside the lower motor cover and remove the rope handle.

11. Remove the bolts holding the power head to the exhaust housing. Remove the power head.

12. Place the power head on a clean workbench and remove the inner exhaust housing. Remove and discard the gasket.

13. Install power head on holding fixture part No. 303605 if further service is necessary.

14. Remove gearcase from exhaust housing. See Chapter Nine.

15. Install water tube in position in the inner exhaust housing.

16. Install inner exhaust housing and adapter to power head with a new gasket.

NOTE
Use a rubber band to hold water tube to exhaust tube. This will simplify proper positioning of the water tube.

17. Lubricate end of water tube with liquid soap. Install power head to exhaust housing and tighten fasteners to specifications (**Table 1**).

18. The remainder of installation is the reverse of removal. Lubricate drive shaft splines with OMC Moly Lube. Install gearcase to exhaust housing and make sure water tube enters water pump grommet. Complete engine synchronization and linkage adjustments. See Chapter Five.

Removal/Installation
(5, 6, 7.5 and 8 hp)

NOTE
The upper main bearing oil seal can be replaced on this model without power head removal or disassembly. With flywheel and armature plate removed, remove old seal with tool part No. 382944 and install new seal with tool part No. 314901.

1. Remove the engine cover.

2. Disconnect the spark plug leads and remove the spark plugs.

3. Remove the air silencer assembly.

4. Disconnect the throttle control screw and nut. Remove the throttle control.

5. Remove the water pump indicator hose.

6. Remove the flywheel as described in this chapter.

7. Disconnect and remove the armature plate as described in this chapter.

8. Remove the ignition coils.

9. Remove the power pack, if so equipped.

10. Remove the manual starter. See Chapter Ten.

11. Disconnect the fuel line and remove the carburetor and fuel pump as an assembly. See Chapter Six.

12. Working from underneath the inner exhaust housing, remove the power head attaching bolts.

13. Remove the power head and gasket. Discard the gasket.

14. Install power head on holding fixture part No. 303605 if further service is necessary.

15. Installation is the reverse of removal. Position water tube in inner exhaust housing. Install inner exhaust housing and adapter to power head with a new gasket. Lubricate drive shaft splines with OMC Moly Lube. Rotate power head slightly while lowering it to align crankshaft and drive shaft splines. Tighten fasteners to specifications (**Table 1**). Complete engine synchronization and linkage adjustments. See Chapter Five.

Removal/Installation (9.5-15 hp)

NOTE
The upper main bearing oil seal can be replaced on this model without power head removal or disassembly. With flywheel and armature plate removed, remove old seal with tool part No. 386629 (1972-1979) or part No. 391060
(1980-on). Install new seal with tool part No. 319872 (1973-1979) or part No. 391060 (1980-on).

1. Remove the flywheel as described in this chapter.

2. Remove the armature plate as described in this chapter.

3. Disconnect the fuel line and remove the carburetor and fuel pump as an assembly. See Chapter Six.

NOTE
A metal shift lock lever is used on older models; newer engines use the plastic lever shown in **Figure 13**.

4. Remove the shift lock lever screw (**Figure 13**). Swing lever and rod out of the way, then remove starter interlock screw.

5A. On electric start models, remove the starter. See Chapter Seven.

5B. On manual start models, remove the starter. See Chapter Ten.

6. Remove the ignition coils. See Chapter Seven. Note that the stop switch ground lead is installed under a coil screw.

7. On CD 2 models, use pin removal tool part No. 322698 to remove the stop switch lead from the A cavity of the 4-wire connector.

8. From underneath the exhaust housing, remove the 3 power head attaching bolts on each side of the unit. Note that the 2 rear bolts are longer. Some models may use a ground lead under one of the front bolts.

9. From inside the lower motor cover, remove the 3 rubber mount screws and washers. Note that a power head ground lead is installed under the starboard mount screw. Additional washers are installed under the rubber mount sleeves.

10. Lift the power head straight up and out of the exhaust housing.

11. Place the power head on a clean workbench and remove the exhaust and

8

water tube assembly. Remove and discard the gasket.

12. Install power head on holding fixture part No. 303605 if further service is necessary.

13. Remove gearcase from exhaust housing. See Chapter Nine.

14. If rubber mount sleeves were removed from power head mounting brackets, reinstall with OMC Adhesive M. Coat the washers with OMC Adhesive M. Position a large washer over each lower motor cover rubber sleeve mounting hole, then place small washers over the large ones.

15. Coat a new power head-to-exhaust housing gasket with OMC Gasket Sealing Compound and install on power head (A, **Figure 14**).

> *NOTE*
> *The 9.5 and 9.9 hp uses a single water tube and grommet in Step 15; the 15 hp model has 2 water tubes and grommets.*

16. Make sure the grommet(s) are properly located in the exhaust tube, then install the exhaust and water tube assembly to the power head. Use a rubber band to hold the long water tube to the exhaust tube (B, **Figure 14**).

17. Coat the outer mating diameter of the crankcase head with Permatex No. 2. See C, **Figure 14**.

18. Lubricate drive shaft splines with OMC Moly Lube.

19. Holding the power head over the exhaust housing, guide the long water tube into the water tube opening in the exhaust housing. On 15 hp models, guide the small water tube into the opening at the rear of the exhaust housing. Guide the vertical control shaft into the shaft gear.

20. Use an awl to align the rubber mount sleeves and washers with the lower motor cover mounting holes, if necessary. Install the mounting screws with the power head ground

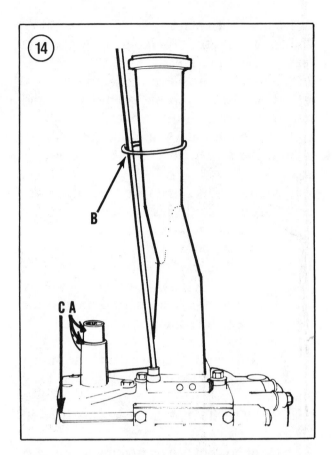

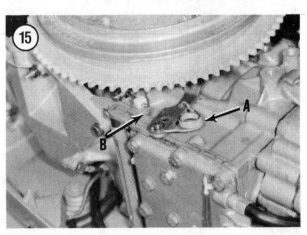

lead under the rear screw. Tighten the screws securely.

21. Wipe the exhaust housing-to-power head screw threads with OMC Gasket Sealing Compound. Install the 2 longer screws in the rear mounting holes, then install the remaining 4 screws. Make sure the ground lead is installed on the front screw, if so

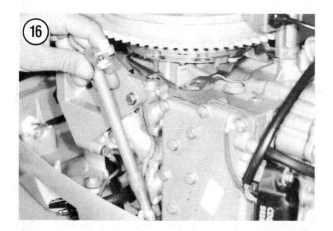

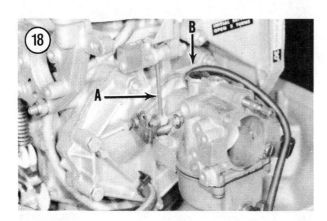

8

> *NOTE*
> *The upper main bearing oil seal can be replaced on this model without power head removal or disassembly. With flywheel and armature plate removed, remove old seal with tool part No. 387780. Wipe new seal casing with OMC Gasket Sealing Compound and install with tool part No. 321539.*

1. Remove the engine cover.
2. Disconnect the battery on electric start models.
3. Disconnect the spark plug leads.
4. Disengage the throttle arm spring (A, **Figure 15**) from the throttle arm. Remove pin from end of throttle control rod (B, **Figure 15**). Separate armature plate link from throttle control lever.
5. Remove the screws and clamp holding the vertical throttle shaft. Lift the shaft from the throttle gear (**Figure 16**).
6. Remove the rewind starter. See Chapter Ten. Remove the starter lockout lever if positioned over the flywheel.
7. On electric models, remove the starter motor and solenoid. See Chapter Seven. On manual models, remove the bracket (**Figure 17**). Note that a ground lead is attached to the bottom rear fastener on both electric and manual start models.
8. Remove the air silencer, if so equipped.
9. Disconnect the throttle cam to cam follower link (A, **Figure 18**). Disconnect the recirculation line (B, **Figure 18**), if so equipped.
10. Remove the fuel filter (**Figure 19**), then remove the fuel pump attaching screws (**Figure 20**). Place the fuel pump and filter assembly to one side.
11. Remove the 2 carburetor mounting nuts. Pull carburetor, gasket and choke bracket (if so equipped) from intake manifold studs

equipped. Tighten the bolts to specifications (**Table 1**).
22. Install the gearcase. See Chapter Nine.
23. Reverse Steps 1-7 to complete installation. Use pin insert tool part No. 322697 to install stop switch lead in A cavity of connector on CD 2 models. Complete engine synchronization and linkage adjustments. See Chapter Five.

(**Figure 21**) while disengaging choke shaft from carburetor choke lever. Remove with fuel pump assembly attached. Discard the gasket.

12. Remove the flywheel as described in this chapter.

13. On electric start models, disconnect all leads at the terminal board. Remove the terminal board.

14. On manual start models equipped with an actuator cam, install a piece of wire through the hole in the top of the shaft (A, **Figure 22**) to keep the shaft from coming out of the bracket. Remove the cotter pin and washer holding the cam link to the cam (B, **Figure 22**).

15. Remove the cam bolt and the 2 bracket nuts. Remove the assembly (**Figure 23**).

16. Disconnect the outboard water indicator hose from the exhaust cover nipple (**Figure 24**). Slide the hose through the J-clamp and remove from the motor.

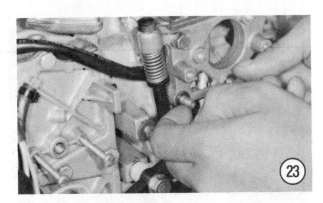

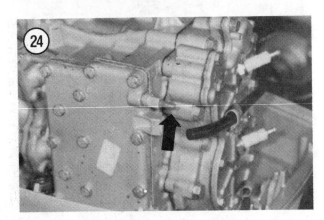

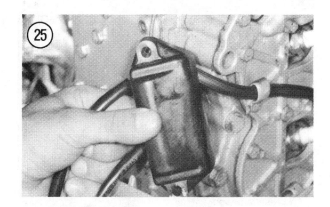

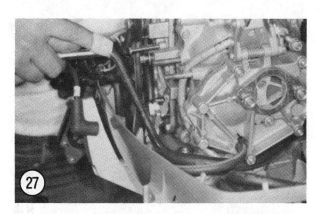

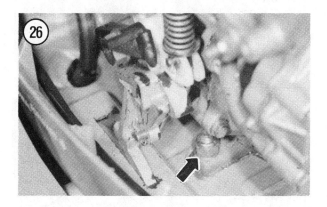

17. Remove the ignition coils. Note that the stop switch ground lead is attached to one of the coil mounting screws.

18. On CD 2 models, use pin removal tool part No. 322698 to remove the stop switch lead from the A cavity of the 4-wire connector.

19. Remove the armature plate as described in this chapter.

20. On CD 2 models, remove the power pack (**Figure 25**). Note the location of the power pack ground lead.

NOTE
At this point, there should be no hoses, wires or linkages connecting the power head to the exhaust housing. Recheck this to make sure nothing will hamper power head removal.

21. From underneath the exhaust housing, remove the 4 bolts holding the power head.

22. Locate the port and starboard power head retaining nuts and washers (**Figure 26**). Remove the nuts with OMC tool part No. 322700 or an offset 1/2 in. box wrench (**Figure 27**).

23. Rock the power head from side to side to break the gasket seal. Carefully lift the power head from the exhaust housing (**Figure 28**) and place on a clean workbench.

24. Remove the inner exhaust tube attaching screws. Tap the end of the tube with a soft hammer (**Figure 29**) to break it loose.

8

Remove the tube. Remove and discard the gasket.

25. Depress water tube guide tab and pull guide from tube. Remove and discard the exhaust tube rubber grommet.

26. Install power head on holding fixture part No. 303605 if further service is necessary.

27. Installation is the reverse of removal. Lubricate drive shaft splines with OMC Moly Lube. Make sure the O-ring is in the end of the crankshaft. Apply OMC Gasket Sealing Compound to exhaust housing surface and lubricate top of water tube with liquid soap. Rotate power head as required to align crankshaft and drive shaft splines. Apply OMC Nut Lock to port and starboard exhaust housing studs. Tighten fasteners to specifications (**Table 1**). Use pin insert tool part No. 322697 to install stop switch lead in A cavity of connector on CD 2 models. Complete engine synchronization and linkage adjustments. See Chapter Five.

Disassembly
(2 hp)

Refer to **Figure 30** for this procedure.

1. Remove the cylinder head bolts. Remove the cylinder head and gasket. Discard the gasket.

2. Remove the exhaust cover bolts. Remove the exhaust cover and gasket. Discard the gasket.

3. Remove the intake manifold and reed valve assembly.

4. Remove the connecting rod cap and 30 needle bearings.

> *NOTE*
> *Main bearing and seal housing are serviced as an assembly. If bearing or seal requires replacement, install a new bearing and seal housing.*

5. Remove the 4 lower main bearing housing bolts. Remove the bearing housing and 28 needle bearings.

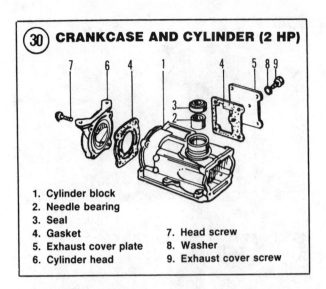

30 CRANKCASE AND CYLINDER (2 HP)

1. Cylinder block
2. Needle bearing
3. Seal
4. Gasket
5. Exhaust cover plate
6. Cylinder head
7. Head screw
8. Washer
9. Exhaust cover screw

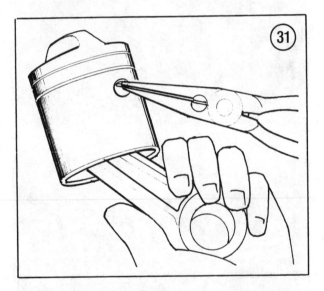

6. Remove the crankshaft through the bottom of the crankcase.

7. Reinstall connecting rod cap on connecting rod. Push the piston toward the cylinder head end of the crankcase until the piston rings can be seen.

8. Remove and discard the piston rings with a ring expander tool.

9. Remove the piston and connecting rod through the carburetor end of the crankcase.

10. Support crankcase and push upper main bearing and seal out with a suitable tool.

11. If the piston is to be removed from the connecting rod, remove the piston pin

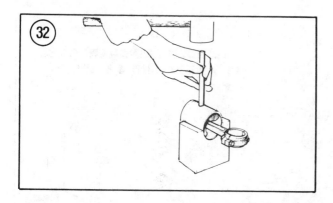

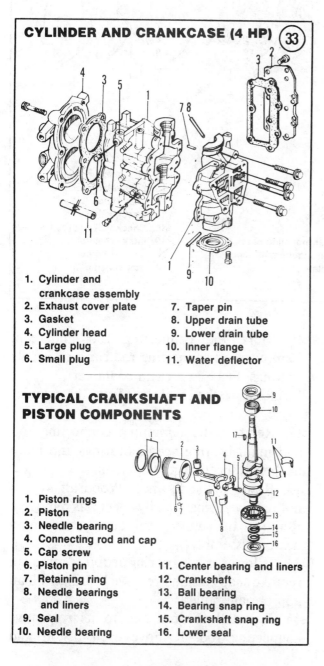

CYLINDER AND CRANKCASE (4 HP) ③③

1. **Cylinder and crankcase assembly**
2. **Exhaust cover plate**
3. **Gasket**
4. **Cylinder head**
5. **Large plug**
6. **Small plug**
7. **Taper pin**
8. **Upper drain tube**
9. **Lower drain tube**
10. **Inner flange**
11. **Water deflector**

TYPICAL CRANKSHAFT AND PISTON COMPONENTS

1. **Piston rings**
2. **Piston**
3. **Needle bearing**
4. **Connecting rod and cap**
5. **Cap screw**
6. **Piston pin**
7. **Retaining ring**
8. **Needle bearings and liners**
9. **Seal**
10. **Needle bearing**
11. **Center bearing and liners**
12. **Crankshaft**
13. **Ball bearing**
14. **Bearing snap ring**
15. **Crankshaft snap ring**
16. **Lower seal**

retaining rings with needlenose pliers. See **Figure 31**.

12. Place piston in cradle part No. 326572 with "L" mark on inside of piston boss facing upward. This positions the driver on the loose end of the piston pin. Drive piston pin through piston with a tool part No. 326624 or a suitable driver. See **Figure 32**.

13. If connecting rod piston pin bearing requires replacement, remove with tool part No. 327637.

Disassembly
(4-8 hp)

Refer to **Figure 33** (4 hp), **Figure 34** (4 Deluxe and 4.5 hp) and **Figure 35** (5, 6, 7.5 and 8 hp) for this procedure.

1. 5-8 hp—Remove the thermostat cap, gasket and components from cylinder head. Discard the seal and gasket.

2. Remove the cylinder head and gasket. Discard the gasket.

NOTE
Check inner exhaust cover (5-8 hp) for signs of pitting. If found, discard the cover.

3. Remove the exhaust cover and gasket. On 5-8 hp, remove the inner exhaust cover and gasket. Discard the gaskets.

4. 4 hp—Remove the inner flange.

5. Remove and discard any crankcase hose clamps. Remove hose from crankcase.

NOTE
Some engines use 2 taper pins. Inspect yours carefully before proceeding with Step 6. Remove both pins, if so fitted, before attempting to separate the crankcase and cylinder in Step 8.

6. With crankcase and cylinder block on a solid surface, drive the taper pins from the back to the front of the crankcase.

8

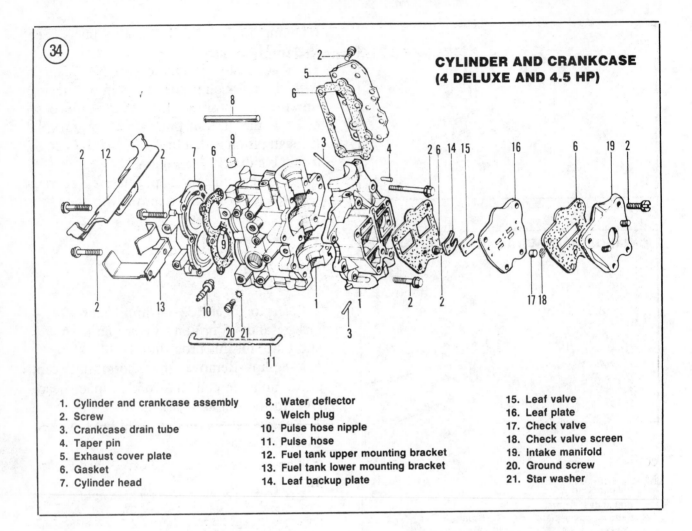

1. Cylinder and crankcase assembly
2. Screw
3. Crankcase drain tube
4. Taper pin
5. Exhaust cover plate
6. Gasket
7. Cylinder head

8. Water deflector
9. Welch plug
10. Pulse hose nipple
11. Pulse hose
12. Fuel tank upper mounting bracket
13. Fuel tank lower mounting bracket
14. Leaf backup plate

15. Leaf valve
16. Leaf plate
17. Check valve
18. Check valve screen
19. Intake manifold
20. Ground screw
21. Star washer

7. Remove the crankcase-to-cylinder block bolts.

8. Tap the top of the crankshaft with a plastic mallet to separate the cylinder and crankcase halves.

NOTE
The main bearing and connecting rod caps must be removed before the crankshaft can be removed from the cylinder block.

9. Remove the center main bearing liner and needle bearings. Place in a clean container.

NOTE
The 30 connecting rod bearings are larger than the 30 center main bearings.

10. Mark the connecting rod and cap. Remove each connecting rod cap and needle bearings. Place in a clean container.

11. Remove the crankshaft from the cylinder block.

12. Remove the remaining connecting rod and main bearing needle bearings and place in their respective container.

13. Remove the flywheel Woodruff key, if not removed when the flywheel was removed. Remove the upper seal and upper main bearing assembly.

14. If lower main bearing requires removal, remove snap ring and remove bearing with an appropriate puller.

15. Reinstall the rod cap to its respective connecting rod. Remove each piston and

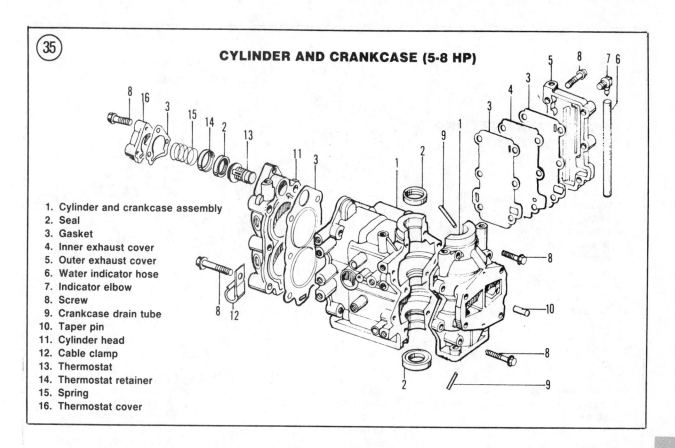

(35) **CYLINDER AND CRANKCASE (5-8 HP)**

1. Cylinder and crankcase assembly
2. Seal
3. Gasket
4. Inner exhaust cover
5. Outer exhaust cover
6. Water indicator hose
7. Indicator elbow
8. Screw
9. Crankcase drain tube
10. Taper pin
11. Cylinder head
12. Cable clamp
13. Thermostat
14. Thermostat retainer
15. Spring
16. Thermostat cover

connecting rod assembly from its cylinder. Mark the cylinder number on the top of the piston with a felt-tipped pen.

16. Pry each ring far enough from the piston to grip it with pliers, then break the rings off the piston and discard.

17. If the piston is to be removed from the connecting rod, remove the piston pin retaining rings with tool part No. 325937. See **Figure 31**.

18A. 1973-1978—Place piston in cradle part No. 326572 (4 hp) or part No. 326573 (6 hp) with "L" mark on inside of piston boss facing upward. This positions the driver on the loose end of the piston pin.

18B. 1979-on—Place piston in cradle part No. 326572 (4-4.5 hp) or part No. 326573 (5-8 hp) with "L" mark on inside of piston boss facing downward. This positions the driver on the tight end of the piston pin.

19. Drive piston pin through piston with tool part No. 326624 (4-4.5 hp), part No. 326573

(5-8 hp) or another suitable driver. See **Figure 32**.

20. If connecting rod piston pin bearing requires replacement, remove with tool part No. 327637 (4-4.5 hp) or part No. 327645 (5-8 hp).

Disassembly
(9.5-15 hp)

Refer to **Figure 36** for this procedure.

1. Remove the crankcase head and discard the O-ring.

2. Remove the cylinder head cover. Remove the thermostat, seal and cover gasket. Discard the seal and gasket.

3. Remove the cylinder head and gasket. Discard the gasket.

4. Remove the bypass cover and gasket. Discard the gasket.

5. Remove the intake manifold, reed valve assembly and gasket. Discard the gasket.

8

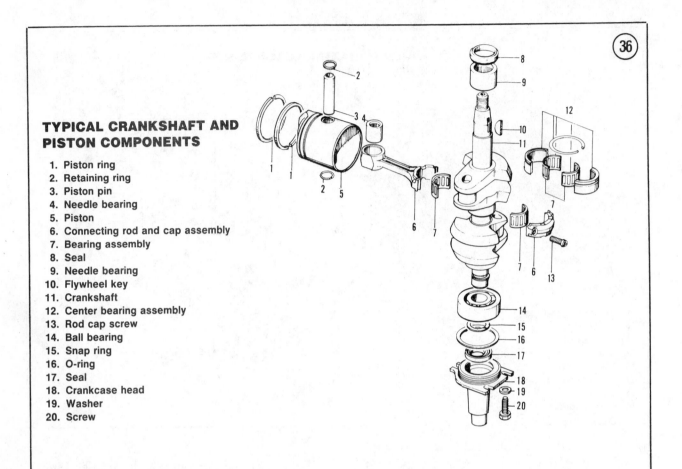

TYPICAL CRANKSHAFT AND PISTON COMPONENTS

1. Piston ring
2. Retaining ring
3. Piston pin
4. Needle bearing
5. Piston
6. Connecting rod and cap assembly
7. Bearing assembly
8. Seal
9. Needle bearing
10. Flywheel key
11. Crankshaft
12. Center bearing assembly
13. Rod cap screw
14. Ball bearing
15. Snap ring
16. O-ring
17. Seal
18. Crankcase head
19. Washer
20. Screw

CYLINDER AND CRANKCASE (9.5-15 HP)

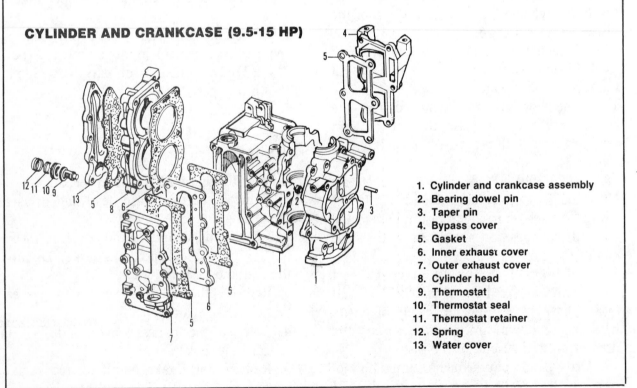

1. Cylinder and crankcase assembly
2. Bearing dowel pin
3. Taper pin
4. Bypass cover
5. Gasket
6. Inner exhaust cover
7. Outer exhaust cover
8. Cylinder head
9. Thermostat
10. Thermostat seal
11. Thermostat retainer
12. Spring
13. Water cover

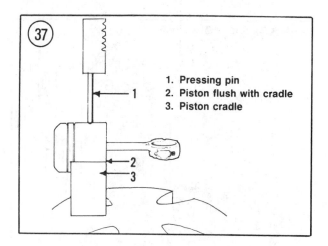

1. Pressing pin
2. Piston flush with cradle
3. Piston cradle

6. With crankcase and cylinder block on a solid surface, drive the taper pin from the back to the front of the crankcase.

7. Remove the crankcase-to-cylinder block bolts.

8. Tap the top of the crankshaft with a plastic mallet to separate the cylinder and crankcase halves.

NOTE
The connecting rod caps must be removed before the crankshaft can be removed from the cylinder block. Note that one side of rod and cap has raised dots and that the corners are chamfered for proper rod/cap alignment. Caps are not interchangeable and cannot be turned.

9. Mark the connecting rod and cap. Remove each connecting rod cap and bearing retainer. Place in a clean container.

10. Remove the crankshaft from the cylinder block.

11. Remove the remaining connecting rod bearing retainer and place in its respective container.

12. Reinstall each rod cap to its respective connecting rod. Remove the piston and rod assemblies from their cylinder. Mark the cylinder number on the top of each piston with a felt-tipped pen.

13. Carefully pry the crankshaft center main bearing retaining ring from its groove. Slide the retaining ring to one side and remove the roller bearing assembly. Place the 23 rollers in a clean container.

14. Slide the top main bearing off the crankshaft.

15. If lower main bearing requires removal, remove snap ring and remove bearing with an appropriate puller.

16. Pry each ring far enough from the piston to grip it with pliers, then break the rings off the piston and discard.

NOTE
When replacing the piston and piston pin on 1976-1980 models, install piston, piston pin and bearing assembly part No. 391526 as a replacement. This assembly supercedes part No. 387660 and contains a larger piston pin/bearing surface for increased durability.

17. If the piston is to be removed from the connecting rod, remove the piston pin retaining rings with tool part No. 325937. See **Figure 31**.

18. Place piston in cradle part No. 319919 (1973-1981) or part No. 326573 (1982-on) with "L" mark on inside of piston boss facing upward. This positions the driver on the loose end of the piston pin. The piston skirt should be flush with the cradle. See **Figure 37**.

19. Heat the piston to 200-400° F with a heat lamp, then drive the piston pin through the piston with tool part No. 319920 (1973-1981) or part No. 392511 (1982-on) and an arbor press.

20. Remove piston from connecting rod along with the 23 needle bearings and 2 washers. Place bearings and washers in a clean container.

Disassembly
(18-40 hp)

Refer to **Figure 38** for this procedure.

1. Remove the lower main bearing seal housing (**Figure 39**). Remove and discard the

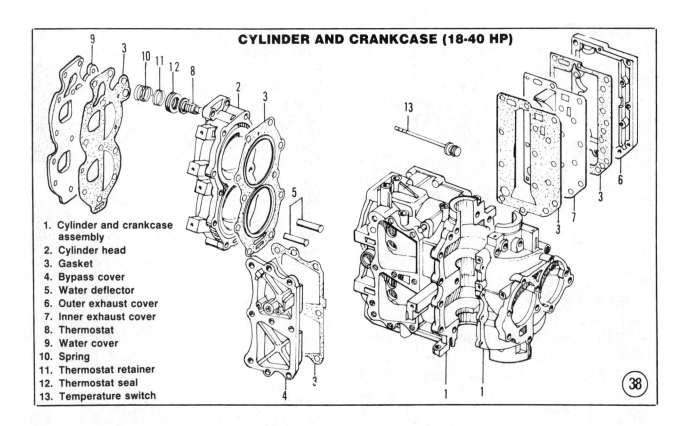

CYLINDER AND CRANKCASE (18-40 HP)

1. Cylinder and crankcase assembly
2. Cylinder head
3. Gasket
4. Bypass cover
5. Water deflector
6. Outer exhaust cover
7. Inner exhaust cover
8. Thermostat
9. Water cover
10. Spring
11. Thermostat retainer
12. Thermostat seal
13. Temperature switch

seal housing O-rings and the O-ring inside the crankshaft. Drive the seal from the housing with an appropriate size punch.

2. Remove the cylinder head cover and gasket (**Figure 40**). Discard the gasket.

3. Remove the thermostat spring, thermostat and seal (**Figure 41**). Discard the seal.

4. Remove the cylinder head and gasket (**Figure 42**). Discard the gasket.

5. Remove the exhaust cover screws. Tap cover if necessary to break the seal. Remove the outer cover and gasket (**Figure 43**). Discard the gasket.

6. Remove the inner exhaust cover and gasket (**Figure 44**). Discard the gasket.

7. Remove the intake bypass covers and gaskets (**Figure 45**). Discard the gaskets.

8. Remove the crankcase taper pin with a punch (**Figure 46**). Drive taper pin from front to back of crankcase.

9. Remove the crankcase-to-cylinder block bolts. Note that 2 are inside the openings and 4 are hidden. See **Figure 47**.

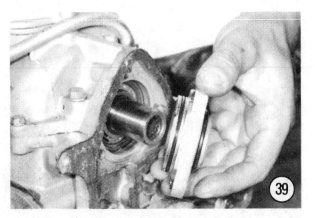

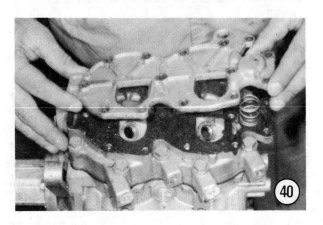

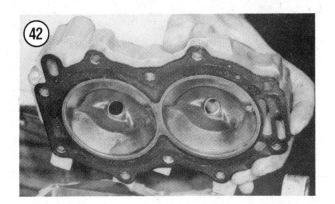

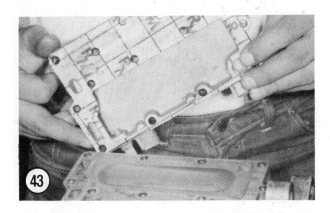

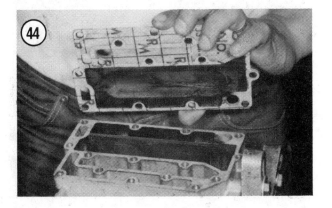

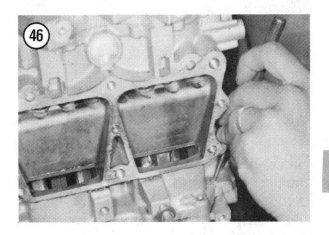

10. Remove the intake manifold and gasket (**Figure 48**). Discard the gasket.

11. Remove the single screw holding the reed valve assembly. Remove the reed valve assembly (**Figure 49**).

12. Tap the side of the crankshaft with a soft mallet to break the gasket seal, then remove the cylinder half from the crankcase. See **Figure 50**.

NOTE
The center main bearing and connecting rod caps must be removed before the crankshaft can be removed from the cylinder block. Note that one side of rod and cap has raised dots and the corners are chamfered for proper rod/cap alignment. Caps are not interchangeable and cannot be turned.

8

13. Remove the center main bearing lower sleeve and the cage/roller assembly. See **Figure 51**.

14. Check connecting rod and cap alignment with a pencil point or dental pick (**Figure 52**). Alignment must be correct at 3 of the 4 corners. Record alignment points of each cap for reassembly reference.

15. Remove each connecting rod cap and bearing retainer. See **Figure 53**. Place in a clean container.

16. Remove the crankshaft from the cylinder block (**Figure 54**).

17. Remove the remaining connecting rod bearing and center main bearing retainers and needle bearings (**Figure 55**). Place bearings and retainer in their respective containers.

18. Orient each rod cap to its respective connecting rod and reinstall cap screws finger-tight.

19. Remove the piston and rod assemblies from their cylinder. Mark the cylinder number on the top of each piston with a felt-tipped pen.

20. Remove the flywheel Woodruff key, if not removed when the flywheel was removed. Slide the upper seal and main bearing assembly off the crankshaft.

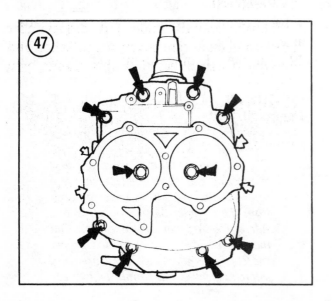

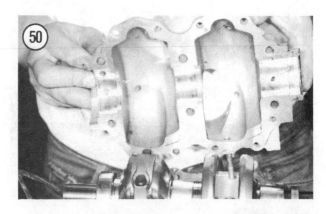

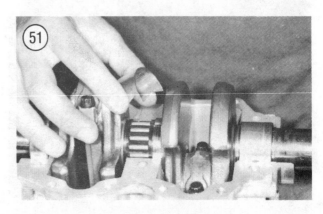

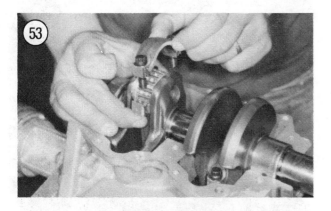

21. If lower main bearing requires removal, remove snap ring then remove bearing with an appropriate puller.

22. Remove and discard O-ring from inside of lower main bearing journal.

23. Pry each ring far enough from the piston to grip it with pliers, then break the rings off the piston and discard.

24. If the piston is to be removed from the connecting rod, remove the piston pin retaining rings with tool part No. 325937. See **Figure 56**.

25. Place piston in cradle part No. 319919 (1973-1981) or part No. 326573 (1982-on) with "L" mark on inside of piston boss facing upward. This positions the driver on the loose end of the piston pin. The piston skirt should be flush with the cradle. See **Figure 37**.

26. Heat the piston to 200-400° F with a heat lamp, then press the piston pin through the piston with tool part No. 321434.

27. Remove piston from connecting rod along with the caged bearing retainer. Slide bearing retainer from connecting rod (**Figure 57**) and place in a clean container.

**Cylinder Block and Crankcase
Cleaning and Inspection
(All Engines)**

Johnson and Evinrude outboard cylinder blocks and crankcase covers are matched and line-bored assemblies. For this reason, you

8

should not attempt to assemble an engine with parts salvaged from other blocks. If inspection indicates that either the block or cover requires replacement, replace both.

WARNING
Remove any jewelry from your from your hands and wrists and wear hand and eye protection when working with Gel Seal and Gasket Remover. The substance is powerful enough to etch holes in a watch crystal or badly irritate any cut in the skin.

Carefully remove all gasket and sealant residue from the cylinder block and crankcase cover mating surfaces. Gel Seal or Gel Seal II should be cleaned from mating parts with OMC Gel Seal and Gasket Remover. After spraying the area to be cleaned, allow the solvent to stand for 5-10 minutes before cleaning off the old Gel Seal and the remover. Since Gel Seal is bright red in color, a visual inspection will quickly tell you when it has been completely removed.

Clean the aluminum surfaces carefully to avoid nicking them. A dull putty knife can be used, but a piece of Lucite with one edge ground to a 45 degree angle is more efficient and will also reduce the possibility of damage to the surfaces. Once the area is clean, apply OMC Cleaning Solvent to remove all traces of the Gel Seal and Gasket Remover.

When sealing the crankcase cover and cylinder block, both mating surfaces must be free of all sealant residue, dirt and oil or leaks will develop.

Once the gasket surfaces are cleaned, place the mating surface of each component on a large pane of glass. Apply uniform downward pressure on the component and check for warpage. Replace each component if more than a slight degree of warpage exists. In cases where there is a slight amount of warpage, it can often be eliminated by placing the mating surface of each component on a large sheet of

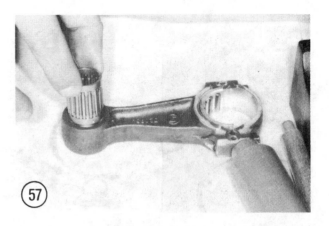

(57)

(58)

120 emery cloth. Apply a slight amount of pressure and move the component in a figure-8 pattern. See **Figure 58**. Remove the component and emery cloth and recheck surface flatness on the pane of glass.

If warpage exists, the high spots will be dull while low areas will remain unchanged in appearance. It may be necessary to repeat this procedure 2-3 times until the entire mating surface has been polished to a dull luster. Do not remove more than a total 0.010 in. from the cylinder block and head. Finish the resurfacing with 180 emery cloth.

1. Clean the cylinder block and crankcase cover thoroughly with solvent and a brush.

2. Carefully remove all gasket and sealant residue from the cylinder block and crankcase cover mating surfaces.

3. Check the cylinder heads and exhaust ports for excessive carbon deposits or varnish.

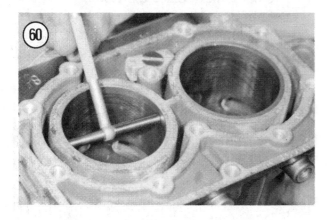

NOTE
With older engines, it is a good idea to have the cylinder walls lightly honed with a medium stone even if they are in good condition. This will break up any glaze that might reduce compression.

9. Check each cylinder bore for signs of aluminum transfer from the pistons to the cylinder walls. If scoring is present but not excessive, have the cylinders honed by a dealer or qualified machine shop.

10. Check each cylinder bore for size and taper in the port area with an inside micrometer or bore gauge. See **Figure 60**. If bore is tapered, worn or out-of-round by less than 0.002 in. (2-8 hp) or 0.003 in. (9.5-40 hp), have the cylinders honed or rebored by a dealer or qualified machine shop. If taper, wear or out-of-round exceeds this dimension, replace the block and cover assembly.

CAUTION
If cylinders are rebored for oversize pistons, be sure to allow 0.003-0.005 in. clearance between the new bore diameter and the oversize pistons.

Crankshaft and Connecting Rod Bearings Cleaning and Inspection (All Engines)

Bearings can be reused if they are in good condition. To be on the safe side, however, it is a good idea to discard all bearings and install new ones whenever the engine is disassembled. New bearings are inexpensive compared to the cost of another overhaul caused by the use of marginal bearings.

1. Place ball bearings in a wire basket and submerge in a suitable container of fresh solvent. The bottom of the basket should not touch the bottom of the container.

2. Agitate basket containing bearings to loosen all grease, sludge and other contamination.

Remove with a scraper or other blunt instrument.

4. Check the block, cylinder head and cover for cracks, fractures, stripped bolt or spark plug holes or other defects.

5. Check the gasket mating surfaces for nicks, grooves, cracks or excessive distortion. Any of these defects will cause a compression leak. Replace as required.

6. Check all oil and water passages in the block and cover for obstructions. Make sure any plugs installed are properly tightened.

7. Make sure all water passage restrictors (**Figure 59**) are in good condition and properly installed. Damaged, loose or missing restrictors will interfere with cooling water circulation and result in possible engine overheating.

8. Check crankcase recirculation orifice, if so equipped, and clean with tool part No. 326623.

8

3. Dry ball bearings with dry filtered compressed air. Be careful not to spin the bearings.

4. Lubricate the dry bearings with a light coat of Johnson or Evinrude 50/1 oil and inspect for rust, wear, scuffed surfaces, heat discoloration or other defects. Replace as required.

5. If needle bearings are to be reused, repeat Steps 1-4, cleaning one set at a time to prevent any possible mixup. Check bearings for flat spots. If one needle bearing is defective, replace the set with new bearings and liners.

6. Repeat Step 5 to check caged piston pin bearings. If bearing is defective, replace the bearing and its corresponding piston pin.

**Piston Cleaning
and Inspection
(All Engines)**

1. Check the piston(s) for signs of scoring, cracking, cracked or worn piston pin bosses or metal damage. Replace piston and pin as a set if any of these defects are noted.

2. Check piston ring grooves for distortion, loose ring locating pins or excessive wear. If the flexing action of the rings has not kept the lower surface of the ring grooves free of carbon, clean with a bristle brush and solvent.

*NOTE
Do not use an automotive ring groove
cleaning tool in Step 3 as it can damage
the piston ring locating pin.*

3. Clean the piston skirt, ring grooves and dome with the recessed end of a broken ring to remove any carbon deposits.

4. Immerse pistons in a carbon removal solution to remove any carbon deposits not removed in Step 3. If the solution does not remove all of the carbon, carefully use a fine wire brush; avoid burring or rounding of the machined edges. Clean the piston skirt with crocus cloth.

5A. Check 1982-on 25, 30 and 35 hp pistons for size and roundness:

   a. Measure the piston at a point 1/8 in. above the bottom edge of the skirt (A, **Figure 61**) and 90° to the piston pin hole (B, **Figure 61**).

   b. Repeat the measurement at a point parallel to the piston pin hole. See **Figure 62**.

   c. Subtract the second measurement from the first one. If the difference is less than 0.0045 in., replace the piston.

   d. Subtract the first measurement from that obtained in Step 10 of *Cylinder Block and Crankcase Cleaning and*

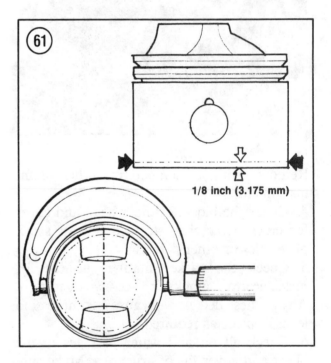
1/8 inch (3.175 mm)

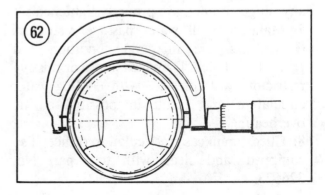

Inspection to determine the piston-to-cylinder clearance. If clearance exceeds 0.0034 ±0.001 in., have the cylinder rebored and install an oversize piston.

e. If the piston side grooves are worn in a pattern similar to that shown in **Figure 63**, replace the piston.

5B. Check all other pistons with a micrometer at the top and piston skirt. See

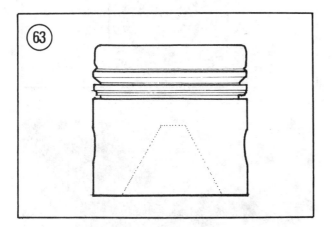

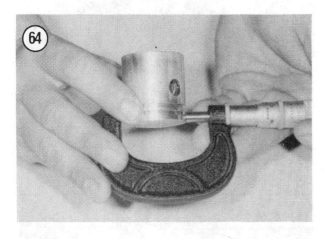

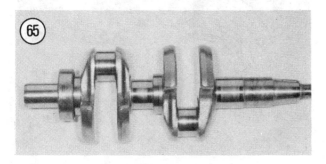

Figure 64. Measure at a point 90° to the piston pin and at a point parallel with the piston pin bosses. Compare the 2 top and skirt measurements to determine if piston is out-of-round. Replace piston and pin as a set if piston is out-of-round by more than 0.0025 in. (2-8 hp) or 0.003 in. (9.5-40 hp).

Crankshaft Cleaning and Inspection (All Engines)

1. Clean the crankshaft thoroughly with solvent and a brush. Blow dry with dry filtered compressed air, if available, and lubricate with a light coat of Johnson or Evinrude 50/1 oil.

2. Check the crankshaft journals and crankpins for scratches, heat discoloration or other defects. See **Figure 65**.

3. Measure the journals and crankpins with a micrometer and compare to **Table 3**. If journals or crankpins are not within specifications, replace the crankshaft.

4. Check drive shaft splines and flywheel taper threads for wear or damage. Replace crankshaft as required.

5. If lower crankshaft ball bearing has not been removed, grasp inner race and try to work it back and forth. Replace bearing if excessive play is noted.

6. Lubricate ball bearing with Johnson or Evinrude 50/1 oil and rotate outer race. Replace bearing if it sounds or feels rough or if it does not rotate smoothly.

Piston and Connecting Rod Assembly (All Engines)

If the pistons were removed from the connecting rods, they must be correctly oriented when reassembling. The exhaust or slanted side of the piston dome must face the exhaust ports when installed (**Figure 66**) and the connecting rod oil hole must face toward

8

the flywheel end of the engine. Double-check rod and piston orientation before installing the piston pin.

1A. If a caged bearing was removed from the connecting rod piston pin end:

    a. Reinstall the bearing with an arbor press.

    b. Fit piston over connecting rod piston pin end with the exhaust (slanted) side of dome facing the starboard side of the connecting rod (oil hole facing up).

1B. If needle bearings were removed from the connecting rod piston pin end:

    a. Position connecting rod with oil hole facing up.

    b. Wipe inside of piston pin bore with OMC Needle Bearing grease.

    c. Install a suitable bushing to act as a spacer and insert needle bearings individually. See **Figure 67**.

    d. When all bearings are in place, fit washers at top and bottom of bearing assembly.

    e. Hold piston with exhaust (slanted) side of dome facing the starboard side of the connecting rod and carefully fit on rod to prevent disturbing the bearings.

2. Lightly coat wrist pin and lubricate each piston pin hole with a drop or two of Johnson or Evinrude 50/1 oil.

> *NOTE*
> *Position piston in Step 3 to drive piston pin in place from the "L" or "LOOSE" side of the piston. See piston pin boss inside piston skirt for marking.*

3. Insert piston pin through piston pin hole and engage connecting rod. Make sure piston dome and connecting rod oil hole are properly oriented. Position piston on the same cradle used to disassemble it and press piston pin in place with the same piston pin tool used to remove it. See **Figure 68**.

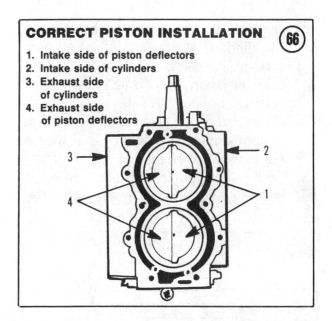

CORRECT PISTON INSTALLATION   66

1. Intake side of piston deflectors
2. Intake side of cylinders
3. Exhaust side of cylinders
4. Exhaust side of piston deflectors

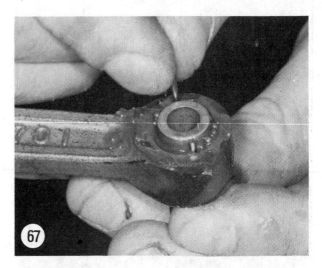

67

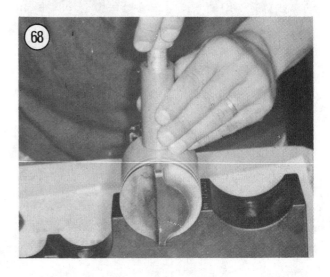

68

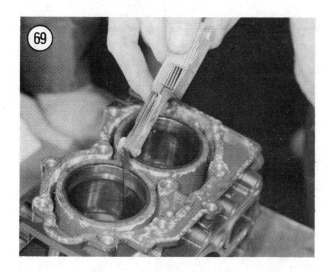

4. Install new piston pin retaining rings on each side of the piston. Make sure rings fit into grooves in piston piston pin bore.

5. Measure the bottom of 2-8 hp piston skirts at a point parallel with the piston pin and 90° from the piston pin. Compare the measurements. If measurements vary more than 0.0025 in., the piston was distorted during assembly and should be replaced.

6. Check end gap of new rings before installing on piston. Place ring in cylinder bore, then square it up by inserting the bottom of an old piston. Do not push ring into bore more than 3/8-1/2 in. Measure the gap with a feeler gauge (**Figure 69**) and compare to specifications (**Table 3**).

7. If ring gap is excessive in Step 5, repeat the step with the ring in the other cylinder. If gap is also excessive in that cylinder, discard and replace with another new ring.

8. If ring gap is insufficient in Step 5, the ends of the ring can be filed slightly. Clean ring thoroughly and recheck gap as in Step 5.

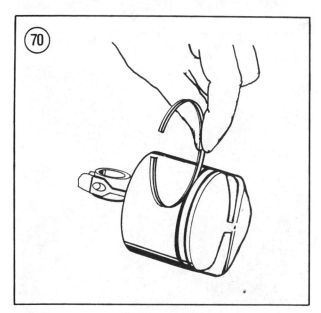

NOTE
The upper ring is a pressure-back type and has a tapered groove which cannot be checked in Step 9.

9. Once the ring gaps are correctly established, roll the lower ring around the piston ring groove to check for binding or tightness. See **Figure 70**.

10. Install the lower ring on the piston with a ring expander. Spread the ring just enough to fit it over the piston head and into position. See **Figure 71**.

11. Repeat Step 10 to install the upper ring.

12. Position each ring so the piston groove locating pin fits in the ring gap. Proper ring positioning is necessary to minimize compression loss and prevent the ring ends from catching on the cylinder ports.

13. Coat the piston and cylinder bore with Johnson or Evinrude 50/1 oil:

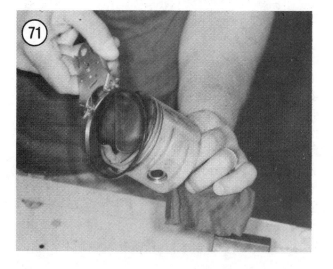

a. Check the piston dome number made during disassembly and match piston with its correct cylinder.

b. Orient exhaust side of piston to exhaust port side of cylinder block.

c. Make sure connecting rod oil hole faces flywheel end of engine.

d. Insert piston into cylinder bore. Recheck ring gap and groove locating pin alignment.

e. Install tool part No. 308479 or part No. 326591 over piston dome and rings.

f. Hold connecting rod end with one hand to prevent it from scraping or scratching the cylinder bore and slowly push piston into cylinder. See **Figure 72**.

14. Remove the ring installer tool and repeat Step 13 to install the other piston on 2-cylinder engines.

15. Reach through exhaust port and lightly depress each ring with a pencil point or small screwdriver blade. See **Figure 73**. The ring should snap back when pressure is released. If it does not, the ring was broken during piston installation and will have to be replaced.

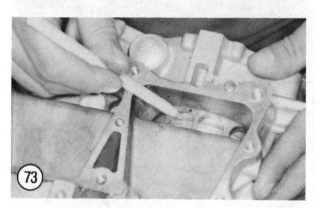

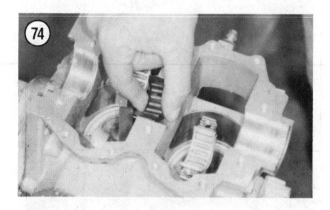

Connecting Rod and Crankshaft Assembly (All Engines)

1. On 2 hp models, install new upper main bearing (lettered side up) through the bottom of the crankcase. Work carefully to prevent losing the bearing needles and press the bearing case until it is recessed 1/16 in. below the crankcase finish thrust surface.

2. Reinstall upper and lower main ball bearings on crankshaft, if removed. Reinstall upper oil seal with lip facing inward.

3. Remove connecting rod caps. Coat connecting rod bearing surfaces with OMC Needle Bearing grease. Install a bearing retainer half and needle bearings in the rod.

4A. If crankshaft center main bearing line uses a sleeve retainer ring, install bearing cages and bearings, fit sleeves in position and install retainer ring.

4B. If center main bearing does not use a sleeve retainer ring, install the center main bearing liner in the block with its pointed end facing the intake side. The locating flange should engage the locating pocket. Install the bearing cage and roller assembly on the liner. See **Figure 74**.

5. Coat outer edge of top crankcase seal with OMC Gasket Sealing Compound.

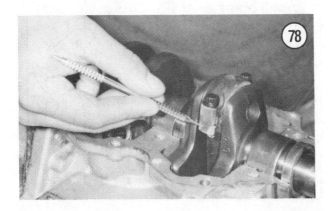

NOTE
Location of upper and lower bearing holes and dowel pins varies according to model. Determine which is in the block and align the bearings accordingly so pin and hole will mate when crankshaft is installed in Step 6.

6. Lubricate the crankshaft assembly with Johnson or Evinrude 50/1 oil and install in cylinder block. Align upper and lower main bearing dowel and pin hole. See **Figure 75** (typical). On crankshafts with a center main bearing sleeve retainer ring, align hole in sleeve with dowel pin in block. Seat crankshaft in place.

7. If crankshaft does not use a retainer sleeve ring, coat the main bearing journal with OMC Needle Bearing grease and install remaining retainer half, needle bearings and sleeve. See **Figure 76**.

8. Draw connecting rod(s) up around crankshaft crankpin journal. Coat crankpins with OMC Needle Bearing grease and install remaining retainer halves and needle bearings on each crankpin (**Figure 77**).

9. Orient the connecting rod cap according to the small raised dots and marks made during disassembly. Install the caps finger-tight.

CAUTION
The procedure detailed in Steps 10-12 is very important to proper engine operation as it affects bearing action. If not done properly, major engine damage can result. It can also be a time-consuming and frustrating process. Work slowly and with patience. If alignment was satisfactory when checked during disassembly, it should be possible to achieve a similar alignment on reassembly.

10. Run a pencil point or dental pick over the rod and cap chamfers to check alignment (**Figure 78**). Refer to notes made during disassembly. Rod and cap must be aligned so that the pencil point or dental pick will pass

smoothly across the break line on at least 3 of the 4 corners.

11. If rod and cap alignment is not satisfactory in Step 10, gently tap cap in direction required with a soft mallet and recheck alignment. Repeat this procedure as many times as necessary to achieve alignment of at least 3 corners.

12. If satisfactory alignment cannot be achieved in Step 10 or Step 11, the connecting rod and cap should be replaced.

13. Once rod and cap alignment is correct, carefully torque rod caps to specifications (**Table 1**).

14. On 2 hp models, install lower bearing housing with a new gasket and tighten to specifications (**Table 1**).

15. Rotate the crankshaft to check for binding. If the crankshaft does not float freely over the full length of the crankpin(s), loosen the rod caps and repeat Steps 10-13.

**Cylinder Block and
Crankcase Assembly
(General Procedures)**

The cylinder head gasket on some models is impregnated with sealant during manufacture and requires no additional sealer when installed. Check the gasket package to determine if it is this type.

All gaskets which have not been impregnated with sealant should be lightly coated on both sides with OMC Gasket Sealing Compound. The outer diameter of the crankshaft upper seal should also be coated with OMC Gasket Sealing Compound.

The crankcase face on some models is grooved for the use of a spaghetti or rubber seal. The new seal should be fully seated in the grooves and then cut 1/2 in. longer at each end to assure a good butt seal against both crankcase bearings. Run a thin bead of OMC Adhesive M in the groove before installing the seal. Force the seal into the groove and let it set 15-20 minutes. Trim the ends of the seal with a sharp knife, leaving about 1/32 in. of the seal end to butt against the bearings. Apply another thin bead of OMC Adhesive M to the crankcase face. Use care not to apply an excessive amount, as it can squeeze over when the parts are mated and may block oil or water passages.

A motor reassembled with Gel Seal II should set overnight before it is started and run. If the motor must be run the same day, spray the surface opposite to the one coated with Gel Seal II with OMC Locquic Primer and allow several hours for the Gel Seal II to cure.

Gel Seal II starts to cure as soon as the parts are mated. The process is shortened when OMC Locquic Primer has also been used. For this reason, it is important that you install and torque all fasteners as soon as possible. If Gel Seal II starts to set up before the fasteners are torqued, it can act as a shim and result in bearing misalignment, mislocation or tight armature plate bearings.

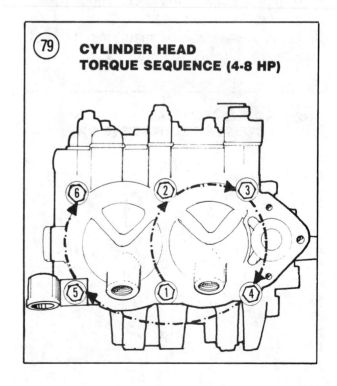

(79) **CYLINDER HEAD
TORQUE SEQUENCE (4-8 HP)**

Cylinder Block and Crankcase Assembly (2 hp)

1. Install the cylinder head with a new gasket.
2. Install the intake manifold and reed valve assembly with a new gasket.
3. Install the exhaust cover with a new gasket.
4. Tighten all fasteners to specifications (**Table 1**).
5. Install the magneto cam drive pin and cam. Cam side marked "TOP" must face the flywheel.
6. Install the power head as described in this chapter.

Cylinder Block and Crankcase Assembly (4-8 hp)

1. Squeeze a 5/16 in. ball of Gel Seal II on each crankcase flange. Spread sealant along flange and inside all bolt holes but keep it at least 1/4 in. from seals.
2. Install crankcase to cylinder block. Install bolts finger-tight, then install crankcase taper pin(s) with a mallet and punch. Tighten bolts to specifications (**Table 1**).
3. Install lower bearing snap ring (beveled edge facing out) in crankcase.

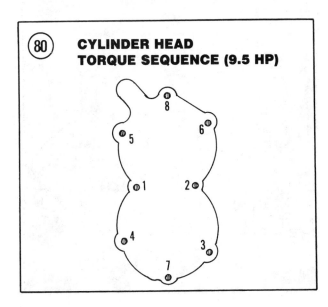

⑧⓪ **CYLINDER HEAD TORQUE SEQUENCE (9.5 HP)**

4. Install lower crankshaft seal (lip facing out) until it bottoms on the snap ring.
5. Rotate the crankshaft several turns to check for binding. If crankshaft does not turn easily, disassemble and correct the interference.
6. Install cylinder head with a new gasket. Tighten bolts to specifications (**Table 1**) following the sequence shown in **Figure 79**.
7. 5-8 hp models—Install thermostat with a new seal. Install retainer, spring, new gasket and thermostat cover. Tighten fasteners to specifications (**Table 1**).
8. Reinstall inner exhaust cover with a new gasket, if so equipped. Install outer exhaust cover with a new gasket. Tighten all fasteners finger-tight, then torque to specifications (**Table 1**).
9. Reinstall crankcase hose with new clamps.
10. 4 hp models—Install inner flange and tighten screws to specifications (**Table 1**).
11. Install the power head as described in this chapter.

Cylinder Block and Crankcase Assembly (9.5-15 hp)

1. Squeeze a 5/16 in. ball of Gel Seal II on each crankcase flange. Spread sealant along flange and inside all bolt holes but keep it at least 1/4 in. from seals.
2. Tap crankshaft toward flywheel end to seat lower bearing.
3. Install crankcase to cylinder block. Wipe the 2 center main bolt threads with Gel Seal II. Install and tighten all fasteners finger-tight.
4. Install crankcase taper pin(s) with a mallet and punch.
5. Rotate the crankshaft several turns to check for binding. If crankshaft does not turn easily, disassemble and correct the interference.
6. Tighten crankcase bolts to specifications (**Table 1**) following the sequence shown in **Figure 80** (9.5 hp) or **Figure 81** (9.9-15 hp).

8

7. Wipe the outer diameter of a new upper main bearing seal with OMC Gasket Sealing Compound and install with tool part No. 319872 (1973-1979) or part No. 391060 (1980-on).

8. Wipe the outer diameter of 2 new crankcase head seals. Fit the smaller diameter seal on tool part No. 330251 with its lip facing the large end of the tool. Install the seal in the crankcase head cover until tool touches cover. Remove the tool and repeat the step with the larger diameter seal (lip facing away from tool). When properly installed, the seal lips will face each other.

9. Lubricate a new O-ring with Johnson or Evinrude 50/1 oil and install on crankcase head.

10. Install crankcase head and tighten fasteners to specifications (**Table 1**).

11. Install the cylinder head with a new gasket. Tighten fasteners following the sequence shown in **Figure 80** (9.5 hp) or **Figure 81** (9.9-15 hp).

12. Install thermostat with a new seal. Install the thermostat spring.

13. Install the cylinder head cover with a new gasket. Tighten fasteners to specifications (**Table 1**).

14. Install inner and outer exhaust covers with new gaskets. Tighten fasteners to specifications (**Table 1**).

15. Install bypass cover and intake manifold/reed valve assembly with new gaskets. Tighten fasteners to specifications (**Table 1**).

16. Install the power head as described in this chapter.

Cylinder Block and Crankcase Assembly (18-40 hp)

1A. Grooved crankcase flange—Install a new spaghetti seal with OMC Adhesive M as described in this chapter.

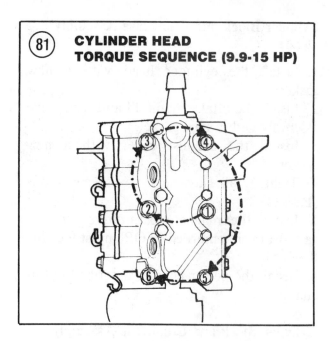

CYLINDER HEAD TORQUE SEQUENCE (9.9-15 HP)

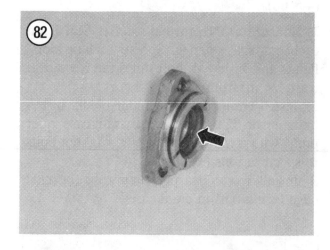

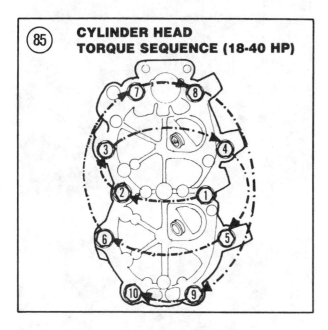

CYLINDER HEAD TORQUE SEQUENCE (18-40 HP)

1B. Flat crankcase flange—Squeeze a 5/16 in. ball of Gel Seal II on each crankcase flange. Spread sealant along flange and inside all bolt holes but keep it at least 1/4 in. from seals.

2. Install crankcase to cylinder block. Install bolts finger-tight, then install crankcase taper pin(s) with a mallet and punch.

3. Tap the bottom of the crankshaft with a mallet to seat the lower main bearing. Wipe the threads of all bolts which enter crankcase cavity through holes with Adhesive M or Gel Seal II as required, then tighten to specifications (**Table 1**). Start with the center bolts and work outwards in a clockwise direction.

4. Drive the old seal from the crankcase head (**Figure 82**) with a punch and mallet. Clean the seal bore and wipe the outer diameter of a new seal with OMC Gasket Sealing Compound. Fit seal on tool part No. 321515 with its lip facing the tool. Press seal into crankcase head until tool bottoms against head.

5. Lubricate 2 new O-rings with Johnson or Evinrude 50/1 oil and install on crankcase head.

6. Install the lower crankcase head with OMC Gasket Sealing Compound on the screw threads. See **Figure 83**. Tighten to specifications (**Table 1**).

> *NOTE*
> *If cylinders have been honed, crankshaft will be more difficult to turn by hand in Step 7. In this case, temporarily install flywheel and crankshaft should turn with a minimal effort.*

7. Rotate the crankshaft several turns to check for binding. If crankshaft does not turn easily, disassemble and correct the interference.

8. Install the cylinder head with a new gasket (**Figure 84**). Tighten bolts to specifications (**Table 1**) following the sequence shown in **Figure 85**.

9. Install the thermostat with a new seal in the cylinder head cavity. Place the spring on top of the thermostat and install the water cover with a new gasket. See **Figure 86**. Tighten the screws to specifications (**Table 1**). The long screw should be installed below the thermostat.

10. Install the inner and outer exhaust covers with new gaskets. See **Figure 87**. Tighten fasteners to specifications (**Table 1**).

11. Install the bypass cover with a new gasket (**Figure 88**). Tighten fasteners to specifications (**Table 1**).

8

12. Install a new reed valve gasket, then install the reed valve. See **Figure 89**. Wipe attaching screw threads with Permatex No. 2 and tighten screw securely.

13. Install the intake manifold with a new gasket (**Figure 90**). Tighten fasteners to specifications (**Table 1**).

14. Connect intake crankcase oil return or recirculation hoses.

15. Install the power head as described in this chapter.

Reed Block Service

The reed block or leaf valve assembly is located behind the intake manifold. **Figure 91** (9.5-15 hp) or **Figure 92** (18-40 hp) show typical reed block assemblies.

The reeds remain in constant contact with the leaf plate until a predetermined crankcase pressure is exerted on them. A reed stop limits the amount of travel from the plate.

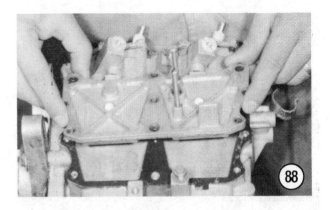

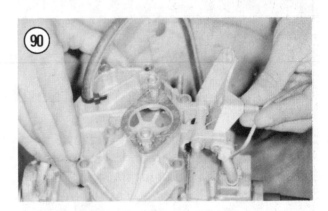

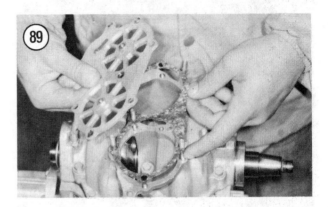

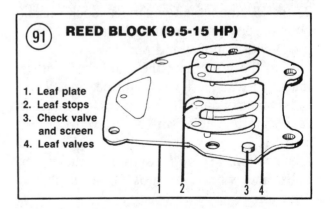

REED BLOCK (9.5-15 HP)

1. Leaf plate
2. Leaf stops
3. Check valve and screen
4. Leaf valves

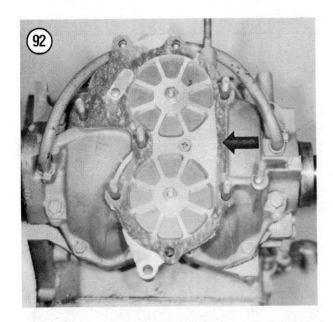

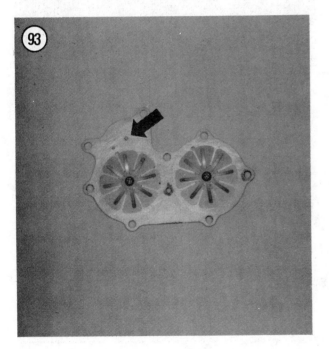

Once the crankcase pressure is removed, the reed returns to contact the plate.

Reeds and reed stops can be disassembled from the plate for cleaning. Do not attempt to bend or flex the reeds if they are distorted or do not contact the plate as designed. If the reeds or reed stops are defective, replace the entire assembly. Whenever the intake manifold is removed, inspect the reed block for signs of gum and varnish, and broken, chipped or distorted reeds. If gum or varnish is present, remove the screws holding the reed stops and reeds to the plate. Carefully clean all components in OMC Engine Cleaner and reinstall.

Some reed blocks contain a recirculation valve hole and reed; others use a recirculation valve and screen assembly. **Figure 93** shows the recirculation valve hole; **Figure 94** shows the recirculation valve reed on the other side of the plate. These require no service beyond an occasional cleaning in OMC Engine Cleaner to remove any gum or varnish.

8

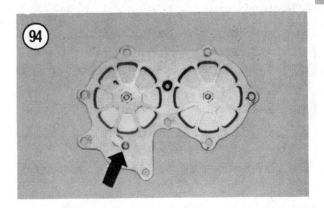

Tables are on the following pages.

Table 1 POWER HEAD TIGHTENING TORQUES

Fastener	in.-lb.	ft.-lb.
Bearing housing-to-cylinder		
2 hp	60-80	
Connecting rod screws		
2, 4, 4.5, 6, 8 hp	60-66	
7.5 hp	60-70	
9.5 hp	90-100	
9.9, 15 hp	48-60	
20 hp (1973)	180-186	
25 hp (1973-1975)	180-186	
25 (1976-on), 35 hp		29-31
Crankcase-to-block bolts		
4, 4.5, 6 (1973),		
7.5 hp	60-80	
5, 6, (1981-on), 7.5		
(1981-on), 8 hp		12-14
9.5 hp	120-145	
9.9, 15 hp	145-170	
20, 25 hp (1973)		
Upper and lower	110-130	
Center	120-130	
20 hp (1982-on)		14-16
25 hp (1974)	120-144	
25, 35 hp		
1976		12-14
1977-1978		18-20
1979-on		14-16
40 hp		
Upper and lower	150-170	
Center	162-168	
Cylinder head bolts		
2, 4, 1973 6 hp	60-80	
5, 6, 8 hp		12-14
7.5 hp	12-14	
9.5, 20 hp (1973)	96-120	
9.9, 15 hp		
1974-1976	145-170	
1977-on		18-20
20 hp (1982-on)		18-20
25 hp (1973-1975)	96-120	
25, 35 hp		
1976		14-16
1977-on		18-20
40 hp		14-16
Intake manifold bolts		
2 hp	60-80	
Power head-to-exhaust housing		
20 hp (1982-on), 25, 35 hp		16-18
Spark plug		17-20

(continued)

Table 1 POWER HEAD TIGHTENING TORQUES (continued)

Fastener	in.-lb.	ft.-lb.
Standard bolts and nuts		
No. 6	7-10	
No. 8	15-22	
No. 10	25-35	2-3
No. 12	35-40	3-4
1/4 in.	60-80	5-7
5/16 in.	120-140	10-12
3/8 in.	220-240	18-20

Table 2 FLYWHEEL NUT TORQUE

	ft.-lb.
2 hp	22-25
4 hp	30-40
6, 9.5 hp	40-45
5, 6, 8 hp	40-50
9.9, 15 hp	45-50
20 hp	
1973	40-45
1982-on	100-105
25 hp (1973-1976)	40-45
25 (1977-on), 35, 40 hp	100-105

Table 3 POWER HEAD SPECIFICATIONS

2 HP	
Standard bore size	1.5668-1.5675 in.
Bore	1.5625 in.
Stroke	1.375 in.
Piston ring	
Width	0.0615-0.0625 in.
Gap	
1973-1975	0.005-0.015 in.
1976-on	0.015-0.025 in.
Side clearance	0.0020-0.0040 in.
Piston-to-cylinder clearance	0.0043-0.0055 in.
Crankshaft bearing clearance	
Upper and lower	Needle bearing
Crankshaft journal diameter	0.7497-0.7502 in.
Connecting rod	
Piston end clearance	0.0004-0.0011 in.
Crankshaft end	Needle bearing
Crankpin diameter	0.6695-0.6700 in.

(continued)

8

Table 3 POWER HEAD SPECIFICATIONS (continued)

4, 4 DELUXE, 4.5 HP	
Standard bore size	1.5643-1.5650 in.
Bore	1.5625 in.
Stroke	1.375 in.
Piston ring	
Width	0.0615-0.0625 in.
Gap	0.005-0.015 in.
Side clearance	0.0020-0.0040 in.
Piston-to-cylinder clearance	
1973-1978	0.0008-0.0020 in.
1979-on	0.0018-0.0030 in.
Crankshaft bearing clearance	
Upper	Needle bearing
Center and lower	0.0013-0.0023 in.
Crankshaft journal diameter	
1973-1978	
Top	0.7515-0.7520 in.
Center	0.6849-0.6854 in.
Bottom	0.6849-0.6854 in.
1979-on	
Top	0.7506-0.7510 in.
Center	0.6685-0.6690 in.
Bottom	0.7498-0.7502 in.
Connecting rod	
Piston end clearance	0.0004-0.0011 in.
Crankshaft end clearance	0.0007-0.0017 in.
Crankpin diameter	
1973-1978	0.6250-0.6255 in.
1979-on	0.6695-0.6700 in.

5, 6, 7.5 AND 8 HP	
Standard bore size	1.9373-1.9380 in.
Bore	1.9375 in.
Stroke	1.700 in.
Piston ring	
Width	0.0615-0.0625 in.
Gap	0.005-0.015 in.
Side clearance	
1973-1979	0.0020-0.0040 in.
1980-on	0.0020-0.0035 in.
Piston-to-cylinder clearance	0.0018-0.0030 in.
Crankshaft bearing clearance	0.0015-0.0025 in.
Crankshaft journal diameter	
1973-1979	0.8075-0.8080 in.
1980-on	
Top	0.87225-0.87725 in.
Center	0.8104-0.81545 in.
Bottom	0.7498-0.7562 in.
Connecting rod	
Piston end clearance	0.0003-0.0010 in.
Crankshaft end clearance	Needle bearing
Crankpin diameter	0.6695-0.6700 in.

(continued)

Table 3 POWER HEAD SPECIFICATIONS (continued)

9.5 HP	
Standard bore size	2.3120-2.3130 in.
Bore	2.3125 in.
Stroke	1.8125 in.
Piston ring	
Width	0.0925-0.0935 in.
Gap	0.007-0.017 in.
Side clearance	0.001-0.0035 in.
Piston-to-cylinder clearance	0.0035-0.0050 in.
Crankshaft bearing clearance	Needle bearings
Crankshaft journal diameter	
Top and bottom	0.8120-0.8125 in.
Center	0.8127-0.8132 in.
Connecting rod	
Piston end	Needle bearing
Crankshaft end	Needle bearing
Crankpin diameter	0.8127-0.8132 in.

9.9 AND 15 HP	
Standard bore size	2.1875-2.1883 in.
Bore	2.188 in.
Stroke	1.760 in.
Piston ring	
Width	
Upper	0.0695-0.0700 in.
Lower	0.0615-0.0625 in.
Gap	0.005-0.015 in.
Side clearance	0.0025-0.0035 in.
Piston-to-cylinder clearance	
1974-1975	0.0040-0.0053 in.
1976-1978	0.0025-0.0053 in.
1979-on	0.0025-0.0038 in.
Crankshaft bearings	Needle bearing
Crankshaft journal diameter	
1974-1975	
Top	0.8752-0.8757 in.
Center and bottom	0.8120-0.8125 in.
1976-on	
Top	0.8757-0.8762 in.
Center and bottom	0.8120-0.8125 in.
Connecting rod	
Piston end clearance	0.000-0.0005 in.
Crankpin diameter	
1974-1979	1.6300-1.6350 in.
1980-on	0.8120-0.8125 in.

8

(continued)

Table 3 POWER HEAD SPECIFICATIONS (continued)

20 AND 25 HP (1973-1976)	
Standard bore size	2.45-2.55 in.
Bore	2.50 in.
Stroke	2.25 in.
Piston ring	
Width	
Upper	0.0895-0.0900 in.
Lower	0.0615-0.0625 in.
Gap	0.007-0.017 in.
Side clearance	0.0020-0.0040 in.
Piston-to-cylinder clearance	0.0033-0.0048 in.
Crankshaft bearings	
Upper and lower	Roller bearing
Center	Needle bearings
Crankshaft journal diameter	0.9995-1.0000 in.
Connecting rod	
Piston end	Needle bearing
Crankshaft end	Needle bearing
Crankpin diameter	1.0000-1.0005 in.

20 HP (1982-ON) 25 HP (1976-ON) 30 HP (1984) 35 HP (1977-ON)	
Standard bore size	2.9995-3.0005 in.
Bore	3.00 in.
Stroke	2.25 in.
Piston ring	
Width	
Upper	0.0895-0.0900 in.
Lower	0.0615-0.0625 in.
Gap	0.007-0.017 in.
Side clearance	0.0015-0.0040 in.
Piston-to-cylinder clearance	
1975-1978	0.0030-0.0050 in.
1979-1982	0.0035-0.0065 in.
1983-on	0.001-0.0034 in.
Crankshaft bearings	
Upper and lower	Roller bearing
Center	Needle bearings
Crankshaft journal diameter	
Top	
1975-1977	1.2495-1.2500 in.
1978-on	1.2510-1.2515 in.
Center	
1975-1977	0.9995-1.0000 in.
1978-1982	1.1810-1.1815 in.
1983-on	1.1833-1.1838 in.
Bottom	0.9842-0.9846 in.
Connecting rod	
Piston end	Needle bearing
Crankshaft end	Needle bearing
Crankpin diameter	1.1823-1.1828 in.

(continued)

Table 3 POWER HEAD SPECIFICATIONS (continued)

40 HP (1973-1976)	
Standard bore size	3.1860-3.1875 in.
Bore	3.1875 in.
Stroke	2.75 in
Piston ring	
Width	
Upper	0.0895-0.0900 in.
Lower	0.0615-0.06525 in.
Gap	0.007-0.017in.
Side clearance	0.0015-0.0040 in.
Piston-to cylinder clearance	0.0030-0.0050 in.
Crankshaft bearings	
Upper and center	Needle bearing
Lower	Roller bearing
Crankshaft journal diameter	
Top	1.4974-1.4979 in.
Center	1.3748-1.3752 in.
Bottom	1.1810-1.1815 in.
Connecting rod	
Piston end	Needle bearing
Crankshaft end	Needle bearing
Crankpin diameter	1.1823-1.1823 in.

8

NOTE: If you own a 1985 or later model, first check the Supplement at the back of the book for any new service information.

Chapter Nine

Gearcase

Torque is transferred from the engine crankshaft to the gearcase by a drive shaft. A pinion gear on the drive shaft meshes with a drive gear in the gearcase to change the vertical power flow into a horizontal flow through the propeller shaft. On Johnson and Evinrude outboards with a shift capability, a sliding clutch engages a forward or reverse gear in the gearcase. This creates a direct coupling that transfers the power flow from the pinion to the propeller shaft.

The gearcase can be removed without removing the entire outboard from the boat. This chapter contains removal, overhaul and installation procedures for the propeller, gearcase and water pump. **Table 1** (specifications) and **Table 2** (tightening torques) are at the end of the chapter.

The gearcases covered in this chapter differ somewhat in design and construction and thus require slightly different service procedures. The chapter is arranged in a normal disassembly/assembly sequence.

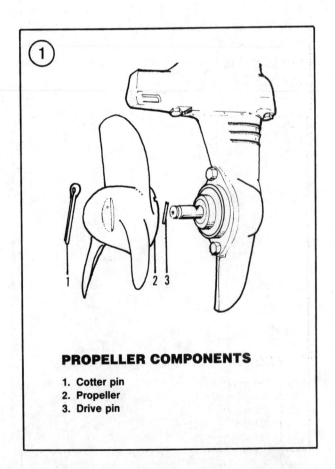

PROPELLER COMPONENTS

1. **Cotter pin**
2. **Propeller**
3. **Drive pin**

When only a partial repair is required, follow the procedure(s) for your gearcase to the point where the faulty parts can be replaced, then reassemble the unit.

Since this chapter covers a wide range of models, the gearcases shown in the accompanying pictures are the most common ones. While it is possible that the components shown in the pictures may not be identical with those being serviced, the step-by-step procedures may be used with all models covered in this manual.

PROPELLER

Johnson and Evinrude outboards use variations of 2 propeller attachment designs. Smaller gearcases use a drive pin that engages a slot in the propeller hub, which is retained by a cotter pin (**Figure 1**). On some models, the cotter pin passes through a cone-type nut that is separate from the propeller.

In this design, a metal pin installed in the propeller shaft engages a recessed slot in the propeller hub. As the shaft rotates, the pin rotates the propeller. The drive pin is designed to break if the propeller hits an obstruction in the water. This design has 2 advantages. The pin absorbs the impact to prevent possible propeller damage. It also alerts the user to the fact that something is wrong, since the engine speed will increase if the pin breaks.

Propellers on the larger gearcases ride on thrust bearings and are retained by a castellated nut and cotter pin (**Figure 2**). An underwater impact is absorbed by the propeller hub.

Removal/Installation

1. To remove the propeller on smaller units:
   a. Remove and discard the cotter pin.
   b. Pull the propeller or propeller and nut off the propeller shaft.
   c. Remove and discard the drive pin from the propeller shaft. Inspect the pin engagement slot in the propeller hub for wear or damage.
   d. Installation is the reverse of removal. Lubricate the propeller shaft with OMC Triple-Guard grease. Use a new drive pin and cotter pin.
2. To remove the propeller on larger units:
   a. Remove and discard the cotter pin.
   b. Remove the castellated nut.
   c. Remove the thrust washer, propeller and thrust bearing assembly from the propeller shaft.
   d. Installation is the reverse of removal. Lubricate propeller shaft with OMC Triple-Guard grease and use a new cotter pin.

WATER PUMP

Johnson and Evinrude outboards use a volume-type or a pressure-type water pump. The 2 can be distinguished by the size and shape of the impeller. Volume-type water pumps use a thin impeller with long vanes;

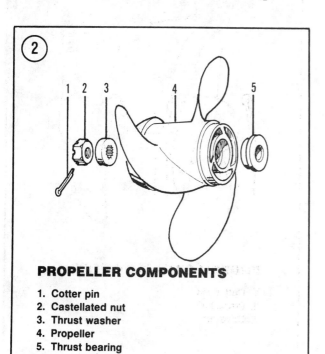

PROPELLER COMPONENTS

1. Cotter pin
2. Castellated nut
3. Thrust washer
4. Propeller
5. Thrust bearing

pressure-type pumps have a thick impeller with short vanes. Both types are serviced in essentially the same manner. An optional chrome water pump available for some models is recommended for use in areas where the water contains considerable sand or silt.

The water pump impeller is secured to the drive shaft by a key that fits between a flat area on the drive shaft and a similar cutout in the impeller hub. As the drive shaft rotates, the impeller rotates with it. Water between the impeller blades and pump housing is pumped up to the power head through the water tube.

All seals and gaskets should be replaced whenever the water pump is removed. Since proper water pump operation is critical to outboard operation, it is also a good idea to install a new impeller at the same time.

Do not turn a used impeller over and reuse it. The impeller rotates clockwise with the drive shaft and the vanes gradually take a "set" in one direction. Turning the impeller over will cause the vanes to move in a direction opposite to that which caused the "set." This will result in premature impeller failure and can damage a power head extensively.

Removal and Disassembly

1. Secure the gearcase in a holding fixture or a vise with protective jaws. If protective jaws are not available, position the gearcase upright in the vise with the skeg between wooden blocks.
2. Remove the water tube from the pump housing. See **Figure 3**.

NOTE
Hold the drive shaft in place on 2 hp gearcases during Step 3 to prevent it from moving up enough to dislodge the pinion gear.

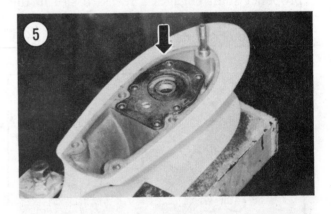
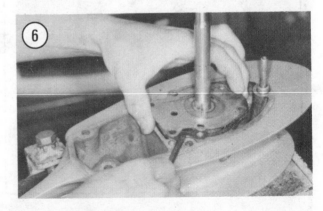

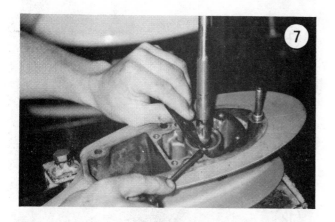

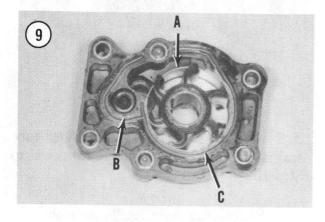

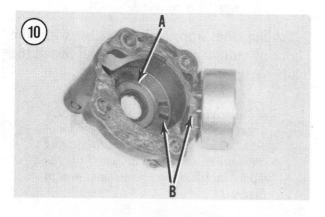

3. Remove the impeller housing screws and washers. Insert screwdrivers at the fore and aft ends of the impeller housing and pry it loose.

NOTE
In extreme cases, the impeller hub may have to be split with a hammer and chisel to remove it in Step 4.

4. Slide the impeller housing up and off the drive shaft (**Figure 4**).

5A. 2 hp gearcase—Remove the impeller from the gearcase cavity. This completes water pump disassembly on this model.

5B. All others—If the impeller did not come off with the impeller housing, carefully pry the impeller up and off the shaft. Remove the drive key.

6. Remove and discard the top impeller plate gasket, if loose. See **Figure 5**. If it is not loose, remove in Step 7 with impeller plate.

7. Carefully pry the impeller plate loose with a screwdriver (**Figure 6**), then slide the plate and gasket (if used) up and off the drive shaft. Discard the gasket.

8. If the bottom impeller plate gasket did not come free with the impeller plate, carefully loosen with a screwdriver tip and scrape off the housing. See **Figure 7**.

9. Remove the nylon water intake screen from the gearcase cavity (**Figure 8**), if so equipped.

Cleaning and Inspection

When removing seals from impeller housing, note and record the direction in which the lip of each seal faces for proper reinstallation.

1. Invert the impeller housing and remove the impeller and impeller cup (A, **Figure 9**).

2. Remove and discard the O-ring or drive shaft seal under the impeller cup. The seal is shown in A, **Figure 10**.

9

3. Remove and discard the shift rod O-ring and bushing (B, **Figure 9**) and spaghetti seal (C, **Figure 9**), if so equipped.

4. Turn the housing right side up and remove and discard the water tube grommet (**Figure 11**). Remove and discard the O-ring, if used.

5. Check the housing for cracks, distortion or melting. Replace as required.

6. Clean all metal parts in solvent and blow dry with compressed air, if available.

7. Carefully remove all gasket residue from the mating surfaces.

8. Check impeller plate and cup for grooving or rough surfaces. Replace if any defects are found.

9. If original impeller is to be reused, check bonding to hub. Check side seal surfaces and vane ends for cracks, tears, wear or a glazed or melted appearance. See **Figure 12**. If any of these defects are noted, do *not* reuse impeller.

10. Check nylon water intake screen for blockage, distortion or other defects. Replace as required.

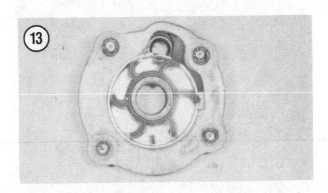

Assembly and Installation

When a new seal is installed in the impeller housing, its lips should face in the direction recorded during disassembly. After installation, wipe the seal lips with OMC Triple-Guard grease.

1A. If impeller housing uses a drive shaft seal, wipe the seal casing with OMC Gasket Sealing Compound and install with a suitable driver.

1B. If impeller housing uses an O-ring, install a new one in the housing groove.

2. Lubricate a new shift rod bushing and O-ring (if used) with OMC HI-VIS Gearcase Lubricant and install in impeller housing.

3. 2-hp gearcase—Install a new water tube seal in the impeller housing and proceed to Step 10.

> *NOTE*
> *Always install a new impeller cup when the impeller is replaced.*

4. Align the impeller cup tabs with the housing cutouts (B, **Figure 10**) and install the cup.

> *CAUTION*
> *If the original impeller is to be reused, install it in the same rotational direction as removed to avoid premature failure. The curl of the blades should be positioned as shown in* ***Figure 13***.

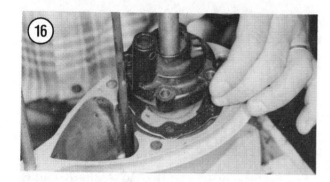

9A. 9.9 and 15 hp—Run a thin bead of OMC Adhesive M on the machined surface of the gearcase that mates with the impeller plate, then install the plate.

9B. All others—Coat both sides of a new impeller plate gasket with OMC Gasket Sealing Compound and install on the gearcase. Install impeller plate. Coat both sides of a second gasket and install. Align gasket and impeller plate holes with those in the gearcase. See **Figure 14**.

10. Coat the drive shaft key flat with OMC Needle Bearing Grease and install the drive key (**Figure 15**).

11. 2-hp gearcase—Coat bottom surface of impeller housing with OMC Adhesive M.

12. Lightly lubricate the drive shaft splines with OMC HI-VIS Gearcase Lubricant and slide the impeller housing and impeller over the drive shaft.

13. Rotate the drive shaft as required to align the drive key with the impeller groove. Press the impeller housing down with a smooth, even motion so impeller hub groove will ride over drive key. See **Figure 16**.

CAUTION
Housing fastener torque is important in Step 14. Excessive torque can cause the pump to crack during operation; insufficient torque may result in leakage and exhaust induction which will cause overheating.

14. Wipe all impeller housing fastener threads with OMC Gasket Sealing Compound and install with washers (if used). See **Figure 17**. Tighten fasteners to specifications (**Table 2**).

GEARCASE

**Removal/Installation
(2 and 4 hp)**

1. Disconnect the spark plug lead as a safety precaution to prevent any accidental starting of the engine during lower unit removal.

5. Lubricate the inside diameter of the impeller cup with a light coat of OMC HI-VIS Gearcase Lubricant and install the impeller with a downward rotating motion.

6. Coat the outside diameter of a new water tube grommet with Scotch Grip Rubber Adhesive 1300. Install grommet so its bosses will fit into the holes in the impeller housing.

7. If impeller housing uses a spaghetti seal (C, **Figure 9**), apply a thin coat of OMC Adhesive M to seal groove, then install the new seal.

8. Install nylon water intake screen in gearcase cavity, if used. See **Figure 8**.

9

2. Remove the propeller as described in this chapter.

3. Remove the 2 screws (2 and 4 hp) or 4 screws (4 hp weedless) holding the gearcase to the exhaust housing. See A, **Figure 18** for 2 and 4 hp.

4. Carefully separate the gearcase from the exhaust housing to prevent damage to the water tube and drive shaft, then remove gearcase.

5. Remove the fill/drain plug(s). The 2 hp, 4 hp weedless and 1973-1980 4 hp use a single plug (B, **Figure 18**); the 1981-on 4 hp has separate fill and drain plugs. Hold the gearcase over a container. Drain the lubricant from the unit.

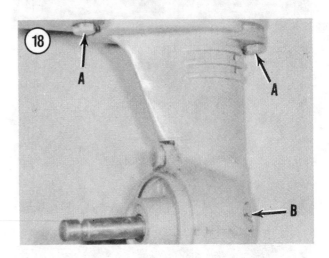

> *NOTE*
> *If the lubricant is creamy in color or metallic particles are found in Step 6, the gearcase must be completely disassembled to determine and correct the cause of the problem.*

6. Wipe a small amount of lubricant on a finger and rub the finger and thumb together. Check for the presence of metallic particles in the lubricant. Note the color of the lubricant. A white or creamy color indicates water in the lubricant. Check the drain container for signs of water separation from the lubricant.

7. If the water tube remained in the exhaust housing, remove it from the grommet.

8. On 4 hp models, remove and discard the drive shaft O-ring.

9. Mount the gearcase in a suitable holding fixture.

10. To reinstall the gearcase, lubricate the exhaust housing water tube grommet with liquid soap.

11. On 4 hp models, install a new drive shaft O-ring.

> *CAUTION*
> *Do not grease the top of the drive shaft in Step 12. This may excessively preload the drive shaft and crankshaft when the mounting bolts are tightened and cause a premature failure of the power head or gearcase.*

12. Lightly lubricate the drive shaft splines with OMC Moly Lube.

> *CAUTION*
> *Do not rotate the flywheel counterclockwise in Step 13. This can damage the water pump impeller.*

13. Position gearcase under exhaust housing and align water tube with grommet and drive shaft splines with the crankshaft. On 1981 and later 4 hp models, also align the shift rod to engage the shift rod bushing. Push the gearcase into place, rotating the flywheel clockwise as required to let the drive shaft and crankshaft engage.

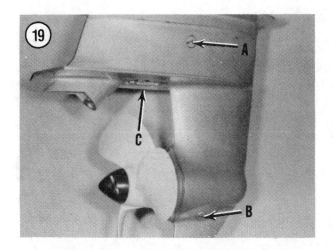

14. Wipe gearcase screw threads with OMC Gasket Sealing Compound. Install screws and tighten to specifications (**Table 2**).

15. Install the propeller as described in this chapter.

16. Reconnect the spark plug lead and refill the gearcase with the proper type and quantity of lubricant. See Chapter Four.

Removal/Installation
(4 Deluxe, 4.5, 5, 6 1982-on,
7.5 and 8 hp)

1. Disconnect the spark plug leads as a safety precaution to prevent any accidental starting of the engine during lower unit removal.

2. Place a container under the gearcase. Remove the oil level plug (A, **Figure 19**), then remove the drain/fill plug (B, **Figure 19**). Drain the lubricant from the unit.

NOTE
If the lubricant is creamy in color or metallic particles are found in Step 3, the gearcase must be completely disassembled to determine and correct the cause of the problem.

3. Wipe a small amount of lubricant on a finger and rub the finger and thumb together. Check for the presence of metallic particles in the lubricant. Note the color of the lubricant. A white or creamy color indicates water in the lubricant. Check the drain container for signs of water separation from the lubricant.

4. Remove the propeller as described in this chapter.

5. Move the shift lever into FORWARD. If necessary, rotate the propeller shaft slightly to help unit engage.

6. Remove the gearcase screw just below the lower steering pivot point (**Figure 20**).

7. Remove the 2 gearcase attaching screws at the rear of the zinc anode cavity (C, **Figure 19**).

8. Separate the gearcase from the exhaust housing and remove from the unit.

9. Remove and discard the drive shaft O-ring.

10. Mount the gearcase in a suitable holding fixture.

11. To reinstall the gearcase, lubricate the exhaust housing water pump grommet with liquid soap.

12. Install a new drive shaft O-ring.

13. Make sure the shift lever is in FORWARD gear.

CAUTION
Do not grease the top of the drive shaft in Step 14. This may excessively preload the drive shaft and crankshaft when the mounting bolts are tightened and cause a premature failure of the power head or gearcase.

14. Lightly lubricate the drive shaft splines with OMC Moly Lube.

9

CAUTION
Do not rotate the flywheel counterclockwise in Step 15. This can damage the water pump impeller.

15. Position gearcase under exhaust housing. Align water tube with grommet, drive shaft with crankshaft splines and the shift rod with the shift rod bushing. Push the gearcase into place, rotating the flywheel clockwise as required to let the drive shaft and crankshaft engage.

16. Install gearcase screws and tighten to specifications (**Table 2**).

17. Install the propeller as described in this chapter.

18. Reconnect the spark plug leads and refill the gearcase with the proper type and quantity of lubricant. See Chapter Four.

Removal/Installation
(1973-1979 6;
All 9.5, 9.9, 15 and 40 hp)

1. Disconnect the spark plug leads as a safety precaution to prevent any accidental starting of the engine during lower unit removal.

NOTE
Figure 21 shows the plugs on the starboard side. On some earlier models, they are located on the port side.

2. Place a container under the gearcase. Remove the oil level plug (A, **Figure 21**), then remove the slotted head drain/fill plug (B, **Figure 21**). Do *not* remove the Phillips head pivot pin (C, **Figure 21**). Drain the lubricant from the unit.

NOTE
If the lubricant is creamy in color or metallic particles are found in Step 3, the gearcase must be completely disassembled to determine and correct the cause of the problem.

3. Wipe a small amount of lubricant on a finger and rub the finger and thumb together.

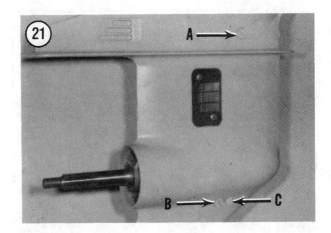

Check for the presence of metallic particles in the lubricant. Note the color of the lubricant. A white or creamy color indicates water in the lubricant. Check the drain container for signs of water separation from the lubricant.

4. Remove the propeller as described in this chapter.

5. Move the shift lever into FORWARD. If necessary, rotate the propeller shaft slightly to help unit engage.

6. Remove the 4 or 6 screws holding the gearcase to the exhaust housing. If equipped with an extension housing, remove the extension-to-exhaust housing screws.

7. Separate the gearcase or gearcase extension from the exhaust housing enough to expose the shift rod connector. Remove the lower connector screw. See **Figure 22**.

8. Remove the gearcase or gearcase and extension from the exhaust housing.

9. Remove and discard the drive shaft O-ring.

10. Mount the gearcase in a suitable holding fixture. On models with a gearcase extension, remove the extension from the gearcase.

11. To reinstall the gearcase, install the extension, if so equipped, and make sure the extension exhaust seal is in place.

12. Install a new drive shaft O-ring.

13. Pull up on the shift rod to engage REVERSE gear. Make sure the shift lever on the motor is in the REVERSE position.

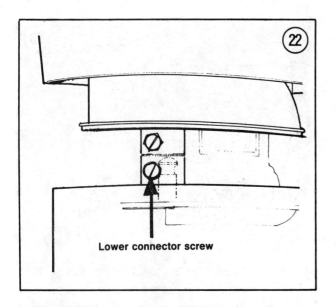

Lower connector screw

CAUTION
Do not grease the top of the drive shaft in Step 14. This may excessively preload the drive shaft and crankshaft when the mounting bolts are tightened and cause a premature failure of the power head or gearcase.

14. Lightly lubricate the drive shaft splines with OMC Moly Lube. Apply a thin bead of OMC Adhesive M to the machined area of the gearcase directly to the rear of the water pump.

CAUTION
Do not rotate the flywheel counterclockwise in Step 15. This can damage the water pump impeller.

NOTE
If drive shaft has a pin installed in its end, the pin must be aligned with the pin slot in the exhaust housing in Step 15.

15. Position gearcase under exhaust housing. Align extension housing water tube with impeller housing grommet, drive shaft with crankshaft splines and the shift rod with the shift rod connector. Push the gearcase into position until the shift rod connector screw can be installed, rotating the flywheel

clockwise as required to let the drive shaft and crankshaft engage.
16. Install and tighten the shift rod connector screw securely. See **Figure 22**. Seat the gearcase against the exhaust housing.
17. Wipe gearcase or extension screw threads with OMC Gasket Sealing Compound. Install screws and tighten to specifications (**Table 2**).
18. Install the propeller as described in this chapter.
19. Reconnect the spark plug leads and refill the gearcase with the proper type and quantity of lubricant. See Chapter Four.

Removal/Installation
(18, 20, 25 and 35 hp)

1. Disconnect the spark plug leads as a safety precaution to prevent any accidental starting of the engine during lower unit removal.
2. Place a container under the gearcase. Remove the oil level plug, then remove the slotted head drain/fill plug. Do *not* remove the Phillips head pivot pin. Drain the lubricant from the unit.

NOTE
If the lubricant is creamy in color or metallic particles are found in Step 3, the gearcase must be completely disassembled to determine and correct the cause of the problem.

3. Wipe a small amount of lubricant on a finger and rub the finger and thumb together. Check for the presence of metallic particles in the lubricant. Note the color of the lubricant. A white or creamy color indicates water in the lubricant. Check the drain container for signs of water separation from the lubricant.
4. Remove the propeller as described in this chapter.
5. Move the shift lever into FORWARD. If necessary, rotate the propeller shaft slightly to help unit engage.
6A. 1982-on 35 hp—Remove the water intake screen on both sides of the gearcase to

9

provide access to the shift rod connector (**Figure 23**). Hold the lower connector with a 1/2 in. open-end wrench and turn the upper connector with a second wrench. When the shift rod disengages, remove and keep the plastic keeper between the connectors.

6B. All others—Remove the exhaust housing cover plate and gasket to provide access to the shift rod connector screw. See **Figure 24**. Remove the lower connector screw.

7. Remove the fasteners holding the gearcase to the exhaust housing. Some models use a nut and 2 screws on each side (**Figure 25**) while others use 5 screws. If equipped with an extension housing, remove the extension-to-exhaust housing fasteners.

8. Carefully withdraw the gearcase or gearcase extension from the exhaust housing. If the impeller housing spacer (arrow, **Figure 26**) does not come out with the gearcase, remove it from the extension housing and discard the O-rings.

9. Mount the gearcase in a holding fixture. On models with a gearcase extension, remove the extension from the gearcase.

10. To reinstall the gearcase, install the extension, if so equipped, and make sure the extension exhaust seal is in place.

11. Shift the gearcase into FORWARD gear. Make sure the shift lever on the motor is in the FORWARD position.

12. Make sure impeller housing spacer is properly positioned at the base of the driveshaft and the water tube is installed in the inner exhaust tube.

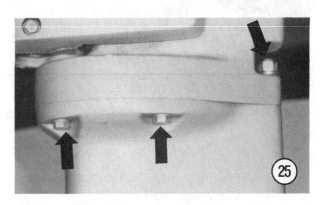

CAUTION
Do not grease the top of the drive shaft in Step 13. This may excessively preload the drive shaft and crankshaft when the mounting bolts are tightened and cause a premature failure of the power head or gearcase.

13. Lightly lubricate the drive shaft splines with OMC Moly Lube.

CAUTION
Do not rotate the flywheel counterclockwise in Step 14. This can damage the water pump impeller.

14. Position gearcase under exhaust housing. Align extension housing water tube with water pump grommet, drive shaft with crankshaft splines and the shift rod with the shift rod connector (**Figure 27**). Rotate the flywheel clockwise as required to let the drive shaft and crankshaft engage.

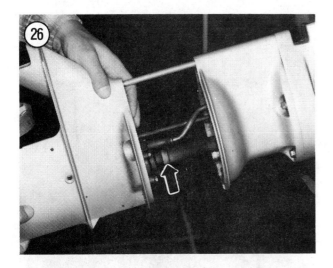

15. Wipe gearcase or extension screw/stud threads with OMC Gasket Sealing Compound. Install screws/nut and tighten to specifications (**Table 2**).

16A. 1982-on 35 hp—Install the plastic keeper on the upper shift rod. Move the shift lever on the motor until the upper shift rod engages the lower shift rod connector. Hold the lower connector with a 1/2 in. open-end wrench and tighten the upper connector with a second wrench. Install the water intake screens.

16B. All others—Align lower shift rod groove with connector screw hole. Install screw with washer and tighten to 10-12 ft.-lb. Install exhaust housing cover plate with a new

gasket coated with OMC Adhesive M. Tighten securely.

17. Install the propeller as described in this chapter.

18. Move shift lever on motor to NEUTRAL position. The propeller should rotate freely. Loosen both shift lever screws. Move shift actuator cam until lockout lever detents into cam notch. Tighten shift lever screws to 60-84 in.-lb.

19. Reconnect the spark plug leads and refill the gearcase with the proper type and quantity of lubricant. See Chapter Four.

Cleaning and Inspection (All Models)

1. Clean all parts in fresh solvent. Blow dry with compressed air, if available.

2. Clean all nut and screw threads thoroughly if OMC Screw Lock or OMC Nut Lock has been used. Soak nuts and screws in solvent and use a fine wire brush to remove residue.

3. Remove and discard all O-rings, gaskets and seals. Clean all residue from gasket mating surfaces.

4. Check drive shaft splines for wear or damage. If gearcase has struck a submerged object, the drive shaft and propeller shaft may suffer severe damage. Replace drive shaft as required and check crankshaft splines for similar wear or damage.

5. Check propeller shaft splines and threads for wear, rust or corrosion. See A, **Figure 28**. Replace shaft as necessary.

6. Install V-blocks under the drive shaft bearing surfaces at each end of the shaft. Slowly rotate the shaft while watching the crankshaft end. Replace the shaft if any signs of wobble are noted.

7. Repeat Step 6 with the propeller shaft. Also check the shaft surfaces where oil seal lips make contact. Replace the shaft as required.

9

8. Check bearing housing and needle bearing for wear or damage. See **Figure 29**. Replace as required.

9. Check bearing housing contact points on the propeller shaft (B, **Figure 28**). If shaft shows signs of pitting, grooving, scoring, heat discoloration or embedded metallic particles, replace shaft and bearings.

10. Check water pump as described in this chapter. Check and clean water intake screen as required.

11. Check all shift components for wear or damage. Look for excessive wear on the shift lever, cradle (A, **Figure 30**), shifter shaft and clutch dog engagement surfaces (B, **Figure 30**). Replace as required.

12. Clean all roller bearings with solvent and lubricate with OMC HI-VIS Gearcase Lube to prevent rusting. Check bearings for rust, corrosion, flat spots or excessive wear. Replace as required.

13. Check pinion gear needle bearing and thrust washers for wear or damage (**Figure 31**). Replace as required.

14. Check the forward, reverse and pinion gear for wear or damage. See A, **Figure 32** (typical). Check clutch engagement dogs (B, **Figure 32**). If clutch dogs or teeth are pitted, chipped, broken or excessively worn, replace the gear.

15. Check gearcase upper drive shaft bearing and pinion bearing for wear or damage. Replace pinion bearing as required. If upper drive shaft bearing requires replacement, replace the bearing and housing as an assembly.

16. Check the propeller for nicks, cracks or damaged blades. Minor nicks can be removed with a file, taking care to retain the shape of the propeller. Replace any propeller with bent, cracked or badly chipped blades.

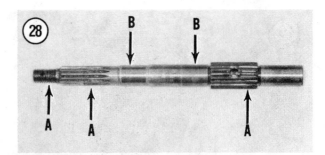

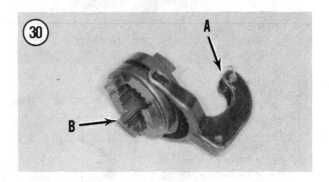

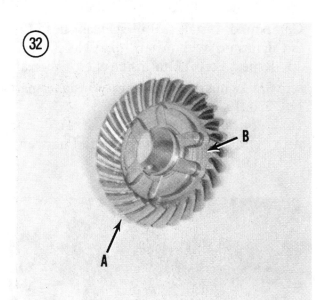

(32)

Disassembly/Assembly
(2 hp and 1973-1980 4 hp)

Refer to **Figure 33** for this procedure.

1. Remove the gearcase as described in this chapter.

2. Secure the gearcase in a holding fixture or a vise with protective jaws. If protective jaws are not available, position the gearcase upright with the skeg between wooden blocks.

3. Remove the water pump attaching screws. Pull the drive shaft and impeller housing assembly up and out of the gearcase. Remove the impeller housing from the drive shaft.

4. Remove the impeller from the gearcase cavity.

5. Remove the 2 gearcase head screws. Tap the gearcase head ears with a mallet to break

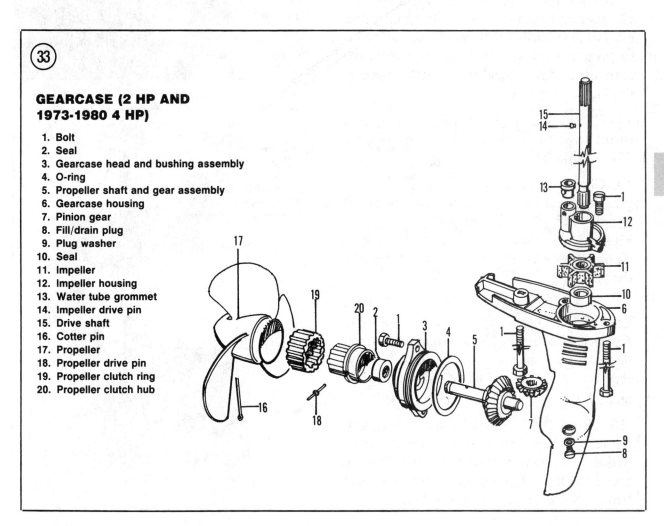

(33)

**GEARCASE (2 HP AND
1973-1980 4 HP)**

1. Bolt
2. Seal
3. Gearcase head and bushing assembly
4. O-ring
5. Propeller shaft and gear assembly
6. Gearcase housing
7. Pinion gear
8. Fill/drain plug
9. Plug washer
10. Seal
11. Impeller
12. Impeller housing
13. Water tube grommet
14. Impeller drive pin
15. Drive shaft
16. Cotter pin
17. Propeller
18. Propeller drive pin
19. Propeller clutch ring
20. Propeller clutch hub

9

the seal (**Figure 34**), then rotate the head off the propeller shaft and gear assembly.

6. Remove and discard the gearcase head O-ring.

7. Remove and discard the gearcase head seal.

8. Remove the propeller shaft and gear assembly.

9A. Standard gearcase—Reach inside the gearcase housing and remove the pinion gear.

9B. Weedless gearcase—Reinsert drive shaft and tap on its end to dislodge the thrust bearing holding the pinion gear. Remove the bearing, pinion gear and drive shaft.

10. Remove the drive shaft seal with universal seal remover part No. 391259.

11. Clean and inspect all parts as described in this chapter. Check drive shaft bushing in gearcase. If worn or damaged, replace the gearcase housing.

12. Coat the metal case of a new gearcase head seal with OMC Gasket Sealing Compound. Install seal in gearcase head (lip facing inward) with installer part No. 330219.

13. Repeat Step 12 to install the drive shaft seal (lip facing downward) with installer part No. 330219.

14. Lubricate a new gearcase head O-ring with OMC HI-VIS Gearcase Lubricant. Install O-ring on gearcase head.

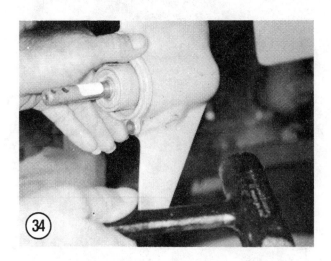

③④

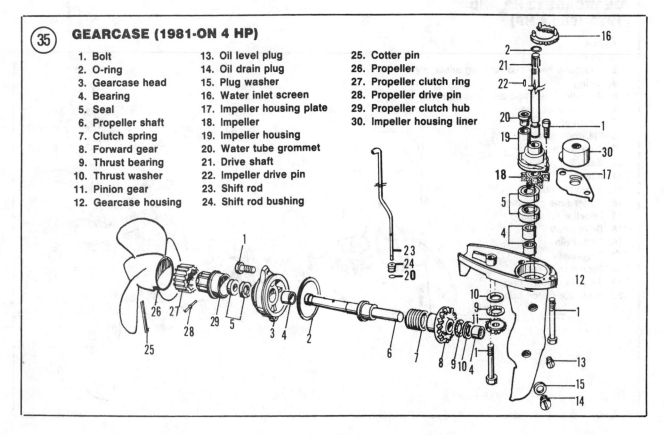

③⑤ **GEARCASE (1981-ON 4 HP)**

1. Bolt
2. O-ring
3. Gearcase head
4. Bearing
5. Seal
6. Propeller shaft
7. Clutch spring
8. Forward gear
9. Thrust bearing
10. Thrust washer
11. Pinion gear
12. Gearcase housing

13. Oil level plug
14. Oil drain plug
15. Plug washer
16. Water inlet screen
17. Impeller housing plate
18. Impeller
19. Impeller housing
20. Water tube grommet
21. Drive shaft
22. Impeller drive pin
23. Shift rod
24. Shift rod bushing

25. Cotter pin
26. Propeller
27. Propeller clutch ring
28. Propeller drive pin
29. Propeller clutch hub
30. Impeller housing liner

15. Slant the gearcase in the holding fixture so the pinion gear can be installed and will remain in place:

   a. Standard gearcase—Insert pinion gear.
   b. Weedless gearcase—Insert pinion gear and thrust bearing. The boss on the bearing must engage the 2 bosses in the gearcase.

16. Install the propeller shaft and gear assembly to engage the pinion gear.

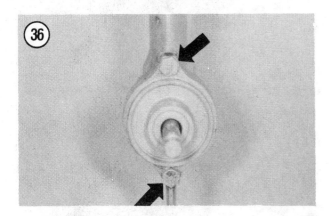

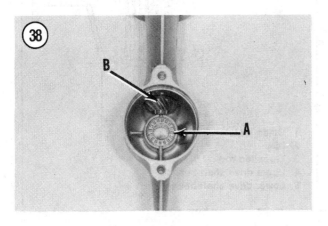

17. Install the drive shaft in the gearcase. Rotate drive shaft to engage pinion gear, hold propeller gear from turning and turn drive shaft until it is fully seated in the pinion gear.

18. Coat gearcase head screw threads with OMC Gasket Sealing Compound. Install standard gearcase head with the flat on the sealing surface facing the upper screw hole in the gearcase. Align gearcase head and gearcase match marks on weedless model. Tighten screws to specifications (**Table 2**).

19. Pressure and vacuum test the gearcase as described in this chapter.

20. Install the water pump assembly as described in this chapter.

21. Install the gearcase as described in this chapter. Fill with the recommended type and quantity of lubricant. See Chapter Four.

22. Check gearcase lubricant level after engine has been run. Change the lubricant after 10 hours of operation (break-in period). See Chapter Four.

Disassembly/Assembly (1981-on 4 hp)

Refer to **Figure 35** for this procedure.

1. Remove the gearcase as described in this chapter.

2. Secure the gearcase in a holding fixture or a vise with protective jaws. If protective jaws are not available, position the gearcase upright with the skeg between wooden blocks.

3. Remove the water pump as described in this chapter.

4. Pull the drive shaft out of the gearcase.

5. Remove the 2 gearcase head screws (**Figure 36**).

6. Tap the gearcase head ears with a mallet to break the seal, then rotate the head free of the gearcase and remove with the propeller shaft and gear assembly. See **Figure 37**.

7. If the forward gear thrust washer and bearing assembly did not come out with the propeller shaft assembly, remove them from the gearcase. See A, **Figure 38**.

9

8. Remove the pinion gear (B, **Figure 38**) and thrust washer/bearing assembly from the gearcase. Place the washer/bearing assembly in a separate container to prevent it from being mixed up with the forward gear washer/bearing assembly.

9. Inspect the propeller shaft, clutch spring and forward gear assembly. Do not disassemble unless necessary:

a. If further disassembly is indicated by your inspection, insert an appropriate size punch in the propeller shaft drive pin hole.

b. Hold the forward gear from moving and rotate the propeller shaft in a counterclockwise direction while pulling outward on it. The shaft and gear will separate (**Figure 39**).

c. Carefully remove the spring to prevent distorting its coils. If the coils do not touch each other at all points, replace the spring.

d. Reassemble the propeller shaft components by reversing steps a-c. The tanged end of the spring should face the gear.

e. Install the forward gear thrust bearing and thrust washer on the propeller shaft in that order.

10. Remove and discard the gearcase head seals (**Figure 40**).

11. Place the gearcase head on a flat surface and remove the needle bearing (A, **Figure 41**) with a suitable driver. Remove and discard the O-ring (B, **Figure 41**).

12. Clean and inspect all parts as described in this chapter.

13. Coat the metal case of 2 new gearcase head seals with OMC Gasket Sealing Compound. Install the inner seal (lip facing inward) with installer part No. 327572, then install the outer seal (lip facing outward) with the same tool.

14. Pack the cavity between the 2 new seals with OMC Triple-Guard grease.

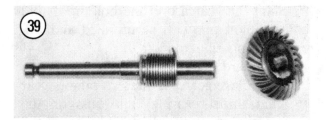

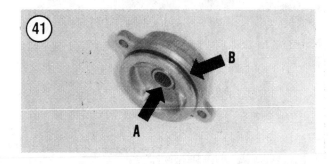

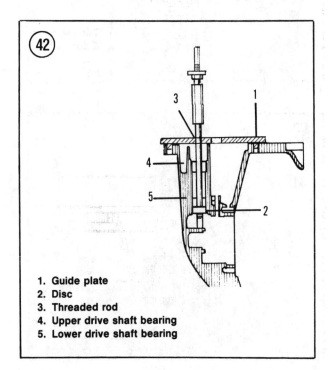

1. Guide plate
2. Disc
3. Threaded rod
4. Upper drive shaft bearing
5. Lower drive shaft bearing

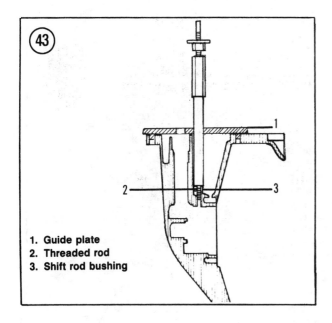

43

1. Guide plate
2. Threaded rod
3. Shift rod bushing

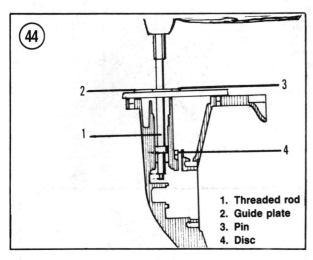

44

1. Threaded rod
2. Guide plate
3. Pin
4. Disc

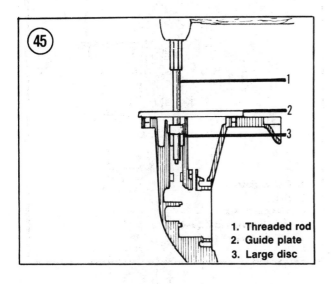

45

1. Threaded rod
2. Guide plate
3. Large disc

15. Lubricate a new O-ring with OMC HI-VIS Gearcase Lubricant and install on gearcase head.

16. Turn the gearcase head over and install a new bearing with tool part No. 392091. Lettered side of bearing must face tool to prevent bearing damage.

17. Remove the 2 drive shaft seals from the gearcase with tool part No. 391259.

18. If the upper and lower drive shaft bearings require removal, assemble the components of tool part No. 392092 as shown in **Figure 42**. Attach a slide hammer and remove the 2 bearings.

19. If the shift rod bushing requires removal, assemble the guide plate and rod from tool part No. 392092 as shown in **Figure 43**. Thread rod into bushing, attach a slide hammer and remove the bushing and O-ring.

20. If the forward gearcase bearing requires removal, assemble tool part No. 391259 with puller jaws in a vertical position and remove the bearing.

21. If shift rod bushing was removed, assemble tool part No. 392092 installer and rod. Fit a new bushing on the installer (O-ring facing down) and coat outside of bushing with OMC Adhesive M. Drive bushing into gearcase with a mallet until fully seated.

22. If forward gearcase bearing was removed, support the gearcase nose on a block of wood. Install a new bearing with tool part No. 392091 and a mallet. Lettered side of bearing should face tool to prevent bearing damage.

23. If upper and lower drive shaft bearings were removed, reinstall as follows:

a. Lower bearing—Assemble tool part No. 392092 components as shown in **Figure 44**. With the lettered side of the bearing facing the tool, drive it in place until the pin touches the guide plate.

b. Upper bearing—Assemble tool part No. 392092 components as shown in **Figure 45**. With the lettered side of the bearing

9

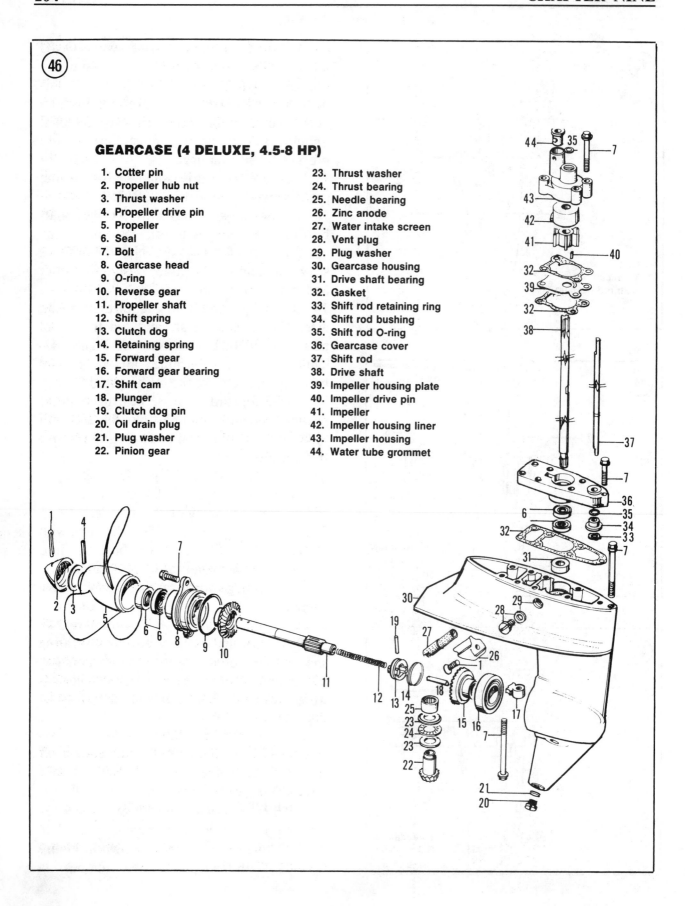

46

GEARCASE (4 DELUXE, 4.5-8 HP)

1. Cotter pin
2. Propeller hub nut
3. Thrust washer
4. Propeller drive pin
5. Propeller
6. Seal
7. Bolt
8. Gearcase head
9. O-ring
10. Reverse gear
11. Propeller shaft
12. Shift spring
13. Clutch dog
14. Retaining spring
15. Forward gear
16. Forward gear bearing
17. Shift cam
18. Plunger
19. Clutch dog pin
20. Oil drain plug
21. Plug washer
22. Pinion gear
23. Thrust washer
24. Thrust bearing
25. Needle bearing
26. Zinc anode
27. Water intake screen
28. Vent plug
29. Plug washer
30. Gearcase housing
31. Drive shaft bearing
32. Gasket
33. Shift rod retaining ring
34. Shift rod bushing
35. Shift rod O-ring
36. Gearcase cover
37. Shift rod
38. Drive shaft
39. Impeller housing plate
40. Impeller drive pin
41. Impeller
42. Impeller housing liner
43. Impeller housing
44. Water tube grommet

facing the tool, drive it in place until firmly seated.

24. Coat the metal case of 2 new gearcase drive shaft seals with OMC Gasket Sealing Compound. Install the inner seal (lip facing inward) with installer part No. 327431, then install the outer seal (lip facing outward) with the same tool. Pack the cavity between the 2 new seals with OMC Triple-Guard grease.

25. Slant the gearcase in the holding fixture so that the pinion gear can be installed and will remain in place. Install the thrust washer, thrust bearing and pinion gear in that order.

26. Lubricate the drive shaft from the pinion gear end to the water pump drive key flat with OMC HI-VIS Gearcase Lubricant. Install drive shaft in gearcase and rotate it until it is secured to the pinion gear.

27. Install the water pump as described in this chapter.

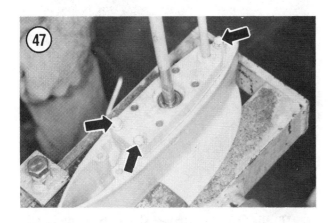

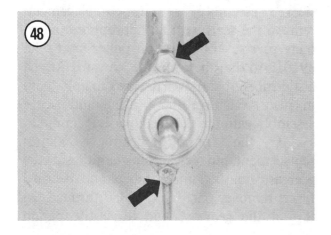

28. Install the propeller shaft and forward gear/bearing assembly in the gearcase.

29. Cover the groove in the propeller shaft with a single layer of cellophane tape to prevent it from damaging the gearcase head seals.

30. Lubricate the gearcase head O-ring with OMC HI-VIS Gearcase Lubricant. Install gearcase head over propeller shaft and seat in the gearcase. Remove the cellophane tape from the shaft groove.

31. Coat the gearcase head screw threads with OMC Gasket Sealing Compound. Install and tighten screws to specifications (**Table 2**).

32. Pressure and vacuum test the gearcase as described in this chapter.

33. Install the gearcase as described in this chapter. Fill with the recommended type and quantity of lubricant. See Chapter Four.

34. Check gearcase lubricant level after engine has been run. Change the lubricant after 10 hours of operation (break-in period). See Chapter Four.

Disassembly/Assembly
(4 Deluxe, 4.5,
5, 6, 7.5 and 8 hp)

Refer to **Figure 46** for this procedure.

1. Remove the gearcase as described in this chapter.

2. Secure the gearcase in a holding fixture or a vise with protective jaws. If protective jaws are not available, position the gearcase upright with the skeg between wooden blocks.

3. Remove the water pump as described in this chapter.

4. Remove the 3 gearcase cover screws (**Figure 47**). Lift the cover up and slide if off the drive shaft and shift rod. Remove and discard the gasket.

5. Pull the drive shaft and shift rod from the gearcase.

6. Remove the 2 gearcase head screws (**Figure 48**).

7. Tap the gearcase head ears with a mallet to turn the cover about 15°, then drive the head rearward by alternately tapping on the ears until the O-ring comes out of the gearcase. Remove the gearcase head and propeller shaft as an assembly. See **Figure 49**.

8. Separate the gearcase head and reverse gear/thrust washer from the propeller shaft. Remove the plunger from the front of the shaft.

9. Carefully lift one end of the clutch dog retaining spring and insert a screwdriver blade under it as shown in **Figure 50**. Holding the screwdriver in one position, rotate the propeller shaft to unwind the spring.

10. Insert tool part No. 390766 in the propeller shaft end to compress the shifter spring. See **Figure 51**.

11. Compress the spring and remove the clutch dog pin. Remove the tool and slide the clutch dog off the shaft. The shifter spring will protrude from the shaft. **Figure 52** shows the components of the disassembled propeller shaft.

12. Reinsert the disassembled propeller shaft in the gearcase and engage the forward gear. Slap the end of the shaft upward with the palm of your hand to pop the forward gear loose. Remove the shaft, reach inside the housing and remove the forward gear.

13. With the forward gear removed, reach inside the housing again and tilt the gearcase until the shift cam falls into your hand. Remove the shift cam from the housing.

14. Move the gearcase back to a vertical position while holding one hand under the pinion gear. The gear, 2 thrust washers and a thrust bearing will drop into your hand (**Figure 53**).

15. If the forward gear bearing race requires replacement, remove with puller part No. 391012 and a slide hammer. Make sure puller jaws fit into the grooves in the gearcase casting behind the bearing race.

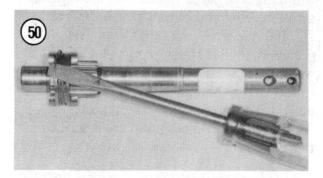

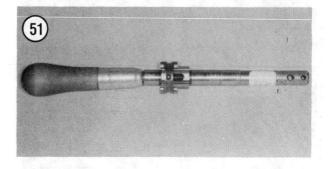

16. If the upper drive shaft bearing and sleeve assembly requires replacement, remove the seals with an appropriate puller, then reverse the jaws of puller part No. 391012 so that their tips face inward. Stretch a stiff rubber band over the jaws to hold them in place. Remove the bearing and sleeve assembly with the puller and a slide hammer.

17. If the pinion bearing requires replacement, put a clean shop cloth inside the gearcase housing under the pinion bearing. Insert remover part No. 319880 through the top of the gearcase and drive the pinion

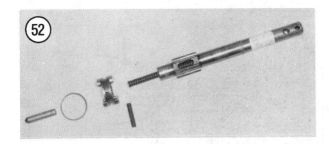

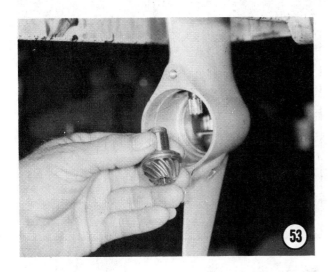

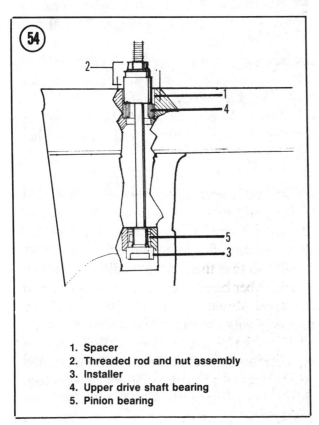

1. Spacer
2. Threaded rod and nut assembly
3. Installer
4. Upper drive shaft bearing
5. Pinion bearing

bearing out. Remove the shop cloth and bearing.

18. Check the water intake screen on the gearcase. If clogged, damaged or otherwise defective, carefully depress the tab and slide the screen from its cavity. If the tab breaks off during screen removal, install a new screen.

19. Check the zinc anode fastened to the bottom of the anti-ventilation plate. If less than 50 percent of the anode remains, remove the attaching screw and install a new anode.

20. Remove the O-ring from the gearcase head. Temporarily reinstall the head in the gearcase with both screws. Install an appropriate puller and slide hammer and remove the 2 seals.

21. Remove the gearcase cover seals with tool part No. 391259.

22. Use the shift rod to pry the shift rod bushing from the gearcase cover. Remove and discard the O-ring.

23. Clean and inspect all components as described in this chapter.

24. Coat the metal case of 2 new gearcase head seals with OMC Gasket Sealing Compound. Install the narrow seal (lip facing inward) with installer part No. 326548, then install the wide seal (lip facing outward) with the same tool. Pack the cavity between the 2 new seals with OMC Triple-Guard grease.

25. Coat the metal case of 2 new gearcase cover seals with OMC Gasket Sealing Compound. Install the seals back-to-back with installer part No. 326547. Pack the cavity between the 2 new seals with OMC Triple-Guard grease.

26. Lubricate a new shift rod O-ring with OMC Triple-Guard grease and install it in the gearcase cover cavity.

27. Run a thin bead of OMC Adhesive M on a new shift rod bushing. Install bushing in gearcase cover and allow Adhesive M to dry.

28. If the pinion and upper drive shaft bearings were removed, refer to **Figure 54**:

9

a. Assemble components of tool part No. 383173 with spacer part No. 383174.

b. Install upper drive shaft bearing (lettered side up) under the spacer.

c. Install pinion bearing (lettered side down) on installer part No. 319878.

d. Insert bearing/installer through propeller bore and thread on installer rod.

e. Tighten the nut at the top of the rod until both bearings are fully seated.

f. If only one of these bearings was removed, the new one can be installed with the same tools and procedure, omitting the use of the tools for the other bearing.

29. Coat the metal case of 2 new drive shaft seals with OMC Gasket Sealing Compound. Install seals back-to-back with installer part No. 326554. Pack the cavity between the seals with OMC Triple-Guard grease.

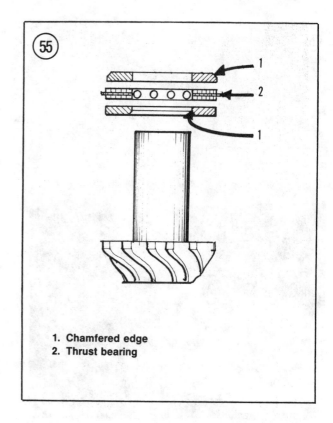

1. Chamfered edge
2. Thrust bearing

NOTE
If either the forward gear bearing or bearing race requires replacement, install a new bearing/race assembly.

30. If the forward bearing race was removed, install with tool part No. 326025 and a mallet until fully seated.

31. If the forward gear or bearing requires replacement, separate the two with a universal puller and arbor press. Install the bearing to the gear with an appropriate mandrel and arbor press.

32. Insert the shift cam in the gearcase housing with the flat on the cam facing the port side of the housing. Hold cam in that position and slide shift rod (retaining ring end first) into the gearcase, rotating it to engage the cam.

33. Coat both sides of a new gearcase cover gasket with OMC Adhesive M. Install the cover and gasket. Wipe the screw threads with OMC Screw Lock and tighten to specifications (**Table 2**).

34. Sandwich the pinion gear bearing between the 2 thrust washers. The thrust washer with the inside chamfer must rest against the pinion shoulder. The chamfered edge of the other thrust washer must face away. See **Figure 55**.

35. Invert the gearcase in the holding fixture and install the pinion gear/bearing/washer assembly.

36. Insert the forward gear in the gearcase, then install the propeller shaft in the gear and pull up sharply on the shaft to snap the gear in its proper position. This will hold the pinion gear in place. See **Figure 56**. Remove the propeller shaft and return the gearcase to an upright position.

37. Insert shifter spring in propeller shaft. Install clutch dog with end marked "PROP" facing the rear of the shaft. Align hole in clutch dog with shaft hole, then insert tool part No. 390766 to compress the shifter spring and install the clutch dog pin. See **Figure 51**.

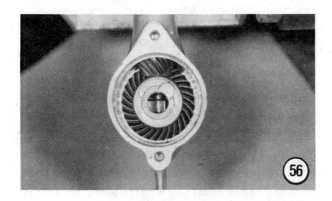

38. Reinstall one end of the clutch dog retaining spring over the clutch dog, then rotate the propeller shaft to wind the spring back in place.

39. Coat the square end of the shift plunger with OMC Needle Bearing grease and insert it in the end of the propeller shaft.

40. Install the propeller shaft in the forward gear.

41. Insert the reverse gear thrust washer in the gear recess and slide the gear on the propeller shaft, rotating as required until it engages the pinion.

42. Apply OMC Gasket Sealing Compound to the gearcase head O-ring and flange. Install the gearcase head and tighten the screws to specifications (**Table 2**).

43. Install the drive shaft with a rotating motion to engage the pinion gear splines.

44. Install the water pump as described in this chapter.

45. Pressure and vacuum test the gearcase as described in this chapter.

46. Install the gearcase as described in this chapter. Fill with the recommended type and quantity of lubricant. See Chapter Four.

47. Check gearcase lubricant level after engine has been run. Change the lubricant after 10 hours of operation (break-in period). See Chapter Four.

**Disassembly/Assembly
(9.9 and 15 hp)**

Refer to **Figure 57** for this procedure.

1. Remove the gearcase as described in this chapter.

2. Secure the gearcase in a holding fixture or a vise with protective jaws. If protective jaws are not available, position the gearcase upright with the skeg between wooden blocks.

3. Remove the water pump as described in this chapter.

4. Remove the 2 propeller shaft bearing housing screws.

5. Install puller part No. 386631 using the propeller nut to hold the puller on the propeller shaft. Turn nut until puller loosens bearing housing in gearcase, then remove the puller. Slide the bearing housing off the propeller shaft and remove it from the gearcase.

6. Remove the propeller shaft and reverse gear assembly with 2 detent balls and a spring.

7. Remove the Phillips head pivot pin screw at the base of the gearcase housing.

8. Pull the drive shaft up and out of the gearcase.

9. Unscrew the shift rod and remove from the gearcase.

10. Reach into the propeller bore with a pair of needlenose pliers and remove the clutch dog.

11. Remove the pinion gear and thrust bearing/washer assembly.

12. Reach into the propeller housing with a pair of needlenose pliers and grasp the shift lever. Move the lever back and forth and remove it with the forward gear and clutch dog yoke.

13. Slant the gearcase enough to remove the forward tapered roller bearing. If one or both detent balls failed to come out in Step 6, it will come out at this time.

14. To remove the shift rod bushing:

   a. Position remover tool and handle part No. 327693 under the bushing.

9

b. Insert a slide hammer adaptor through the bushing and thread it into the remover tool.

c. Remove the handle from the remover tool and pull the bushing out with the slide hammer.

d. Remove and discard bushing O-ring. Examine bushing for wear or damage and replace as required.

15. Attach a slide hammer to a narrow 2-jaw puller (part No. 391010). Insert puller jaws behind the drive shaft seals and remove the seals.

16. Drive the upper drive shaft bearing from its sleeve with remover tool part No. 319880 and a mallet.

17. Attach a slide hammer to a wide 2-jaw puller (part No. 390012). Insert puller jaws in the gearcase recesses behind the forward bearing cup and remove the cup.

18. If the lower pinion bearing requires removal, assemble the components of tool part No. 391257 as shown in **Figure 58**. Insert the assembled tool in the gearcase and drive the pinion bearing out.

19. Remove and discard the gearcase bearing housing O-ring.

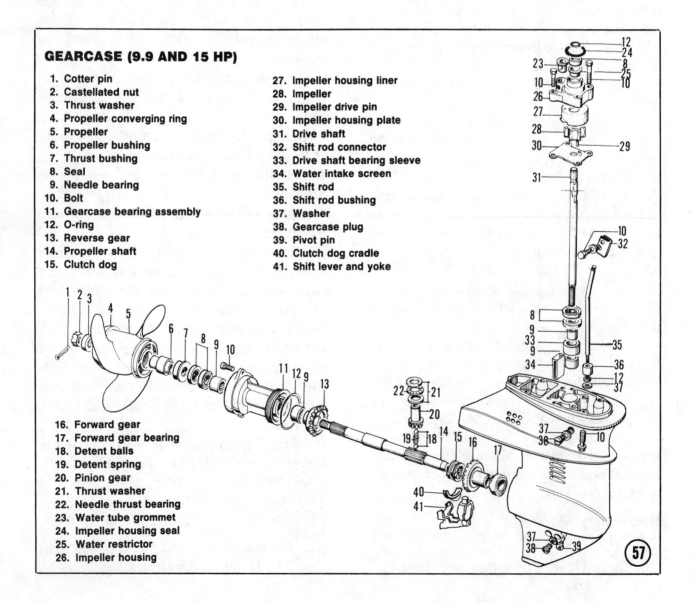

GEARCASE (9.9 AND 15 HP)

1. Cotter pin
2. Castellated nut
3. Thrust washer
4. Propeller converging ring
5. Propeller
6. Propeller bushing
7. Thrust bushing
8. Seal
9. Needle bearing
10. Bolt
11. Gearcase bearing assembly
12. O-ring
13. Reverse gear
14. Propeller shaft
15. Clutch dog
16. Forward gear
17. Forward gear bearing
18. Detent balls
19. Detent spring
20. Pinion gear
21. Thrust washer
22. Needle thrust bearing
23. Water tube grommet
24. Impeller housing seal
25. Water restrictor
26. Impeller housing
27. Impeller housing liner
28. Impeller
29. Impeller drive pin
30. Impeller housing plate
31. Drive shaft
32. Shift rod connector
33. Drive shaft bearing sleeve
34. Water intake screen
35. Shift rod
36. Shift rod bushing
37. Washer
38. Gearcase plug
39. Pivot pin
40. Clutch dog cradle
41. Shift lever and yoke

57

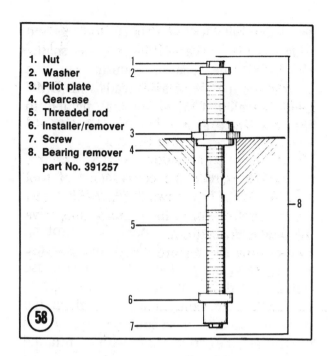

1. Nut
2. Washer
3. Pilot plate
4. Gearcase
5. Threaded rod
6. Installer/remover
7. Screw
8. Bearing remover
   part No. 391257

58

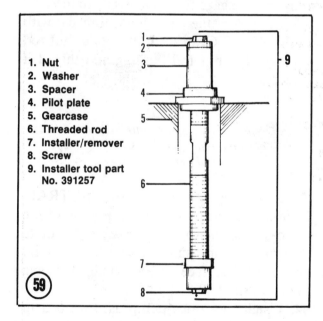

1. Nut
2. Washer
3. Spacer
4. Pilot plate
5. Gearcase
6. Threaded rod
7. Installer/remover
8. Screw
9. Installer tool part
   No. 391257

59

20. Secure the bearing housing in a vise with protective jaws and remove the 2 bearings and the seals with tool part No. 391259 or a slide hammer and narrow 2-jaw puller.

21. Clean and inspect all components as described in this chapter.

22. Install a new large bearing (lettered side facing tool) in the gearcase bearing housing with installer part No. 319876.

23. Install a new small bearing (lettered side facing tool) in the gearcase bearing housing with installer part No. 319875.

24. Coat the metal case of 2 new gearcase head seals with OMC Gasket Sealing Compound. Install the inner seal (lip facing inward) with installer part No. 326553, then install the outer seal (lip facing outward) with the same tool. Pack the cavity between the 2 new seals with OMC Triple-Guard grease.

25. Install a new O-ring on the bearing housing and lubricate with OMC HI-VIS Gearcase Lube.

NOTE
If either the forward gear bearing or bearing cup requires replacement, install a new bearing/cup assembly.

26. If the forward gear bearing cup was removed, remove the gearcase from the holding fixture. Place nose of gearcase on a block of wood and drive the bearing in place with installer tool part No. 319929, handle part No. 311880 and a mallet, rotating the tool during installation.

27. If the lower pinion bearing was removed, assemble the components of tool part No. 391257 as shown in **Figure 59**. Use OMC Needle Bearing Grease to hold the bearing on the tool (lettered side facing up). Insert the tool and bearing in the gearcase and tighten the tool screw until the washer on the tool touches the spacer.

28. If the drive shaft bearing was removed, install bearing (lettered side up) in the bearing sleeve with an arbor press and installer part No. 319931 or part No. 326566.

29. Install the bearing and sleeve (lettered side up) in the gearcase with installer part No. 319931 and handle part No. 311880.

30. Coat the metal case of 2 new drive shaft seals with OMC Gasket Sealing Compound. Install the inner seal (lip facing toward gearcase) with installer part No. 326554, then install the outer seal (lip facing away from

9

gearcase) with the same tool. Pack the cavity between the 2 new seals with OMC Triple-Guard grease.

31. Lubricate a new shift rod bushing O-ring with OMC HI-VIS Gearcase Lube. Install O-ring on bushing. Fit the bushing and a new washer on tool part No. 304515. Wipe outer diameter of bushing with OMC Gasket Sealing Compound and drive bushing into the gearcase with a mallet.

32. Lubricate the forward gear bearing with OMC HI-VIS Gearcase Lube and install in the forward gear bearing cup.

33. Thread tool part No. 319991 through the shift rod bushing and into the shifter yoke. Pull on the tool and guide the yoke/lever/forward gear assembly into the gearcase. When properly located, the gear will rest against the forward bearing and the shift lever will fit in the gearcase slot.

34. Sandwich the pinion gear bearing between the 2 thrust washers. The thrust washer with the inside chamfer must rest against the pinion shoulder. The chamfered edge of the other thrust washer must face away. See **Figure 55**.

NOTE
If pinion binding occurs in Step 35, temporarily install drive shaft to align pinion. If this does not relieve the binding condition, the forward bearing cup is not fully seated.

35. Guide the pinion gear in place in the gearcase while pushing on the top of the forward gear with a long screwdriver.

36. Position the clutch dog with its grooves facing the forward gear and install in the cradle with needlenose pliers.

37. Coat the propeller shaft spring and 2 detent balls with OMC Needle Bearing Grease. Install the spring and balls in the propeller shaft.

38. Install the propeller shaft in the clutch dog, forward gear and forward bearing. Align the detent balls with the clutch dog lugs and slide the reverse gear on the propeller shaft.

39. Install the bearing housing in the gearcase. Wipe the screw threads with OMC Gasket Sealing Compound and tighten to specifications (**Table 2**).

NOTE
If the pivot pin seal condition is doubtful, install a new pin in Step 40.

40. Locate the shift yoke pin hole by probing through the pivot pin hole in the gearcase with an awl. Align the yoke and gearcase holes. Coat the pivot pin threads with OMC Gasket Sealing Compound and tighten the screw to specifications (**Table 2**).

41. Install the drive shaft with a rotating motion to engage the pinion gear splines.

42. Lubricate the shift rod threads with OMC HI-VIS Gearcase Lube. Slide shift rod through the shift rod bushing and thread it into the yoke.

NOTE
On models equipped with a gearcase extension, make the adjustment in Step 43 after installing the extension.

43. Shift the gearcase into NEUTRAL. Measure the distance between the top of the gearcase and the top of the shift rod. Rotate shift rod until measurement is 13/32-7/16 in. with the flat surface on the connector facing the drive shaft.

44. Install the water pump as described in this chapter.

45. Pressure and vacuum test the gearcase as described in this chapter.

46. Install the gearcase as described in this chapter. Fill with the recommended type and quantity of lubricant. See Chapter Four.

47. Check gearcase lubricant level after engine has been run. Change the lubricant after 10 hours of operation (break-in period). See Chapter Four.

Disassembly/Assembly
(9.5, 20, 25 and 40 hp)

Refer to **Figure 60** for this procedure.

1. Remove the gearcase as described in this chapter.

2. Secure the gearcase in a holding fixture or a vise with protective jaws. If protective jaws are not available, position the gearcase upright with the skeg between wooden blocks.

3. Remove the water pump as described in this chapter.

4. Remove the drive shaft from the gearcase.

5. Invert the gearcase in the holding fixture. Remove the Phillips head pivot pin. Remove and discard the O-ring.

6. Remove the 6 screws holding the lower half of the gearcase to the upper half. Tap the skeg with a soft hammer to break the seal and

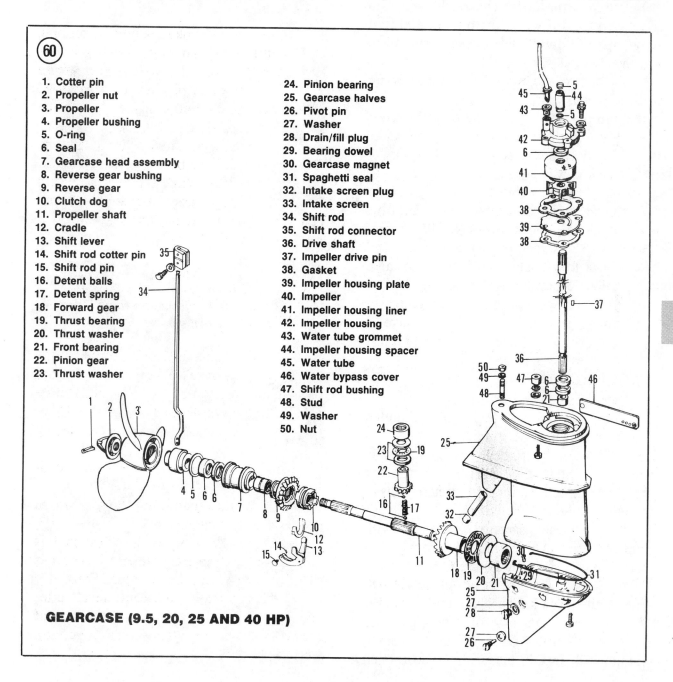

60

1. Cotter pin
2. Propeller nut
3. Propeller
4. Propeller bushing
5. O-ring
6. Seal
7. Gearcase head assembly
8. Reverse gear bushing
9. Reverse gear
10. Clutch dog
11. Propeller shaft
12. Cradle
13. Shift lever
14. Shift rod cotter pin
15. Shift rod pin
16. Detent balls
17. Detent spring
18. Forward gear
19. Thrust bearing
20. Thrust washer
21. Front bearing
22. Pinion gear
23. Thrust washer
24. Pinion bearing
25. Gearcase halves
26. Pivot pin
27. Washer
28. Drain/fill plug
29. Bearing dowel
30. Gearcase magnet
31. Spaghetti seal
32. Intake screen plug
33. Intake screen
34. Shift rod
35. Shift rod connector
36. Drive shaft
37. Impeller drive pin
38. Gasket
39. Impeller housing plate
40. Impeller
41. Impeller housing liner
42. Impeller housing
43. Water tube grommet
44. Impeller housing spacer
45. Water tube
46. Water bypass cover
47. Shift rod bushing
48. Stud
49. Washer
50. Nut

GEARCASE (9.5, 20, 25 AND 40 HP)

9

remove the lower half (**Figure 61**). Remove and discard the spaghetti seal (**Figure 62**).

7. Pivot the shifter lever to the rear and remove the cradle (**Figure 63**).

8. Slide the propeller shaft assembly straight up and to the side, then remove it from the gearcase. See **Figure 64**.

9. Remove the pinion gear/bearing/washer assembly from the gearcase (**Figure 65**).

10. Examine the upper end of the shift rod for burrs and remove with No. 400 grit sandpaper, if found. Slide the shift rod out of the gearcase.

11. To check, clean or replace the water intake screen:

    a. Remove the 2 screws holding the cover plate in the side of the gearcase. Remove the cover plate and check for blocked water passages.

    b. If the water intake screen requires replacement, drill a 5/32 in. hole in the plug and remove with a No. 3 Easy-out.

    c. Slide the screen from the gearcase and check for damage, blockage or metallic chips. Replace as required.

    d. Slide the screen back into the gearcase.

    e. Coat a new plug with OMC Adhesive M and drive it into the gearcase until it just touches the screen.

    f. Reinstall the cover plate and tighten the screws snugly.

12. Slide all components except the clutch dog from the propeller shaft.

13. With a hand cupped over the clutch dog, slowly slide it to the front of the propeller shaft, catching the spring and 2 detent balls as the clutch dog uncovers them.

14. Remove the gearcase head seals with remover part No. 391259. Remove and discard the O-ring. See **Figure 66**.

15. Soak the gearcase head in solvent to remove the dried sealant from the seal bore.

16. Coat the metal case of 2 new gearcase head seals with OMC Gasket Sealing Compound. Install the seals back-to-back

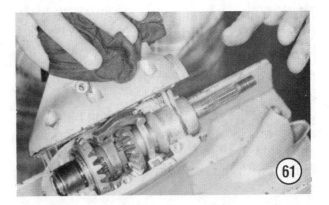

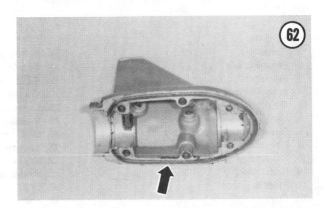

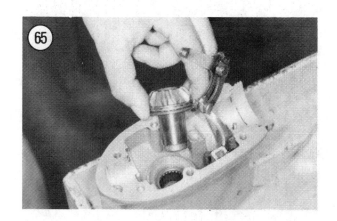

with installer part No. 326691. Pack the cavity between the 2 new seals with OMC Triple-Guard grease.

17. Lubricate a new O-ring with OMC HI-VIS Gearcase Lube and install on gearcase head.

18. Drive the upper drive shaft seals and bearing (**Figure 67**) from the gearcase with tool part No. 326570 (9.5-25 hp) or part No. 320018 (40 hp) and a mallet.

19. Lubricate a new bearing with OMC HI-VIS Gearcase Lube and install in the gearcase (lettered side up) with tool part No. 326564 (9.5-25 hp) or part No. 319926 (40 hp).

20. Coat the metal case of 2 new gearcase head seals with OMC Gasket Sealing Compound. Install the inner seal (lip facing toward gearcase) and the outer seal (lip facing away from gearcase) at the same time with installer part No. 330655 (9.5-25 hp) or part No. 3119927 (40 hp) and drive handle part No. 378737. Pack the cavity between the 2 new seals with OMC Triple-Guard grease.

21A. 9.5-25 hp—Remove the pinion bearing with remover part No. 326571 and remover part No. 326570. Install remover part No. 326571 with its slide ring behind the bearing cage, then drive the bearing out with remover part No. 326570 and a mallet.

21B. 40hp—Remove the pinion bearing with puller part No. 379445 and puller jaws part No. 308093.

22A. 9.5-25 hp—Lubricate a new pinion bearing with OMC HI-VIS Gearcase Lube and install (lettered side up) in gearcase with tool part No. 326565 until tool seats against gearcase flange.

22B. 40hp—Lubricate thrust washers and bearing with Johnson or Evinrude 50/1 oil. Install washer with large hole, bearing and washer with small hole in that order, then install new pinion bearing (lettered side up) in gearcase with tool part No. 378098 and driver part No. 378737.

23. Drive the shift rod bushing from the gearcase with tool part No. 304514 and a mallet.

24. Fit a new shift rod bushing on the end of tool part No. 304515. Lubricate a new O-ring with OMC HI-VIS Gearcase Lube and install on the end of the bushing along with a new bushing gasket. Position the tool and bushing assembly in the gearcase and drive in place until the bushing is fully seated.

9

25. Insert the spring in the propeller shaft. Position a detent ball on each side of the spring and hold in place while sliding the clutch dog in place. Chamfered and grooved lugs of the shift dog should face the front of the shaft.

26. Lubricate the remaining propeller shaft components with OMC HI-VIS Gearcase Lube. Install the roller bearing (lettered end facing forward), thrust washer, thrust bearing and gear in that order.

27. Turn the shaft around and install the reverse gear, bushing and gearcase head in that order.

28. Lubricate the end of the shift rod with OMC HI-VIS Gearcase Lube. Insert rod through shift rod bushing.

29. Sandwich the pinion gear bearing between the 2 thrust washers. The thrust washer with the inside chamfer must rest against the pinion shoulder. The chamfered edge of the other thrust washer must face away. See **Figure 55**.

30. Install the pinion gear/bearing/washer assembly in the gearcase (**Figure 68**).

31. Run a bead of OMC Adhesive M on the upper gearcase at point A, **Figure 69**.

32. Install the cradle on the shift lever (B, **Figure 69**).

33. Install the propeller shaft assembly in the upper gearcase (**Figure 69**). Make sure the hole in the gearcase head engages the locating pin in the gearcase. Pry the clutch dog forward into gear with a flat-blade screwdriver while rotating the propeller shaft, then position the shift cradle.

34. 9.5-25 hp—Install alignment tool part No. 390880 on propeller shaft (**Figure 70**) to seat the forward gear and thrust bearing against the gearcase and prevent them from cocking. Leave the tool in place until the other half of the gearcase is installed.

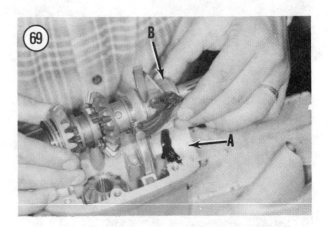

NOTE
Spaghetti seal is sold in bulk rolls. Obtain at least 13 inches for use in Step 35.

35. Coat the machined surfaces of both gearcase halves and the exposed area of the gearcase head with OMC Adhesive M. Place the spaghetti seal in the lower gearcase groove and cut the ends of the seal flush with the end of the groove using a sharp knife. Apply OMC RTV Adhesive Sealant on each end of the seal for a distance of 1/2 inch.

36. Coat the gearcase screw threads with OMC Gasket Sealing Compound. Install the lower gearcase half with the 2 front and 2 rear screws. Tighten the 4 screws alternately and evenly until finger-tight to draw the halves together.

37. Install the remaining screws finger-tight, then tighten all screws to specifications (**Table**

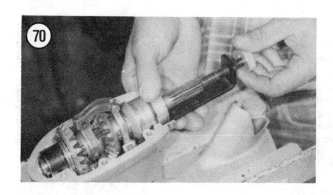

2), working from side-to-side and front-to-rear. Remove the alignment tool.

38. Locate the shift yoke pin hole by probing through the pivot pin hole in the gearcase with an awl. Align the yoke and gearcase holes. Install a new O-ring on the pivot pin. Coat the pin threads and O-ring with OMC Gasket Sealing Compound and tighten the screw to specifications (**Table 2**).

39. Install the drive shaft with a rotating motion to engage the pinion gear splines.

40. Install the water pump as described in this chapter.

41. Pressure and vacuum test the gearcase as described in this chapter.

42. Install the gearcase as described in this chapter. Fill with the recommended type and quantity of lubricant. See Chapter Four.

43. Check gearcase lubricant level after engine has been run. Change the lubricant after 10 hours of operation (break-in period). See Chapter Four.

Disassembly/Assembly
(30 and 35 hp)

Refer to **Figure 71** for this procedure.

1. Remove the gearcase as described in this chapter.

2. Secure the gearcase in a holding fixture or a vise with protective jaws. If protective jaws are not available, position the gearcase upright with the skeg between wooden blocks.

3. Remove the water pump fasteners. Pull up on the drive shaft and remove it from the gearcase with the water pump attached. Disassemble the water pump as described in this chapter.

4. Remove the 2 screws holding the bearing housing in the propeller bore. Use a long screwdriver or a screwdriver tip socket and extension to reach the screws. See **Figure 72**.

5. Install puller part No. 378103 components as shown in **Figure 73** and remove the bearing housing from the gearcase.

6. Remove the large snap ring from the gearcase with snap ring pliers part No. 303859 or equivalent.

7. Holding one hand around the propeller shaft, tilt the gearcase in the holding fixture and catch the retainer plate as it drops out.

8. Turn the lower shift rod counterclockwise with an open-end wrench and remove the rod from the shift yoke.

9. Reach into the gearcase with needlenose pliers and remove the shift yoke (**Figure 74**).

10. Remove the Phillips head pivot pin from the outside of the gearcase. Remove and discard the pivot pin O-ring.

11. Start to pull the propeller shaft out carefully and slowly. Two clutch dog detent balls will dislodge and drop into the gearcase bore. Tilt the gearcase and catch the clutch dog and shift cradle, reverse gear and the detent spring and balls.

12. Remove the forward gear and bearing assembly. Remove the pinion gear/bearing/washer assembly with a right angle rod, if necessary. See **Figure 75**.

13. Attach a slide hammer to a narrow 2-jaw puller (part No. 391010). Insert the puller jaws in the grooves at each side of the gearcase behind the forward gear bearing cup and remove the cup.

14. Lubricate the forward bearing cup with OMC HI-VIS Gearcase Lube and install with tool part No. 319929 and handle part No. 311880. Make sure cup is completely seated in the gearcase.

9

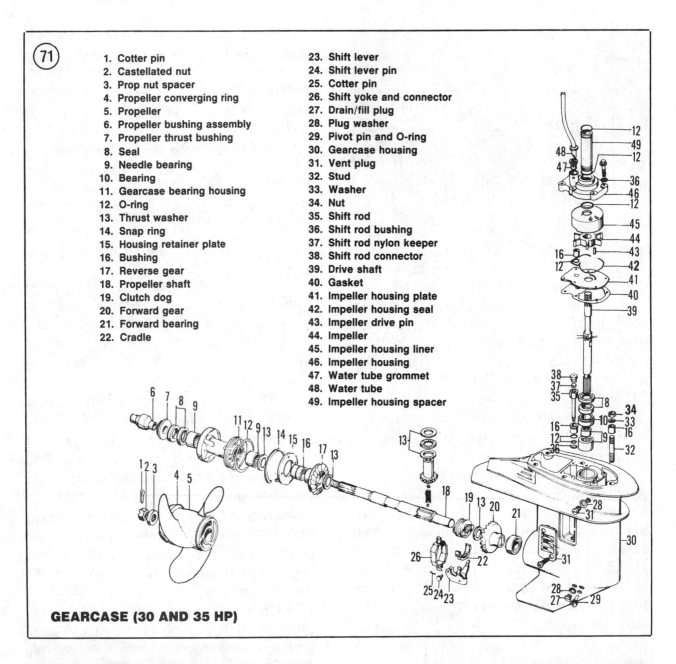

71.
1. Cotter pin
2. Castellated nut
3. Prop nut spacer
4. Propeller converging ring
5. Propeller
6. Propeller bushing assembly
7. Propeller thrust bushing
8. Seal
9. Needle bearing
10. Bearing
11. Gearcase bearing housing
12. O-ring
13. Thrust washer
14. Snap ring
15. Housing retainer plate
16. Bushing
17. Reverse gear
18. Propeller shaft
19. Clutch dog
20. Forward gear
21. Forward bearing
22. Cradle

23. Shift lever
24. Shift lever pin
25. Cotter pin
26. Shift yoke and connector
27. Drain/fill plug
28. Plug washer
29. Pivot pin and O-ring
30. Gearcase housing
31. Vent plug
32. Stud
33. Washer
34. Nut
35. Shift rod
36. Shift rod bushing
37. Shift rod nylon keeper
38. Shift rod connector
39. Drive shaft
40. Gasket
41. Impeller housing plate
42. Impeller housing seal
43. Impeller drive pin
44. Impeller
45. Impeller housing liner
46. Impeller housing
47. Water tube grommet
48. Water tube
49. Impeller housing spacer

GEARCASE (30 AND 35 HP)

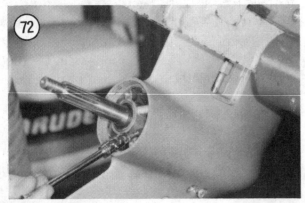

72.

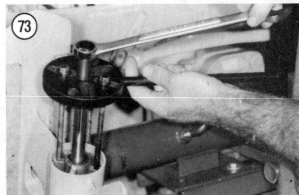

73.

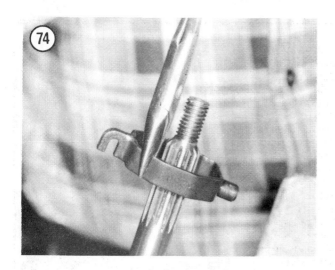

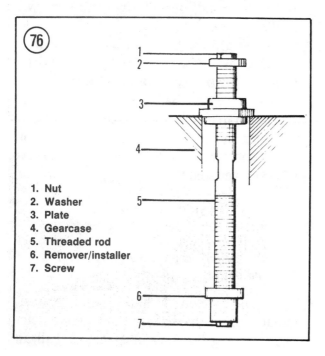

1. Nut
2. Washer
3. Plate
4. Gearcase
5. Threaded rod
6. Remover/installer
7. Screw

15. Remove the drive shaft seals with remover tool part No. 391259. Remove the upper drive shaft bearing and bearing housing assembly with the same tool. If the bearing is worn or damaged, press it from the housing and discard it.

16. Lubricate a new drive shaft bearing with OMC HI-VIS Gearcase Lube and install in bearing housing (lettered side up) with tool part No. 322923. Use the same tool to install the drive shaft bearing housing (lettered side up) in the gearcase.

17. Coat the metal case of 2 new drive shaft seals with OMC Gasket Sealing Compound. Install seals back-to-back with installer part No. 326554. Pack the cavity between the seals with OMC Triple-Guard grease.

NOTE
Pinion bearings cannot be serviced separately. If one requires removal, both must be removed.

18. To remove the pinion bearings, assemble the components of tool part No. 391257 as shown in **Figure 76**. Install the assembled tool in the gearcase and drive the pinion bearings into the propeller shaft bore.

19. To install the pinion bearings, assemble the components of tool part No. 391257 and spacers part No. 330067 and part No. 330068 (spacers are not included with tool part No. 391257) as shown in **Figure 77**. Use OMC Needle Bearing Grease to hold the bearing on the tool (lettered side facing up). Insert the tool and bearing in the gearcase and tighten the tool screw until the washer on the tool touches the spacer.

20. To remove the shift rod bushing:
   a. Position remover tool and handle part No. 327693 under the bushing.
   b. Insert a slide hammer adaptor through the bushing and thread it into the remover tool.

9

c. Remove the handle from the remover tool and pull the bushing out with the slide hammer.

d. Remove and discard bushing O-ring. Examine bushing for wear or damage and replace as required.

21. To install the shift rod bushing, lubricate 2 new O-rings with OMC HI-VIS Gearcase Lube and install on bushing. Coat outside of bushing with OMC Adhesive M. Install bushing and washer with tool part No. 304515.

22. Remove and discard the bearing housing O-ring. Remove and discard the bearing housing seals and bearings with tool part No. 391259.

23. Clean and inspect all components as described in this chapter.

24. Lubricate a new bearing with OMC HI-VIS Gearcase Lube and install (lettered side against tool) in the rear of the bearing housing with tool part No. 321429. Repeat this step to install front bearing with tool part No. 321428.

25. Coat the metal case of 2 new bearing housing seals with OMC Gasket Sealing Compound. Install the seals back-to-back with installer part No. 326546. Pack the cavity between the 2 new seals with OMC Triple-Guard grease.

26. Lubricate a new bearing housing O-ring with OMC HI-VIS Gearcase Lube and install on the housing.

27. Lubricate the forward gear bearing with OMC HI-VIS Gearcase Lube and install in bearing cup.

28. Sandwich the pinion gear bearing between the 2 thrust washers. The thrust washer with the inside chamfer must rest against the pinion shoulder. The chamfered edge of the other thrust washer must face away. See **Figure 55**. Install the assembly in the gearcase with a right angle rod. See **Figure 75**.

29. Install the forward gear in the gearcase.

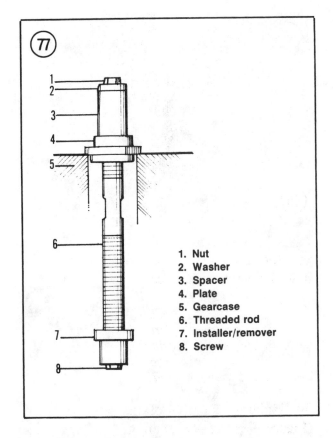

1. Nut
2. Washer
3. Spacer
4. Plate
5. Gearcase
6. Threaded rod
7. Installer/remover
8. Screw

30. Coat clutch shifter and clutch dog with OMC Needle Bearing Grease. Assemble clutch dog (grooved end facing forward gear) to shifter and install in gearcase with needlenose pliers.

31. Align gearcase and shifter holes with an awl, then install pivot pin with a new O-ring. Tighten pin to specifications (**Table 2**).

32. Coat detent balls with OMC Needle Bearing Grease. Install detent spring in propeller shaft hole and set one ball on one side of the spring. Slide detent sleeve part No. 328081 over shaft.

> *WARNING*
> *Detent balls are under considerable pressure in Step 33. Wear safety glasses for eye protection in case the ball flies out during installation.*

33. Align detent sleeve groove with remaining hole in shaft and put second detent ball in tool groove. Depress detent ball and

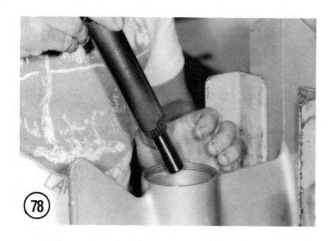

pull tool back until detent ball engages shaft hole. Leave tool in place.

NOTE
Work slowly and carefully in Step 34. Detent balls and spring will not engage clutch dog if tool legs and clutch dog ramps are misaligned.

34. Holding detent tool on propeller shaft (**Figure 78**), insert shaft in gearcase and engage forward gear. Push shaft forward, aligning tool legs with clutch dog ramps until detent balls and spring enter the clutch dog. Remove the detent tool.

35. Lubricate reverse gear and reverse gear bushing with OMC HI-VIS Gearcase Lubricant. Install reverse gear, then install the bushing in the gear.

36. Grasp shifter yoke with needlenose pliers. Install the yoke in the gearcase bore, engaging its top in the upper gearcase cavity and locating its bottom hook on the shift lever clevis pin at the bottom of the gearcase cavity.

37. Lubricate the lower shift rod with OMC HI-VIS Gearcase Lubricant. Install rod through the water intake opening until it engages the shifter yoke. Thread rod into yoke until it bottoms.

38. Position the retainer plate on the propeller shaft with its tab facing the skeg and slide plate in position.

39. Install the large snap ring with snap ring pliers part No. 303869. Sharp outside edge of ring should face to the rear and the rings should face the skeg.

40. Thread guide pins (part No. 383175) into the retainer plate holes.

41. Lubricate the bearing housing thrust washer and O-ring with OMC HI-VIS Gearcase Lubricant. Install thrust washer in bearing housing recess. Position bearing housing on guide pins with the word "UP" facing the top of the gearcase. Slide housing into gearcase cavity and seat by tapping in place with a brass punch and mallet.

42. Install new O-rings on the bearing housing screws. Coat screw threads with OMC Gasket Sealing Compound. Remove one guide pin and install the screw with a long screwdriver or a screwdriver tip socket and extension. See **Figure 72**. Remove the other guide pin and install the second screw. Tighten both screws to specifications (**Table 2**).

43. Lightly lubricate drive shaft pinion splines with OMC HI-VIS Gearcase Lubricant. Install the drive shaft with a rotating motion to engage the pinion gear splines.

44. Install the water pump as described in this chapter.

45. Pressure and vacuum test the gearcase as described in this chapter.

46. Install the gearcase as described in this chapter. Fill with the recommended type and quantity of lubricant. See Chapter Four.

47. Check gearcase lubricant level after engine has been run. Change the lubricant after 10 hours of operation (break-in period). See Chapter Four.

Pressure and Vacuum Test

Whenever a gearcase is overhauled, it should be pressure and vacuum tested before refilling it with lubricant. If the gearcase fails either the pressure or vacuum test, it must be disassembled and the source of the problem located and corrected. Failure to perform a pressure and vacuum test or ignoring the results and running a gearcase which failed one or both portions of the test will result in major gearcase damage.

1. Install a new seal on the oil level plug.

2. Thread a pressure test gauge into the fill/drain plug hole. See **Figure 79** (typical).

3. Pump the pressure to 3-6 psi. If pressure holds, increase it to 16-18 psi. If it does not hold, submerge the gearcase in water and check for the presence of air bubbles to indicate the source of the leak.

4. If pressure holds at 16-18 psi, release the pressure and remove the pressure tester. If pressure does not hold at this level, submerge the gearcase in water and check for the presence of air bubbles to indicate the source of the leak.

5. Thread a vacuum test gauge into the fill/drain plug hole. See **Figure 79** (typical).

6. Draw 3-5 in. Hg vacuum. If vacuum holds, increase it to 15 in. Hg. If vacuum does not hold at this level, coat suspected seal with lubricant to see if the leak stops or the lubricant is sucked in.

7. If vacuum holds at 15 in. Hg, release the vacuum and remove the tester. If vacuum does not hold, coat the suspected seal with lubricant to see if the leak stops or the lubricant is sucked in.

8. If the source of a pressure or vacuum leak cannot be determined visually, disassemble the gearcase and locate it.

9. If gearcase passes the pressure and vacuum test, fill it with the required type and quantity of lubricant. See Chapter Four.

SHIFT LEVER ADJUSTMENT

(9.9-15 hp)

Refer to **Figure 80** for this procedure.

1. Disconnect the fuel line at the carburetor.

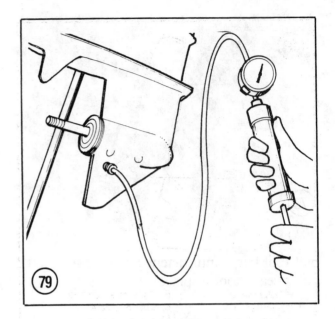

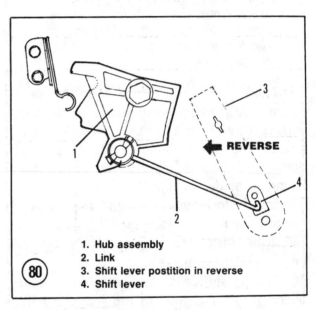

1. Hub assembly
2. Link
3. Shift lever postition in reverse
4. Shift lever

2. Remove the cotter pin and washer from the shift lever link.

3. Move shift lever and hub assembly to REVERSE.

4. Adjust the link to align with the shift lever hole without moving shift lever.

5. When link aligns with shift lever hole, shorten it one turn. Apply a slight pressure to the shift lever and reinstall the link.

6. Install washer and a new cotter pin, then reconnect the carburetor fuel line.

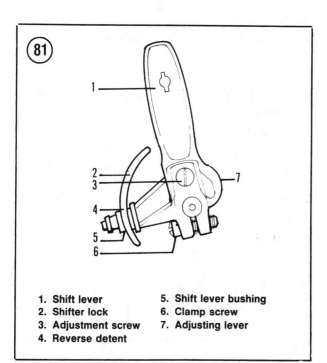

1. Shift lever
2. Shifter lock
3. Adjustment screw
4. Reverse detent
5. Shift lever bushing
6. Clamp screw
7. Adjusting lever

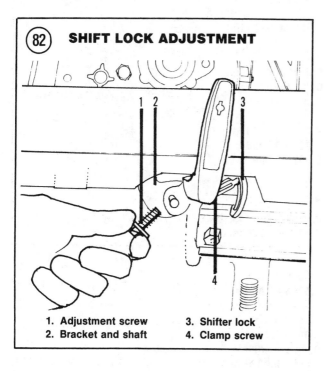

SHIFT LOCK ADJUSTMENT

1. Adjustment screw
2. Bracket and shaft
3. Shifter lock
4. Clamp screw

7. Check and adjust neutral start switch. See Chapter Three.

20-35 hp

Refer to **Figure 81** for this procedure.
1. Move shift lever to REVERSE.
2. Loosen adjustment and clamp screws.
3. Rotate adjustment lever counterclockwise until full engagement of clutch dog is felt in reverse gear.
4. Rotate shift lever counterclockwise until the lever roller contacts the end of the shifter lock reverse detent.
5. Tighten adjustment and clamp screws to 5-7 ft.lb.

40 hp

Refer to **Figure 82** for this procedure.
1. Move the shift handle to FORWARD while rotating the propeller clockwise to engage the clutch dog with forward gear.
2. Note the point at which engagement takes place and the point at which the shift lever pin rides in the shifter lock forward detent.
3. Move the shift handle from FORWARD through NEUTRAL and into REVERSE. Note the points of engagement and the points at which the shift lever pin rides in the shifter lock neutral and reverse detents.
4. If the shifter lever pin does not fully engage the forward and reverse detents and return to the neutral detent when the shift lever is placed in NEUTRAL, loosen the shift handle clamp and adjustment screws.
5. Position handle as required and tighten the screws. Repeat procedure to check adjustment.

9

Tables are on the following pages.

Table 1 GEARCASE CLEARANCE SPECIFICATIONS

Bearing housing bushing	
to drive shaft	
6 hp	
1973	0.0015-0.0030 in.
1974-1979	0.0015-0.0025 in.
Drive shaft and bushing	
in gear case	
2 hp	0.0010-0.0028 in.
4 hp weedless	0.001-0.003 in.
Front gear to gearcase bushing	
6 hp (1973-1979)	0.0010-0.0022 in.
Gearcase bushing to	
propeller shaft	
2 hp	0.0007-0.0022 in.
4 hp (1973-1980)	0.0005-0.0020 in.
Gearcase head and propeller shaft	
2 hp	0.0007-0.0022 in.
6 hp (1973-1979)	0.0010-0.0020 in.
Gear head and bushing assembly	
4 hp	
1973	0.0005-0.0020 in.
1974-1980	0.0007-0.0022 in.
4 hp weedless	0.0005-0.0015 in.
Pinion and bushing in gearcase	
4 hp (1973-1980)	0.0005-0.0018 in.
Propeller on shaft	
2 hp	
1973	0.0022-0.0057 in.
1974-on	0.0022-0.0067 in.
4 hp	0.0030-0.0055 in.
4 hp weedless	
1973	0.0020-0.0063 in.
1974-on	0.0020-0.0053 in.
6 hp (1973-1979)	0.0070-0.009 in.
Propeller shaft in front	
gear bushing	
6 hp (1973-1979)	0.0005-0.0015 in.
9.9 and 15 hp	0.0002-0.0087 in.
20-40 hp	0.0010-0.0020 in.
Propeller shaft to reverse	
gear bushing	
6 hp (1973-1979)	0.0005-0.0015 in.
20-40 hp	0.0005-0.0015 in.
Rear reverse gear bushing	
6 hp	
1973	0.0005-0.0020 in.
1974-1979	0.0005-0.0025 in.
20-40 hp	0.0005-0.0020 in.

Table 2 GEARCASE TIGHTENING TORQUE

Fastener	in.-lb.	ft.-lb.
Bearing housing screws	60-84	
Drain/fill/oil level plugs	60-84	
Gearcase cover screws	60-80	
Gearcase head screws		
2, 4 hp	60-84	
4 Deluxe-8 hp	60-80	
Gearcase mounting screws		
2, 4 hp	60-80	
4 Deluxe-8 hp		
Front		10-12
Rear	60-84	
9.5-40 hp		10-12
Lower-to-upper gearcase screws		
9.5, 20, 25 and 40 hp	60-80	
Pivot pin	48-84	
Upper shift rod connector	60-84	
Water pump fasteners		
2, 4 hp	25-35	
4 Deluxe-8 hp	60-80	
9.5-40 hp	60-84	
Zinc anode screw	60-84	

9

NOTE: If you own a 1985 or later model, first check the Supplement at the back of the book for any new service information.

Chapter Ten

Automatic Rewind Starters

All models are equipped with a rope-operated rewind starter. The starter assembly may be mounted in the engine cover (all 2 hp and 1979-on 4 hp), beside the flywheel (1973-1978 4 hp and all 4.5-15 hp) or above the flywheel (18-40 hp). See **Figures 1-3** (typical). Pulling the rope handle causes the starter spindle shaft to rotate against spring tension, moving the drive pawl or pinion to engage the flywheel and turn the engine over. When the rope handle is released, the spring inside the assembly reverses direction of the spindle shaft and winds the rope around the pulley.

All 5 hp and larger outboards are equipped with a starter interlock feature. This prevents operation of the rewind starter whenever the throttle is advanced beyond the START position.

Automatic rewind starters are relatively trouble-free, with a broken or frayed rope the most common malfunction. This chapter covers rewind starter and rope/spring service.

ENGINE COVER STARTER

This starter type is used on all 2 hp and 1979-on 4 hp outboards.

Removal/Installation

1. Disconnect the spark plug lead to prevent the engine from accidentally starting.
2. Remove the fuel tank cap. Remove the engine cover. Reinstall the cap on the fuel tank.
3. Installation is the reverse of removal. Tighten cover screws to 60-80 in.-lb.

Starter Rope Replacement

1. Place the engine cover upright on a flat surface.
2. Pull the starter rope out as far as it will go and tie a slip knot in the rope near the cover.
3. Untie the knot in the handle end of the rope and remove the handle assembly.
4. Invert the engine cover and pull the rope out enough to release the slip knot tied in Step 2.

NOTE
Some models use a pulley plate installed over the pulley. This plate must be removed before the rope can be disconnected from the pulley in Step 6.

5. If equipped with a pulley plate, remove the plate screws and plate.

6. Hold the pulley firmly and pull knotted end of rope from pulley. Slowly allow pulley to rotate until it is completely unwound.
7. Tie a knot in the end of a new rope.
8. Rotate the pulley 3 1/2 turns counterclockwise to tension the spring and hold in that position.
9. Insert the unknotted end of the rope in the pulley hole. If pulley uses a plate, reinstall plate and tighten screws. Thread the rope around the pulley and out the starter housing hole, then pull the rope until the knot bottoms in the pulley.
10. Holding the free end of the rope, carefully release pressure on the pulley and allow it to slip slowly. Wind all but approximately 12 in. of the rope on the pulley in this manner.
11. Tie a slip knot in the rope to hold it in place and install the handle assembly. Tie a knot in the end of the rope and seat the knot in the handle.
12. Release the slip knot and allow the starter pulley to rewind the remaining rope.

Disassembly

WARNING
Disassembling this starter mechanism without holding the spring in place can result in the spring unwinding violently, causing serious personal injury. Wear safety glasses and gloves during this procedure.

Refer to **Figure 4** for this procedure.
1. Remove the starter rope as described in this chapter.
2. Remove the circlip holding the starter pawl in place. Lift the pawl off its shaft and disengage the friction spring and links. Remove the pawl and spring/link assembly.
3. Place the engine cover on its side. Hold the pulley and spindle in place with one hand and remove the starter spindle screw from the top of cover.

4. Invert the engine cover and remove the spindle while holding the pulley in place.

5. Slowly lift the pulley straight up and out of the starter housing in the engine cover. The spring should remain in the housing.

6. Position the cover right-side up on the workbench or floor and rap it sharply. The spring will fly out of the engine cover starter housing and be contained inside the cover.

Cleaning and Inspection

1. Wash all metal parts in solvent and blow dry with compressed air.

2. Check spring for wear or broken end loops. Replace as required.

3. Check pawl, friction spring and spindle for wear.

4. Remove any sharp edges or rough surfaces from pulley and housing that might fray the rope.

5. Check rope for fraying. Replace as required.

Assembly
(Models With Pulley Plate)

1. Lubricate the spring and housing spring cavity with Lubriplate 777 or OMC Triple-Guard grease.

2. Loosely coil the spring and insert it in the engine cover. Locate the inside coil in the housing slot with its loop facing the center of the spring cavity.

3. Position rope pulley over the spring and engage the pulley pin in the spring loop. See **Figure 5**.

4. Wipe the outer diameter of the spindle with Lubriplate 777 or OMC Triple-Guard grease. Insert spindle through pulley and engage spindle slot with housing rib.

5. Dip spindle screw threads in OMC Screw Lock and install screw.

6. Rotate pulley counterclockwise to wind spring into housing until the outer spring loop engages the outer face of the spring cavity.

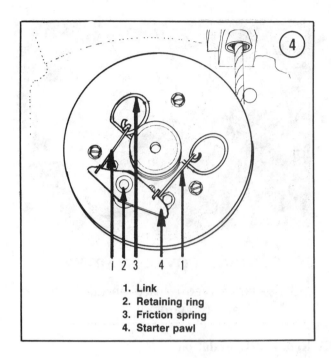

1. Link
2. Retaining ring
3. Friction spring
4. Starter pawl

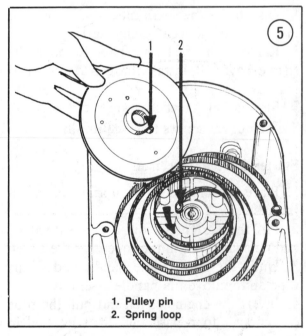

1. Pulley pin
2. Spring loop

7. Insert knotted end of rope in pulley slot. Wrap the rope counterclockwise around the pulley flange.

8. Install pulley plate with 3 screws and tighten securely. Wind pulley counterclockwise 3 1/2 turns to preload the spring, then insert a punch through the remaining screw hole (**Figure 6**) and engage one of the

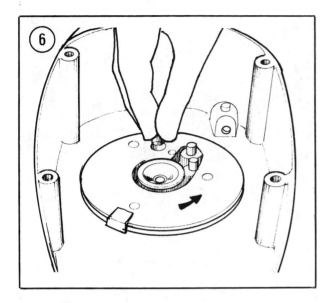

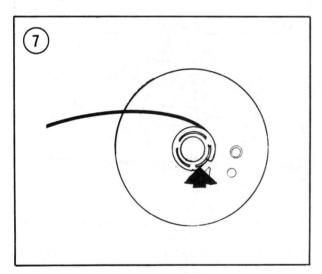

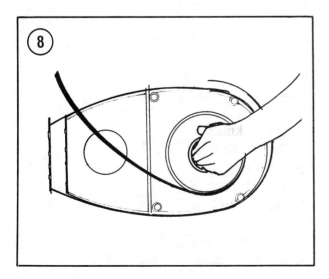

starter housing ribs to hold the pulley against spring tension.

9. Feed the rope through the starter housing hole and install the handle assembly. Tie a knot in the end of the rope.

10. Remove the punch and install the remaining plate screw.

11. Install the starter pawl, friction spring assembly and secure the pawl in place with the circlip.

12. Test the starter action by pulling the rope handle. The pawl should extend when the rope is pulled and retract when released.

Assembly
(Models Without Pulley Plate)

1. Lubricate the spring and housing spring cavity with Lubriplate 777 or OMC Triple-Guard grease.

2. Wipe the outer diameter of the spindle with Lubriplate 777 or OMC Triple-Guard grease.

3. Install spring on pulley as shown in **Figure 7**.

4. Install pulley in housing with spring passing through the spring cavity gate. The rib in the center of the housing should engage the spindle slot.

5. Clean the spindle screw threads of all old adhesive. Spray threads with OMC Locquic Primer. Install lockwasher on screw and wipe screw threads with OMC Screw Lock. Install and tighten screw.

6. Rotate pulley counterclockwise until outer spring loop engages outer face of spring cavity (**Figure 8**).

7. Install the starter pawl and friction spring assembly and secure the pawl in place with the circlip.

8. Install rope as described in this chapter.

9. Test the starter action by pulling the rope handle. The pawl should extend when the rope is pulled and retract when released.

10

SWING ARM GEAR DRIVE STARTER

This starter type is used on 1973-1978 4 hp, Deluxe 4 hp and 4.5 hp outboards. It must be partially disassembled to replace the rope.

Removal/Installation

1. Disconnect the armature plate-to-power pack connector to prevent the engine from accidentally starting.

2. Pull the starter rope out enough to tie a slip knot behind the handle. Untie the knot holding the rope in the handle and remove the handle assembly.

3. Release the slip knot made in Step 2 and gradually allow the starter to unwind while holding the pulley.

4. Disconnect the starter spring at the cup and stop assembly and pull it out as far as possible to relieve spring tension.

NOTE
On some models, removal of the ignition coil will increase access for screw removal and subsequent starter assembly removal.

5. Remove the shoulder screw (A, **Figure 9**) and the adjustment screw (B, **Figure 9**). Remove the starter assembly from the power head.

6. Clean threads of the 2 screws to remove all old adhesive. Spray the threads with OMC Locquic Primer.

7. Wipe the shoulder screw threads with OMC Screw Lock. Make sure the idler gear arm is located between the 2 tabs of the cup and stop assembly. Position the starter assembly to the power head and install the shoulder and adjustment screws finger-tight.

8. Coat starter spring with a light coat of Lubriplate 777 or OMC Triple-Guard grease.

9. Install OMC tool part No. 383967 in lower motor cover groove at side of idler arm.

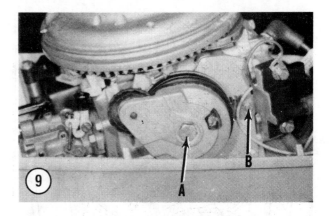

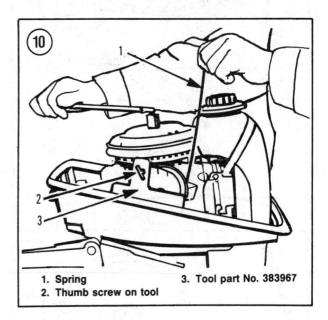

1. Spring
2. Thumb screw on tool
3. Tool part No. 383967

1. Pull rope out fully
2. Extend spring

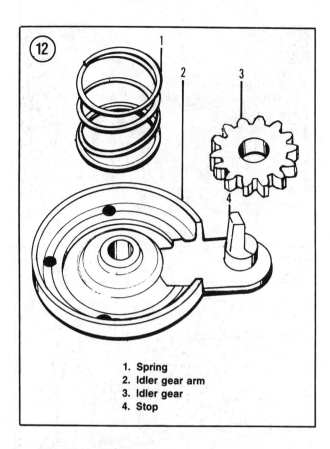

1. Spring
2. Idler gear arm
3. Idler gear
4. Stop

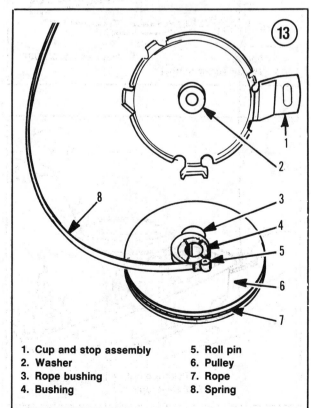

1. Cup and stop assembly
2. Washer
3. Rope bushing
4. Bushing
5. Roll pin
6. Pulley
7. Rope
8. Spring

Rotate tool thumbscrew as required to position it in the idler arm hole.

10. Make sure idler gear engages flywheel, then turn flywheel clockwise and wind starter spring into cup and stop assembly until the spring loop touches the pulley slot. See **Figure 10**.

11. Hold pulley from turning and remove tool, then let pulley rotate slowly until spring tension is relieved.

12. Reinstall tool part No. 383967 and turn flywheel clockwise enough to rotate starter pulley 1 1/2 turns to preload the spring. Hold pulley and remove tool.

13. Release the end of the rope and feed it through the lower motor cover hole, pulling it out as far as possible. Hold rope fully extended and grasp the spring end loop. Pull spring from cup and stop assembly. See **Figure 11**. If spring can be pulled out 8-18 in., preload is satisfactory. If not, repeat Steps 10-13.

14. Install rope handle assembly and tie a knot in the end of the rope.

15. Hold the idler gear arm stop against the cup stop. Make sure the idler gear teeth engage the flywheel properly, then tighten the adjustment screw.

16. Tighten the shoulder screw to 10-12 ft.-lb.

17. Install the ignition coil, if removed.

18. Reconnect the 4-wire connector.

10

Disassembly

1. Remove the idler gear arm, gear and gear arm spring from the starter assembly. See **Figure 12**.

2. Separate the pulley from the cup and stop assembly. Note spring loop position and disconnect the spring from the pulley roll pin. See **Figure 13**.

3. Remove the rope from the pulley, then remove the rope bushing.

4. Remove the idler gear arm bushing. Remove the bushing from each side of the pulley.

Cleaning and Inspection

1. Wash all metal parts in solvent and blow dry with compressed air.
2. Check metal parts for corrosion. Remove corrosion, if found, and wipe parts with an oil-dampened cloth.
3. Check spring for wear or broken end loops. Replace as required.
4. Check rope for fraying. Replace as required.

Assembly

1. Insert pulley bushing.
2. Tie a knot in one end of the rope. Insert the other end through the bushing rope hole. See **Figure 14**.
3. Pull the rope through until the knot seats in the pulley bushing. Hold the pulley with the knot facing you, then wind the pulley clockwise. Tape or install a rubber band to hold rope in pulley.
4. Wipe bushings with Lubriplate 777 or OMC Triple-Guard grease and insert in pulley and idler gear arm.
5. Install washer in cup and pulley assembly, hooking spring end loop to pulley roll pin. See **Figure 13**.
6. Sandwich pulley and spring to cup and stop assembly. The spring should extend through the cup slot. See **Figure 15**.
7. Assemble idler gear with shoulder resting against gear arm, then install arm and spring to pulley and cup. Locate the idler gear shaft stop between the cup and stop assembly tabs without turning pulley and disengaging spring end. See **Figure 16**.
8. Install starter mechanism to power head as described in this chapter.

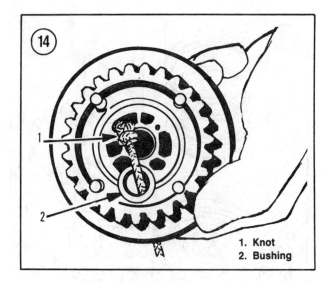

1. Knot
2. Bushing

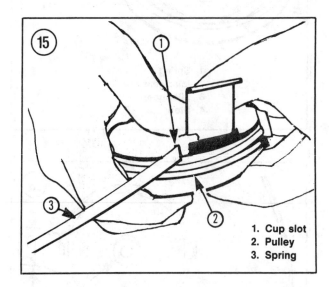

1. Cup slot
2. Pulley
3. Spring

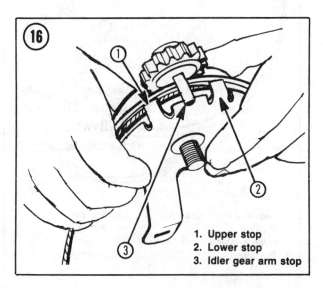

1. Upper stop
2. Lower stop
3. Idler gear arm stop

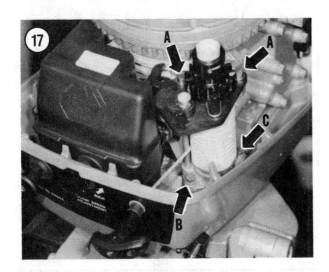

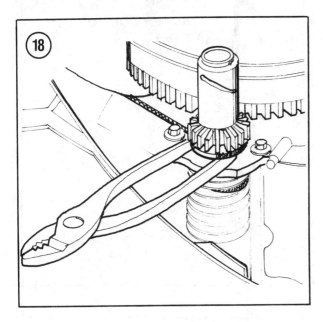

SIDE-MOUNTED
PINION GEAR STARTER

This starter type operates in a manner similar to an automotive starter. The nylon pinion slides up to engage the flywheel as the rope is pulled, then disengages when the engine starts.

Removal/Installation
(5-9.5 hp)

1. Disconnect the armature plate-to-power pack connector to prevent the engine from accidentally starting.

2. Pull the starter rope out enough to tie a slip knot behind the handle. Untie the knot holding the rope in the handle and remove the handle assembly.

NOTE
The version used on the 9.5 hp engine has no lower retainer plate fasteners.

3. Remove the 2 top starter screws (A, **Figure 17**). Remove the front spring retainer plate screw (B, **Figure 17**).
4. Loosen the rear retainer plate screw (C, **Figure 17**). Let the plate drop enough to release the starter spring hook.
5. Remove the starter and main spring from the power head.
6. Lubricate the lower retainer bushing with several drops of Johnson or Evinrude 50/1 outboard lubricant.
7. Fit the external tang of the starter assembly main spring into the lower retainer plate slot. Tighten both lower retainer plate screws.
8. Install the starter spool assembly so that the spool slot engages the internal rewind spring tang. Install and tighten the top starter screws to 60-84 in.-lb.
9. Disengage the cam follower and insert a flat-blade screwdriver in the lever arm slot. Install an O-ring or rubber band above the pinion teeth to prevent engagement with the flywheel.
10. Rotate the spool counterclockwise 12 1/2-14 turns (except 9.5 hp) or 20 1/2 turns (9.5 hp) using a speeder or ratchet wrench and a flat tip driver which fits into the inner slot of the spool.
11. With 9.5 hp models, raise pinion gear to engage flywheel and lock in place by sliding plier handles under the gear. See **Figure 18**.
12. With all others, insert a pin punch in the pinion gear roll pin hole to prevent the spool from unwinding. See **Figure 19**.
13. Insert the knot end of the starter rope through the spool slot. Hold the rope and

10

remove the pliers or pin punch. Let the starter slowly wind the rope up.

14. Insert the rope through the lower motor cover eyelet and tie a slip knot. Install the handle assembly and tie a knot in the end of the rope to fit into the handle.

15. Release the slip knot and remove the screwdriver and O-ring or rubber band. Pull the starter handle several times to make sure it engages with the flywheel.

16. Make sure the starter interlock functions properly. The starter should lock when the throttle is opened beyond the START position.

17. Reconnect the 4-wire connector.

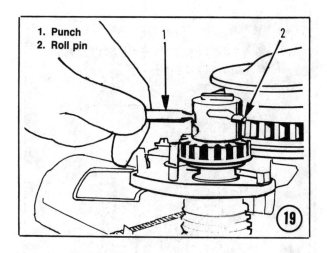

1. Punch
2. Roll pin

Starter Rope
Replacement (5-9.5 hp)

1. Disconnect the armature plate-to-power pack connector to prevent the engine from accidentally starting.

2. Pull the starter rope out until it is fully extended. On 9.5 hp models, raise the pinion gear to engage the flywheel and lock in place by inserting plier handles under the gear. See **Figure 18**. On all others, insert a small punch in the roll pinhole to lock the starter in the extended position. See **Figure 19**.

3. Untie the knot holding the rope in the handle and remove the handle assembly. Pull the rope from the spool.

4. If the rope has broken while in service, rotate the spool counterclockwise 20 1/2 turns (9.5 hp) or 12 1/2-14 turns (all others) using a speeder or ratchet wrench and a flat tip driver which fits into the inner slot of the spool.

5. Tie a knot in the new rope about 1/2 in. from the end, then feed the rope through the pulley slot until the knot rests snugly against the pulley.

6. Feed the rope counterclockwise around the pulley once and between the spool and guide.

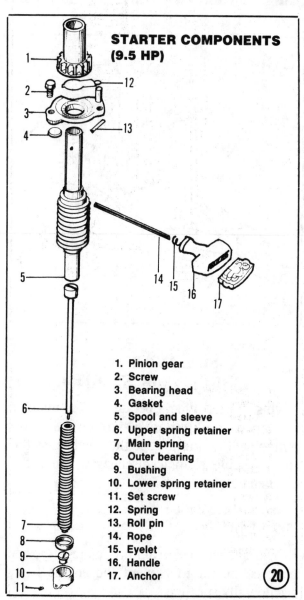

STARTER COMPONENTS (9.5 HP)

1. Pinion gear
2. Screw
3. Bearing head
4. Gasket
5. Spool and sleeve
6. Upper spring retainer
7. Main spring
8. Outer bearing
9. Bushing
10. Lower spring retainer
11. Set screw
12. Spring
13. Roll pin
14. Rope
15. Eyelet
16. Handle
17. Anchor

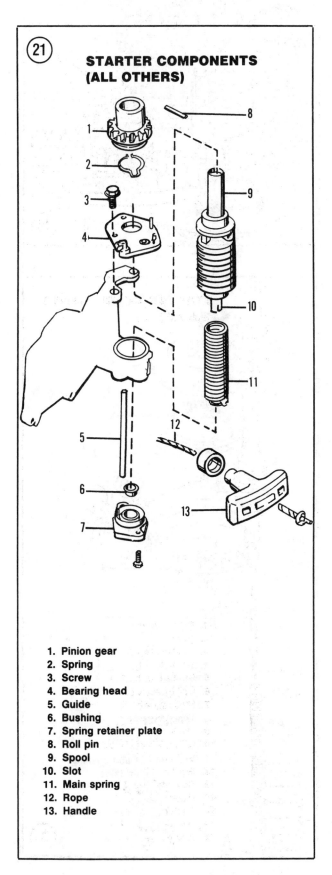

STARTER COMPONENTS (ALL OTHERS)

1. Pinion gear
2. Spring
3. Screw
4. Bearing head
5. Guide
6. Bushing
7. Spring retainer plate
8. Roll pin
9. Spool
10. Slot
11. Main spring
12. Rope
13. Handle

7. Insert the rope through the lower motor cover and install the handle assembly.

8. Hold rope handle securely and remove pliers or punch holding starter pinion gear. Let starter rope rewind slowly.

Disassembly/Assembly (5-9.5 hp)

Starter disassembly should only be necessary if the pinion gear is damaged. Refer to **Figure 20** (9.5 hp) or **Figure 21** (all others) for this procedure.

1. Remove the roll pin with a pin punch.

2. Remove the pinion. Release the cam follower and slide the bearing head off the starter spool.

3. Remove the main spring from the spool assembly.

4. On 9.5 hp models, remove the lower spring retainer set screw. Remove retainer, bushing and outer bearing.

5. To assemble, install outer bearing, bushing and retainer on 9.5 hp models. Tighten setscrew.

6. Install the pinion spring. Position bearing head and pinion gear on starter spool. Spring loop must fit over bearing head post.

7. Align pinion slot with spool holes. Install roll pin with split seam facing to the side to prevent dragging against the pinion gear slot.

8. Install main spring in spool assembly.

Cleaning and Inspection (5-9.5 hp)

1. Wash all parts in solvent and blow dry with compressed air.

2. Check all parts for excessive wear or damage. Replace as required.

3. Check rope for fraying. Replace as required.

10

Removal/Installation
(9.9 and 15 hp)

1. Disconnect the armature plate-to-power pack connector to prevent the engine from accidentally starting.

2. Pull the starter rope out enough to tie a slip knot behind the handle. Untie the knot holding the rope in the handle and remove the handle assembly.

3. Release the slip knot made in Step 2 and gradually allow the pulley to slowly rewind the rope.

4. Remove the air silencer assembly.

5. Loosen the starter mounting screw. Hold pulley and cup together to keep the spring in the cup and remove the mounting screw.

6. If starter does not require disassembly, install a 3/8 in.×16 nut on the mounting screw and finger-tighten to prevent the cup and pulley from coming apart.

7. Installation is the reverse of removal.

Starter Rope Replacement
(9.9 and 15 hp)

> *WARNING*
> *Disassembling this starter mechanism without holding the spring in place can result in the spring unwinding violently, causing serious personal injury. Wear safety glasses and gloves during this procedure.*

Refer to **Figure 22** for this procedure.

1. Remove the starter as described in this chapter.

2. Carefully secure the starter housing horizontally in a vise with protective jaws.

3. Remove the mounting screw and washer.

4. Unclip the pinion spring and remove from the starter pulley with the pinion gear.

5. Insert a putty knife or similar instrument between the pulley and cup to hold the spring in place. Remove the pulley from the cup.

6. Remove the rope from the pulley.

7. Thread the new rope through the hole in the pulley. Tie a knot in the end of the rope

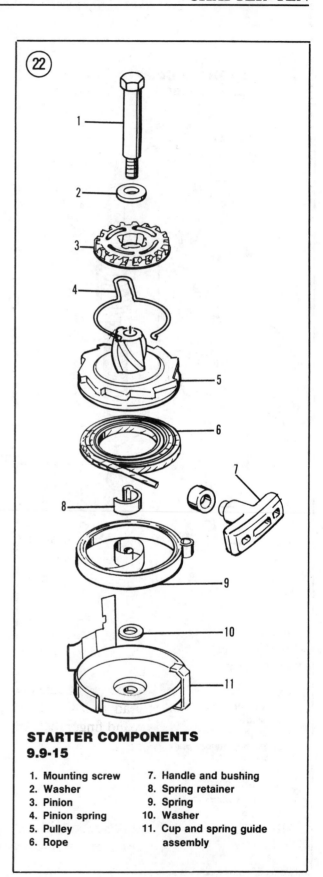

STARTER COMPONENTS
9.9-15

1. Mounting screw
2. Washer
3. Pinion
4. Pinion spring
5. Pulley
6. Rope
7. Handle and bushing
8. Spring retainer
9. Spring
10. Washer
11. Cup and spring guide assembly

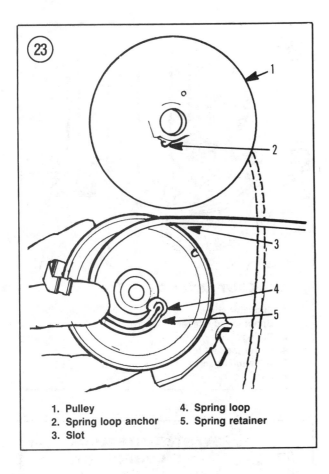

1. Pulley   4. Spring loop
2. Spring loop anchor   5. Spring retainer
3. Slot

and wind the rope onto the pulley in a counterclockwise direction.

8. Fit the pulley to the cup so that the spring loop will engage the pulley shaft cutout.

9. Install the pinion and pinion spring on the pulley.

10. Lubricate the mounting screw and washer with Johnson or Evinrude 50/1 outboard lubricant. Install screw through pulley, cup washer and cup.

11. If starter is not to be immediately installed on manifold, thread a 3/8 in. $\times$ 16 nut on the mounting screw and finger-tighten to keep the assembly together.

**Starter Disassembly
(9.9 and 15 hp)**

1. Remove the starter from the manifold and install a nut on the mounting screw as described in this chapter.

2. Carefully secure the starter assembly vertically in a vise with protective jaws.

*WARNING
Wear safety glasses and gloves during
Step 3.*

3. Slip a flat screwdriver blade through the exposed spring loop and withdraw the spring from the cup.

4. Remove the starter from the vise. Remove the nut, mounting screw and washer.

5. Unclip the pinion spring and remove from the starter pulley with the pinion gear.

6. Remove the pulley, spring, cup washer and spring retainer from the cup assembly.

7. Remove the rope from the pulley, if required.

**Cleaning and Inspection
(9.9 and 15 hp)**

1. Clean all metal and plastic parts in solvent. Blow dry with compressed air.

2. Check spring for wear or broken end loops. Replace as required.

3. Check pinion and pulley for excessive wear and chipped or broken teeth.

4. Check cup for corrosion or damage. Clean or replace as required.

5. Check rope for fraying. Replace as required.

Assembly (9.9 and 15 hp)

Refer to **Figure 22** for this procedure.

1. Install starter rope as described in this chapter.

2. Lubricate spring surface in cup with Lubriplate 777 or OMC Triple-Guard grease.

3. Install spring and retainer in cup as shown in **Figure 23**.

4. Position cup washer and install pulley with spring loop engaging the pulley loop anchor (**Figure 23**).

5. Place pinion on pulley. Wipe mounting screw threads with Johnson or Evinrude 50/1

10

outboard oil and install screw with washer through pulley, cup washer and cup.

6. Install a 3/8 in.×16 nut on the mounting screw finger-tight.

7. Hold cup in one hand and wind spring into cup by turning pulley counterclockwise (as seen from top of pulley). As spring is wound and resistance felt, feed the spring into the cup through the slot to relieve tension.

8. When spring is completely wound into cup with outer loop drawn up against the cup, wind the rope counterclockwise around the pulley and install pinion spring.

9. Install starter on manifold as described in this chapter.

10. Pull the rope out as far as possible, then pull out the spring loop end. It should extend at least 1/2 in. from the cup.

11. Make sure the starter interlock functions properly. The starter should lock when the throttle is opened beyond the START position.

12. Reconnect the 4-wire connector.

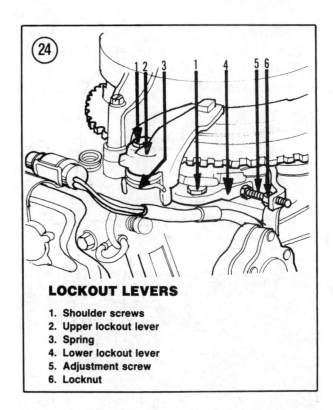

LOCKOUT LEVERS

1. **Shoulder screws**
2. **Upper lockout lever**
3. **Spring**
4. **Lower lockout lever**
5. **Adjustment screw**
6. **Locknut**

FLYWHEEL MOUNTED STARTER

This starter type is used on 18-40 hp outboards. A locking plunger connected to the gear shift lockout lever prevents starter engagement if the motor is in gear. **Figure 24** shows the older type lockout system; **Figure 25** shows the late model system. The starter must be disassembled to replace the rope.

Removal/Installation

1. Remove the 3 housing screws.

2. Remove the starter housing from the power head (**Figure 26**).

> *NOTE*
> *The starter lockout cable should be disconnected at the power head in Step 3 if power head is to be removed.*

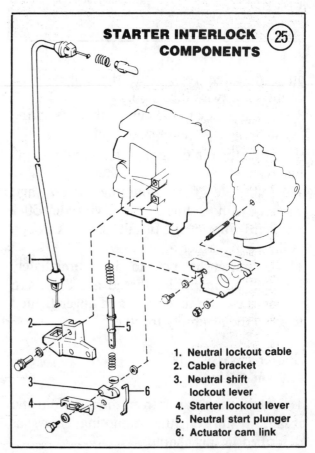

STARTER INTERLOCK COMPONENTS

1. **Neutral lockout cable**
2. **Cable bracket**
3. **Neutral shift lockout lever**
4. **Starter lockout lever**
5. **Neutral start plunger**
6. **Actuator cam link**

3. Disconnect the lockout cable connector (arrow, **Figure 26**) from the starter housing with a screwdriver, if so equipped.

4. Installation is the reverse of removal.

Disassembly

WARNING
Disassembling this starter mechanism without holding the spring in place can result in the spring unwinding violently, causing serious personal injury. Wear safety glasses and gloves during this procedure.

Refer to **Figure 27** (typical) for this procedure.

1. Pull the starter rope out enough to tie a slip knot behind the handle. Pry the rope anchor from the handle.

2. Remove the handle, untie the slip knot and gradually allow the starter to unwind while holding the pulley.

3. Remove the circlip holding the starter pawl in place (**Figure 28**).

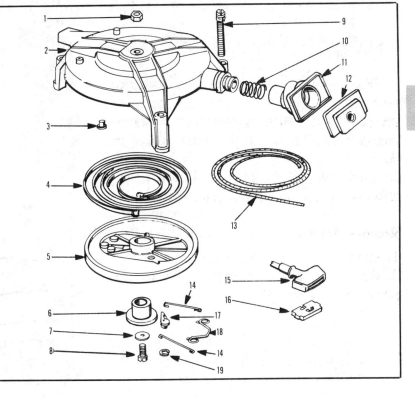

**FLYWHEEL MOUNTED
STARTER COMPONENTS**

1. Spindle screw nut
2. Rewind starter assembly
3. Guide pin
4. Spring
5. Pulley
6. Starter spindle
7. Spindle washer
8. Screw
9. Mounting screw
10. Spring
11. Handle support
12. Support plate
13. Rope
14. Pawl link spring
15. Handle
16. Handle anchor
17. Starter pawl
18. Friction spring
19. Circlip

10

4. Lift the pawl off its shaft and disengage the friction spring and links. Remove the pawl and spring/link assembly. See **Figure 29**.

5. Remove the screw and washer from the spindle (**Figure 30**). It may be necessary to hold the nut on the top of the starter housing with a wrench while loosening the screw.

6. Remove the spindle (**Figure 31**) and hold pulley in housing while turning it over (legs downward) on the workbench or floor.

7. Release the pulley and rap the housing sharply to dislodge the pulley and spring. The spring should uncoil within the starter housing legs.

8. Lift the housing up and remove the spring and pulley.

Cleaning and Inspection

1. Wash all metal parts in solvent and blow dry with compressed air.

2. Check spring for wear or broken end loops. Replace as required.

> *NOTE*
> *If starter pawl is replaced on 1973-1978 models, use part No. 324755. This redesigned pawl is used on 1979 and later models and can be fitted to previous models.*

3. Check pawl, friction spring and spindle for wear.

4. Remove any sharp edges or rough surfaces from pulley and housing that might fray the rope.

5. Check rope for fraying. Replace as required.

6. Check starter interlock components for wear or damage. Replace as required.

Assembly

> *WARNING*
> *During starter mechanism assembly the spring may unwind violently, causing serious personal injury. Wear safety glasses and gloves during this procedure.*

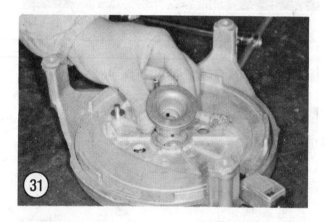

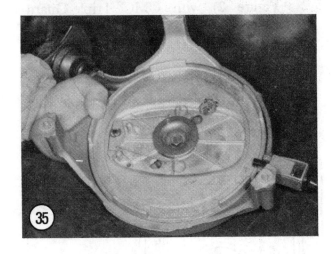

Refer to **Figure 27** for this procedure.

1. Lubricate the spindle and housing spindle area with Lubriplate 777 or OMC Triple-Guard grease.

2. Insert one spring loop over the pin in the housing cutout (**Figure 32**).

3. Carefully coil the spring into the housing. See **Figure 32**.

4. Install pulley in housing, making sure that pin on pulley engages the inner spring loop.

5. Install spindle in housing. Install spindle screw with washer. Thread nut on screw as it protrudes through the top of the housing. Hold nut with one wrench and tighten the spindle screw with a second wrench.

6. Wind pulley counterclockwise until spring is tight, then back pulley off 1/2-1 turn and align the pulley and housing holes (arrow, **Figure 33**). Insert a nail, punch or drill in holes to lock pulley in place.

7. Tie a knot in the end of a new rope. Insert the opposite end of the rope in the pulley hole and feed the rope until it comes out the side of the housing. Pull the rope through the pulley until the knot rests against it.

8. Lubricate the handle end of the rope with Lubriplate 777 or OMC Triple-Guard grease. Thread rope through handle using Johnson or Evinrude tool part No. 378774.

9. Press rope into channel in rope anchor with end of rope butted tightly against channel. See **Figure 34**. Install anchor in handle.

10. Pull on the end of the rope to make sure the knot seats against the pulley, then remove the locking nail, punch or drill and slowly let rope wind onto pulley.

11. Lightly lubricate the pawl pin with Lubriplate 777 or OMC Triple-Guard grease. Install pawl and link assembly. Install circlip. **Figure 35** shows the finished assembly.

12. Pull starter rope out and check pawl operation. Pawl should extend when rope is pulled out and retract when rope is released.

13. Pull the rope out and release it several times, then check to make sure the housing arrow aligns with the pulley mark. If not aligned properly, pull rope out and release several more times. A new rope must lose some of its stiffness before the marks will properly align.

10

NOTE: If you own a 1985 or later model, first check the Supplement at the back of the book for any new service information.

Chapter Eleven

Electric Motors

A variety of Johnson and Evinrude Scout models have been offered since the electric trolling motor was introduced in 1975. Scout electrics are available with foot or hand controls in bow or transom mount models. They have been offered in 12-volt and 12/24-volt models. The propeller connects directly to the motor armature in all models, eliminating the need for gears.

This chapter covers lubrication, maintenance, propeller replacement, lower unit and control housing troubleshooting and repair. **Figure 1** shows the major components of a basic electric model.

LUBRICATION

Electric models require a minimum of care. For this reason, proper lubrication and maintenance is all the more important.

Perform the following every 60 days (fresh water) or 30 days (salt water).

1. Foot control model:
   a. Remove the steering cover housing and lubricate the steering gear and pinion (**Figure 2**) with OMC Triple-Guard grease.
   b. Invert the foot control and lubricate the steering cable (**Figure 3**) with OMC Triple-Guard grease.
   c. With the foot control inverted, lubricate the hinge pin (**Figure 4**) with SAE 30W engine oil.

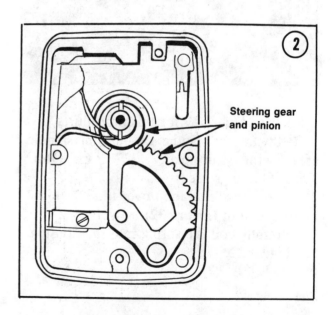

Steering gear and pinion

ELECTRIC MODEL COMPONENTS

1. Control housing
2. Reset button
3. Adjusting knob and collar
4. Steering friction knob
5. Swivel bracket
6. Battery clamps
7. Motor housing
8. Propeller
9. Skeg
10. Adaptor
11. Motor tube
12. Serial No./model No. plate
13. Stern bracket
14. Clamp screw
15. Tilt button
16. Steering handle
17. Directional switch
18. Master switch
19. Speed control knob
20. Bow arm assembly
21. Mounting bracket
22. Latch release

23. Rest pad and strap
24. Mounting tube bracket
25. On/off switch
26. Serial No./Model No. plate
27. Master switch
28. Steering foot pedal
29. Speed control wheel

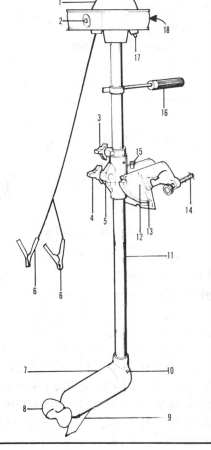

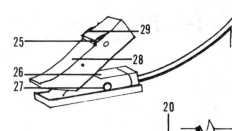

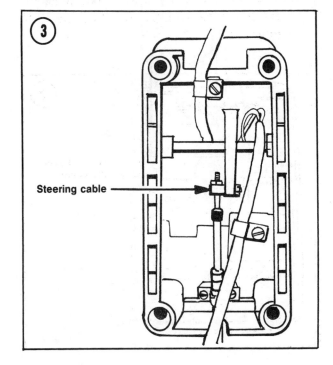

①

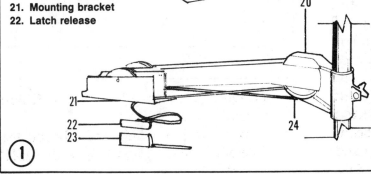

③

Steering cable

④

Hinge pin

11

2. Hand steering model:
   a. Lubricate the steering adjustment mechanism (1, **Figure 5**) with OMC Triple-Guard grease.
   b. Lubricate the mounting bracket hinges with SAE 30W engine oil.
3. Transom mount model:
   a. Lubricate the clamps screws (1, **Figure 6**) with OMC Triple-Guard grease.
   b. Lubricate the tilt button and hinge points (2, **Figure 6**) with SAE 30W engine oil.

PERIODIC MAINTENANCE

Perform the following on a periodic basis. Johnson and Evinrude recommends the maintenance interval be based on the type of use and frequency with which the motor is used. At a minimum, such maintenance should be performed once a season.

NOTE
If the electric is used in salt water, flush all external surfaces with fresh water after each use to prevent salt accumulation.

1. Clean the entire motor thoroughly.
2. Check for damaged or corroded areas on the finish. Clean such areas and repaint with OMC spray paint.
3. Look for any loose, damaged or missing components. Tighten or replace as necessary.
4. Check steering and battery cable condition. Service as required.
5. Service the battery. See Chapter Seven.

BATTERY

Johnson and Evinrude recommend the use of a marine-type deep-cycle battery with a minimum 80 ampere hour rating. If a cranking type battery is used, it should have a minimum 100 ampere hour rating.

Where the electric is used in conjunction with a primary motor, separate batteries

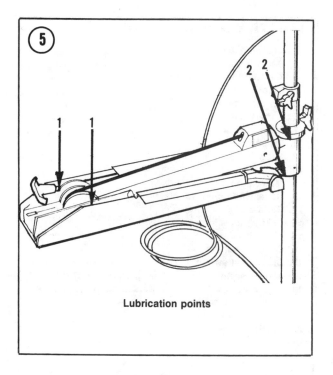

Lubrication points

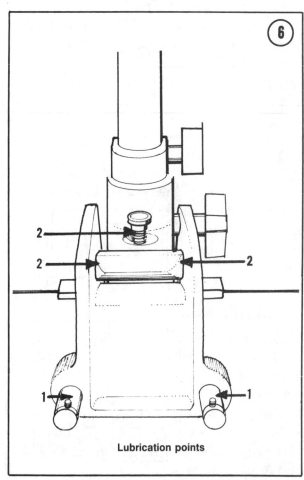

Lubrication points

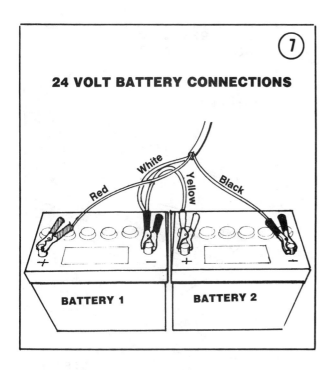

24 VOLT BATTERY CONNECTIONS

should be provided for each motor. When a common battery is used for both motors, the electric may discharge it to a point where the primary motor cannot be started. All procedures and specifications in Chapter Seven except the following apply to electric use.

1. Connect 24-volt models to the 2 batteries as shown in **Figure 7**.
2. Recharge deep-cycle batteries after every use. Use a 10-15 amp charger set to provide a slow charge. Check the battery state of charge with a hydrometer and do not charge in excess of 16 hours.

PROPELLER

Propeller Replacement

1. Disconnect the negative battery cable.
2. Hold propeller with one hand to prevent it from rotating. Remove and discard the cotter pin from the plastic propeller.
3. Remove propeller from prop shaft.
4. Installation is the reverse of removal. Make sure the shear pin engages the propeller hub recess.

Shear Pin Replacement

1. Support the prop shaft on a block of wood to protect shaft, seals and bearings from shock.
2. Remove shear pin from shaft with a hammer and punch.
3. Installation is the reverse of removal. Center pin in shaft.

1975-1981 12 VOLT BOW MOUNT MODEL

The electrical system consists of a master on/off toggle switch, a spring-loaded foot-operated on/off switch, a potentiometer, transistor, the electric motor and connecting wiring. A direction indicator light is provided for night operation.

The propeller must be removed for all troubleshooting as a safety precaution. All electrical connections and terminal screws are coated with OMC Liquid Neoprene Dip to provide insulation. This material must be scraped off before testing to assure good electrical connections. When testing has been completed, cover all connections and terminals with a fresh application of OMC Liquid Neoprene Dip.

Troubleshooting

Motor does not run

Refer to **Figure 8** (1975-1976) or **Figure 9** (1977-1981) for this procedure.

1. With the foot control cable connected to the battery, connect the black voltmeter lead to the negative battery terminal.
2. Turn the foot control master switch ON.
3. Probe the master switch terminal at point 1 with the red voltmeter lead. The meter should show battery voltage.
4. If the meter does not show battery voltage in Step 3, probe the master switch terminal at point 1A with the red voltmeter lead. If battery voltage is shown here, replace the

11

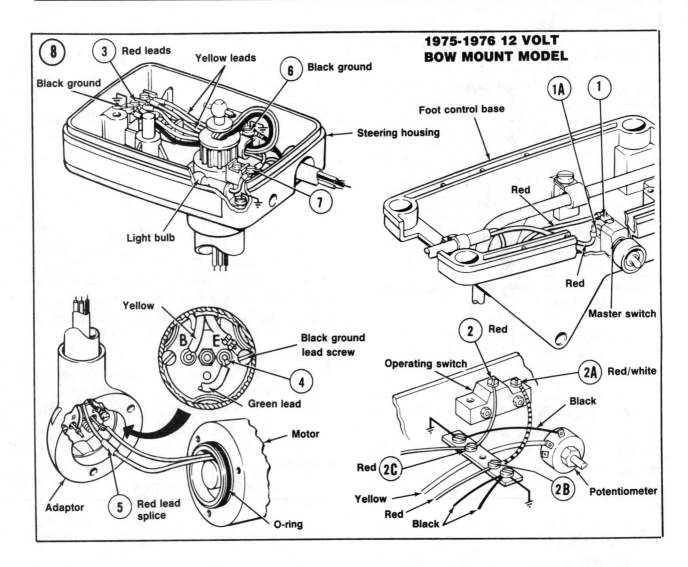

master switch. If battery voltage is not shown, check the continuity of the foot control cable-to-battery terminal leads.

5. Depress operating switch (master switch ON) and probe point 2 with the red voltmeter lead. The meter should read battery voltage and the direction indicator lamp in the steering housing should light.

6. If no voltage is shown in Step 5, probe point 2B with the red voltmeter lead. If battery voltage is shown here, the operating switch is defective. If no voltage is shown, there is an open in the wiring between point 1 and point 2A. With 1975-1976 models, also check for a poor contact, loose terminal screw or an open lead at point 2B, **Figure 8**.

7. Remove the 4 screws underneath the steering housing and remove the housing cover. Depress operating switch (master switch ON) and probe point 3 with the red voltmeter lead. The meter should show battery voltage.

8. If battery voltage is not shown in Step 7, move the red voltmeter lead to point 7. If battery voltage is now shown, there is an open in the wiring between point 3 and point 7.

9. If no voltage is shown in Step 8, check continuity between point 2 and point 7. If there is no continuity, replace the wiring cable between the steering housing and the foot control.

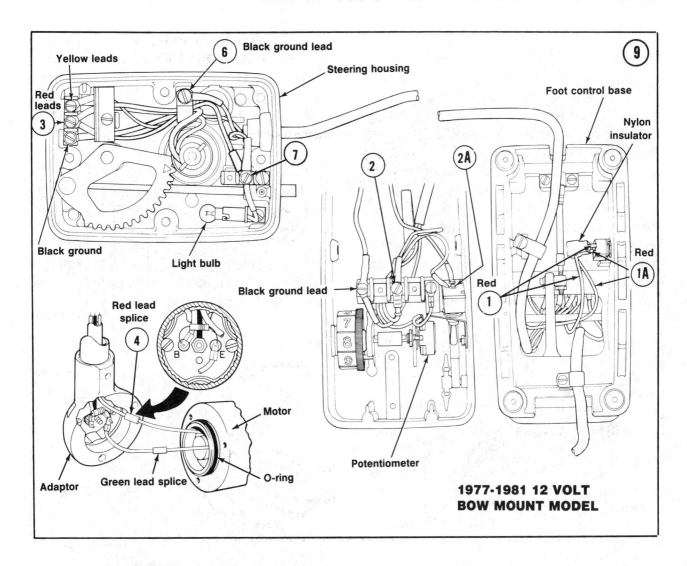

Yellow leads

Red leads

3

Black ground

Red lead splice

4

Adaptor

Green lead splice

6

Black ground lead

Steering housing

7

Light bulb

B E

Motor

O-ring

2

2A

Foot control base

Nylon insulator

Red

1A

Red

1

Black ground lead

Potentiometer

9

1977-1981 12 VOLT BOW MOUNT MODEL

10. Separate motor from adaptor but do not disconnect the wires for this step. Depress the operating switch (master switch ON):

a. 1975-1976—Probe point 4, **Figure 8** with the red voltmeter lead. If battery voltage is not shown, there is an open between point 3 and point 4. Remove the heat shrink tube on the red lead splice at point 5 and check for battery voltage. If voltage is not shown, there is an open between point 3 and point 4. If voltage is shown and the motor does not run, perform *Motor Runs Fast, No Speed Control* test to check potentiometer and *Motor Test* to check motor.

b. 1977-1981—Remove the heat shrink tube on the red lead splice at point 4, **Figure 9** and check for battery voltage. If voltage is not shown, there is an open between point 3 and point 4. If voltage is shown and the motor does not run, perform *Motor Runs Fast, No Speed Control* test to check potentiometer and *Motor Test* to check motor.

Motor runs fast, no speed control (1975-1976)

Refer to **Figure 10** for this procedure.
1. Disconnect the battery cables.

11

2. Separate motor from the adaptor. Unsolder the green lead at point 1 (transistor emitter terminal). Set the ohmmeter on the low scale and connect the red test lead to point 1 and the black test lead to point 2. Note the reading and reverse the leads. If the meter does not show an open circuit in one direction and a low ohms reading in the other, replace the transistor.

3. Unsolder the yellow lead at point 3 (transistor base terminal). Connect the red test lead to point 3A and the black test lead to point 4. Move the speed control wheel to position 1 (as seen through opening in top of pedal). The meter should read 500 ohms.

4. Rotate the speed control wheel to position 9. The meter reading should decrease to approximately zero ohms. If it does not, check for continuity of yellow lead between point 3A and point 5 and between point 5 and point 6.

5. Move the red test lead to point 6 and rotate the speed control wheel from position 9 to position 1. The meter reading should increase from almost zero to 500 ohms. If it does not, move the red test lead to point 7. If there is no increase in the reading at point 7, check for continuity between point 7 and point 4. If there is continuity, replace the

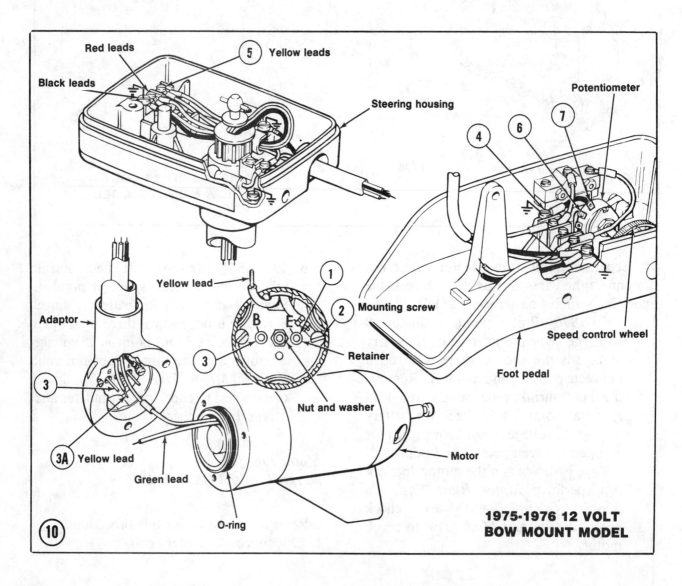

1975-1976 12 VOLT
BOW MOUNT MODEL

potentiometer. If there is no continuity, replace the wire between point 7 and point 4.

Motor runs fast,
no speed control (1977-1981)

Refer to **Figure 11** for this procedure.

1. Disconnect the battery cables.

2. Separate the motor from the adaptor. Unsolder one end of resistor from the transistor.

3. Disconnect the red lead at point 5. Set the ohmmeter on the high scale and connect the red test lead to the disconnected lead at point 5. Connect the black meter lead to ground at point 8 and note the meter reading. Reverse the meter leads and note this reading. One reading should show high resistance and the other should show low resistance. If the meter shows low resistance in both directions, check for a pinched or shorted lead. If none is found, replace the transistor.

4. Disconnect the yellow foot control cable lead at point 9. Set the ohmmeter on the low scale and connect the red test lead to the disconnected yellow lead. Connect the black test lead to point 4. Move the speed control wheel to position 1 (as seen through opening in top of pedal). The meter should read 150 ohms.

5. Rotate the speed control wheel to position 9. The meter reading should decrease to approximately zero ohms.

6. If it does not, move the red test lead to point 6. Continuity indicates an open in the yellow lead between the upper housing and the foot control.

7. If continuity is not shown in Step 6, move the black test lead to point 7. Replace the potentiometer if continuity is not shown here.

8. If continuity is shown in Step 7, move the black test lead back to point 4. No continuity at this point indicates an open in the ground

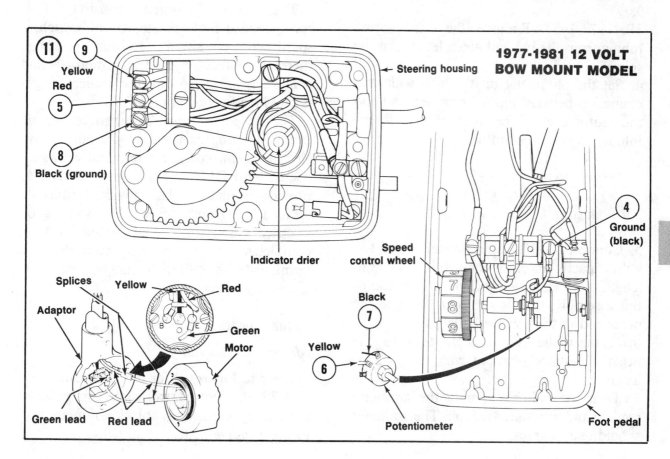

lead. Check connections and replace lead as required.

9. Disconnect yellow indicator driver lead at point 9. Set the ohmmeter on the high scale and connect the red test lead to the disconnected yellow lead. Connect the black test lead to the red indicator driver lead at point 5. The meter should show continuity. If it does not, test the motor as described in this chapter. If the motor is satisfactory, replace the adaptor.

Motor Test

1. Disconnect the battery leads.
2. Remove the 3 screws holding the motor to the adaptor. Gently tap the motor frame and separate it from the adaptor.
3A. 1975-1976—Remove the heat shrink tubing from the red lead and cut the splice. Unsolder green lead from terminal E, **Figure 9**.
3B. 1977-1981—Remove the heat shrink tubing from the red and green leads. Cut the splices.
4. Set the ohmmeter on the high scale and connect it between the red or green lead and the motor case. If the meter does not read infinity, replace the motor.

> *NOTE*
> *The battery used in Step 5 must be fully charged.*

5. Connect a 0-10 amp ammeter and a 100 amp capacity on/off switch within a 4 1/2 ft. length of 14 gauge wire. Connect one end of this assembly to the red motor lead and the other end to the positive battery terminal.
6. Connect the green motor lead to the negative battery terminal with a 4 1/2 ft. length of 14 gauge wire.
7. Turn the switch on, note the ammeter reading and turn the switch off. The ammeter should read 4 amps.

8. Replace the 0-10 amp ammeter with one that reads 125 amps. Hold the motor shaft with an in.-lb. torque wrench.
9. Turn switch on, note ammeter and torque wrench readings and turn switch off within 10 seconds. The ammeter should read 110 amps at 32 in.-lb. (1975-1976) or 105 amps at 31 in.-lb. (1977-1981).
10. Replace the motor if it does not meet the specifications in Step 7 and/or Step 9.
11. Reconnect motor to adapter. Use a new O-ring lubricated with SAE 30W oil. Install heat shrink tubing as required, resolder the leads using a heat sink to protect the transistor, slide tubing over splice and apply heat to shrink it in place. Coat screw threads with OMC Screw Lock and tighten to 2-3 ft.-lb.

1982-ON 12 VOLT BOW MOUNT MODEL

The electrical system consists of a spring-loaded foot-operated on/off switch, a speed control switch, resistor assembly, thermal cutout, electric motor and connecting wiring. A direction indicator light is provided for operation at night.

The propeller must be removed for all troubleshooting as a safety precaution. All electrical connections and terminal screws are coated with OMC Liquid Neoprene Dip to provide insulation. This material must be scraped off before testing to assure good electrical connections. When testing has been completed, cover all connections and terminals with a fresh application of OMC Liquid Neoprene Dip.

Troubleshooting

Motor does not run

Refer to **Figure 12** for this procedure.
1. With the foot control cable connected to the battery, connect the black voltmeter lead to the negative battery terminal.

**1982-ON 12 VOLT
BOW MOUNT MODEL**

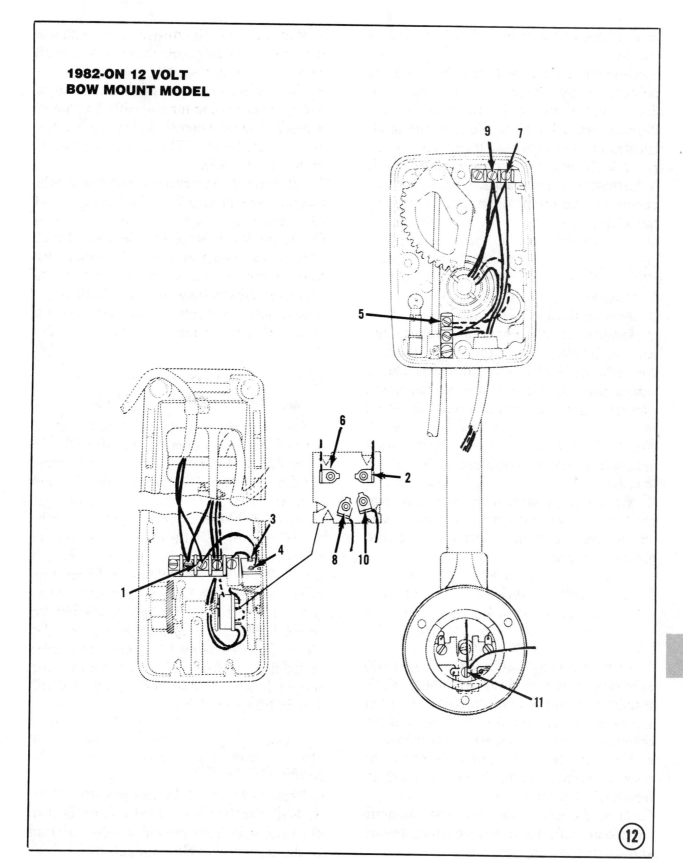

12

2. Connect the red voltmeter lead to terminal A. If the meter does not read battery voltage, check continuity between terminal A and the positive battery terminal.

3. Rotate speed control wheel to LOW. Depress operating switch and probe terminal B with the red test lead. If battery voltage is not shown, move red test lead to terminal C. Voltage at this point indicates an open in the circuit between terminal B and terminal C. If no voltage is shown, move red test lead to terminal D. Replace the operating switch if voltage is shown at terminal D. If no voltage is shown, move red test lead to terminal A. Voltage at this point indicates an open between terminal A and terminal D.

4. Remove the 4 screws underneath the steering housing and remove the housing cover. Move the red test lead to terminal E and depress the operating switch. The meter should read battery voltage and the direction indicator lamp in the steering housing should light.

5. If no voltage is shown in Step 4, probe terminal F with the red voltmeter lead. If battery voltage is shown here, there is an open in the circuit between terminal E and terminal F. If no voltage is shown, check the rotary switch as described in this chapter.

6. Rotate speed control wheel to NORMAL. Depress operating switch and probe terminal G with the red test lead. If battery voltage is not shown, move red test lead to terminal H. Voltage at this point indicates an open in the circuit between terminal G and terminal H. If no voltage is shown, check the rotary switch as described in this chapter.

7. Rotate speed control wheel to HIGH. Depress operating switch and probe terminal I with the red test lead. If battery voltage is not shown, move red test lead to terminal J. Voltage at this point indicates an open in the circuit between terminal I and terminal J. If no voltage is shown, check the rotary switch as described in this chapter.

8. Separate the motor from the adaptor. Connect the red test lead to terminal K. With speed control wheel at HIGH and operating switch depressed, the meter should show voltage. If not, there is an open in the circuit between terminal I and terminal K.

9. Rotate speed control wheel to NORMAL. With red test lead connected to terminal K and operating switch depressed, meter should read voltage. If not, check the resistor and thermal cutout.

10. Repeat Step 9 with the speed control wheel at LOW. If voltage is not shown, check the resistor and thermal cutout.

11. If voltage is shown in Steps 8-10 but the motor does not run, test the motor as described in this chapter.

Motor runs, no speed control

Refer to **Figure 13** for this procedure.

1. Disconnect the battery cables.

2. Remove the 4 screws underneath the steering housing and remove the housing cover. Disconnect the leads at terminals A, B and C.

3. Set an ohmmeter on the low scale and connect the black test lead to point D. Connect the red test lead to the red wire disconnected from terminal A in the steering housing.

4. Rotate the speed control wheel to HIGH. There should be no continuity. Move the wheel to NORMAL. There should be continuity. Move the wheel to LOW and then to OFF. There should be no continuity in either position.

5. Move the red test lead to the green wire disconnected from terminal B and repeat Step 4. There should be continuity only in NORMAL.

6. Move the red test lead to the green/white wire disconnected from terminal C and repeat Step 4. There should be continuity in all positions except OFF.

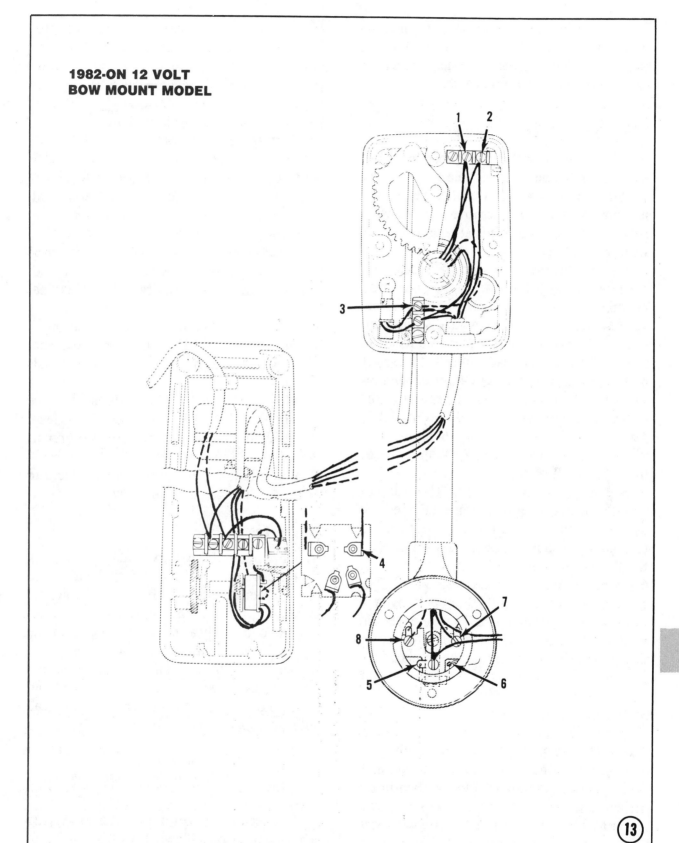

**1982-ON 12 VOLT
BOW MOUNT MODEL**

13

7. If the ohmmeter readings are not as specified in Steps 4-6, check the terminals and wiring for defects. If none are found, replace the speed control switch.

Motor runs only at high speed

Refer to **Figure 13** for this procedure.
1. Disconnect the battery cables.
2. Remove the 4 screws underneath the steering housing and remove the housing cover. Disconnect the leads at terminals A, B and C.
3. Set an ohmmeter on the low scale and connect the black test lead to the green lead disconnected from terminal B. Connect the red test lead to the red wire disconnected from terminal A. The meter should read 0.14-0.20 ohms. If it reads infinity, there may be an open in the thermal cutout or resistor.
4. Connect the black test lead to the green/white wire disconnected at terminal C. The meter should read 0.4-0.6 ohms. If it reads infinity, there may be an open in the thermal cutout or resistor.
5. Separate the motor from the adaptor without cutting the leads. Connect the red test lead to terminal E and the black test lead to terminal F. If continuity is not shown, replace the thermal cutout.
6. Move the red test lead to terminal G. The meter should read 0.14-0.20 ohms. Move the red test lead to terminal H. The meter should read 0.4-0.6 ohms. If an open circuit is shown at terminal G or terminal H, replace the resistor.

Rotary Switch Test

Refer to **Figure 14** for this procedure.
1. Disconnect the battery cables.
2. Disconnect all leads at the rotary switch.
3. Set the ohmmeter on the low scale. Connect black test lead to terminal A for entire test.

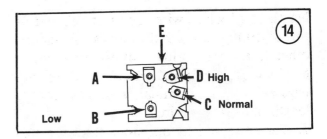

4. With switch OFF, probe terminals B, C, D and metal switch case with red test lead. There should be no continuity shown at any position.
5. Move the switch to LOW and probe terminals B, C and D with the red test lead. There should be continuity only at terminal B.
6. Move the switch to NORMAL and probe terminals B, C and D with the red test lead. There should be continuity only at terminals B and C.
7. Move the switch to HIGH and probe terminals B, C and D with the red test lead. There should be continuity only at terminals B and D.
8. If continuity is not shown as indicated in Steps 4-7, replace the rotary switch.

Motor Test

1. Disconnect the battery leads.
2. Remove the 3 screws holding the motor to the adaptor. Gently tap the motor frame and separate it from the adaptor.
3. Remove the heat shrink tubing from the red and green leads. Cut the splices.
4. Set the ohmmeter on the high scale and connect it between the red or green lead and the motor case. If the meter does not read infinity, replace the motor.

NOTE
The battery used in Step 5 must be fully charged.

5. Connect a 0-10 amp ammeter and a 125 amp capacity on/off switch within a 4 1/2 ft.

length of 14 gauge wire. Connect one end of this assembly to the red motor lead and the other end to the positive battery terminal.

6. Connect the green motor lead to the negative battery terminal with a 4 1/2 ft. length of 14 gauge wire.

7. Turn the switch on, note the ammeter reading and turn the switch off. The ammeter should read 6 amps.

8. Replace the 0-10 amp ammeter with one that reads 125 amps. Hold the motor shaft with an in.-lb. torque wrench.

9. Turn the switch on, note the ammeter and torque wrench readings and turn the switch off within 10 seconds. The ammeter should read 105 amps at 31 in.-lb.

10. Replace the motor if it does not meet the specifications in Step 7 and/or Step 9.

11. Reconnect motor to adapter. Use a new O-ring lubricated with SAE 30W oil. Install heat shrink tubing as required, resolder the leads using a heat sink to protect the transistor, slide tubing over splice and apply heat to shrink it in place. Coat screw threads with OMC Screw Lock and tighten to 2-3 ft.-lb.

1975-1976 12 VOLT
TRANSOM MOUNT MODEL

The electrical system consists of a master on/off switch, circuit breaker, directional switch, potentiometer, transistor, diode, the electric motor and connecting wiring.

The propeller must be removed for all troubleshooting as a safety precaution. All electrical connections and terminal screws are coated with OMC Liquid Neoprene Dip to provide insulation. This material must be scraped off before testing to assure good electrical connections. When testing has been completed, cover all connections and terminals with a fresh application of OMC Liquid Neoprene Dip.

Troubleshooting

Motor does not run

Refer to **Figure 15** for this procedure.

1. Connect the control housing battery clamps to the battery.

2. Remove the 4 screws underneath the control housing and remove the housing cover.

3. Connect the black voltmeter lead to point 1 for all checks in this procedure.

4. Connect the red voltmeter lead to the circuit breaker terminal at point 2. If meter does not indicate battery voltage, move lead to point 2A.

5. If no voltage is indicated at point 2A, depress the circuit breaker reset button. If there is still no voltage shown, remove the red lead at point 2A and probe the terminal with the red test lead while depressing the reset button. If no voltage is shown, replace the circuit breaker. If voltage is shown with red lead disconnected, look for a short in the wiring.

6. Reconnect the red lead at point 2A and move the voltmeter test lead to point 3A. Turn switch on. If battery voltage is not shown at point 3A, move the test lead to point 3. If voltage is shown here, replace the master switch.

7. Move the test lead to point 4. With directional switch in FORWARD, battery voltage should be shown. If not, check the directional switch as described in this chapter.

8. If battery voltage is indicated as described in this procedure and the motor still does not run, disconnect the motor from the adaptor and check continuity of leads between motor and adapter. If leads are good, test the motor as described in this chapter.

11

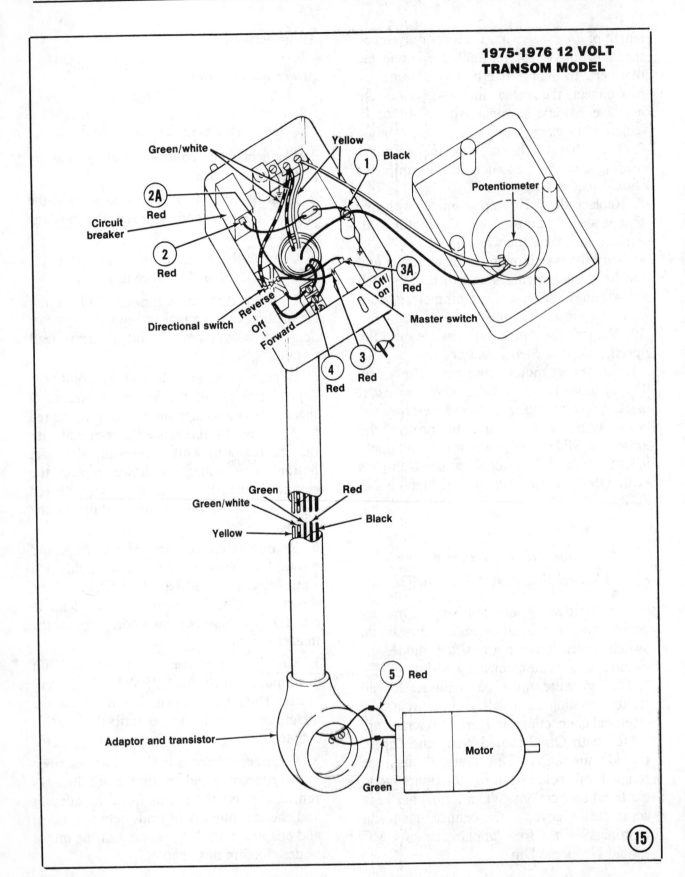

1975-1976 12 VOLT
TRANSOM MODEL

Green/white

Yellow

1 Black

2A
Red

Circuit
breaker

2
Red

Potentiometer

3A
Red

Reverse

Off/
on

Directional switch

Off

Master switch

Forward

4
Red

3
Red

Green   Red

Green/white

Black

Yellow

5 Red

Adaptor and transistor

Motor

Green

15

Potentiometer Test

Refer to **Figure 16** for this procedure.

1. Disconnect the battery cables at the battery.
2. Remove the 4 screws underneath the control housing and remove the housing cover.
3. Disconnect the yellow potentiometer lead at point 2.
4. Set the ohmmeter on the high scale and connect the black test lead to point 1. Connect the red test lead to the disconnected yellow lead. Rotate speed control knob. The ohmmeter needle should move from zero to 150 ohms. If no reading is obtained, check the wiring for opens or shorts. If wiring checks out good, replace the potentiometer.

Transistor Test

Refer to **Figure 16** for this procedure.

1. Disconnect the battery cables at the battery.
2. Remove the 4 screws underneath the control housing and remove the housing cover.
3. Disconnect the green/white wire at the terminal board.
4. Set the ohmmeter on the low scale and connect the black test lead to point 1. Connect the red test lead to the disconnected green/white wire. Note the ohmmeter reading and reverse the test leads. The meter should read low in one direction and high in the other. If the meter reads low or high in both directions replace the transistor in the adaptor.

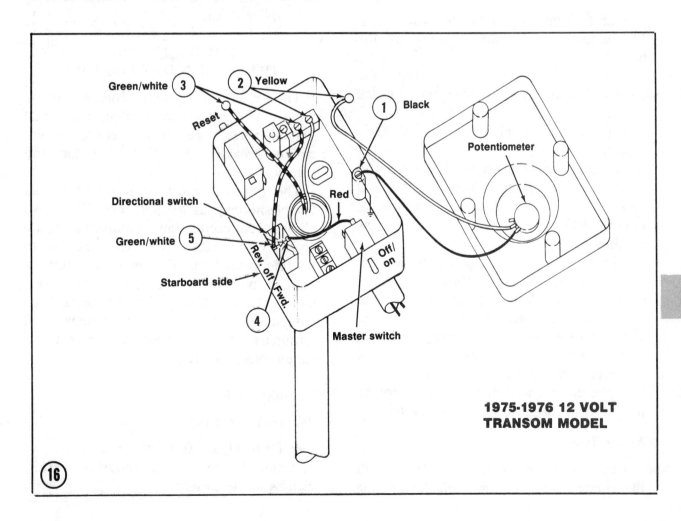

1975-1976 12 VOLT TRANSOM MODEL

16

11

Diode Test

Refer to **Figure 16** for this procedure.
1. Disconnect the battery cables at the battery.
2. Remove the 4 screws underneath the control housing and remove the housing cover.
3. Make sure the directional switch is OFF.
4. Set the ohmmeter on the low scale and connect the test leads between point 4 and point 5. Note the ohmmeter reading and reverse the test leads. The meter should read low in one direction and high in the other. If there is no reading in either direction or a high reading in both directions, replace the directional switch.

Directional Switch Test

Refer to **Figure 17** for this procedure.
1. Disconnect the battery cables at the battery.
2. Remove the 4 screws underneath the control housing and remove the housing cover.
3. Set the directional switch in the OFF position.
4. Set the ohmmeter on the low scale and connect the test leads between point 1 and point 2. Place the directional switch in FORWARD. The meter should show continuity.
5. Move the test leads to point 3 and point 4. The meter should show continuity.
6. Move the test leads to point 1 and point 3. Place the directional switch in REVERSE. The meter should show continuity.
7. Move the test leads to point 2 and point 4. The meter should show continuity.
8. If the directional switch does not provide the specified readings, replace the switch.

Motor Test

The transom mount motor is tested with the same procedure described for the

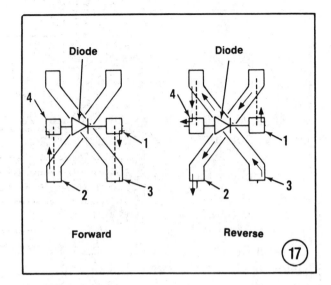

1975-1976 12 volt bow mount model in this chapter. The red and green transom mount motor leads should both be disconnected at their splice points.

1981-ON 12 VOLT TRANSOM MOUNT MODEL

The electrical system consists of a 5-position speed control switch, directional switch, resistor assembly, thermal cutout, circuit breaker, the electric motor and connecting wiring.

The propeller must be removed for all troubleshooting as a safety precaution. All electrical connections and terminal screws are coated with OMC Liquid Neoprene Dip to provide insulation. This material must be scraped off before testing to assure good electrical connections. When testing has been completed, cover all connections and terminals with a fresh application of OMC Liquid Neoprene Dip.

Troubleshooting

Motor does not run

Refer to **Figure 18** for this procedure.
1. Connect the control housing battery clamps to the battery.

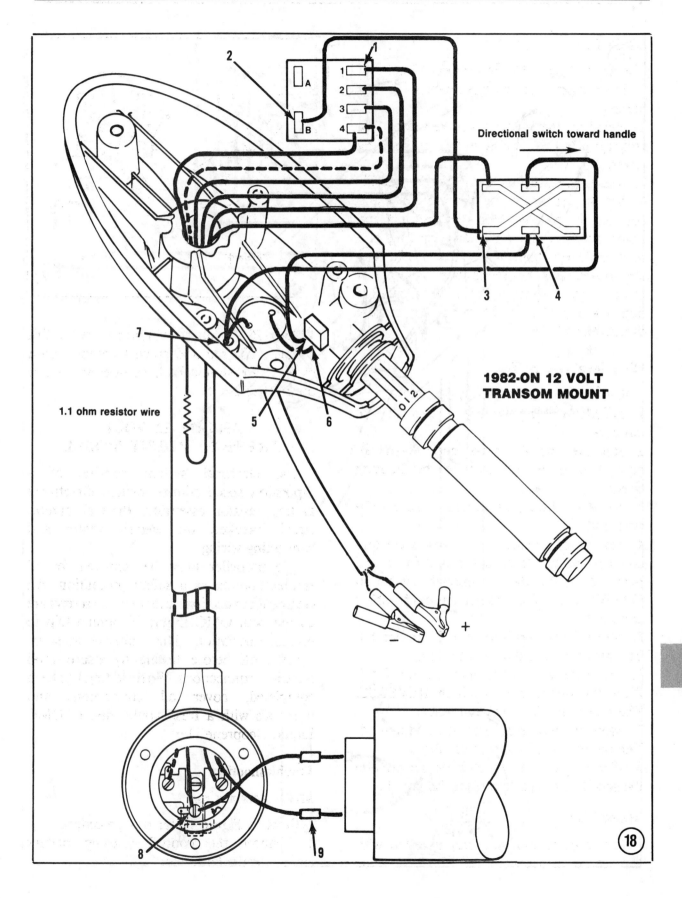

Directional switch toward handle

1982-ON 12 VOLT TRANSOM MOUNT

1.1 ohm resistor wire

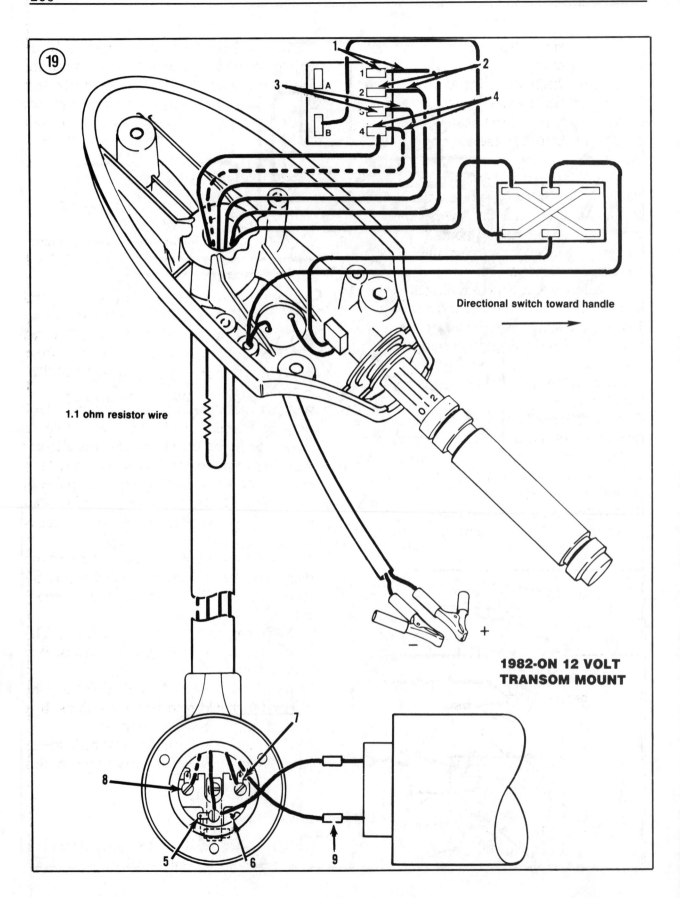

Directional switch toward handle

1.1 ohm resistor wire

**1982-ON 12 VOLT
TRANSOM MOUNT**

2. Remove the 3 housing screws. Remove the housing cover.

3. Connect the black voltmeter lead to point 7 for all checks in this procedure.

4. Move the directional switch to FORWARD. Rotate the steering handle to position 4.

5. Connect the red voltmeter test lead to point 1. If battery voltage is indicated, separate the motor from the adaptor and move the red test lead to point 8. If battery voltage is still indicated, test the motor as described in this chapter.

6. If battery voltage is not indicated at point 1 in Step 5, move the test lead to point 2. Replace the rotary switch if battery voltage is indicated. If no voltage is shown, move the test lead to point 3. Voltage at point 3 indicates an open in the circuit between point 2 and point 3.

7. Move the test lead to point 4. Replace the directional switch if voltage is shown. If no voltage is shown, move the test lead to point 5. Voltage at point 5 indicates an open in the circuit between point 4 and point 5.

8. If voltage is not shown at point 5 in Step 7, move the test lead to point 6. If voltage is

shown, replace the circuit breaker. If no voltage is shown, check for continuity in the lead between point 6 and the positive battery terminal. If continuity is present but the motor will not run, the problem is a poor ground.

Motor runs only at high speed

Refer to **Figure 19** for this procedure.

1. Disconnect the battery cables.

2. Remove the 3 housing cover screws. Remove the housing cover. Unsolder the 5 leads at points 1, 2, 3 and 4.

3. Set an ohmmeter on the low scale and connect the black test lead to the green lead disconnected from point 2. Connect the red test lead to the red wire disconnected from point 1. The meter should show 0.14-0.20 ohms resistance.

4. If the meter reads infinity in Step 3, there may be an open in the thermal cutout or resistor. Separate the motor from the adaptor without cutting the leads. Connect the red test lead to the white lead removed at point 3. Connect the black test lead to the white lead removed at point 4. If the meter reads infinity, replace the resistor wire.

5. Move the red test lead to point 5 and the black test lead to point 6. If there is no ohmmeter reading, replace the thermal cutout.

6. Move the red test lead to point 7. The ohmmeter should read 0.14-0.20 ohms. If it reads infinity, replace the resistor.

7. Move the red test lead to point 8. The ohmmeter should read 0.45-0.55 ohms. If it reads infinity, replace the resistor.

8. If the motor still runs only at high speed, test the rotary switch as described in this chapter.

Rotary Switch Test

Refer to **Figure 20** for this procedure.

1. Disconnect the battery cables.

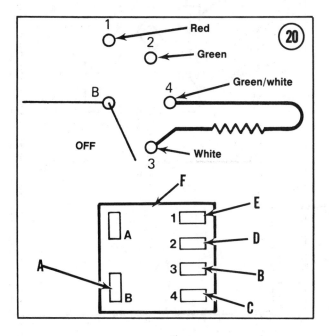

11

2. Disconnect all leads at the rotary switch.

3. Set the ohmmeter on the low scale. Connect black test lead to terminal A for entire test.

4. With steering handle in the OFF position, probe terminals B, C, D, E and metal switch case with red test lead. There should be no continuity shown at any position.

5. Move the steering handle to position 1 and probe terminals B, C, D and E with the red test lead. There should be continuity only at terminal B.

6. Move the steering handle to position 2 and probe terminals B, C, D and E with the red test lead. There should be continuity only at terminal C.

7. Move the steering handle to position 3 and probe terminals B, C, D and E with the red test lead. There should be continuity only at terminal D.

8. Move the steering handle to position 4 and probe terminals B, C, D and E with the red test lead. There should be continuity only at terminal E.

9. If continuity is not shown as indicated in Steps 4-8, replace the rotary switch.

Directional Switch Test

Refer to **Figure 21** for this procedure.

1. Disconnect the battery cables at the battery.

2. Remove the 3 control housing screws. Remove the housing cover.

3. Set the directional switch in the FORWARD position and unsolder all leads connected to it.

4. Set the ohmmeter on the low scale. Connect the red test lead to outer switch terminal point 1. Connect the black test lead to point 2 in the center of the switch. The meter should show continuity.

5. Move red test lead to point 3. The meter should not show continuity.

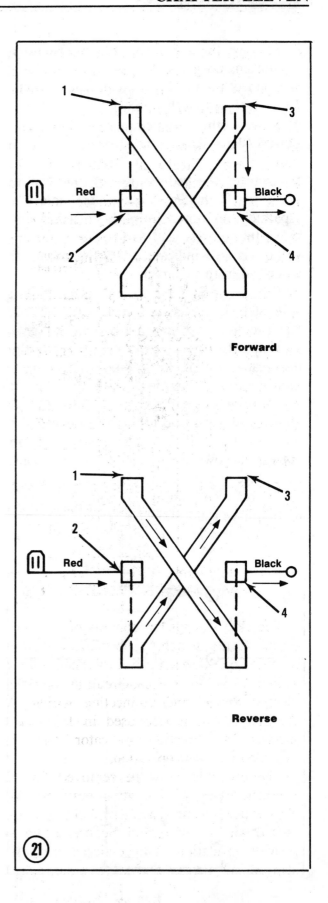

6. Connect the red test lead to outer switch terminal point 3. Connect the black test lead to point 4 in the center of the switch. The meter should show continuity.

7. Move red test lead to point 1. The meter should not show continuity.

8. Set the directional switch in the REVERSE position. Connect the red lead to point 3 and the black lead to point 2. The meter should show continuity.

9. Move the red test lead to point 1 and the black test lead to point 4. The meter should show continuity.

10. Move the red test lead to point 3. The meter should not show continuity.

11. Connect the black test lead to the metal switch case. Connect the red test lead to point 1 and then to point 4. The meter should not show continuity at either point.

12. If the directional switch does not provide the specified readings, replace the switch.

Motor Test

The transom mount motor is tested with the same procedure described for the 1981-on 12 volt bow mount model in this chapter.

1975-1981 12/24 VOLT BOW MOUNT MODEL

The electrical system consists of a master on/off toggle switch, a spring-loaded foot operated on/off switch, a rotary speed control switch, 12/24 volt switch, circuit breaker, the electric motor and connecting wiring. A thermal cutout is also used in 1977-1981 models. A direction indicator light is provided for night operation.

The propeller must be removed for all troubleshooting as a safety precaution. All electrical connections and terminal screws are coated with OMC Liquid Neoprene Dip to provide insulation. This material must be scraped off before testing to assure good

electrical connections. When testing has been completed, cover all connections and terminals with a fresh application of OMC Liquid Neoprene Dip.

Troubleshooting

Motor does not run

Refer to **Figure 22** (1975-1976) or **Figure 23** (1977-1981) for this procedure.

1. With the foot control cable properly connected to the batteries, connect the black voltmeter lead to the black ground wire on the foot control terminal block (point 1A). The lead will remain connected to this terminal for all voltage checks.

2. Connect the red voltmeter lead to the center terminal of the 12/24 volt switch (point 1).

3. Set the switch first in the 12 volt and then the 24 volt position. The meter should read battery voltage in each position.

4. If there is no reading at one or both positions in Step 3, probe point 1B with the red test lead for 12 volts (switch set for 12 volts) and point 1C for 24 volts (switch set for 24 volt). If voltage is obtained at each terminal, replace the switch. If no voltage is obtained at one or both terminals, there is an open in the wiring between the 12/24 volt switch terminals and the batteries.

5. Set the 12/24 volt switch in the 24 volt position. Connect the red test lead to point 2. If the meter does not read 24 volts, disconnect the red wire at point 2. Depress and release the circuit breaker reset button. Recheck for voltage with the red wire disconnected. If the meter reads battery voltage, the circuit breaker is good.

6. If there is no voltage shown in Step 5, reconnect the red wire to the circuit breaker and recheck for voltage with the test lead at point 2. If there is no voltage, there is a short in the wiring or the circuit breaker is defective. Check the wiring for continuity. If

11

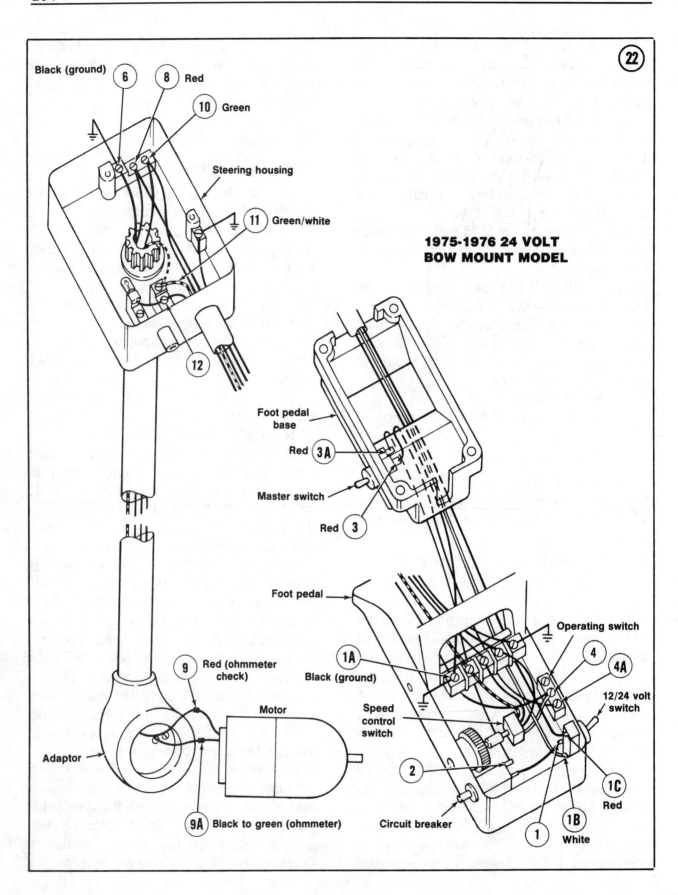

Black (ground)

6

8 Red

10 Green

Steering housing

11 Green/white

22

1975-1976 24 VOLT BOW MOUNT MODEL

12

Foot pedal base

Red 3A

Master switch

Red 3

Foot pedal

Operating switch

9 Red (ohmmeter check)

1A

Black (ground)

4

4A

12/24 volt switch

Motor

Speed control switch

Adaptor

2

1C

Red

9A Black to green (ohmmeter)

Circuit breaker

1

1B

White

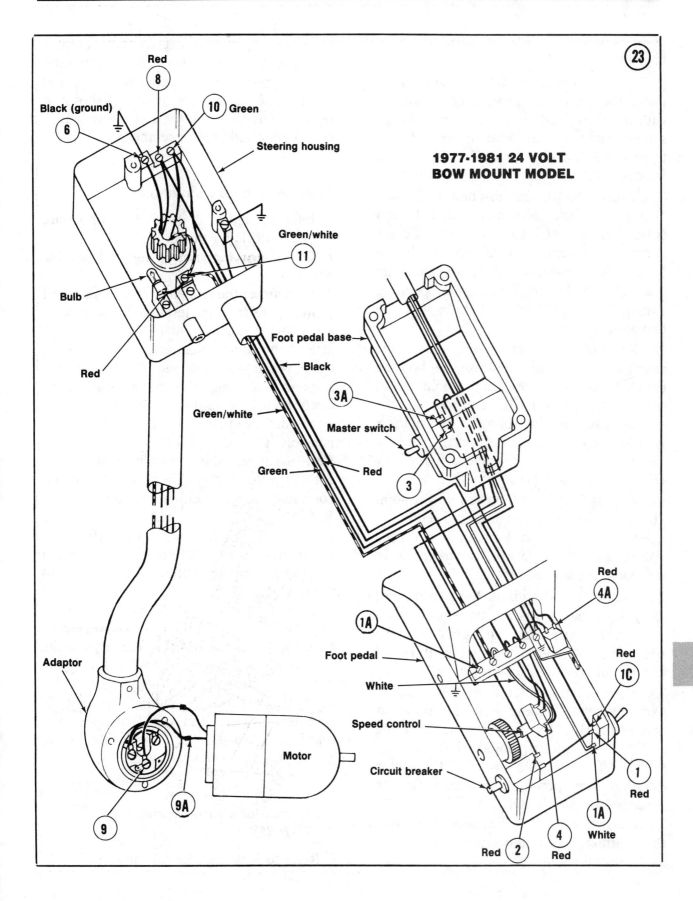

Red
8

Black (ground)
6

10 Green

Steering housing

**1977-1981 24 VOLT
BOW MOUNT MODEL**

Green/white
11

Bulb

Red

Foot pedal base

Black

Green/white

Master switch

Green

Red

3A

3

Adaptor

Red
4A

1A

Foot pedal

White

Speed control

Red
1C

Circuit breaker

1

Red

Motor

9A

1A

White

9

Red **2**

4

Red

11

no open or short is found, replace the circuit breaker.

7. Turn the master switch ON and probe under the plastic terminal cover at point 3 with the test lead. If there is no voltage shown, move the test lead to point 3A. If there is no voltage at point 3A, replace the master switch.

8. Connect the test lead to point 4. Depress operating switch. The meter should read battery voltage and the direction indicator lamp in the steering housing should light.

9. If no voltage is shown in Step 8, move the test lead to point 4A. Depress the operating switch. If voltage is shown here, replace the operating switch.

10. Remove the 4 screws underneath the steering housing and remove the housing cover. Move the red test lead to point 8. Set speed control on HIGH and depress the operating switch. If no voltage is shown, there is either an open in the red wiring circuit or the speed control switch is defective. If wiring checks out good, replace the switch.

11. Repeat Step 10 with the test lead at point 10. If no voltage is shown, there is either an open in the green wiring circuit or the speed control switch is defective. If wiring checks out good, replace the switch.

12. Repeat Step 10 with the test lead at point 11. If no voltage is shown, there is either an open in the green/white wiring circuit or the speed control switch is defective. If wiring checks out good, replace the switch.

13. Separate the motor from the adaptor. Connect the red test lead to point 9. Set speed control on HIGH and depress the operating switch. The meter should show battery voltage. If voltage is shown and the motor does not run, perform the *Motor Test* as described in this chapter.

14. If no voltage is shown in Step 13, remove the voltmeter and disconnect the battery leads from the batteries.

15. Connect an ohmmeter between point 8 and point 9 and check for continuity. Connect the ohmmeter between point 6 and point 9A. If there is no continuity shown at either test connection, there is a problem in the adaptor and cable assembly.

Motor runs, no speed control

Refer to **Figure 24** (1975-1976) or **Figure 25** (1977-1981) for this procedure.

1. Disconnect the battery cables from the batteries.

2. Disconnect the red, green and white speed control leads from the terminal block at point 8A, point 10A and point 11A.

3. Set the ohmmeter on the low scale. Connect the black test lead to the white lead at point 4. Connect the red test lead to the disconnected red lead at point 8B.

4. Set the speed control switch at the HIGH position. The meter should show continuity. Turn the speed control switch to MEDIUM and then to LOW. There should be no continuity shown in either position.

5. Connect the red test lead to the disconnected green lead at point 10B. The meter should show continuity with the switch in HIGH. Turn the speed control switch to MEDIUM and then to LOW. There should be continuity in MEDIUM and no continuity in LOW.

6. Move the red test lead to the green/white lead at point 11B and repeat Step 4. There should be continuity in all switch positions.

7. If the ohmmeter readings are not as specified in Steps 3-6, check the terminals and wiring for defects. If none are found, replace the speed control switch.

Motor runs at high speed only (1977-1981)

Refer to **Figure 26** for this procedure.

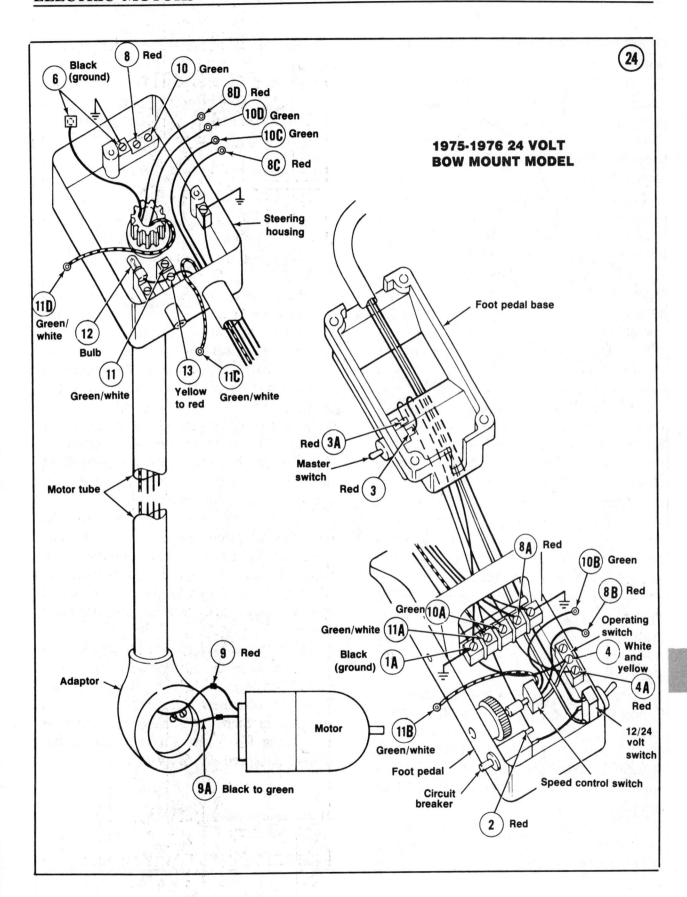

1975-1976 24 VOLT BOW MOUNT MODEL

11

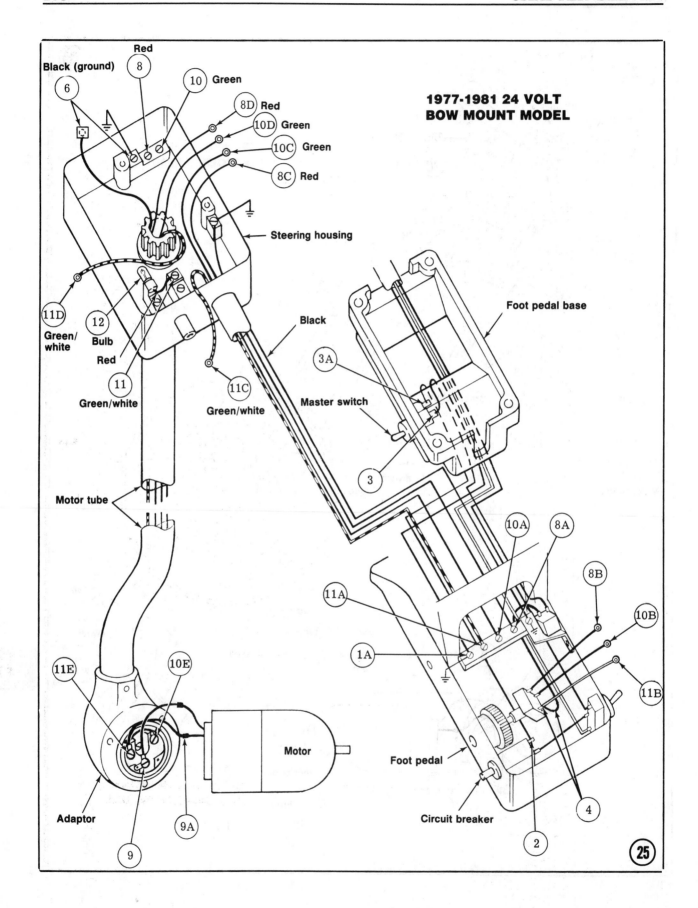

Red
Black (ground)
(8)
(6)
(10) Green
(8D) Red
(10D) Green
(10C) Green
(8C) Red

**1977-1981 24 VOLT
BOW MOUNT MODEL**

Steering housing

Black

Foot pedal base

(3A)

(11D)
Green/
white
(12)
Bulb
Red
Master switch

(3)

(11)
Green/white
(11C)
Green/white

Motor tube

(10A)
(8A)

(8B)

(11A)

(10B)

(1A)

(11B)

(11E)
(10E)

Motor

Foot pedal

(9A)
Adaptor
Circuit breaker
(4)

(9)
(2)

(25)

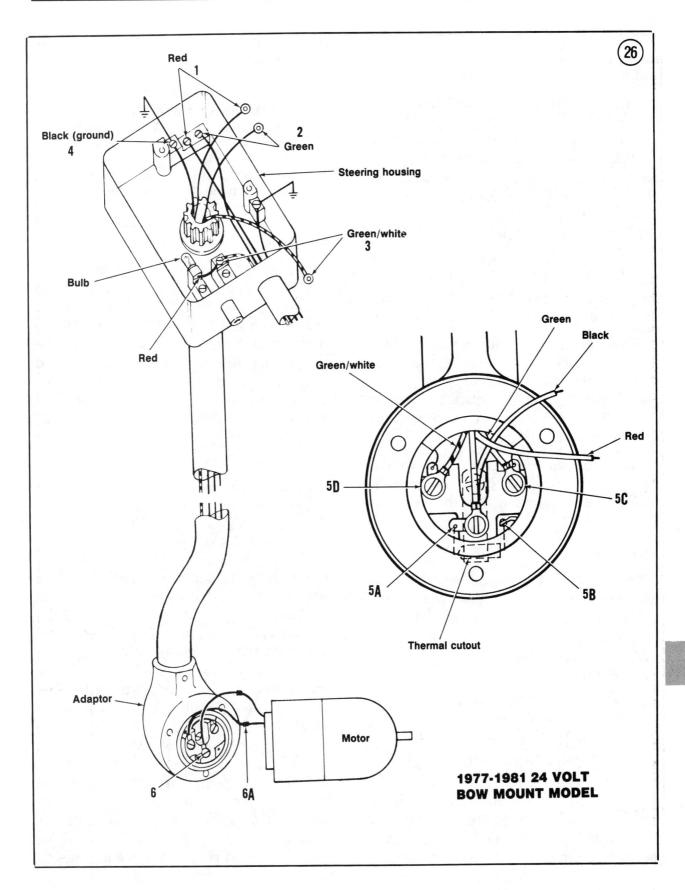

1977-1981 24 VOLT BOW MOUNT MODEL

1. Disconnect the red, green and green/white leads from the motor tube at point 1, point 2 and point 3.

2. Set the ohmmeter on the low scale. Connect the red test lead to the red lead disconnected at point 1. Connect the black test lead to the green lead disconnected at point 2. The meter should read 0.72-0.78 ohms indicating thermal cutout continuity. If the meter reads infinity, there may be an open in the resistor or thermal cutout.

3. Move the black test lead to the green/white lead disconnected at point 3. The meter should read 1-2 ohms indicating thermal cutout continuity.

4. If the meter reads infinity in Step 2 or Step 3, separate the motor from the adaptor without cutting the leads. Connect the red test lead to point 5A and the black test lead to point 5B. If there is no reading, replace the thermal cutout.

5. Move the red test lead first to point 5C and then to point 5D. If the meter reads infinity at either point, replace the resistor.

Motor Test

The 12/24 volt bow mount motor is tested with the same procedure described for the 1975-1981 12 volt bow mount model in this chapter. The motor should draw 4 amps in the no-load test and 100 amps at 38 in.-lb. in the load test.

1982-ON 12/24 VOLT BOW MOUNT MODEL

The electrical system consists of a spring-loaded foot-operated on/off switch, a speed control switch, 12/24 volt resistor assembly, thermal cutout, electric motor and connecting wiring. A direction indicator light is provided for night operation.

NOTE
If the on/off switch tends to stick in the ON position on 1982-1983 models, install switch and arc suppressor kit part No. 394837 to prevent arcing across the switch contacts under high load conditions. Follow the kit installation directions carefully to assure proper wire routing and connections.

The propeller must be removed for all troubleshooting as a safety precaution. All electrical connections and terminal screws are coated with OMC Liquid Neoprene Dip to provide insulation. This material must be scraped off before testing to assure good electrical connections. When testing has been completed, cover all connections and terminals with a fresh application of OMC Liquid Neoprene Dip.

Troubleshooting

Motor does not run

Refer to **Figure 27** for this procedure.

1. With the foot control cable properly connected to the batteries, connect the black voltmeter test lead to point 2 for all steps in this test.

2. Connect the red test lead to the center terminal of the 12/24 volt switch (point 1). With the switch set to the 12 volt position, the meter should indicate 12 volts. Move the switch to the 24 volt position. The meter should indicate 24 volts.

3. If there is no reading at one or either of the switch positions, check for 12 volts at point 3 and 24 volts at point 4. If voltage is correct at these test points, replace the 12/24 volt switch. If no voltage is obtained at one or both of the test points, check the wiring between the test point(s) and the batteries.

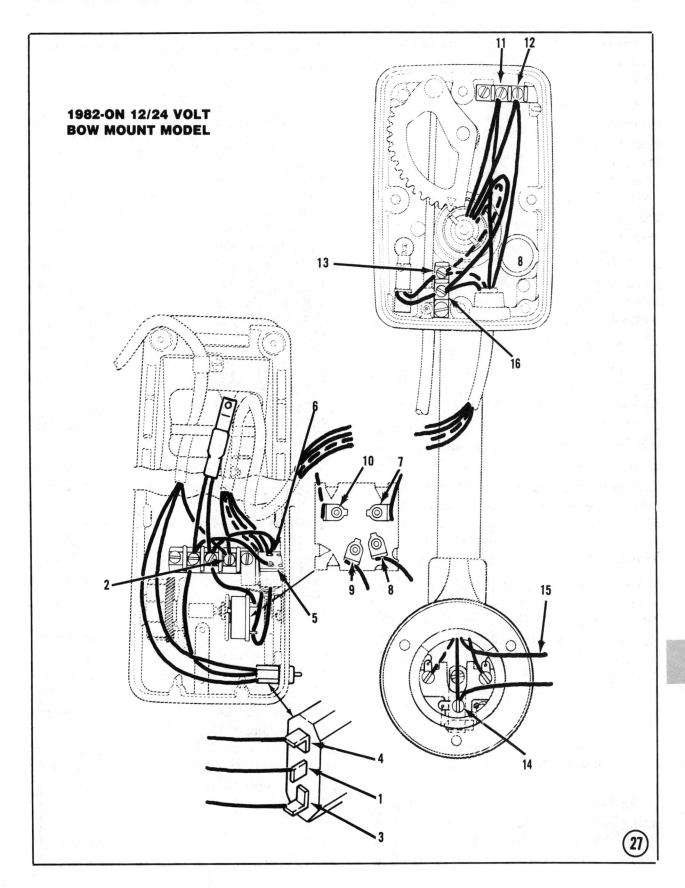

**1982-ON 12/24 VOLT
BOW MOUNT MODEL**

27

4. Set the switch to the 24 volt position. Connect the red test lead to point 5. If the meter does not show 24 volts, there is an open in the wiring between point 5 and point 1.

5. Connect the red test lead to point 6 and depress the operating switch. The meter should read voltage and the direction indicator lamp should light. If no voltage is shown, replace the operating switch.

6. Move the red test lead to point 7. If voltage is not shown, there is an open in the wiring between point 6 and point 7.

7. Move the red test lead to point 8 on the rotary switch. Set the speed control on HIGH and depress the operating switch. If battery voltage is not shown, replace the rotary switch.

8. Repeat Step 7 with the red test lead on point 9 and the speed control set on NORMAL, then with the test lead on point 10 and the speed control on LOW. If battery voltage is not shown at each test point, replace the rotary switch.

9. Remove the 4 screws underneath the steering housing and remove the housing cover. Connect the red test lead to point 11. Set the speed control on HIGH and depress the operating switch. If battery voltage is not shown, there is an open in the wiring between point 8 and point 11.

10. Move the red test lead to point 12. Set the speed control on NORMAL and depress the operating switch. If battery voltage is not shown, there is an open in the wiring between point 9 and point 12.

11. Move the red test lead to point 13. Set the speed control on LOW and depress the operating switch. If battery voltage is not shown, there is an open in the wiring between point 10 and point 13.

12. Separate the motor from the adaptor without disconnecting the wiring. Connect the red test lead to point 14. Set the speed control on HIGH and depress the operating

switch. If voltage is shown but the motor does not run, test the motor as described in this chapter.

13. If no voltage is shown in Step 12, disconnect the battery cable from the batteries. Connect an ohmmeter between the red leads at point 11 and point 14. There should be continuity.

14. Probe the green-to-black wire splice at point 15 with the black ohmmeter test lead. Connect the red test lead to point 16. There should be continuity.

15. If continuity is not shown in Step 13 or Step 14, replace or repair the adaptor and cable assembly as required. If continuity is shown in both steps, test the motor as described in this chapter.

Motor runs, no speed control

Refer to **Figure 28** for this procedure.

1. Disconnect the battery cable from the batteries.

2. Disconnect the rotary switch red, green and green/white leads at points 1, 2, and 3.

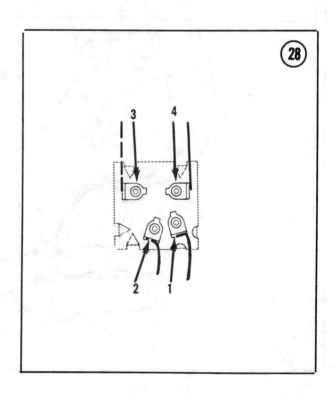

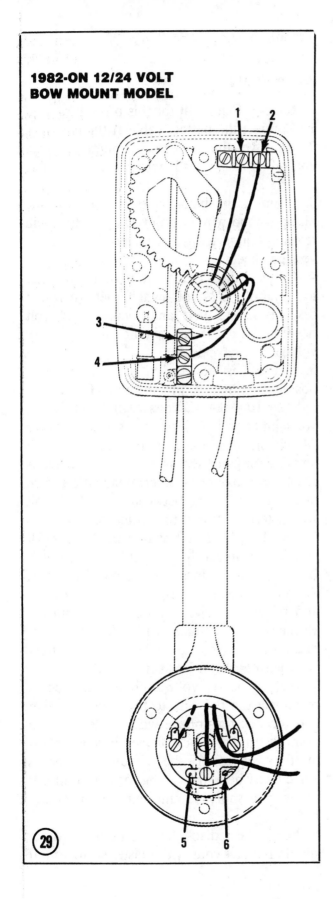

1982-ON 12/24 VOLT BOW MOUNT MODEL

③

3. Set an ohmmeter on the low scale and connect the black test lead to point 4 on the switch. Connect the red test lead to the red wire disconnected from point 1.

4. Rotate the speed control wheel to HIGH. The ohmmeter should show continuity. Move the wheel to NORMAL, LOW and OFF. There should be no continuity in any of the 3 positions.

5. Move the red test lead to the green wire disconnected from point 2. Move the speed control wheel through all positions. There should be continuity only in NORMAL.

6. Move the red test lead to the green/white wire disconnected from point 3. Move the speed control wheel through all positions. There should be continuity in all positions except OFF.

7. If the ohmmeter readings are not as specified in Steps 4-6, check the terminals and wiring for defects. If none are found, replace the speed control switch.

Motor runs only at high speed

Refer to **Figure 29** for this procedure.

1. Disconnect the battery cable from the batteries.

2. Remove the 4 screws underneath the steering housing and remove the housing cover. Disconnect the leads at terminals 1-4.

3. Set an ohmmeter on the low scale and connect the black test lead to the green wire disconnected from terminal 2. Connect the red test lead to the red wire disconnected from terminal 1. The meter should read 0.14-0.20 ohms. If it reads infinity, there may be an open in the thermal cutout or resistor.

4. Connect the black test lead to the green/white wire disconnected at terminal 3. The meter should read 0.45-0.55 ohms. It it reads infinity, there may be an open in the thermal cutout or resistor.

5. Separate the motor from the adaptor without cutting the leads. Connect the red test

11

lead to terminal 5 and the black test lead to terminal 6. If continuity is not shown, replace the thermal cutout.

6. Move the red test lead to terminal 2. The meter should read 0.14-0.20 ohms. Move the red test lead to terminal 3. The meter should read 0.45-0.55 ohms. If an open circuit is shown at terminal 2 or terminal 3, replace the resistor.

Rotary Switch Test

See *1982-on 12 Volt Bow Mount Model Rotary Switch Test* in this chapter.

Motor Test

The 12/24 volt bow mount motor is tested with the same procedure described for the 1982-on 12 volt bow mount model in this chapter. Use a 30 in. length of 14 gauge wire to connect the ammeter and switch between the motor and the positive battery terminal. Connect the green motor lead to the negative terminal of the second battery. The motor should draw 5 amps in the no-load test and 90 amps at 38 in.-lb. in the load test.

1975-1976 12/24 VOLT TRANSOM MOUNT MODEL

The electrical system consists of a master on/off switch, a directional switch, a 3-speed rotary control switch, 12/24 volt switch, circuit breaker, electric motor and connecting wiring.

The propeller must be removed for all troubleshooting as a safety precaution. All electrical connections and terminal screws are coated with OMC Liquid Neoprene Dip to provide insulation. This material must be scraped off before testing to assure good electrical connections. When testing has been completed, cover all connections and terminals with a fresh application of OMC Liquid Neoprene Dip.

Troubleshooting

Motor does not run

Refer to **Figure 30** for this procedure.
1. Connect the battery cable at the batteries.
2. Remove the 4 screws underneath the control housing and remove the housing cover.
3. Connect the black voltmeter lead to the black ground wire at point 1A. The lead will remain connected to this terminal for all voltage checks.
4. Connect the red test lead to point 1 (center terminal of 12/24 volt switch). Set the switch first in the 12 volt and then the 24 volt position. The meter should read battery voltage in each position.
5. If there is no reading in one or both positions in Step 4, probe point 1B with the red test lead for 12 volts (switch set for 12 volts) and point 1C for 24 volts (switch set for 24 volts). If voltage is obtained at each terminal, replace the switch. If no voltage is obtained at one or both terminals, there is an open in the wiring between the 12/24 volt switch terminals and the batteries.
6. Set the 12/24 volt switch in the 24 volt position. Connect the red test lead to point 2. If the meter does not read 24 volts, disconnect the red wire at point 2. Depress and release the circuit breaker reset button. Recheck for voltage with the red wire disconnected. If the meter reads battery voltage, the circuit breaker is good.
7. If there is no voltage shown in Step 6, reconnect the red wire to the circuit breaker and recheck for voltage with the test lead at point 2. If there is no voltage, there is a short in the wiring or the circuit breaker is defective. Check the wiring for continuity. If no open or short is found, replace the circuit breaker.
8. Move the red test lead to point 3. Meter should read 24 volts with master switch on. If

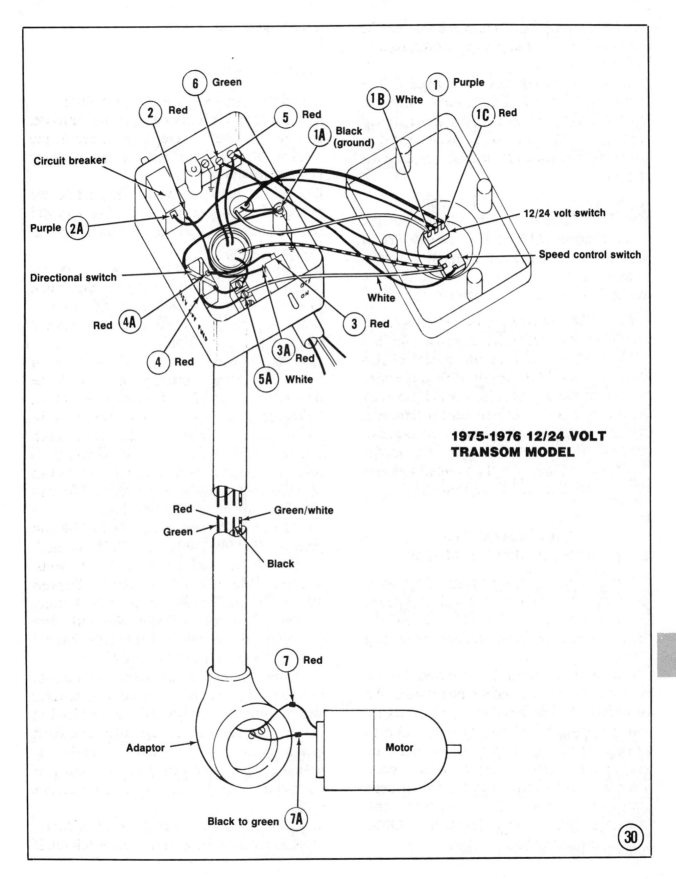

6 Green

2 Red

5 Red

1B White

1 Purple

1C Red

1A Black (ground)

Circuit breaker

12/24 volt switch

Purple 2A

Speed control switch

Directional switch

White

Red 4A

3 Red

4 Red

3A Red

5A White

1975-1976 12/24 VOLT TRANSOM MODEL

Red

Green/white

Green

Black

7 Red

Adaptor

Motor

Black to green 7A

30

no voltage is shown, move the test lead to point 3A. If voltage is shown at point 3A, replace the master switch.

9. Connect the test lead to point 4. The meter should read battery voltage with the switch in FORWARD. If no voltage is shown, move the test lead to point 4A. If voltage is shown at point 4A, replace the directional switch.

10. Move the red test lead to point 5. The meter should read battery voltage with the speed control on HIGH. If no voltage is shown, check the red and white wire circuits at terminal 5A for an open or short. If the wiring checks out good, replace the speed control switch.

11. Move the red test lead to point 6 and set the speed control on MEDIUM. If no voltage is shown, check the green wire circuit to the control housing for an open or short. If the wiring checks out good, replace the speed control switch.

12. Separate the motor from the adaptor without cutting the leads. Probe the red wire splice at point 7 with the red test lead. If no voltage is shown, disconnect the battery cable from the batteries.

13. Connect an ohmmeter between point 7 and point 5 and check for continuity. Probe the green wire splice at point 7A with the black ohmmeter test lead and connect the red test lead to point 1A. Check for continuity.

14. If continuity is indicated in Step 13 and the motor does not run, test the motor as described in this chapter.

Directional Switch Test

Refer to **Figure 31** for this procedure.

1. Disconnect the battery cable from the batteries.

2. Set the directional switch in the OFF position.

3. Set an ohmmeter on the low scale and connect it between point 1 and point 2. Move

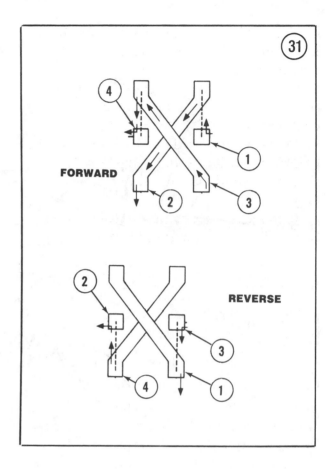

the directional switch to FORWARD. The meter should show continuity.

4. Move the test leads to point 3 and point 4. The meter should show continuity (switch in FORWARD).

5. Move the test leads to point 1 and point 3. Move the directional switch to REVERSE. The meter should show continuity.

6. Move the test leads to point 2 and point 4. The meter should show continuity (switch in REVERSE).

Speed Control Switch Test

1. Disconnect the battery cable from the batteries.

2. Disconnect all speed control switch leads at their respective terminals.

3. Connect the red ohmmeter test lead to the red switch lead. Connect the black test lead to the white switch lead.

4. Turn the switch to HIGH, MEDIUM, LOW and OFF. There should be continuity only in HIGH.

5. Connect the red test lead to the green switch lead. Repeat Step 4. There should be continuity only in HIGH and MEDIUM.

6. Connect the red test lead to the green/white switch lead. Repeat Step 4. There should be continuity in all positions except OFF.

7. If continuity is not shown as indicated in Steps 4-6, replace the speed control switch.

Motor Test

The 12/24 volt transom mount motor is tested with the same procedure described for the 1975-1981 12 volt bow mount model in this chapter. The motor should draw 4 amps in the no-load test and 100 amps at 38 in.-lb. in the load test. Use a 12 ft. length of 12 gauge wire to connect the ammeter and switch between the motor and the positive battery terminal. Connect the green motor lead to the negative terminal of the second battery with an equal length of 12 gauge wire.

1980-1981 12/24 VOLT HAND CONTROL MODEL

The electrical system consists of a rotary speed control switch, 12/24 volt switch, directional switch, circuit breaker, thermal cutout, electric motor and connecting wiring.

The propeller must be removed for all troubleshooting as a safety precaution. All electrical connections and terminal screws are coated with OMC Liquid Neoprene Dip to provide insulation. This material must be scraped off before testing to assure good electrical connections. When testing has been completed, cover all connections and terminals with a fresh application of OMC Liquid Neoprene Dip.

Troubleshooting

Motor does not run

Refer to **Figure 32** for this procedure.

1. Connect the battery cable to the batteries.

2. Remove the 4 screws underneath the control housing and remove the housing cover.

3. Connect the black voltmeter lead to the black ground wire at point G. The lead will remain connected to this terminal for all voltage checks.

4. Connect the red test lead to point 1 (center terminal of 12/24 volt switch). Set the switch first in the 12 volt and then the 24 volt position. The meter should read battery voltage in each postion.

5. If there is no reading in one or both positions in Step 4, probe point 1B with the red test lead for 12 volts (switch set for 12 volts) and point 1A for 24 volts (switch set for 24 volts). If voltage is obtained at each terminal, replace the switch. If no voltage is obtained at one or both terminals, there is an open in the wiring between the 12/24 volt switch terminals and the batteries.

6. Set the 12/24 volt switch in the 24 volt position. Connect the red test lead to point 2. If the meter does not read 24 volts, disconnect the red wire at point 2. Depress and release the circuit breaker reset button. Recheck for voltage with the red wire disconnected. If the meter reads battery voltage, the circuit breaker is good.

7. If there is no voltage shown in Step 6, reconnect the red wire to the circuit breaker and recheck for voltage with the test lead at point 2. If there is no voltage, there is a short in the wiring or the circuit breaker is defective. Check the wiring for continuity. If no open or short is found, replace the circuit breaker.

8. Move the red test lead to point 3. Meter should read 24 volts with directional switch

11

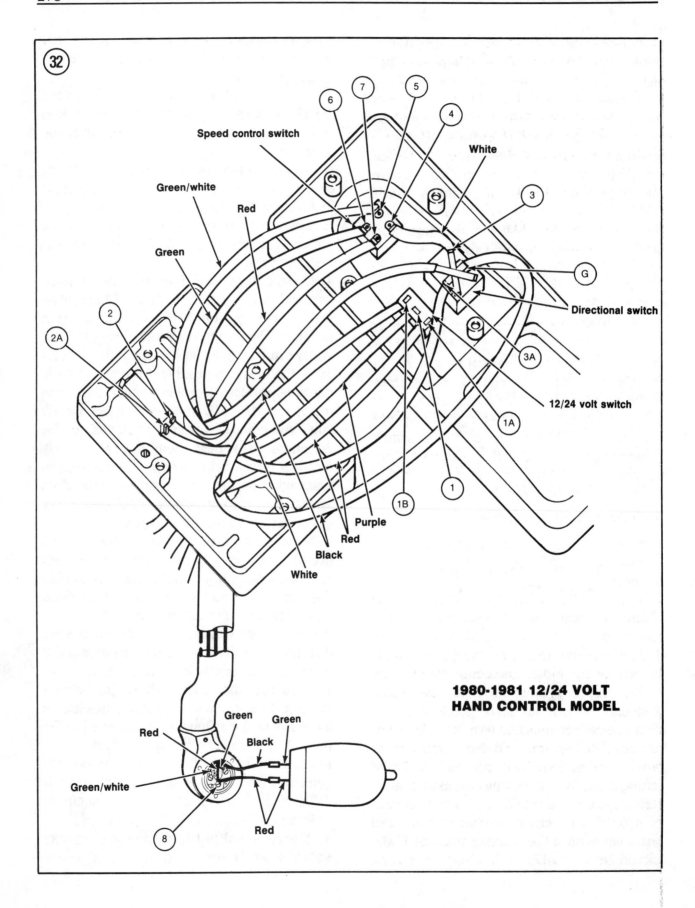

32

Speed control switch

Green/white

Green

Red

White

6 7 5 4 3

G

2 2A

1A 1B 1

3A

Directional switch

12/24 volt switch

Purple

Red

Black

White

**1980-1981 12/24 VOLT
HAND CONTROL MODEL**

Green Green

Red Black

Green/white

Red

8

in FORWARD. If no voltage is shown, move the test lead to point 3A. If voltage is shown at point 3A, replace the directional switch.

9. Connect the test lead to point 4. The meter should read battery voltage with the switch in FORWARD. If no voltage is shown, check for an open or short between point 3 and point 4.

10. Move the red test lead to point 5. The meter should read battery voltage with the speed control on LOW. If no voltage is shown, replace the speed control switch.

11. Move the red test lead to point 6 and set the speed control on MEDIUM. If no voltage is shown, replace the speed control.

12. Move the red test lead to point 7 and set the speed control on HIGH. If no voltage is shown, replace the speed control.

13. Separate the motor from the adaptor without cutting the leads. Connect the red test lead to point 8. If no voltage is shown, replace the wiring between point 7 and point 8 and check for opens in the adaptor wiring circuit. If voltage is shown at point 8, test the motor as described in this chapter.

Motor runs only at high speed

Refer to **Figure 33** for this procedure.
1. Disconnect the battery cable from the batteries.
2. Remove the 4 screws underneath the control housing and remove the housing cover.
3. Unsolder the red, green and green/white leads at points 1-3 respectively.
4. Set the ohmmeter on the low scale. Connect the red test lead to the red wire disconnected at point 1. Connect the black test lead to the green wire disconnected at point 2. The meter should read 0.72-0.78 ohms. If the meter reads infinity, there may be an open in the resistor or thermal cutout.
5. Move the black test lead to the green/white lead disconnected at point 3. The meter should read 1-2 ohms indicating

thermal cutout continuity. If the meter reads infinity, there may be an open in the resistor or thermal cutout.

6. Move the red test lead to point 4 and the black test lead to point 5. If the meter does not show continuity, replace the thermal cutout.

7. Move the red test lead to point 6. If the meter does not read 0.72-0.78 ohms, replace the resistor.

8. Move the red test lead to point 7. If the meter does not read 1-2 ohms, replace the resistor.

9. Separate the motor from the adaptor without disconnecting the leads. Connect the red test lead to point 4 and the black test lead to point 1. If the meter does not show continuity, look for an open in the circuit between point 1 and point 4.

10. Move the red test lead to point 6 and the black test lead to point 2. If the meter does not show continuity, look for an open in the circuit between point 2 and point 6.

11. Move the red test lead to point 7 and the black test lead to point 3. If the meter does not show continuity, look for an open in the circuit between point 3 and point 7.

12. Move the black test lead to point 8 and the red test lead to point 4. If the meter does not show continuity, there is either an open in the circuit between point 4 and point 8 or inside the motor.

13. Probe the splice at point 9 with the red test lead. Connect the black test lead at point 8. If there is continuity but the motor does not run, test the motor as described in this chapter. If there is no continuity, look for an open in the wiring between point 8 and point 9.

Directional Switch Test

Refer to **Figure 34** for this procedure.
1. Disconnect the battery cable at the batteries.

11

**1980-1981 12/24 VOLT
HAND CONTROL MODEL**

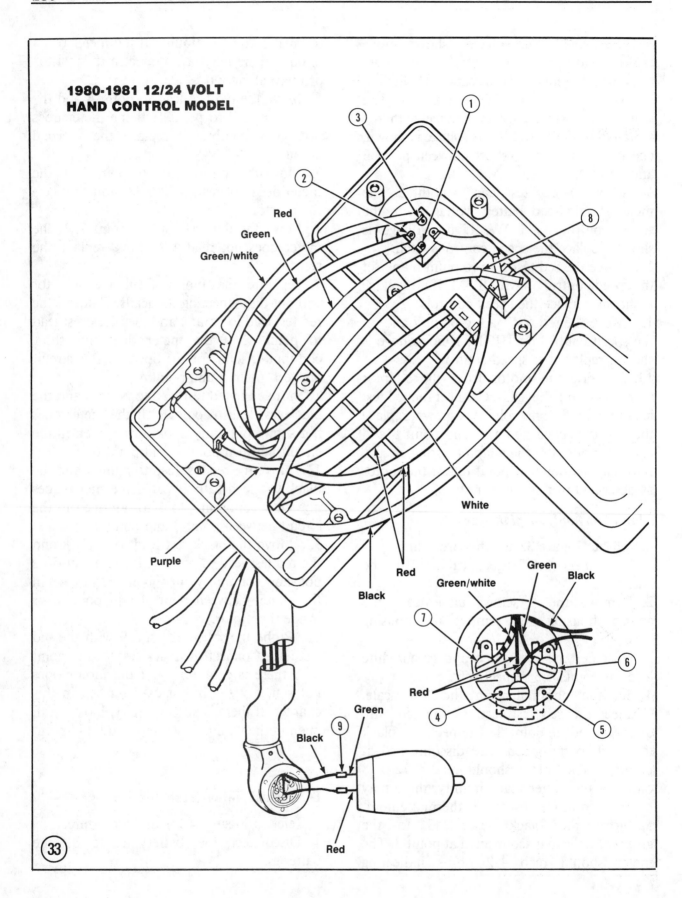

Red

Green

Green/white

Purple

Black

Red

White

Green/white

Green

Black

Red

Black

Green

Red

33

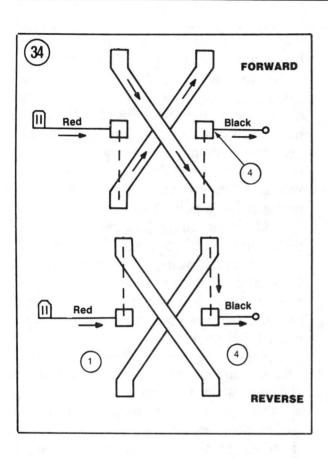

2. Remove the 4 control housing screws. Remove the housing cover.

3. Set the directional switch in the FORWARD position and unsolder all leads connected to it.

4. Set the ohmmeter on the low scale. Connect the test leads between points 1 and 2, then between points 3 and 4. If continuity is not shown at both test connections, replace the switch.

5. Connect the test leads between point 1 and point 4. Replace the switch if continuity is shown.

6. Set the directional switch in REVERSE. Connect the test leads between point 1 and 3, then between point 2 and point 4. If continuity is not shown at both test connections, replace the switch.

7. Connect the test leads between points 1 and 4. Replace the switch if continuity is shown.

Speed Control Switch Test

Refer to **Figure 35** for this procedure.

1. Disconnect the battery cable from the batteries.

2. Disconnect all speed control switch leads at their respective terminals.

3. Connect the black test lead to point 1. With the switch off, probe points 2, 3 and 4 with the red test lead. There should be no continuity at any test point.

4. Turn the switch to LOW and repeat Step 3. There should be continuity only at point 2.

5. Turn the switch to MEDIUM and repeat Step 3. There should be continuity only at point 2 and point 3.

6. Turn the switch to HIGH and repeat Step 3. There should be continuity only at point 2 and point 4.

7. If continuity is not shown as indicated in Steps 3-6, replace the speed control switch.

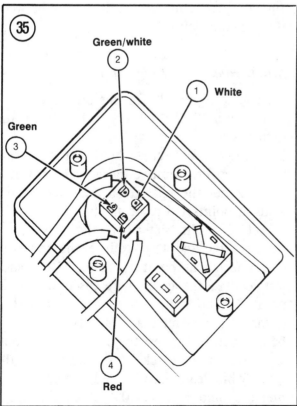

11

Motor Test

The 12/24 volt hand control motor is tested with the same procedure described for the 1975-1981 12 volt bow mount model in this chapter. The motor should draw 4 amps in the no-load test and 100 amps at 38 in.-lb. in the load test.

1982-ON 12/24 VOLT HAND CONTROL MODEL

The electrical system consists of a rotary speed control switch, 12/24 volt switch, directional switch, resistor, thermal cutout, electric motor and connecting wiring.

The propeller must be removed for all troubleshooting as a safety precaution. All electrical connections and terminal screws are coated with OMC Liquid Neoprene Dip to provide insulation. This material must be scraped off before testing to assure good electrical connections. When testing has been completed, cover all connections and terminals with a fresh application of OMC Liquid Neoprene Dip.

Troubleshooting

Motor does not run

Refer to **Figure 36** for this procedure.
1. With the battery cable properly connected to the batteries, connect the black voltmeter test lead to point 7 for all steps in this test.
2. Connect the red test lead to the center terminal of the 12/24 volt switch (point 1). With the switch set to the 12 volt position, the meter should indicate 12 volts. Move the switch to the 24 volt position. The meter should indicate 24 volts.
3. If there is no reading at one or both of the switch positions, check for 12 volts at point 2 and 24 volts at point 3. If voltage is correct at these test points, replace the 12/24 volt switch. If no voltage is obtained at one or

both of the test points, check the wiring between the test point(s) and the batteries.
4. Set the switch to the 24 volt position. Connect the red test lead to point 4. Place the directional switch in FORWARD. If the meter does not show 24 volts, move the red test lead to point 5. If voltage is shown at point 5, replace the directional switch. If no voltage is shown, there is an open in the wiring between point 1 and point 5.
5. Connect the red test lead to point 6 and set the rotary switch to position 3. If the meter does not read 24 volts, move the red test lead to point 8. If voltage is shown at point 8, replace the rotary switch. If no voltage is shown, there is an open in the wiring between point 4 and point 8.
6. Separate the motor from the adaptor without disconnecting the wiring. Connect the red test lead to point 9. Set the rotary switch to position 3. If voltage is shown but the motor does not run, test the motor as described in this chapter. If no voltage is shown, there is an open in the wiring between point 6 and point 9.

Motor runs only at high speed

Refer to **Figure 37** for this procedure.
1. Disconnect the battery cable from the batteries.
2. Remove the 3 screws holding the steering housing cover. Remove the housing cover.
3. Unsolder the red, green and green/white leads at points 1-3 respectively.
4. Set the ohmmeter on the low scale. Connect the red test lead to the red wire disconnected at point 1. Connect the black test lead to the green wire disconnected at point 2. The meter should read 0.14-0.20 ohms. If the meter reads infinity, there may be an open in the resistor or thermal cutout.
5. Move the black test lead to the green/white lead disconnected at point 3. The meter should read 0.4-0.6 ohms indicating

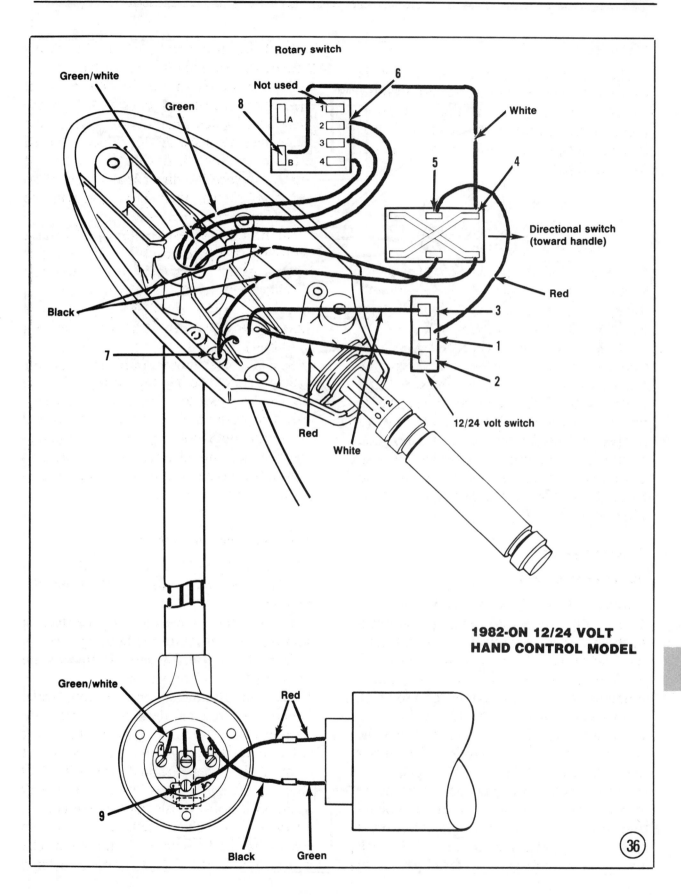

Rotary switch

Green/white

Green

Not used

8

6

White

A

1

2

3

4

B

5

4

Directional switch
(toward handle)

Red

Black

3

1

2

7

Red

White

12/24 volt switch

**1982-ON 12/24 VOLT
HAND CONTROL MODEL**

11

Green/white

Red

9

Black

Green

36

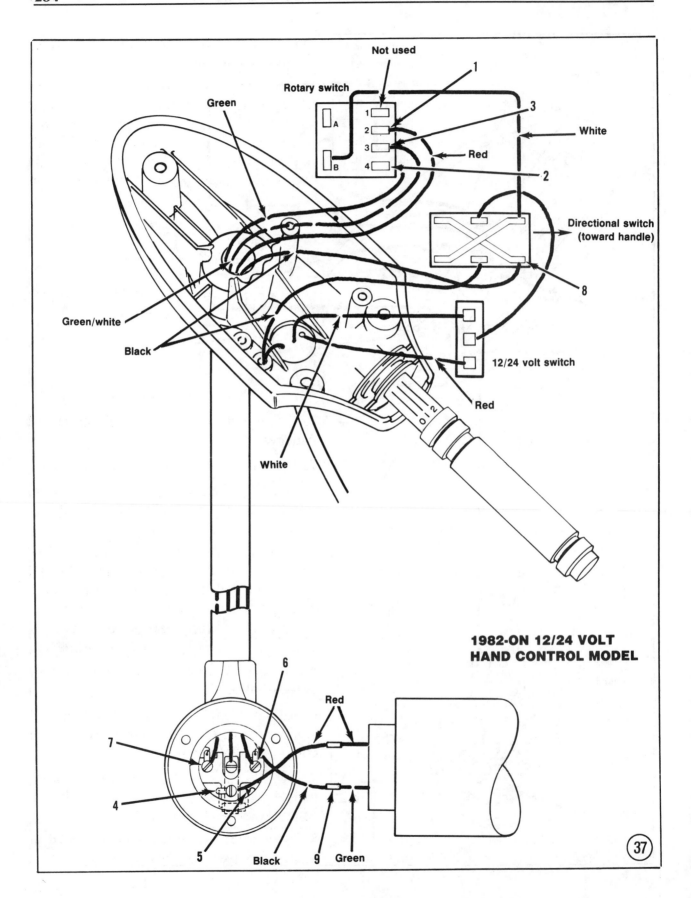

Not used

Rotary switch

Green

White

Red

Directional switch
(toward handle)

Green/white

Black

12/24 volt switch

Red

White

**1982-ON 12/24 VOLT
HAND CONTROL MODEL**

Red

Black   Green

(37)

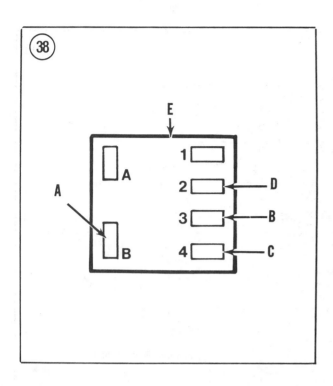

thermal cutout continuity. If the meter reads infinity, there may be an open in the resistor or thermal cutout.

6. Separate the motor from the adaptor without disconnecting the leads. Connect the red test lead to point 4 and the black test lead to point 5. If the meter does not show continuity, replace the thermal cutout.

7. Move the red test lead to point 6. The meter should read 014-0.20 ohms. If it reads infinity, replace the resistor.

8. Move the red test lead to point 7. The meter should read 0.4-0.6 ohms. If it reads infinity, replace the resistor.

9. Connect the ohmmeter between the wire at point 1 and point 4 (red), at point 2 and point 5 (green) and at point 3 and point 6 (green/white). There should be continuity in each case. If not, there is an open in that wiring circuit between the adaptor and steering housing.

10. Connect the black test lead at point 8 and the red lead at point 4. If continuity is not

shown, there is an open in the black wiring circuit or in the motor.

11. With the red test lead at point 4, probe the splice at point 9 with the black test lead. If there is continuity but the motor does not run, test the motor as described in this chapter. If there is no continuity, look for an open in the wiring between point 8 and point 9.

Directional Switch Test

See *12 Volt Transom Mount Directional Switch Test (1981-on)* in this chapter.

Rotary Switch Test

Refer to **Figure 38** for this procedure.

1. Disconnect the battery cable from the batteries.

2. Disconnect all leads at the rotary switch.

3. Set the ohmmeter on the low scale. Connect black test lead to terminal A for entire test.

4. With speed control handle in the OFF position, probe terminals B, C, D and metal switch case with red test lead. There should be no continuity shown at any position.

5. Move the speed control handle to position 1 and probe terminals B, C and D with the red test lead. There should be continuity only at terminal B.

6. Repeat Step 5 with the speed control handle in position 2. There should be continuity only at terminal C.

7. Repeat Step 5 with the speed control handle in position 3. There should be continuity only at terminal D.

8. If continuity is not shown as indicated in Steps 4-7, replace the rotary switch.

11

⓷⓽

TRANSOM MOUNT COMPONENTS

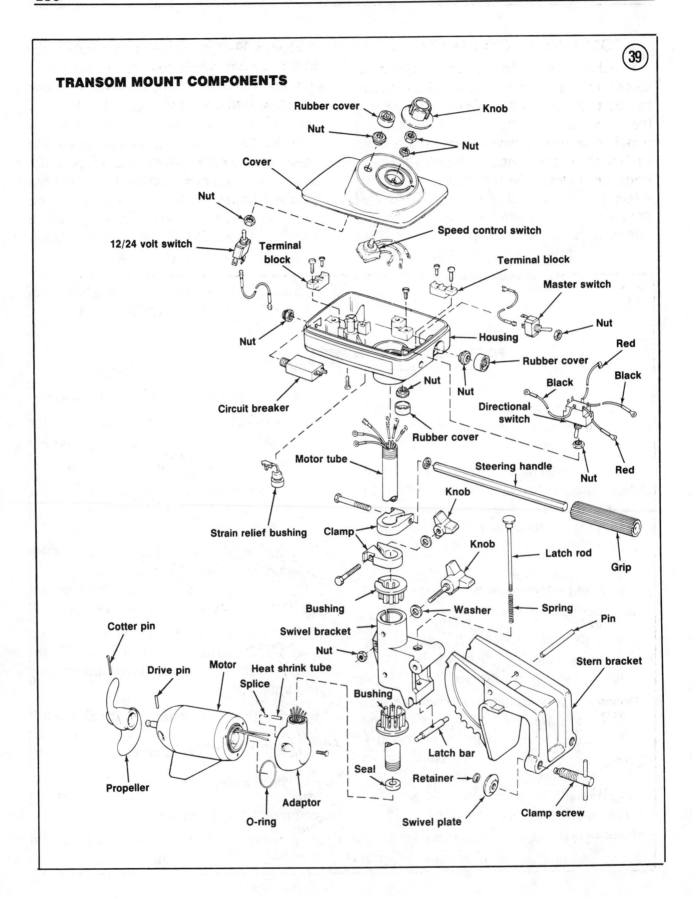

Rubber cover — Knob

Nut

Nut

Cover

Nut

12/24 volt switch — Terminal block

Speed control switch

Terminal block

Master switch

Nut

Nut

Housing

Red

Rubber cover

Black

Black

Nut   Nut

Directional switch

Nut   Red

Circuit breaker

Rubber cover

Motor tube

Steering handle

Knob

Strain relief bushing   Clamp

Knob

Latch rod

Grip

Bushing

Washer   Spring

Pin

Swivel bracket

Nut

Stern bracket

Cotter pin

Drive pin   Motor   Heat shrink tube

Splice

Bushing

Latch bar

Propeller

Seal   Retainer

O-ring   Adaptor   Swivel plate   Clamp screw

COMPONENT REPLACEMENT

Switches are the major operating components in electric motors. After a switch has been diagnosed as defective, disconnect the necessary switch leads. Remove the switch and install a new one. Reconnect the leads to the proper switch terminals. If switch leads are soldered, be sure to use rosin core solder and work with a heat sink to avoid damage to the new switch or nearby components.

Figures 39-41 show the major components of the transom mount, foot pedal and steering housing respectively. Use these to locate defective switches for replacement.

Other than switch replacement, an electric motor should not require service unless it has struck an underwater object or received similar damage. In such cases, damage will likely be severe and the motor should be serviced by your Johnson or Evinrude dealer.

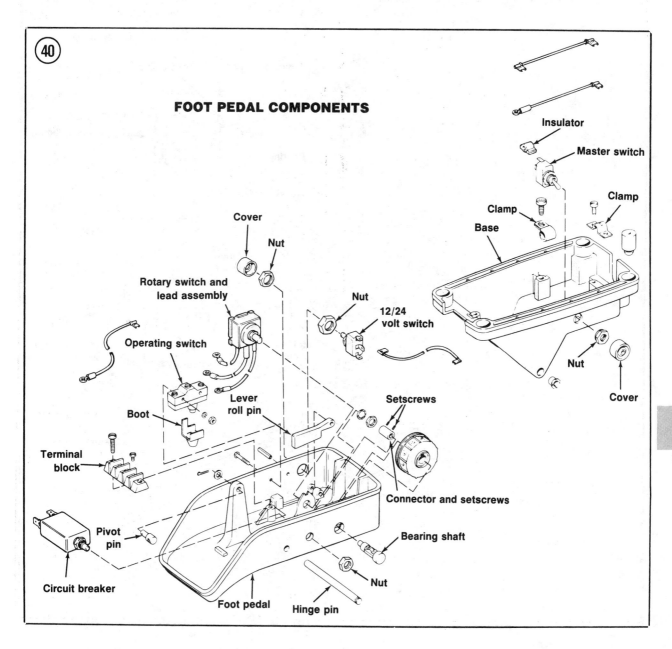

FOOT PEDAL COMPONENTS

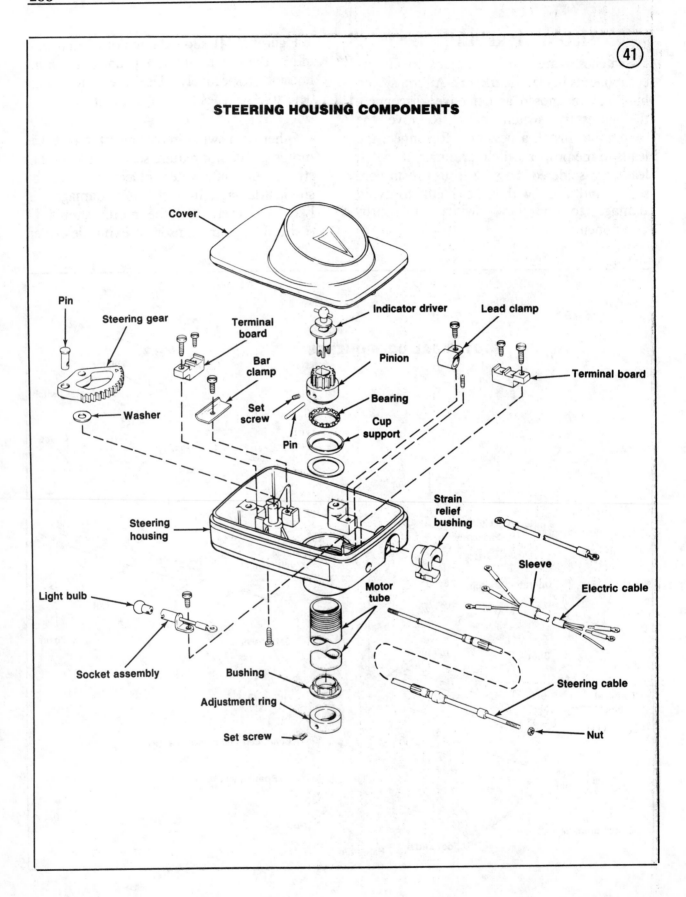

STEERING HOUSING COMPONENTS

SUPPLEMENT

1985 and Later Service Information

This supplement contains service and maintenance procedures for 1985 and later Johnson and Evinrude 2-40 hp outboards. The information supplements the procedures in the main body (Chapters One through Eleven) of the book, referred to in this supplement as the "basic book."

The chapter headings and titles in this supplement correspond to those in the basic book. If a chapter is not included in the supplement, there are no changes affecting 1985 and later models.

If your model is covered by this supplement, carefully read the supplement and then read the appropriate chapters in the basic book before beginning any work.

Chapter Three
Troubleshooting

STARTING SYSTEM

The 1985 and later 9.9 and 15 hp starting system requires a different troubleshooting method than earlier models. Refer to **Figure 1** for this procedure.

1. Remove the engine cover.

2. Remove the fuel pump to permit access to the neutral start switch terminals. See Chapter Six of the basic book.

3. Place the control box shift lever in NEUTRAL, if so equipped.

4. Disconnect the power pack-to-armature plate connector.

5. Connect the red voltmeter lead to point 1, **Figure 1**. Connect the black lead to a good engine ground. Depress the starter switch button. The voltmeter should indicate battery voltage (approximately 12 volts).

6. If no voltage is shown in Step 5, move the red voltmeter lead to point 2 and depress the button. If voltage is now shown, look for an open in the wiring between point 1 and point 2. If voltage is still not shown, disconnect the neutral start switch and check for continuity as described in Chapter Three of the basic book.

7. Move the red voltmeter lead to point 4 and depress the button. If voltage is indicated, adjust the neutral start switch as described in Chapter Three of the basic book. If no voltage is indicated, depress the neutral start switch manually. If voltage is now indicated, the neutral start switch requires adjustment. See Chapter Three of the basic book.

8. Move the red voltmeter lead to point 5 and depress the starter switch button. There should be voltage. If not, there is an open in the wiring between point 4 and point 5.

9. If there is voltage in Step 8 but the starter motor will not turn over, replace the starter.

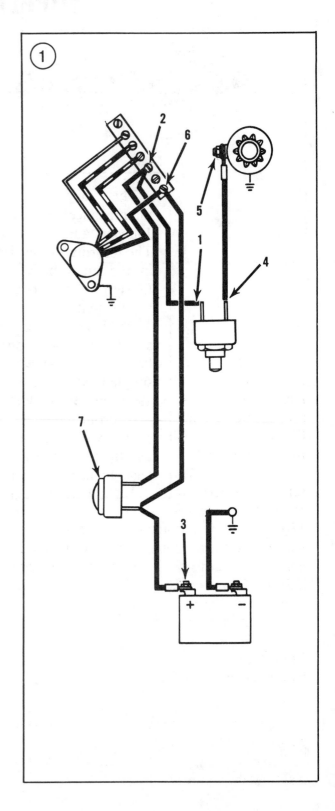

CD 2 IGNITION TROUBLESHOOTING

A 5-wire connector is used between the power pack and armature plate on 1985 and later models. Test procedures and/or specifications that differ from those in Chapter Three of the basic book are provided in this supplement.

If the ignition system produces a satisfactory spark and the engine backfires but will not start, the ignition timing may be 180° off. Check to make sure the black/white wire in the 5-wire connector is positioned in connecter terminal B of both connector halves. Also check to make sure the orange/blue power pack lead is connected to the No. 1 ignition coil.

Stop Button/Key Switch Elimination Test

Refer to **Figure 2** for this procedure.
1. Connect a spark tester as shown in **Figure 2**. Set the tester air gap to 1/2 in.
2. Separate the power pack-to-armature plate 5-wire connector.

3. Insert jumper wires between the connector A, B, C and D terminals.
4. Crank the engine with a starter rope while watching the spark tester.
   a. If there is no spark at either gap, test the charge coil as described in this supplement.
   b. If there is a spark at only one gap, test the sensor coil as described in this supplement.
   c. If a spark jumps both gaps alternately, the problem is in the stop button circuit or the emergency ignition cutoff switch.

Sensor Coil Resistance Test

See Chapter Three of the basic book.

Charge Coil Resistance Test

See Chapter Three of the basic book. Resistance should be between 550-600 ohms.

Sensor Coil Output Test

See Chapter Three of the basic book. Output should be 2 volts or more. If less than 2 volts, check the component wiring and

12

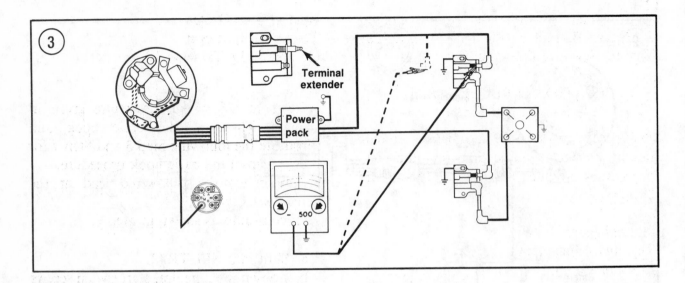

connector. Repair or replace as required, then retest. If wiring and connector are satisfactory, replace the sensor coil.

Charge Coil Output Test

See Chapter Three of the basic book.

Power Pack Output Test

Refer to **Figure 3** for this procedure.
1. Set the CD voltmeter switches to NEGATIVE and 500.
2. Disconnect the ignition coil primary leads. Install a terminal extender (A, **Figure 3**) on each coil terminal, then reconnect the primary leads.
3. Connect the black test lead to a good engine ground. Connect the red test lead to the metal portion of the No. 1 coil terminal extender. Crank the engine and note the meter reading.
4. The meter should read 200 volts or more in Step 3. If it does not, disconnect the the coil primary lead from the terminal extender. Connect the red test lead directly to the spring clip in the primary lead boot. Crank the engine and note the meter reading.
   a. If the meter now reads at least 200 volts, test the ignition coil as described in this supplement.

   b. If the meter still reads less than 200 volts, check the spring clip and primary lead condition. Repair or replace as required, then retest. If condition is satisfactory, replace the power pack.
4. Repeat Step 3 with the red test lead on the metal portion of the No. 2 coil terminal extender. If the reading is less than 200 volts, repeat Step 4.
5. Disconnect the primary leads, remove the terminal extenders from the coil terminals and reconnect the primary leads. Make sure the orange/blue lead is connected to the No. 1 ignition coil.

Ignition Coil Resistance Test

1. Disconnect the primary and high tension (secondary) coil leads at the ignition coil to be tested.
2. With an ohmmeter set on the low scale, connect the red test lead to the coil primary terminal. Connect the black test lead to a good engine ground (if the coil is mounted) or the coil ground tab (if the coil is unmounted). The meter should read 0.1 ± 0.05 ohms.
3. Set the ohmmeter on the high scale. Move the black test lead to the ignition coil high tension terminal. The meter should read 225-325 ohms.

4. If the readings are not as specified in Step 2 or Step 3, replace the ignition coil. See Chapter Seven of the basic book.

IGNITION AND NEUTRAL START SWITCH

Wiring changes on 1985 and later models require slight modification of the test procedures provided in Chapter Three of the basic book.

Neutral Start Switch
Test and Adjustment
(9.9 and 15 hp)

Refer to Chapter Three of the basic book and substitute the following Step 5 for that given in the basic book procedure. If required, plunger adjustment should be 0.090-0.150 in.

5. Connect one ohmmeter test lead to the starter motor cable. Connect the other test lead to the neutral start switch lead at the terminal board.

Neutral Start Switch
Test and Adjustment
(25 and 30 hp TE Models)

Refer to *(18-35 hp)* procedure given in Chapter Three of the basic book and substitute the following Step 3 and Step 7 for those given in the basic book procedure.

3. Disconnect the yellow/red lead at the neutral start switch.

7. If continuity is shown in Step 6:

  a. Shift into NEUTRAL.
  b. Loosen the 2 neutral start switch screws and insert a 1/16 in drill bit between the top of the plunger and bottom of the switch. Move the switch until the switch and plunger contact the drill bit, then tighten the screws securely.
  c. Shift into FORWARD and then REVERSE. If the light or meter shows continuity in either gear, replace the switch.

Chapter Four

Lubrication, Maintenance and Tune-up

Recommended Fuel Mixture

The use of reduced friction bearings in all 1985 and later 2-30 hp and 1985 and later 40 hp engines with tiller steering allows these models to be operated with a 100:1 fuel-oil mixture. The 1985 40 hp electric start and 1986 25 and 30 hp models are equipped with variable ratio oil (VRO) injection. AutoBlend oil injection is standard on 1986 9.9-30 hp and optional on 4-8 hp models. A variation of the AutoBlend system for boats with built-in fuel tanks is optional with all 1986 4-30 hp models. See Chapter Six of this supplement.

Test Wheel Recommendations

Test wheel recommendations for 1985 and later models that differ from those provided in Chapter Four of the basic book are given in **Table 1**.

Spark Plugs

All 1985-on 4 Deluxe through 40 hp engines use a surface gap spark plug for sustained high speed operation. The gap on this plug type is non-adjustable. See **Table 2** for spark plug recommendations and **Figure 4** for spark plug analysis.

12

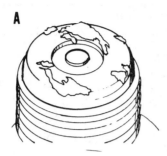
A

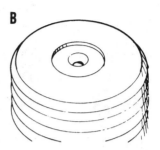
B

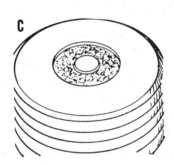
C

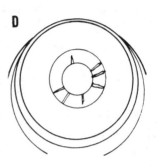
D

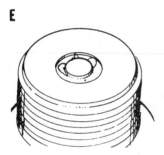
E

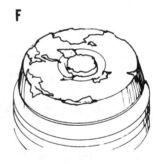
F

SURFACE GAP
SPARK PLUG ANALYSIS

A. Normal—Light tan or gray colored deposits indicate that the engine/ignition system condition is good. Electrode wear indicates normal spark rotation.

B. Worn out—Excessive electrode wear can cause hard starting or a misfire during acceleration.

C. Cold fouled—Wet oil-fuel deposits are caused by "drowning" the plug with raw fuel mix during cranking, overrich carburetion or an improper fuel-oil ratio. Weak ignition will also contribute to this condition.

D. Carbon tracking—Electrically conductive deposits on the firing end provide a low—resistance path for the voltage. Carbon tracks form and can cause misfires.

E. Concentrated arc—Multi-colored appearance is normal. It is caused by electricity consistently following the same firing path. Arc path changes with deposit conductivity and gap erosion.

F. Aluminum throw-off—Caused by preignition. This is not a plug problem but the result of engine damage. Check engine to determine cause and extent of damage.

Table 1 TEST WHEEL RECOMMENDATIONS

Model	Test wheel	Engine rpm
4 deluxe	390123	5,100
5 hp	390239	4,900
20 hp	386891	4,550
25 hp	394145	4,800
30 hp	394145	5,400
40 hp		
Manual	382861	4,900
Electric	387635	5,200

Table 2 RECOMMENDED SPARK PLUGS

Model	hp/cyl.	Champion plug type	Gap (in.)
2	2/1	RJ6C or J6C	0.030
4	4/2	RL86C or L86C	0.030
All others			
Sustained low speed	—	QL77J4 or L77J4	0.040
Sustained high speed	—	QL78V or L78V	NA

Chapter Five

Engine Synchronization and Linkage Adjustments

2-15 HP MODELS

Throttle Cam Adjustment

Refer to Chapter Five of the basic book. However, the cam position is no longer adjusted by loosening its attaching screws and moving the cam itself. Instead, a special adjustment screw is provided on the cam follower and requires the use of special tool part No. 327622 or an equivalent ballhex driver. The screw is backed out until the throttle valve is completely closed, then turned in until the throttle shaft just starts to move.

Carburetor Mixture Adjustment

1. Install the engine in a test tank with the proper test wheel or on the boat in the water with the correct propeller.
2. If carburetor has been overhauled, temporarily install low- and high-speed knobs. If carburetor has not been overhauled, loosen high-speed needle packing nut.
3. Start the engine and run at half throttle until the engine reaches operating temperature.
4. Connect a tachometer according to manufacturer's instructions.

12

5. Increase engine speed to full throttle and adjust the high-speed needle to obtain the highest consistent rpm.

NOTE
The engine requires approximately 15 seconds to respond to adjustment in Step 6.

6. Bring engine speed back to 700-800 rpm and adjust the low-speed needle to obtain the highest consistent rpm.

7. Once low-speed mixture adjustment is satisfactory, turn low-speed needle 1/8 turn counterclockwise to prevent an excessively lean condition at idle.

8. Repeat Step 5. Once high-speed mixture adjustment is satisfactory, turn high-speed needle 1/8 turn counterclockwise to prevent an excessively lean condition at wide-open throttle, then tighten needle packing nut securely.

9. Without changing needle position, install low-speed knob with pointer facing down and high-speed knob with pointer facing up.

Low-speed Adjustment

See *Needle Valve Adjustment* in Chapter Five of the basic book.

40 HP R AND TE MODELS

Initial Throttle Cam Adjustment

1. Rotate the tiller handle idle speed adjustment knob counterclockwise to the slow speed position.

2. Rotate the twist grip to the full open position and check the throttle roller position in the throttle cam slot (**Figure 5**). It should be approximately 1/4 in. from the end of the slot.

3. Rotate the twist grip to the fully closed position and check the throttle roller position in the throttle cam slot (**Figure 6**). It should be approximately 1/4 in. from the end of the slot.

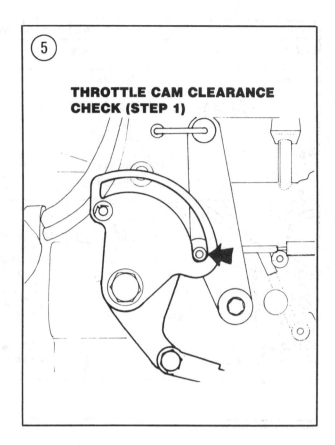

⑤ THROTTLE CAM CLEARANCE CHECK (STEP 1)

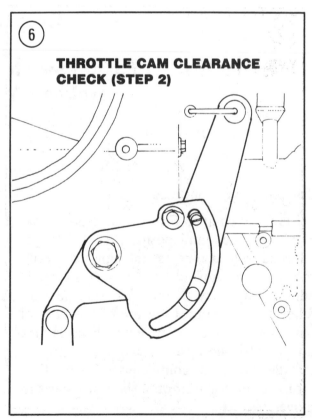

⑥ THROTTLE CAM CLEARANCE CHECK (STEP 2)

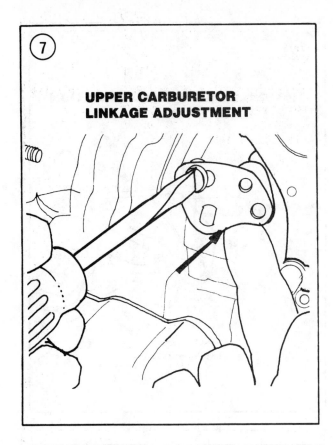

UPPER CARBURETOR
LINKAGE ADJUSTMENT

THROTTLE PICKUP POINT ADJUSTMENT

1. Adjustment screw
2. Lower cam mark
3. Cam follower roller
4. Depress here

4. If the roller is not properly positioned in the cam slot in Step 2 or Step 3, loosen the throttle cable connector retaining screw. Rotate the cable connector until the roller comes to rest about 1/4 in. from each end of the cam slot as the twist grip is opened and closed. Tighten the retaining screw.

Throttle Valve Synchronization

1. Remove the engine cover.
2. Remove the air silencer cover.
3. Retard the throttle lever to a point where the throttle cam roller does not touch the cam.
4. Loosen the upper carburetor lever adjustment screw (**Figure 7**).
5. Rotate the throttle shaft partially open, then let it snap back to the closed position. Depress the adjusting link tab slightly to remove any backlash and tighten the adjustment screw.
6. Move the cam follower while watching the throttle valves. If the throttle valves do not start to move at the same time, repeat Steps 3-5.

Cam Follower Pickup Point Adjustment

1. Connect a throttle shaft amplifier tool (see Chapter Five of the basic book) to the top carburetor throttle shaft.
2. Watching the amplier tool, slowly rotate the throttle cam. As the end of the tool starts to move, check the cam and cam follower alignment. The lower embossed mark on the cam (2, **Figure 8**) should align with the center of the cam follower (3, **Figure 8**).
3. If the cam follower and cam mark do not align in Step 2, loosen the cam follower screw (**Figure 9**) and let the throttle spring close the throttle valves. Align the cam mark and follower and press on the cam follower lever (4, **Figure 8**) to maintain the alignment while tightening the screw.

12

4. Repeat Step 2 to check the adjustment. If incorrect, repeat Step 3, then repeat Step 2 as required.

Cam Follower Pickup Timing

1. Install the engine in a test tank with the proper test wheel or on the boat in the water with the correct propeller.

2. Connect a timing light to the No. 1 cylinder according to manufacturer's instructions.

3. Slowly move the throttle lever until the tip of the amplifier tool starts to move. Remove the tool without disturbing the throttle lever position.

4. Start the engine and check the spark advance with the timing light, advancing the idle speed adjustment knob as required to keep the engine running. Spark advance should be 2-4° BTDC.

5. If the spark advance is incorrect in Step 4, remove the throttle cam shoulder screw (1, **Figure 9**). Rotate the cam on the throttle lever link (2, **Figure 9**) clockwise to advance or counterclockwise to retard timing as required. One full turn of the cam will change timing approximately 2°. Install and tighten the shoulder screw.

6. Repeat Step 3 and Step 4 to check the adjustment. If incorrect, repeat Step 5, then repeat Step 3 and Step 4 as required.

Maximum Spark Advance Adjustment

1. Install the engine in a test tank with the proper test wheel. Do not use a propeller or flushing device.

2. Connect a timing light to the No. 1 cylinder according to manufacturer's instructions.

3. Connect a tachometer according to manufacturer's instructions.

4. Start the engine and run in forward gear at a minimum 3,500 rpm.

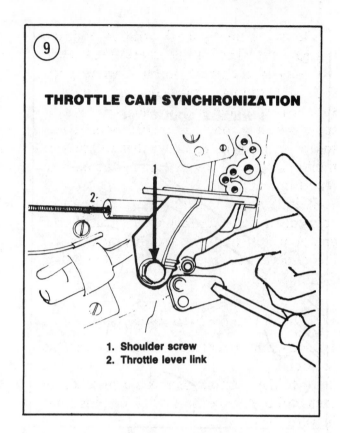

THROTTLE CAM SYNCHRONIZATION

1. Shoulder screw
2. Throttle lever link

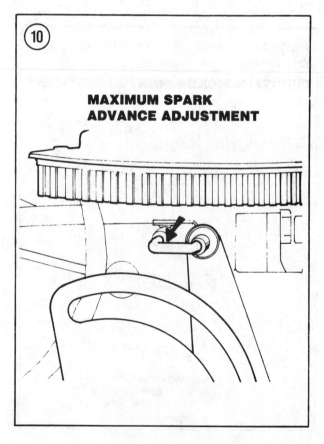

MAXIMUM SPARK ADVANCE ADJUSTMENT

5. Check the timing mark position with the timing light. The timing mark must align with the 19° ± 1° mark on the flywheel grid.

6. If the timing marks do not align as specified, shut the engine off. Remove the spark advance rod (**Figure 10**). Shorten the rod by bending its ends together to advance timing; lengthen it by expanding the ends to retard timing.

7. Reinstall the spark advance rod if adjustment was necessary and repeat Step 4 and Step 5. If timing mark alignment is still incorrect, repeat Step 6, then Step 4 and Step 5 as required.

Wide-open Throttle Stop Adjustment

1. Open the throttle to the full throttle position.

2. Note the position of the pin installed in each carburetor thottle shaft. The pins must be vertical.

3. If the pins are not correctly located in Step 2, loosen the locknut on the wide-open stop screw located behind the slotted throttle cam. Turn the stop screw as required to locate the throttle shaft pins vertically, then tighten the locknut.

Shift Lever Detent Adjustment

1. Place the shift lever in NEUTRAL.

2. Note the position of the lower detent spring (located below the throttle cam follower). It should be fully engaged in the shift lever detent.

3. If the spring is not properly positioned in Step 2, loosen the detent spring screw, move the spring until it engages the detent properly and tighten the screw securely.

Idle Speed Adjustment

This procedure should be performed with the boat floating in the water and tied securely at the slip or dock to prevent any fore or aft motion.

1. Remove the engine cover.

2. Connect a tachometer according to manufacturer's instructions.

3. Start the engine and warm to operating temperature.

4. Shift the engine into FORWARD gear and note the idle speed on the tachometer. It should be 750 rpm.

5. If idle speed requires adjustment, loosen the idle speed screw locknut (located above slotted throttle cam). Turn the idle speed screw as required to bring the idle speed within specifications, then tighten the locknut.

6. When idle speed adjustment is completed, shut the engine off. Remove the tachometer and install the engine cover.

12

Chapter Six

Fuel System

CARBURETORS

Carburetors used on the 1985 and later 20 hp and 40 hp engines are essentially the same as those described in Chapter Six of the basic book for 20-40 hp models. Removal/installation procedures are provided in this supplement.

A new carburetor design with phenolic cover and float bowl is used on 1986 5-8 hp engines. Complete service procedures are provided in this supplement.

Removal/Installation
(1985-on 20 hp)

1. Remove the engine cover.
2. Disconnect the primer hose from the intake manifold and remove the screw holding the hose clamp to the carburetor.
3. If equipped with an electric starter, unbolt the starter bracket and place to one side.
4. Disconnect throttle link from cam follower.
5. Unbolt the primer solenoid and place to one side.
6. Remove the carburetor mounting nuts. Remove the carburetor and gasket. Discard the gasket.
7. Disconnect the fuel line at the carburetor. Plug the line to prevent leakage.
8. Installation is the reverse of removal. Use a new gasket. Adjust the carburetor as described in Chapter Five of the basic book. Squeeze primer bulb and check for leaks.

Removal/Installation
(1985-on 40 hp)

1. Remove the engine cover.
2. Remove the air silencer cover and gasket. Discard the gasket.

3. Remove and discard the air silencer base attaching screws.

NOTE
Do not disconnect the hoses connected to the VRO pump in Step 4.

4. On electric start models, remove the 2 screws holding the VRO pump bracket to the power head. Remove the VRO pump and bracket and place to one side.
5. Disconnect the drain hose at the air silencer base. Remove the base and gasket. Discard the gasket.
6. Disconnect the fuel line at the carburetor. Plug the line to prevent leakage.
7. Disconnect the linkage at the throttle lever.
8. Remove the carburetor mounting nuts. Remove the carburetor and gasket. Discard the gasket.
9. Installation is the reverse of removal. Use new carburetor and air silencer gaskets. Adjust the carburetor as described in Chapter Five of the basic book. Squeeze primer bulb and check for fuel leaks.

Removal/Installation
(1986 5-8 hp)

1. Remove the engine cover.
2. Remove the air silencer cover and hose.
3. Remove the automatic rewind (manual) starter. See Chapter Ten of the basic book.
4. Disconnect the cam follower and link at the carburetor.
5. Remove the 2 carburetor mounting nuts. Remove the carburetor and gasket. Discard the gasket.
6. Disconnect the primer and fuel lines at the carburetor. Plug the lines to prevent leakage.

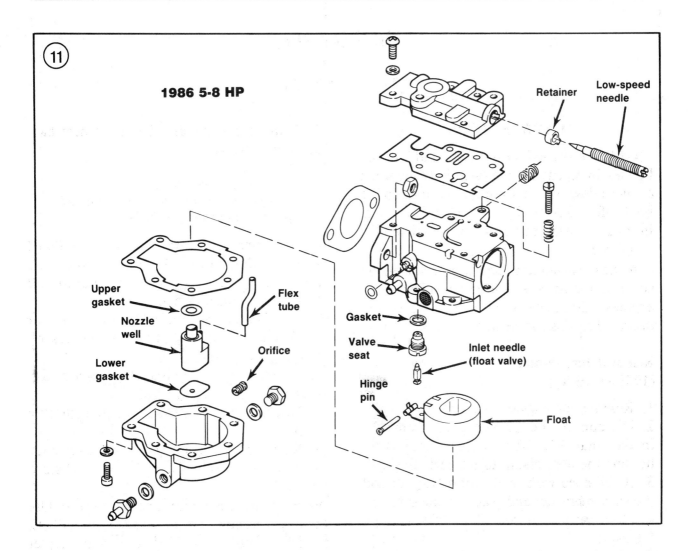

⑪

1986 5-8 HP

Retainer

Low-speed needle

Upper gasket

Nozzle well

Lower gasket

Flex tube

Orifice

Gasket

Valve seat

Inlet needle (float valve)

Hinge pin

Float

7. Installation is the reverse of removal. Use new carburetor and air silencer gaskets. Adjust the carburetor to idle at 850-900 rpm (6SL and 8SRL) or 650-700 rpm (all others) as described in Chapter Five of the basic book. Squeeze primer bulb and check for fuel leaks.

Disassembly/Assembly

Refer to **Figure 11** for this procedure.
1. Unscrew and remove the low-speed needle and retainer from the carburetor body cover.
2. Remove the cover and gasket. Discard the gasket.
3. Remove the float chamber and gasket. Discard the gasket and check the condition of the lower gasket in the float chamber.

4. Remove the float assembly hinge pin. Lift the float and needle valve from the carburetor body.
5. Remove the needle valve seat with a wide-blade screwdriver. Discard the seat gasket.
6. Cut the flex tube from the 2 nipples to which it is connected. Discard the tube.
7. Remove the orifice plug from the float chamber. Remove the high-speed orifice with fixed jet screwdriver part No. 317002.
8. Remove the nozzle well and upper gasket. Discard the upper gasket.
9. Assembly is the reverse of disassembly. Compare new gaskets to old ones to make sure all holes are properly punched. Remove any loose gasket fibers or stamping crumbs

12

adhering to the new gaskets. Adjust the float as described in this supplement chapter. Lightly seat low-speed needle, then back it out 2 1/2 turns. Install on engine and adjust carburetor (Chapter Five).

Float Adjustment

1. Invert the carburetor body with its gasket surface horizontal, allowing the float weight to close the needle valve.
2. Place float gauge (part No. 324891) on the gasket surface and hold it next to the float (**Figure 12**). Use "9.9-15 hp" notch for this carburetor. Do not let gauge pressure hold float down.
3. If the top of the float is not between the gauge notches (**Figure 12**), bend the metal float arm carefully (to avoid forcing the needle valve into its seat) and bring the level within specifications.
4. Return the carburetor body to its normal running position and check float drop. The distance between the carburetor body and the float as shown in **Figure 13** should be 1-1 3/8 in.
5. If the float drop is incorrect, carefully bend the tang (**Figure 13**) until it comes within specifications.

OIL INJECTION SYSTEM

The variable ratio oiling (VRO) system is a factory-installed standard feature on 1985 electric start 40 hp models and 1986 25 and 30 hp models. This system uses a self-contained pump on the power head instead of the conventional fuel pump. A remote mounted oil tank with pump and primer bulb and a warning horn complete the basic system.

One design uses a spark or flame arrestor installed in the pulse hose leading to the VRO pump and clamped in position to prevent it from moving and causing damage to the pump. An oil inlet filter is installed in the oil

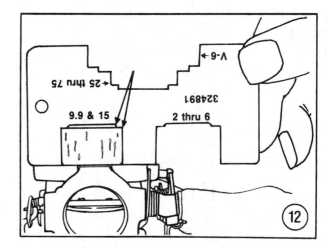

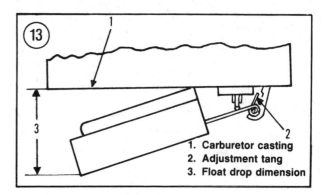

1. Carburetor casting
2. Adjustment tang
3. Float drop dimension

tank pickup unit and an inline filter is installed in the transparent oil inlet hose to the VRO pump on these models to protect the pump from contamination.

The other design has the arrestor installed in the pulse hose fitting. The arrestor should not be removed from the fitting; they are serviced as an assembly. These models have the oil inlet filter installed in the oil tank pickup unit and an inline filter canister (serviced as a complete assembly) installed in the fuel line on the power head.

Operation

The VRO system works on crankcase pressure in a manner similar to the conventional fuel pump, drawing fuel and oil from separate tanks and mixing them in the VRO pump at a ratio varying from 50:1 to 150:1 according to engine requirements.

VRO-equipped models can also be run on a 50:1 fuel-oil mixture drawn from the fuel tank if the user premixes the fuel and oil as described in Chapter Four of the basic book.

Break-in Procedure

All VRO models should be run on a 50:1 fuel-oil mixture from the fuel tank (see Chapter Four of the basic book) *in addition* to the lubricant supplied by the VRO system. Mark the oil level on the translucent VRO remote oil tank and periodically check to make sure the system is working (oil level drops) before switching over to plain gasoline at the end of the 10-hour break-in period.

Warning Horn

A warning horn is installed in the accessory or remote control wiring harness. The horn has 2 functions.

The sending unit in the remote oil tank is connected to the warning horn through the key switch and grounded to the engine. If the oil level in the tank drops below the 1/4 full point, the warning horn sounds for 1/2 second every 20 seconds to alert the user to a low oil level. A no-oil warning feature is incorporated in 1986 circuits. If the system runs completely out of oil, the warning horn sounds for 1/2 second every second.

A temperature sending unit is installed in the cylinder head and connected to the warning horn through the key switch to warn of an overheat condition. If the power head temperature exceeds 211° F, the horn sounds continuously. Backing off on the throttle will shut the horn off as soon as power head temperature reaches 175°degrees F, unless a restricted engine water intake is causing the overheat condition. If the water pump indicator does not deliver a steady stream or if the horn continues sounding after 2 minutes, the engine should be shut off immediately to prevent power head damage.

CAUTION
If the engine overheats and the warning horn sounds, retorque the cylinder head after the engine cools to minimize the possibility of power head damage from a blown head gasket.

Warning Horn Test

The warning horn should be tested periodically to make sure it is functioning properly.
1. Locate the electrical wire between the warning horn and temperature switch. Move the insulating sleeve back to provide access to the disconnect point in the wire.
2. Turn the key switch ON and ground the disconnect point to the engine.
3. If the horn does not sound, check the wiring and horn.
4. Reposition the insulating sleeve over the disconnect point in the wire.

Troubleshooting

The VRO pump is sealed at the factory and is serviced by replacement if defective. Any attempt to disassemble the pump will void the factory warranty.

If the oil inlet hose is disconnected from the pump, it must be reinstalled with the same type of clamps as removed. The use of worm clamps will damage the vinyl hose while tie straps will not provide sufficient clamping pressure.

Refer to **Figure 14** for inlet and outlet identification.

CAUTION
The pump nipples are plastic and can be broken if excess pressure is used when disconnecting or connecting the lines.

12

1. Disconnect the fuel outlet line. Install a tee to the end of the line and connect a 4 inch length of 5/16 in. ID hose to the tee.

2. Lubricate the pump outlet fitting with a drop of oil and connect the vinyl hose and tee assembly to the pump.

3. Connect a 0-15 psi pressure gauge to the tee.

4. Secure all hose connections with tie straps or hose clamps.

5. Start the engine and run at wide-open throttle in gear. The gauge should read between 3-15 psi and drop to 1-2 psi (accompanied by a clicking sound) each time the pump discharges oil.

6. If no pressure is shown in Step 5:
   a. Check for fuel in the tank.
   b. Check for a pinched, kinked or restricted fuel line.
   c. Check for a pinched or leaking VRO pump pulse line (2, **Figure 14**).

7. If low pressure is shown in Step 5:
   a. Check fuel filter for restrictions.
   b. Check for a pinched or leaking VRO pump pulse line (2, **Figure 14**).
   c. Check for a pinched, kinked or restricted fuel line.
   d. Squeeze the fuel primer bulb several times to remove any possible vapor lock condition in the line.

8. If no pressure or low pressure is shown in Step 5 and the items in Step 6 or Step 7 are satisfactory, replace the VRO pump.

Oil Flow Test

1. Make sure there is sufficient oil in the VRO tank. Top up as required.

2. Connect a remote fuel tank containing the 50:1 fuel/oil mixture to the engine.

3. With the engine in a test tank or on the boat in the water, start the engine and note the flow through the transparent hose at the VRO pump.

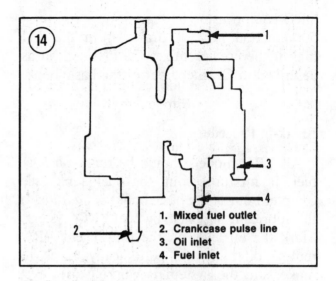

1. Mixed fuel outlet
2. Crankcase pulse line
3. Oil inlet
4. Fuel inlet

4. If a reduced flow or no flow is noted in Step 3, shut the engine off. Check the oil pickup filter as described in this chapter.

5A. If filter is not clogged or obstructed, proceed to Step 6.

5B. If filter required cleaning or replacement, repeat Step 3 to see if this service restored full oil flow. If it did not, continue with Step 6.

6. Disconnect the oil hose at the inlet fitting on the lower engine cover. Have an assistant hold the hose in a suitable clean container.

7. Loosen oil hose clamp at pickup unit. Grasp pickup unit firmly to prevent it from moving on its support rods and disconnect the hose. Blow the line out with low-pressure compressed air.

8. Remove the oil pickup mounting screws with a T-25 Torx driver. Remove the pickup unit from the tank and let it drain into a suitable clean container.

9. Insert a suitable plug in the end of the hose attached to the pickup unit. Install a clamp to hold the plug in place.

10. Connect a Stevens gearcase vacuum tester or a hand vacuum pump to the oil hose at the lower engine cover end and install a clamp to secure the connection.

11. Draw approximately 7 in. Hg vacuum. If the system does not hold the vacuum, check the oil hose for damage. If the hose is good,

apply oil at each connection while drawing a vacuum to determine the point of leakage. Correct as required.

12. If the system holds vacuum in Step 10, replace the VRO pump assembly.

Excessive Engine Smoke

Check fuel system and filters for restrictions. The engine may smoke on a cold start. This is normal for cold starting a 2-cycle engine. It will also smoke if the oil hose primer bulb is squeezed prior to starting the engine. This priming is unnecessary and loads the carburetors with an excessively rich mixture.

Low Oil Warning Sounds at 20 Second Intervals

If the oil level in the tank is satisfactory, the pickup unit disc/contacts are either out of position or dirty. Remove the pickup unit from the tank and clean the float chamber in fresh solvent. If the float does not raise the disc clear of the contacts, replace the pickup unit.

Pickup Unit and Filter Service

Other than filter replacement, the oil pickup unit is serviced as an assembly if it does not function properly.

1. Remove the oil pickup mounting screws with a T-25 Torx driver. Remove the pickup unit from the tank and let it drain into a suitable clean container.
2. Note the position of the foam baffle (if so equipped) for reinstallation and remove from the pickup unit.
3. Pull the plastic filter assembly from the end of the pickup tube with needlenose pliers.
4. Clean filter in fresh solvent and blow dry with low-pressure compressed air, if available. Replace filter if damaged or badly clogged.

5. To reinstall filter, insert it in the plastic cap from a felt-tip marker. Marker cap should be large enough to hold filter but no larger than the outer diameter of the filter head.
6. Use the marker cap to press the filter into the pickup tube.
7. Reinstall the foam baffle (if so equipped) in the position noted in Step 2.
8. Reinstall pickup unit in oil tank and tighten the 4 retaining screws securely.

CAUTION
Failure to properly purge air from the system in Step 9 can result in serious engine damage caused by lack of proper lubrication.

9. Disconnect the oil hose at the inlet fitting on the lower engine cover. Hold the hose in a suitable clean container and squeeze the VRO primer bulb *50* times to purge any air from the line.
10. Reinstall the oil hose to the engine inlet fitting and tighten the clamp securely.

AUTOBLEND OIL INJECTION

This electro-mechanical oil injection system consists of a fuel-pump activated oil metering pump built into a portable 6-gallon fuel tank (**Figure 15**). A similar metering pump design is available for boats with built-in fuel tanks. The 1 1/2 quart oil reservoir provides sufficient oil to blend a precise 100:1 mixture for 5 full tanks of gasoline. AutoBlend should *not* be used with 1985 or earlier outboards.

A low-oil warning indicator is triggered whenever the oil in the reservoir reaches the 1/2 quart level. This allows the use the one full tank of gasoline before the reservoir requires refilling. If the oil level should drop to a critical level, the sensor will automatically shut down the motor to prevent damage.

12

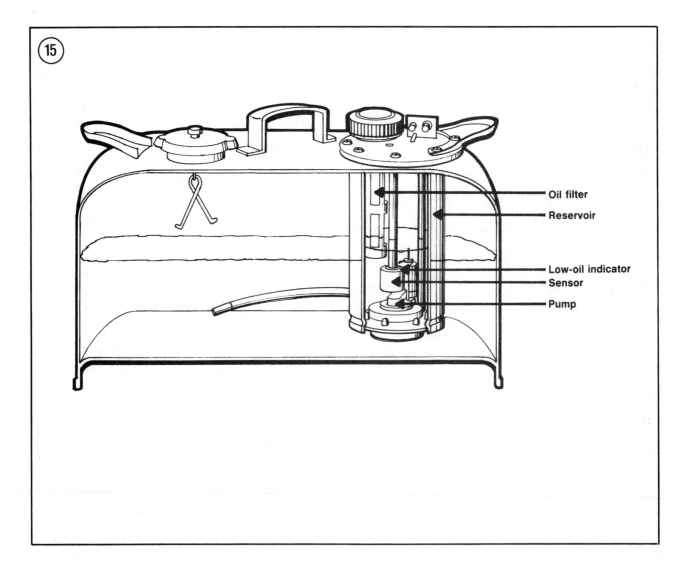

⑮

Oil filter
Reservoir

Low-oil indicator
Sensor
Pump

Owner service of the AutoBlend injection system is limited to draining and flushing of the fuel tank at each tune-up or major overhaul, or at least once per year. The AutoBlend unit is serviced by replacement.

Removal/Installation

1. Remove the 8 screws holding the oil reservoir to the fuel tank. Lift the reservoir up and out of the tank. Remove and discard the reservoir gasket.
2. Remove the cover from the reservoir. Discard the cover seal.
3. Wash the oil reservoir components with a mild cleaner and blow dry with low-pressure compressed air.

4. Insert the pickup hose in the clip and position the reservoir on the fuel tank with a new gasket.

5. Fit a new cover seal in position and wipe the outer diameter of the fuel tube with a light coat of OMC Triple-Guard grease.

6. Fit the cover on the reservoir, making sure the fuel tube enters the cavity in the cover.

7. Insert the reservoir in the tank opening. Install the screws and washers, adding an extra washer under each tank bracket fastener. Tighten screws to 10-12 in.-lb.(1.1-1.3 N•m).

Chapter Eight

Power Head

1985 20 and 40 hp

The 20 hp is a detuned 25 hp model; the 40 hp is a detuned 50 hp model. Both can be serviced using the procedures provided for the 18-40 hp models in Chapter Four of the basic book.

Power head specifications and tightening torques for these new designs are provided in **Table 3** and **Table 4** respectively.

Table 3 POWER HEAD SPECIFICATIONS

20 HP	
Bore	3.000 in. (76.2 mm)
Stroke	2.250 in. (57.15 mm)
Displacement	31.8 cu. in. (521 cc)
Full throttle operating range	4,500-5,500 rpm
Idle rpm (in forward gear)	750 rpm
Crankshaft	
Journal diameter	
Top	1.2510-1.2515 in. (31.775-31.788 mm)
Center	1.1833-1.1838 in. (30.056-30.069 mm)10
Bottom	0.9842-0.9846 in. (24.999-30.030 mm)
Crankpin diameter	1.1823-1.1828 in. (30.030-30.043 mm)
Standard bore size	2.9995-3.0005 in. (76.187-76.213 mm)
Piston Ring	
End gap	0.007-0.017 in. (0.18-0.43 mm)
Groove side	
clearance (lower)	0.004 in. (0.10 mm) max.
40 HP	
Bore	3.1875 in. (80.96 mm)
Stroke	2.820 in. (71.63 mm)
Displacement	45 cu. in. (737 cc)
Full throttle operating range	4,500-5,500 rpm
Idle rpm (in forward gear)	750 rpm
(continued)	

12

Table 3 POWER HEAD SPECIFICATIONS (continued)

40 HP (continued)	
Crankshaft	
Journal diameter	
Top	1.4974-1.4979 in. (38.034-38.047 mm)
Center	1.3748-1.3752 in. (34.920-34.930 mm)
Bottom	1.1810-1.1815 in. (29.997-30.110 mm)
Crankpin diameter	1.1823-1.1828 in. (30.030-30.043 mm)
Standard bore size	3.1870-3.1880 in. (80.950-80.975 mm)
Piston Ring	
End gap	0.007-0.017 in. (0.18-0.43 mm)
Groove side	
clearance (lower)	0.004 in. (0.10 mm) max.

Table 4 20 AND 40 HP POWER HEAD TORQUES

Fastener	in.-lb.	ft.-lb.	N·m
Connecting rod screws		29-31	40-42
Crankcase main bearing screws			
20 hp		14-16	19-22
40 hp		18-20	24-27
Cylinder head screws		18-20	24-27
Flywheel nut		100-105	135-140
Ignition coil mounting screws	60-84		7-9
Lower journal bearing screws	96-120		11-14
Manual starter mounting screws		8-10	11-14
Power pack mounting screws	60-84		7-9
Power head to exhaust housing			
20 hp		16-18	22-25
40 hp		18-20	24-27
Spark plugs		18-21	24-27
Stator screws	60-80		7-9
Starter motor mounting bolts		10-12	14-16

Chapter Nine

Gearcase

The 2-piece gearcase used with 1984 25 hp models has been discontinued. All 1985 and later 20, 25 and 30 hp models use a one-piece gearcase. Refer to *Disassembly/Assembly (30 and 35 hp)* in Chapter Nine of the basic book for service procedures. Tightening torques are provided in **Table 5**.

The 1985 and later 40 hp model uses the same one-piece gearcase as the 50 hp model.

Service procedures are provided in this supplement and tightening torques given in **Table 5**.

Disassembly

Refer to **Figure 16** (typical) for this procedure.

1. Secure the gearcase in a holding fixture or a vise with protective jaws. If protective jaws

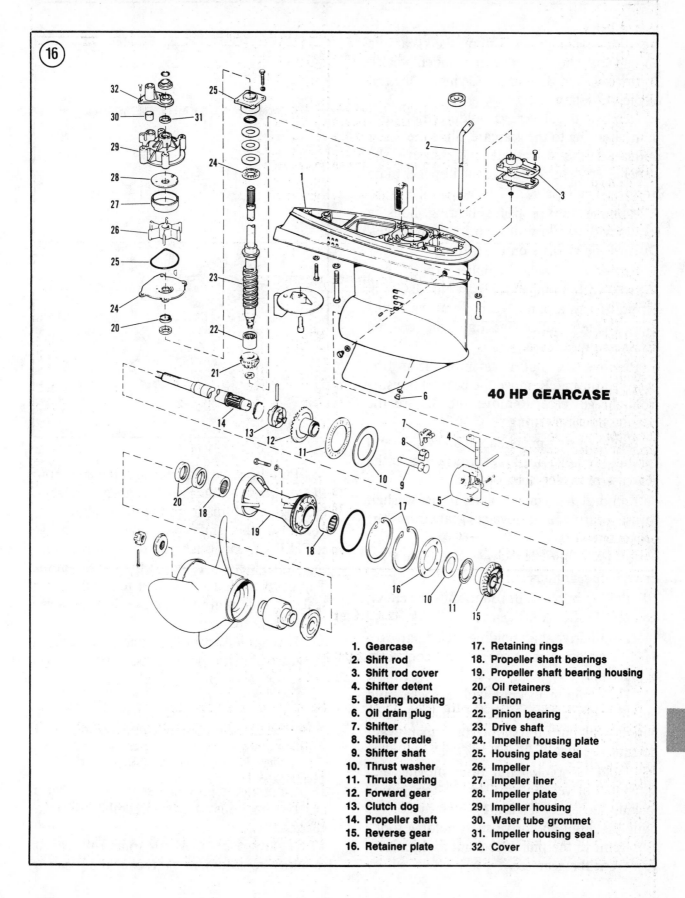

40 HP GEARCASE

1. Gearcase
2. Shift rod
3. Shift rod cover
4. Shifter detent
5. Bearing housing
6. Oil drain plug
7. Shifter
8. Shifter cradle
9. Shifter shaft
10. Thrust washer
11. Thrust bearing
12. Forward gear
13. Clutch dog
14. Propeller shaft
15. Reverse gear
16. Retainer plate
17. Retaining rings
18. Propeller shaft bearings
19. Propeller shaft bearing housing
20. Oil retainers
21. Pinion
22. Pinion bearing
23. Drive shaft
24. Impeller housing plate
25. Housing plate seal
26. Impeller
27. Impeller liner
28. Impeller plate
29. Impeller housing
30. Water tube grommet
31. Impeller housing seal
32. Cover

12

are not available, position the gearcase upright with the skeg between wooden blocks.

2. Remove and discard the O-ring on the top of the driveshaft.

3. Remove the 4 screws holding the water pump housing to the gearcase. Slide the water pump off the driveshaft and retrieve the impeller drive pin. Remove the impeller plate from the gearcase.

4. Remove the propeller bearing housing screws with a thin wall 5/16 in. deep socket. Discard the O-rings on the screws.

5. Assemble flywheel puller (part No. 378103) with 3 puller legs (part No. 320737). Fit puller legs around bearing housing flange legs. Tighten puller nut until the bearing housing comes loose.

6. Remove the puller assembly from the bearing housing. Remove the bearing housing from the gearcase. Remove and discard the bearing housing O-ring.

7. Use snap ring pliers part No. 311879 and carefully remove the 2 large snap rings in the gearcase propeller bore.

8. Remove the retainer plate, thrust washer, thrust bearing and reverse gear from the propeller shaft.

9. Remove the 4 screws holding the driveshaft seal housing.

10. Pull up on the shift rod to shift the clutch dog into FORWARD gear.

11. Install drive shaft holding socket part No. 316612 on drive shaft splines and connect a breaker bar.

12. Hold pinion locknut with a socket and flex handle. Pad the gearcase where the flex handle will hit with shop cloths to prevent housing damage.

13. Hold the pinion nut from moving and turn the drive shaft to break the pinion locknut loose. See **Figure 17**. Remove the pinion locknut and drive shaft holding tool.

14. Remove the pinion locknut and pinion gear from the gearcase.

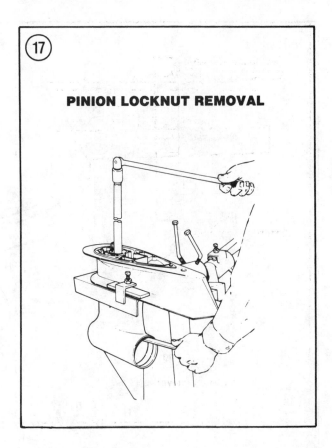

PINION LOCKNUT REMOVAL

15. Pull the drive shaft and seal housing from the gearcase. Remove the thrust washer, bearing and shims from the drive shaft.

16. Push the shift rod down to engage REVERSE gear. Unthread the shift rod from the shifter detent. Remove the cover screws. Tap cover with a soft mallet to break gasket seal and slide it upward on the shift rod away from the gearcase.

17. Disengage the shift rod and remove from the gearcase with the shift rod cover. Discard the cover gasket and O-ring.

NOTE
The shift detent must be in REVERSE to provide necessary clearance for propeller shaft removal in Step 18.

18. Remove the propeller shaft, forward gear and bearing housing as an assembly from the gearcase.

19. If lower drive shaft (pinion) bearing requires replacement, remove the bearing

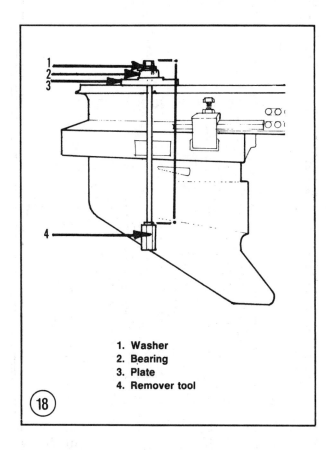

1. Washer
2. Bearing
3. Plate
4. Remover tool

18

retaining screw from the gearcase. Remove and discard the O-ring on the screw.

20. Assemble bearing remover/installer tool (part No. 391257) as shown in **Figure 18** and tighten screw to pull bearing from gearcase.

21. Drive oil seals and bearings from each end of bearing housing with a suitable punch and mallet.

22. Carefully lift one end of the clutch dog retaining spring and insert a screwdriver blade or the tip of an awl under it. Holding the screwdriver or awl in a stationary position, rotate the propeller shaft to unwind the spring.

23. Remove the clutch dog retainer pin (**Figure 19**) and separate the bearing housing, forward gear, thrust washer and bearing assembly and clutch dog from the propeller shaft.

24. Remove the shift lever pin from the bearing housing with a suitable punch.

25. Disconnect the shift lever from the shifter shaft cradle, then remove the shaft, cradle and lever. See **Figure 20**.

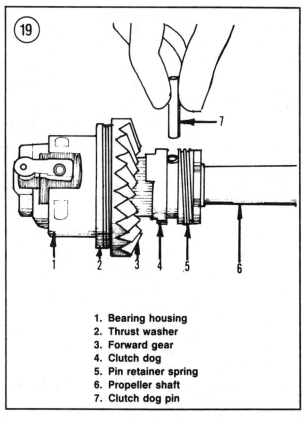

19

1. Bearing housing
2. Thrust washer
3. Forward gear
4. Clutch dog
5. Pin retainer spring
6. Propeller shaft
7. Clutch dog pin

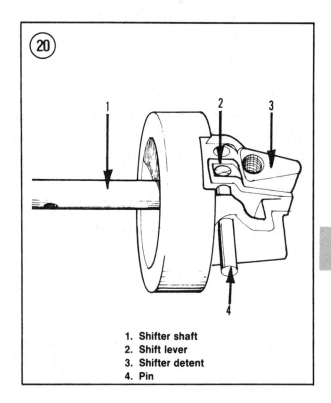

20

1. Shifter shaft
2. Shift lever
3. Shifter detent
4. Pin

12

26. Depress the detent ball and spring by rotating the shifter detent 180°. Catch ball and spring as detent is removed from bearing housing. See **Figure 21**.

Cleaning and Inspection

See Chapter Nine of basic book. The forward gear bearing and bearing housing are serviced as an assembly. Replace the assembly if either is worn or damaged.

Assembly

Refer to **Figure 16** (typical) for this procedure.
1. Reassemble the bearing housing as follows:
   a. Coat end of forward bearing housing detent spring and ball with OMC Needle Bearing Grease. Insert spring and ball in forward bearing housing.
   b. Install shifter detent in forward bearing housing. Depress ball and spring with a suitable punch and push detent into housing.
   c. Coat shifter cradle with OMC HI-VIS Gearcase Lubricant and install on shift shaft. Rotate shifter detent 180°, then insert cradle and shaft in housing.
   d. Insert the shift lever to engage the cradle and shifter detent, then install retaining pin.
2. Position the clutch dog with the end stamped PROP facing the propeller end of the shaft. Align the clutch dog holes and propeller shaft slot, then install clutch dog on shaft.
3. Place thrust bearing on forward gear shoulder. Place thrust washer on bearing housing shoulder. Install forward gear in bearing housing.
4. Install the propeller shaft over the shift shaft and align the clutch dog and shift shaft holes. Insert the retaining pin.

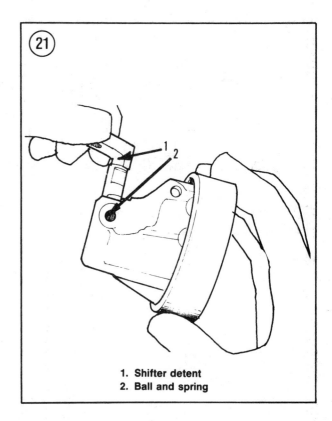

1. Shifter detent
2. Ball and spring

5. Install one end of a new clutch dog retaining spring over the clutch dog, then rotate the propeller shaft to wind the spring back in place.
6. Push shifter detent into REVERSE position, then install bearing housing, forward gear and propeller shaft assembly in the gearcase. The locating pin on the bearing housing must engage the locating hole in the gearcase.
7. If lower drive shaft (pinion) bearing was removed, lubricate a new bearing with OMC Needle Bearing Grease. Assemble bearing remover/installer tool part NO. 391257. Position new bearing on tool with lettered side facing tool shoulder. Insert assembly into gearcase and drive the bearing in until the tool washer touches the tool spacer. Remove the tool.
8. Wipe a new bearing setscrew O-ring with OMC Gasket Sealing Compound and install setscrew in gearcase. Tighten to specifications (**Table 5**).

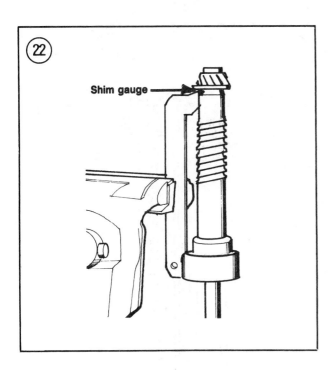

Shim gauge

9. If drive shaft tapered roller bearing requires replacement, remove and install the bearing with an arbor press and universal bearing plate.

10. Install pinion gear on drive shaft and tighten locknut to specifications (**Table 5**).

11. Measure and record the thickness of the shims removed during disassembly. Install 0.020 in. shimming on drive shaft shoulder, then install the drive shaft in shim gauge part No. 320739. See **Figure 22**.

12. Measure the clearance between the shim gauge and pinion gear. If the same pinion and forward gear assembly is being reinstalled, check the gearcase trim tab pocket.

   a. If there is an "S" stamped inside the pocket, adjust the thickness of the shim(s) removed during disassembly to match the feeler gauge reading.

   b. If there is no stamping in the gearcase trim tab pocket, subtract 0.007 in. from the feeler gauge reading, then adjust the thickness of the shim(s) removed during disassembly to match that reading.

13. If a new pinion and forward gear assembly is being installed, adjust the thickness of the shim(s) removed during disassembly to match the feeler gauge reading.

14. Remove the drive shaft from the shim gauge. Remove the 0.020 shim. Remove the pinion gear from the drive shaft.

15. Coat the outside diameter of 2 new drive shaft bearing housing seals with OMC Gasket Sealing Compound. Install the seals back-to-back in the housing (one lip facing in and the other facing out).

Pack the cavity between the seals with OMC Triple-Guard grease.

16. Install a new bearing housing O-ring and lubricate it with OMC Triple-Guard grease.

17. Install the drive shaft thrust bearing, thrust washer and shim pack on the drive shaft.

18. Coat both sides of a new drive shaft seal housing gasket with OMC Gasket Sealing Compound. Install gasket to seal housing.

19. Wrap drive shaft splines with one thickness of masking tape and carefully slide seal housing and gasket over drive shaft.

20. Wipe the seal housing screw threads with OMC Gasket Sealing Compound and install the screws. Tighten screws to specifications (**Table 5**).

21. Remove the masking tape from the drive shaft splines and clean splines as required.

22. Coat both sides of a new shift cover gasket with OMC Gasket Sealing Compound and install on gearcase.

23. Insert shift rod through shift rod cover bushing and thread it into the shifter detent until it stops, then back it out enough to position offset on top of rod with the port side of the gearcase. Tighten shift rod cover screws to specifications (**Table 5**).

NOTE
After adjustment in Step 24, shift rod offset should face drive shaft.

24. Place shift rod in NEUTRAL. Position a universal shift rod gauge (part No. 389997)

12

on the gearcase beside the vertical shift rod and align gauge and shift rod holes. Insert gauge pin in gauge hole. See **Figure 23**. Screw the shift rod in or out of the shifter detent to obtain a dimension of 15 29/32 ±1/32 in. (standard shaft) or 20 29/32 ±1/32 in. (long shaft), then pull up on the shift rod to engage clutch dog with forward gear.

25. Install pinion gear in gearcase propeller shaft bore and mesh with forward gear teeth.

26. Install drive shaft to engage pinion gear and install locknut.

27. Install drive shaft holding socket part No. 316612 on drive shaft splines and connect a breaker bar.

28. Hold pinion locknut with a socket and flex handle. Pad the gearcase where the flex handle will hit with shop cloths to prevent housing damage.

29. Hold the pinion nut from moving and turn the drive shaft to tighten the pinion locknut to specifications (**Table 5**). See **Figure 17**. Remove the pinion locknut and drive shaft holding tools.

30. Install the thrust bearing and thrust washer on reverse gear. Install reverse gear assembly with retainer plate on propeller shaft.

31. Slip one snap ring (flat side facing out) over the propeller shaft and install with snap ring pliers part No. 311879. Repeat this step to install the other snap ring.

32. If the bearing was removed from the propeller shaft bearing housing, install a new one with a suitable mandrel.

33. Wipe the outer diameter of 2 new propeller bearing housing seals with OMC Gasket Sealing Compound. Install the seals back-to-back (one lip facing in, the other facing out) with a suitable seal installer. Pack the cavity between the seals with OMC Triple-Guard grease.

34. Install a new O-ring on the bearing housing and lubricate with OMC Triple-Guard grease. Install new O-rings on

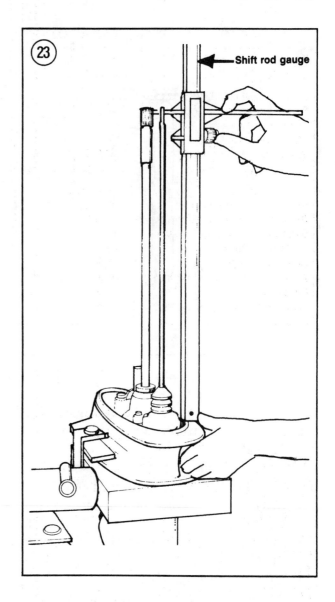

the housing screws and wipe the screw threads with OMC Gasket Sealing Compound.

35. Install the guide pins used for bearing housing removal. Position the housing on the guide pins with drain slot facing downward or "UP" mark facing upward and slide the housing into the gearcase. Tighten screws to specifications (**Table 5**).

36. Install the water pump assembly using new gaskets. Tighten housing screws to specifications (**Table 5**).

37. Pressure and vacuum test the gearcase. See Chapter Nine of the basic book.

Table 5 20 AND 40 HP GEARCASE TORQUES

Fastener	in.-lb	ft.-lb.	N•m
20 hp			
Bearing housing screws	60-84		7-9
Gearcase mounting screws		16-18	22-25
Shift cradle pivot pin	48-84		5-9
Water pump housing screws	60-84		7-9
40 hp			
Bearing housing screws		8-10	11-14
Driveshaft seal housing screws	96-120		11-14
Gearcase mounting screws		18-20	24-27
Oil level/drain plugs	60-84		7-9
Shift rod cover	60-84		7-9
Pinion bearing retaining screw	48-80		5.5-9
Pinion nut		40-45	54-60
Water pump housing screws	60-84		7-9

Chapter Ten

Automatic Rewind Starters

Refer to Chapter Ten of the basic book to service the flywheel mounted manual starter used on 1985 20 hp models.

The flywheel mounted manual starter used on 1985 40 hp models is a heavy-duty version similar in design to that used on previous 18-40 hp models. Service procedures are provided in this supplement.

Removal/Installation (40 hp)

1. Remove the engine cover. Disconnect the power pack-to-armature plate 5-wire connector.

NOTE
Disconnect the starter lockout cable at the power head in Step 2 if the power head is to be removed.

2. Remove the screw holding the starter lockout cable clamp on the starter housing. Remove the lockout slide from the housing.

3. Remove the 3 housing attaching screws with lockwashers and washers.

4. Remove the 2 screws holding the starter handle bracket to the power head. Remove the starter from the power head.

5. Installation is the reverse of removal, plus the following:

a. Make sure the washers are installed between the rubber starter mounts and power head.
b. Tighten bracket screws to 60-84 in.-lb. (7-9 N•m) and housing attaching screws to 10-12 ft.-lb. (14-16 N•m).
c. Lubricate lockout slide area on housing with OMC Triple-Guard grease or Lubriplate 777.
d. Shift engine into NEUTRAL and adjust lockout cable to center lockout slide on lockout lever. Tighten cable clamp screw snugly.

12

Disassembly

WARNING
Disassembling this starter mechanism without holding the spring in place can result in the spring unwinding violently, causing serious personal injury. Wear safety glasses and gloves during this procedure.

1. Pull the starter rope out enough to tie a slip knot behind the handle. Pry the rope anchor from the handle.
2. Remove the handle, untie the slip knot and gradually allow the starter to unwind while holding the pulley.
3. With the starter housing placed upright on a clean workbench, remove the lockout lever shoulder screw. Remove the lockout lever, spring and washer from the housing.
4. Remove the nut from the center of the housing holding the pawl retaining screw.
5. Carefully invert the starter housing and remove the pawl retaining screw, washer, pawl plate and return spring.
6. Remove the spring from the pawl screw cavity. Remove the pawl and spring washer.
7. Carefully open the pulley lockring with a screwdriver and remove it from the housing.
8. Remove the friction plate and spring washer.
9. Hold pulley in housing while turning the housing upright (legs downward) on the workbench or floor.
10. Release the pulley and rap the housing sharply to dislodge the pulley and spring. The spring should uncoil within the starter housing legs.
11. Lift the housing up and remove the spring and pulley.
12. Remove the bushing from the pulley. If necessary, remove the rope guide shoulder screw and guide from the housing.

Cleaning and Inspection

See Chapter Ten of the basic book.

Asssembly

WARNING
During starter mechanism assembly, the spring may unwind violently, causing serious personal injury. Wear safety glasses and gloves during this procedure.

1. Lubricate the pulley bushing with Lubriplate 777 or OMC Triple-Guard grease.
2. Position the spring shield in the starter housing.
3. Inserting the open loop of the spring first, carefully coil the spring into the housing cutout.
4. Install the pulley bushing in the pulley and position the pulley shim on the pulley.
5. Install the pulley in the starter housing, making sure the outer loop of the spring engages the pin in the housing.
6. Position the friction plate spring washer and plate on the pulley hub, then install the lockring.
7. Coat the starter pawl boss with Lubriplate 777 or OMC Triple-Guard grease. Position spring washer on pawl boss and install pawl in pulley.
8. Install the spring in the retaining screw cavity.
9. Install the return spring on the pawl plate, press the other end of the spring on the pulley boss and position the pawl plate on the pulley.
10. Install the pawl plate retaining screw and washer. Tighten screw to 10-12 ft.-lb. (14-16 N•m).
11. With starter housing upright on workbench, spray the threads of the retaining screw and nut with OMC Locquic Primer. Coat nut threads with OMC Screw Lock. Install and tighten nut securely.
12. If rope guide shoulder screw and guide were removed, reinstall and tighten screw snugly.

13. Tie a knot in the end of a new rope. Invert starter housing on workbench and wind pulley counterclockwise as far as possible. Back off the rewind spring until the pulley rope cavity aligns with the rope guide.

14. Insert new rope through pulley, rope guide and handle bracket outlet. Feed the rope until it comes out the side of the housing. Pull the rope through the pulley until the knot seats against it, then tie a slip knot in the rope to hold it in position.

15. Lubricate the handle end of the rope with Lubriplate 777 or OMC Triple-Guard grease. Thread rope through handle using Johnson or Evinrude tool part No. 378774.

16. Press rope into channel in rope anchor with end of rope butted tightly against channel. Install anchor in handle.

17. Pull on the end of the rope to make sure the knot seats against the pulley, then untie the slip knot and slowly let rope wind onto pulley.

18. Pull starter rope out and check pawl operation. Pawl should extend when rope is pulled out and retract when rope is released.

19. Pull the rope out and release it several times, then check to make sure the housing arrow aligns with the pulley mark. If not properly aligned, pull rope out and release several more times. A new rope must lose some of its stiffness before the marks will properly align.

20. Position the starter lockout lever, spring and washer on the starter housing. Install the shoulder screw and tighten snugly.

Chapter Eleven

Electric Motors

COMPONENT REPLACEMENT

Switch design, location and method of attachment has changed. Refer to **Figure 24** (12-volt foot pedal) or **Figure 25** (12/24-volt foot pedal) as required.

12

㉔

12-VOLT
FOOT PEDAL COMPONENTS

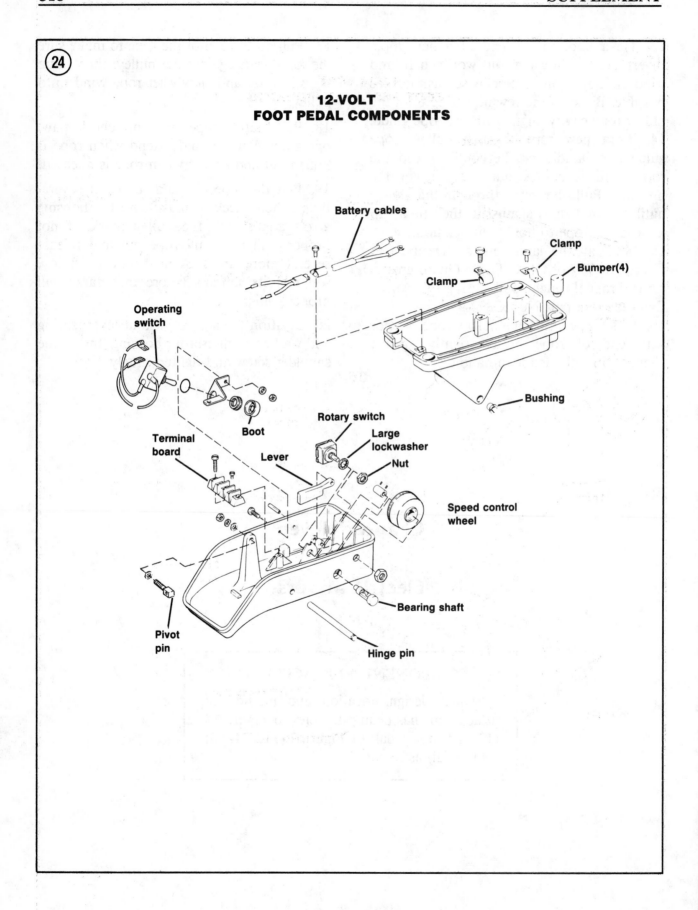

Battery cables

Clamp

Clamp

Bumper(4)

Operating switch

Bushing

Rotary switch

Large lockwasher

Terminal board

Boot

Lever

Nut

Speed control wheel

Bearing shaft

Pivot pin

Hinge pin

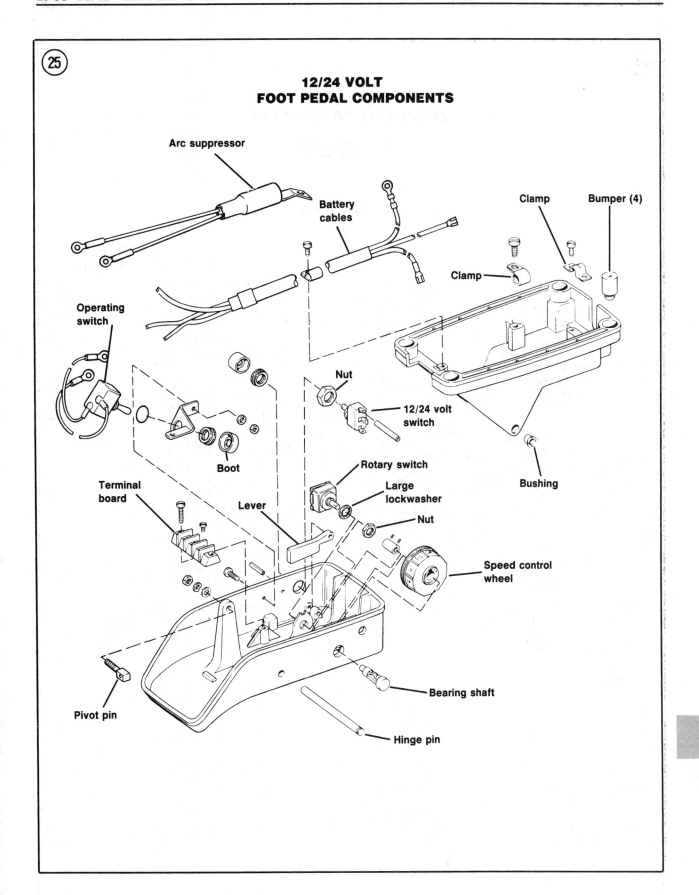

(25)

**12/24 VOLT
FOOT PEDAL COMPONENTS**

Arc suppressor

Battery cables

Clamp

Bumper (4)

Clamp

Operating switch

Nut

12/24 volt switch

Bushing

Boot

Rotary switch

Large lockwasher

Terminal board

Lever

Nut

Speed control wheel

Pivot pin

Bearing shaft

Hinge pin

12

Index

13

1978-1980 4 HP

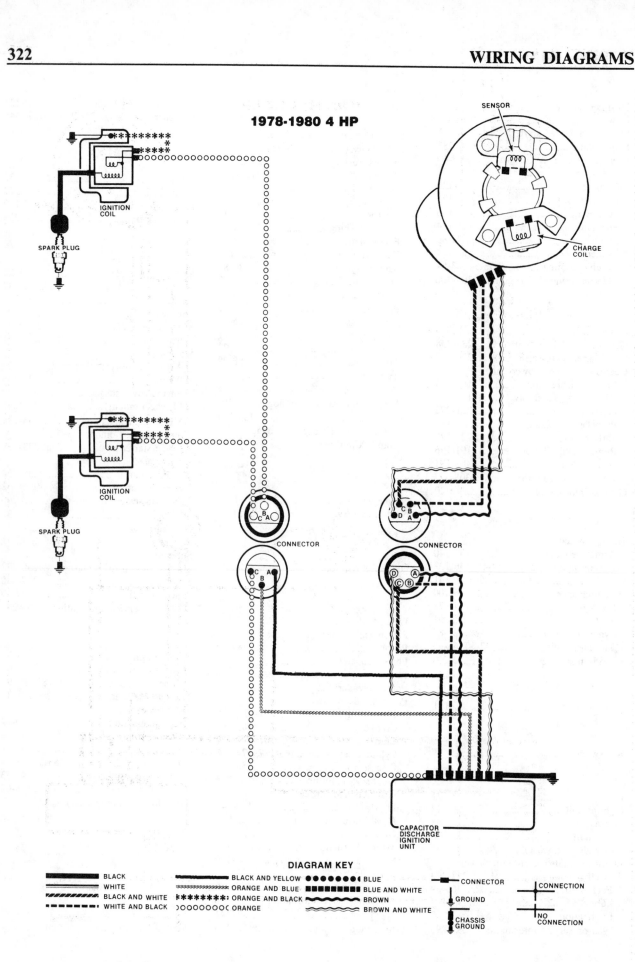

DIAGRAM KEY

BLACK	BLACK AND YELLOW	BLUE
WHITE	ORANGE AND BLUE	BLUE AND WHITE
BLACK AND WHITE	ORANGE AND BLACK	BROWN
WHITE AND BLACK	ORANGE	BROWN AND WHITE

CONNECTOR

CONNECTION

GROUND

CHASSIS GROUND

NO CONNECTION

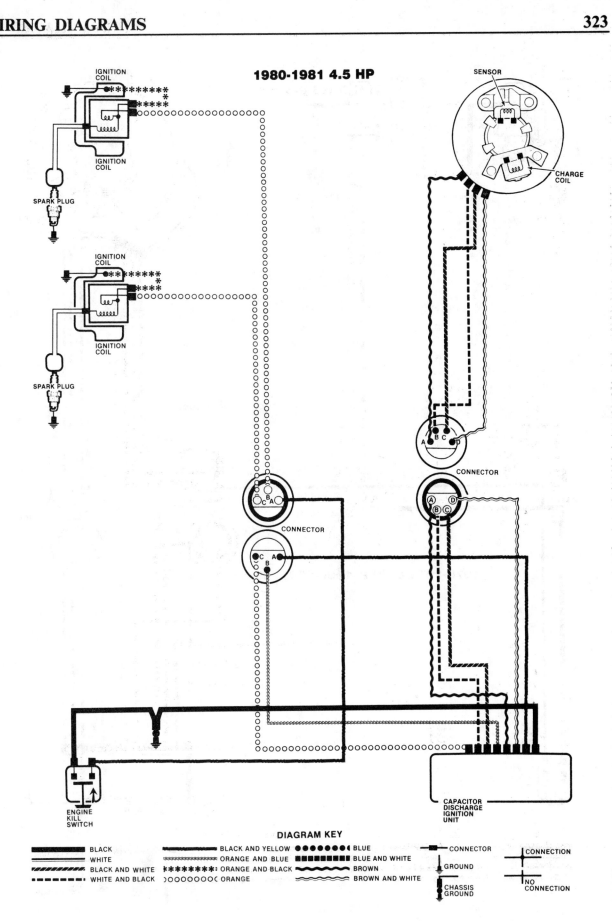

1980-1981 4.5 HP

IGNITION COIL

IGNITION COIL

SPARK PLUG

IGNITION COIL

IGNITION COIL

SPARK PLUG

SENSOR

CHARGE COIL

CONNECTOR

CONNECTOR

CONNECTOR

ENGINE KILL SWITCH

CAPACITOR DISCHARGE IGNITION UNIT

DIAGRAM KEY

BLACK	BLACK AND YELLOW	BLUE	CONNECTOR	CONNECTION
WHITE	ORANGE AND BLUE	BLUE AND WHITE	GROUND	
BLACK AND WHITE	ORANGE AND BLACK	BROWN	CHASSIS GROUND	NO CONNECTION
WHITE AND BLACK	ORANGE	BROWN AND WHITE		

14

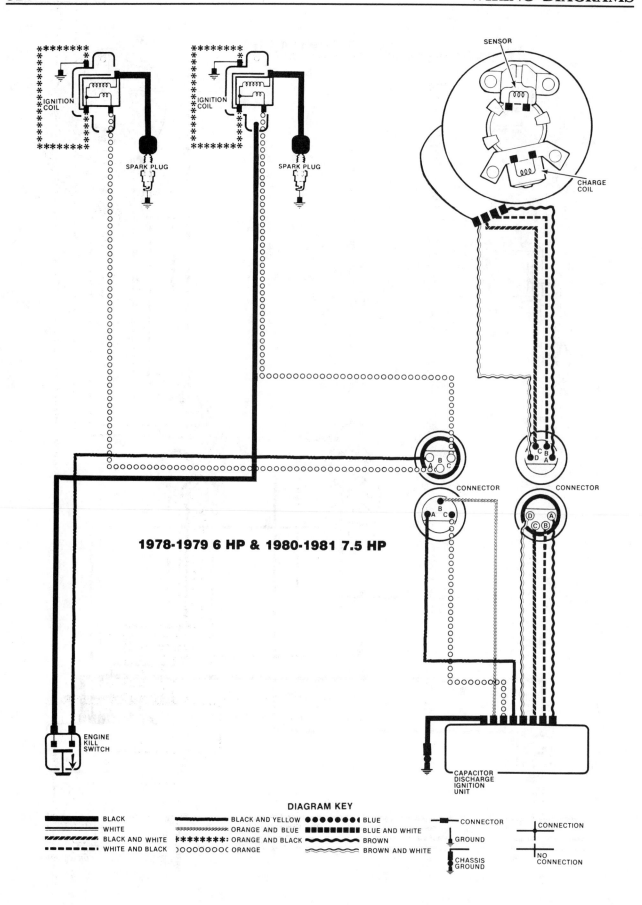

1978-1979 6 HP & 1980-1981 7.5 HP

SENSOR

CHARGE
COIL

IGNITION
COIL

SPARK PLUG

IGNITION
COIL

SPARK PLUG

CONNECTOR

CONNECTOR

ENGINE
KILL
SWITCH

CAPACITOR
DISCHARGE
IGNITION
UNIT

DIAGRAM KEY

BLACK	BLACK AND YELLOW	BLUE	CONNECTOR
WHITE	ORANGE AND BLUE	BLUE AND WHITE	CONNECTION
BLACK AND WHITE	ORANGE AND BLACK	BROWN	GROUND
WHITE AND BLACK	ORANGE	BROWN AND WHITE	CHASSIS GROUND
			NO CONNECTION

1982-1984 4-35 HP MANUAL START

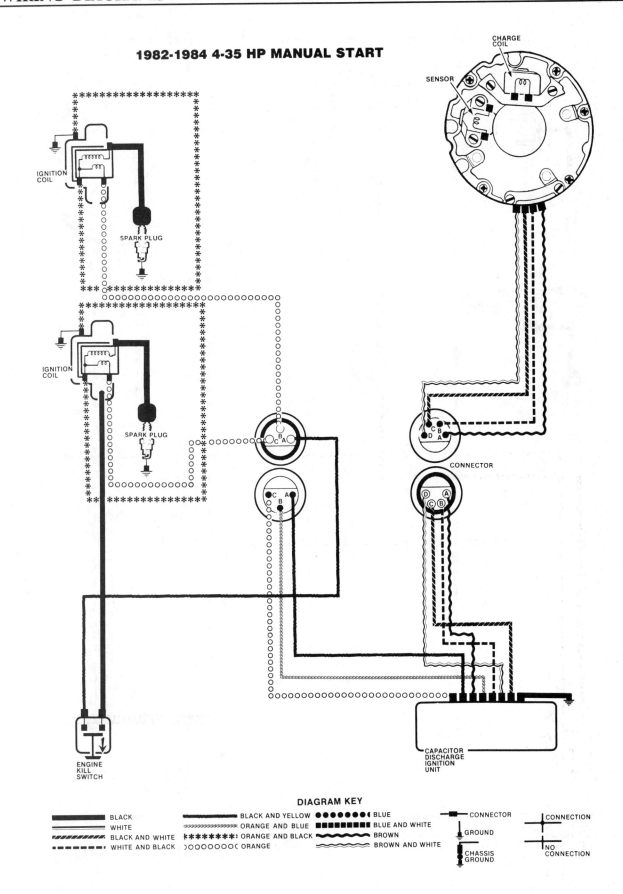

IGNITION COIL

SPARK PLUG

IGNITION COIL

SPARK PLUG

ENGINE KILL SWITCH

CHARGE COIL

SENSOR

CONNECTOR

CAPACITOR DISCHARGE IGNITION UNIT

DIAGRAM KEY

BLACK	BLACK AND YELLOW	BLUE
WHITE	ORANGE AND BLUE	BLUE AND WHITE
BLACK AND WHITE	ORANGE AND BLACK	BROWN
WHITE AND BLACK	ORANGE	BROWN AND WHITE

CONNECTOR

GROUND

CHASSIS GROUND

CONNECTION

NO CONNECTION

1984 5-35 HP MANUAL START/AC LIGHTING

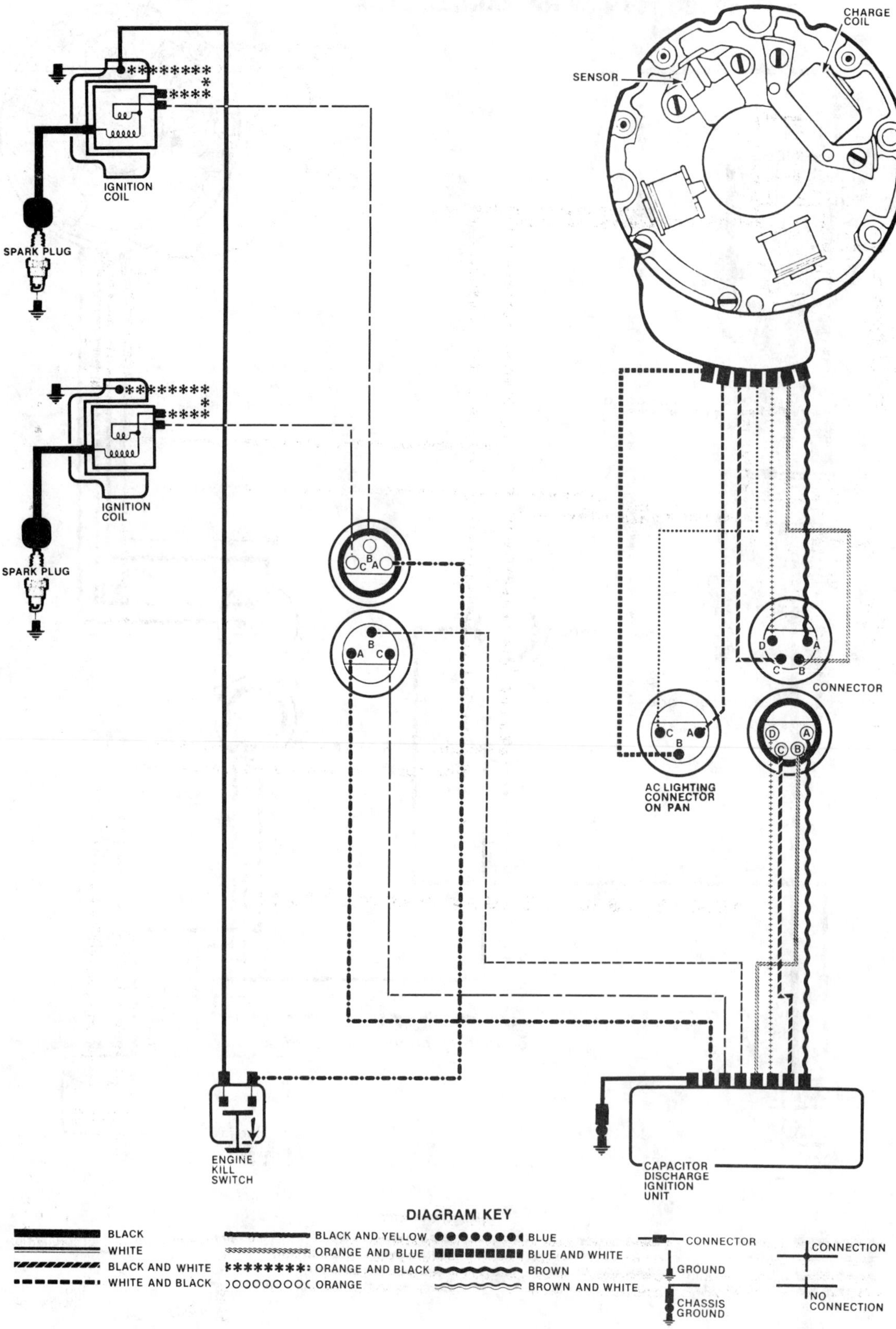
CHARGE COIL
SENSOR
IGNITION COIL
SPARK PLUG
IGNITION COIL
SPARK PLUG
C B A
B A C
D A C B
CONNECTOR
C A B
D A C B
AC LIGHTING CONNECTOR ON PAN
ENGINE KILL SWITCH
CAPACITOR DISCHARGE IGNITION UNIT
DIAGRAM KEY
BLACK
WHITE
BLACK AND WHITE
WHITE AND BLACK
BLACK AND YELLOW
ORANGE AND BLUE
ORANGE AND BLACK
ORANGE
BLUE
BLUE AND WHITE
BROWN
BROWN AND WHITE
CONNECTOR
GROUND
CHASSIS GROUND
CONNECTION
NO CONNECTION

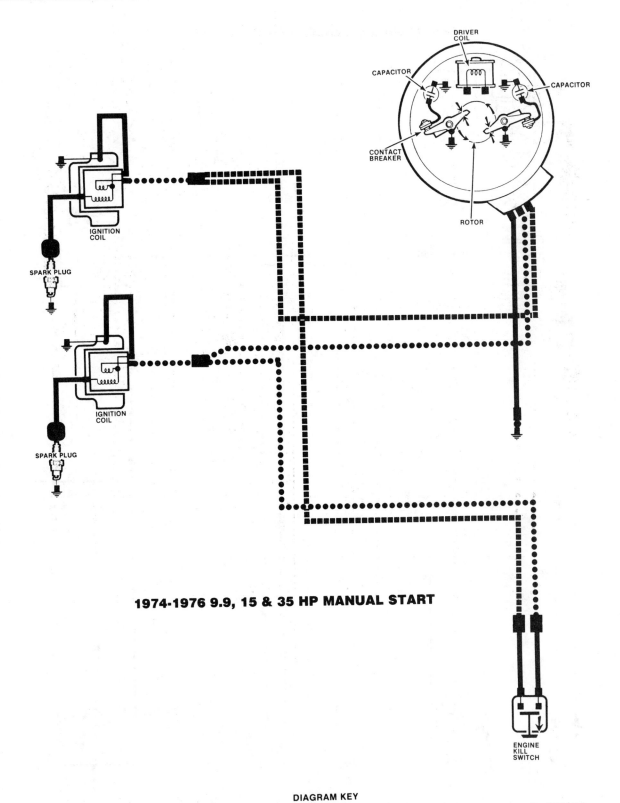

1974-1976 9.9, 15 & 35 HP MANUAL START

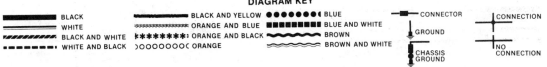

DIAGRAM KEY

BLACK	BLACK AND YELLOW	BLUE
WHITE	ORANGE AND BLUE	BLUE AND WHITE
BLACK AND WHITE	ORANGE AND BLACK	BROWN
WHITE AND BLACK	ORANGE	BROWN AND WHITE

CONNECTOR
GROUND
CHASSIS GROUND

CONNECTION
NO CONNECTION

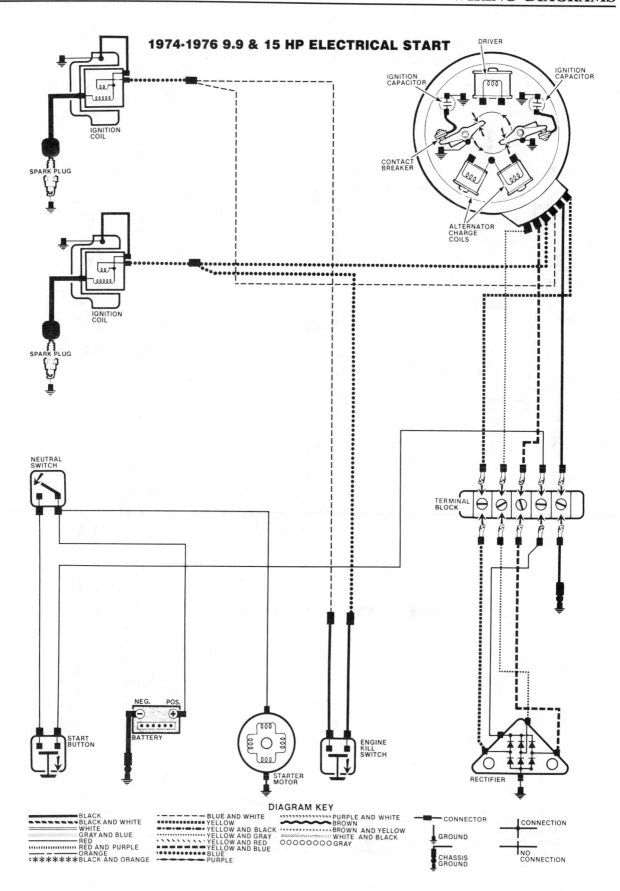

1974-1976 9.9 & 15 HP ELECTRICAL START

DRIVER

IGNITION CAPACITOR

IGNITION CAPACITOR

CONTACT BREAKER

ALTERNATOR CHARGE COILS

IGNITION COIL

SPARK PLUG

IGNITION COIL

SPARK PLUG

NEUTRAL SWITCH

TERMINAL BLOCK

START BUTTON

NEG.   POS.

BATTERY

STARTER MOTOR

ENGINE KILL SWITCH

RECTIFIER

DIAGRAM KEY

BLACK	BLUE AND WHITE
BLACK AND WHITE	YELLOW
WHITE	YELLOW AND BLACK
GRAY AND BLUE	YELLOW AND GRAY
RED	YELLOW AND RED
RED AND PURPLE	YELLOW AND BLUE
ORANGE	BLUE
BLACK AND ORANGE	PURPLE

PURPLE AND WHITE
BROWN
BROWN AND YELLOW
WHITE AND BLACK
GRAY

CONNECTOR

GROUND

CHASSIS GROUND

CONNECTION

NO CONNECTION

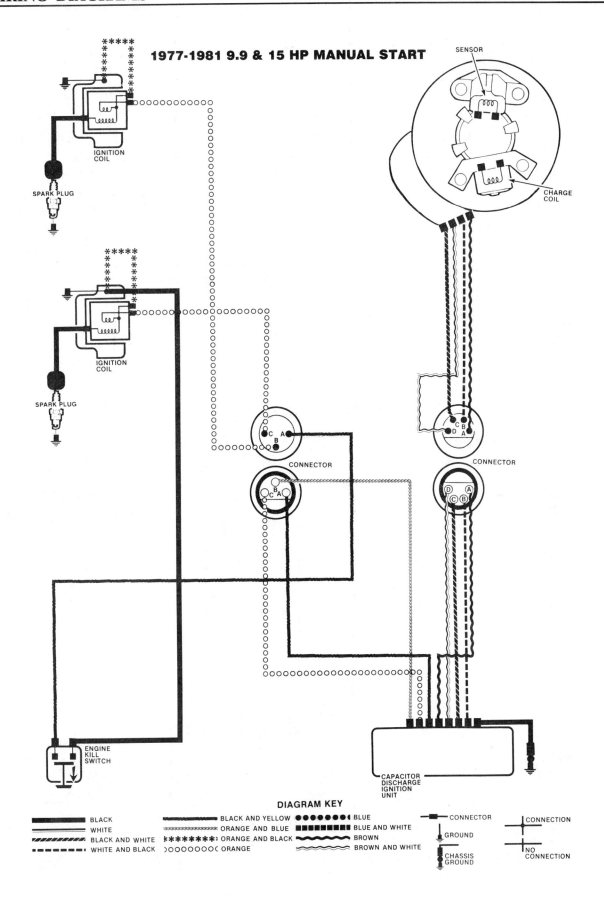

1977-1981 9.9 & 15 HP MANUAL START

SENSOR

CHARGE
COIL

IGNITION
COIL

SPARK PLUG

IGNITION
COIL

SPARK PLUG

CONNECTOR

CONNECTOR

ENGINE
KILL
SWITCH

CAPACITOR
DISCHARGE
IGNITION
UNIT

DIAGRAM KEY

BLACK	BLACK AND YELLOW	BLUE
WHITE	ORANGE AND BLUE	BLUE AND WHITE
BLACK AND WHITE	ORANGE AND BLACK	BROWN
WHITE AND BLACK	ORANGE	BROWN AND WHITE

CONNECTOR

GROUND

CHASSIS
GROUND

CONNECTION

NO
CONNECTION

14

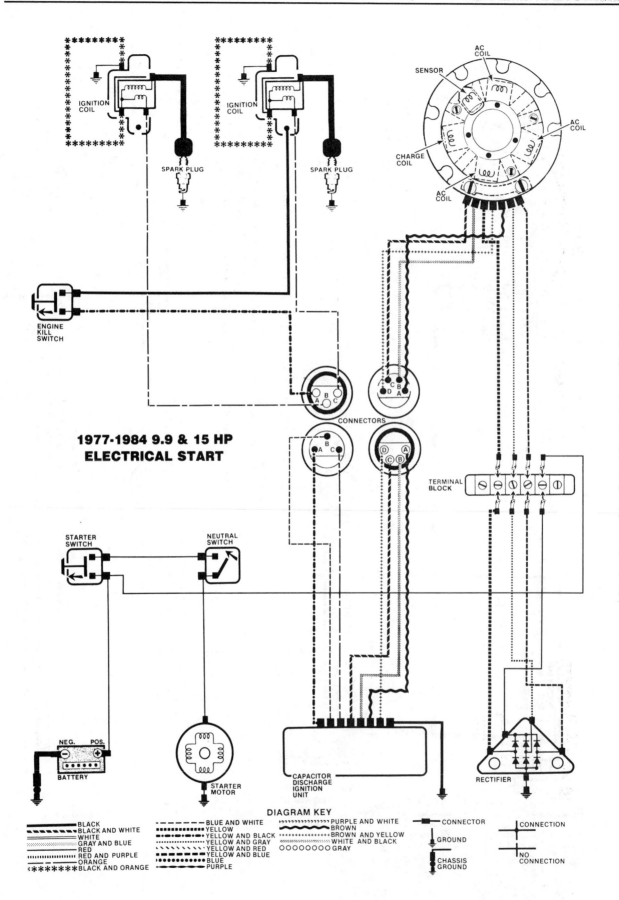

IGNITION COIL

SPARK PLUG

IGNITION COIL

SPARK PLUG

SENSOR

AC COIL

AC COIL

CHARGE COIL

AC COIL

ENGINE KILL SWITCH

CONNECTORS

1977-1984 9.9 & 15 HP ELECTRICAL START

TERMINAL BLOCK

STARTER SWITCH

NEUTRAL SWITCH

NEG. POS.

BATTERY

STARTER MOTOR

CAPACITOR DISCHARGE IGNITION UNIT

RECTIFIER

DIAGRAM KEY

BLACK	BLUE AND WHITE	PURPLE AND WHITE
BLACK AND WHITE	YELLOW	BROWN
WHITE	YELLOW AND BLACK	YELLOW AND GRAY	BROWN AND YELLOW
GRAY AND BLUE	YELLOW AND RED	WHITE AND BLACK
RED	YELLOW AND BLUE	GRAY
RED AND PURPLE	BLUE	
ORANGE	PURPLE	
BLACK AND ORANGE		

CONNECTOR

GROUND

CHASSIS GROUND

CONNECTION

NO CONNECTION

1973-1976 18, 20 & 25 HP MANUAL START

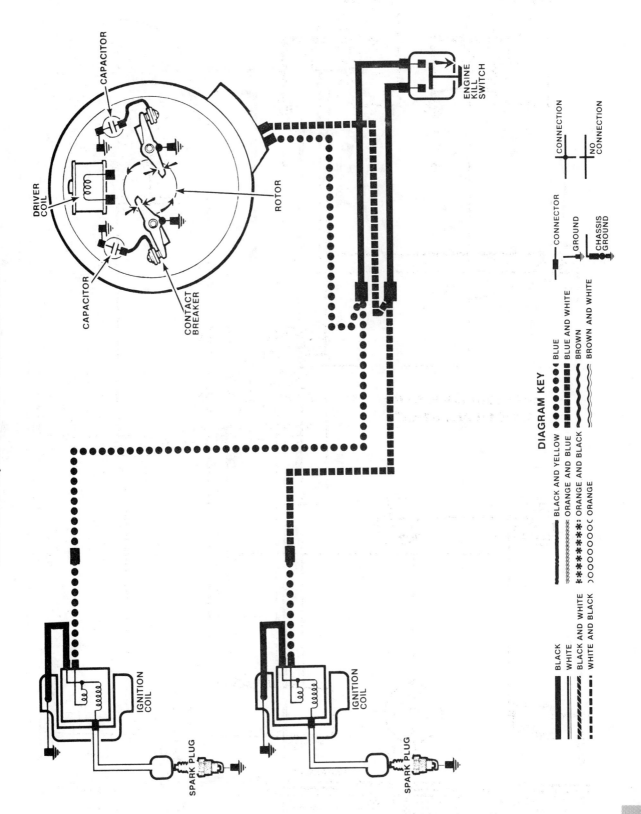

DIAGRAM KEY

BLACK

WHITE

BLACK AND WHITE

WHITE AND BLACK

BLACK AND YELLOW

ORANGE AND BLUE

BLUE

BLUE AND WHITE

ORANGE AND BLACK

BROWN

ORANGE

BROWN AND WHITE

CONNECTION

NO CONNECTION

CONNECTOR

GROUND

CHASSIS GROUND

CAPACITOR

DRIVER COIL

CAPACITOR

CONTACT BREAKER

ROTOR

ENGINE KILL SWITCH

IGNITION COIL

IGNITION COIL

SPARK PLUG

SPARK PLUG

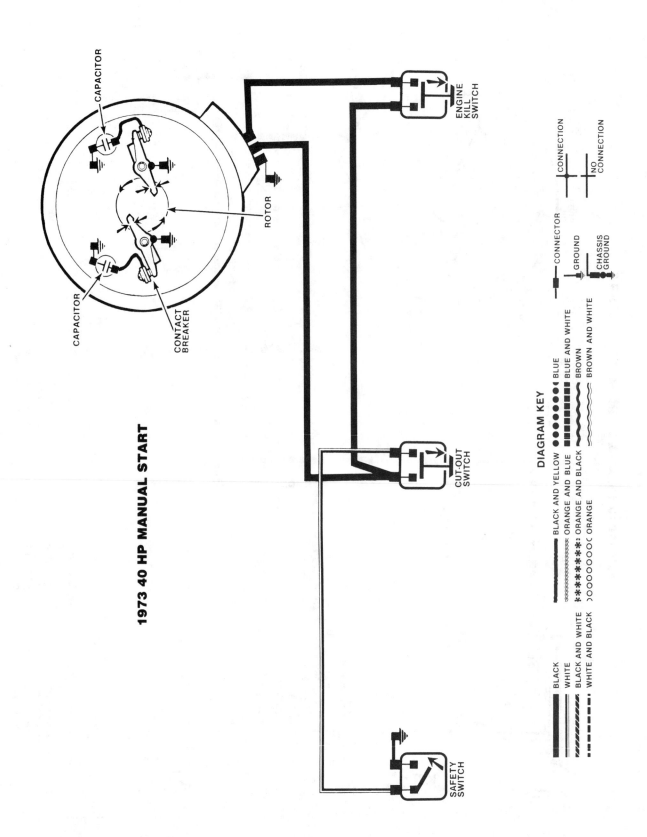

1973 40 HP MANUAL START

CAPACITOR

CAPACITOR

CONTACT BREAKER

ROTOR

ENGINE KILL SWITCH

CUT-OUT SWITCH

SAFETY SWITCH

DIAGRAM KEY

CONNECTION

NO CONNECTION

CONNECTOR

GROUND

CHASSIS GROUND

BLACK

WHITE

BLACK AND WHITE

WHITE AND BLACK

BLACK AND YELLOW

ORANGE AND BLUE

ORANGE AND BLACK

ORANGE

BLUE

BLUE AND WHITE

BROWN

BROWN AND WHITE

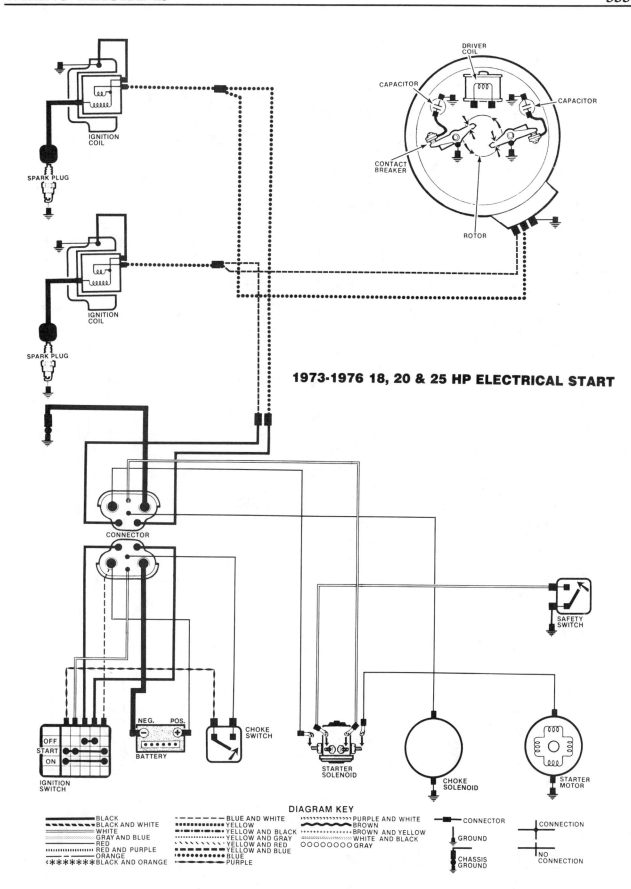

DRIVER COIL

CAPACITOR

CAPACITOR

IGNITION COIL

SPARK PLUG

IGNITION COIL

SPARK PLUG

CONTACT BREAKER

ROTOR

1973-1976 18, 20 & 25 HP ELECTRICAL START

CONNECTOR

SAFETY SWITCH

OFF
START
ON

IGNITION SWITCH

NEG. POS.

BATTERY

CHOKE SWITCH

STARTER SOLENOID

CHOKE SOLENOID

STARTER MOTOR

DIAGRAM KEY

BLACK	BLUE AND WHITE	PURPLE AND WHITE	CONNECTOR
BLACK AND WHITE	YELLOW	BROWN	
WHITE	YELLOW AND BLACK	BROWN AND YELLOW	GROUND
GRAY AND BLUE	YELLOW AND GRAY	WHITE AND BLACK	
RED	YELLOW AND RED	GRAY	CONNECTION
RED AND PURPLE	YELLOW AND BLUE		CHASSIS GROUND
ORANGE	BLUE		NO CONNECTION
BLACK AND ORANGE	PURPLE		

14

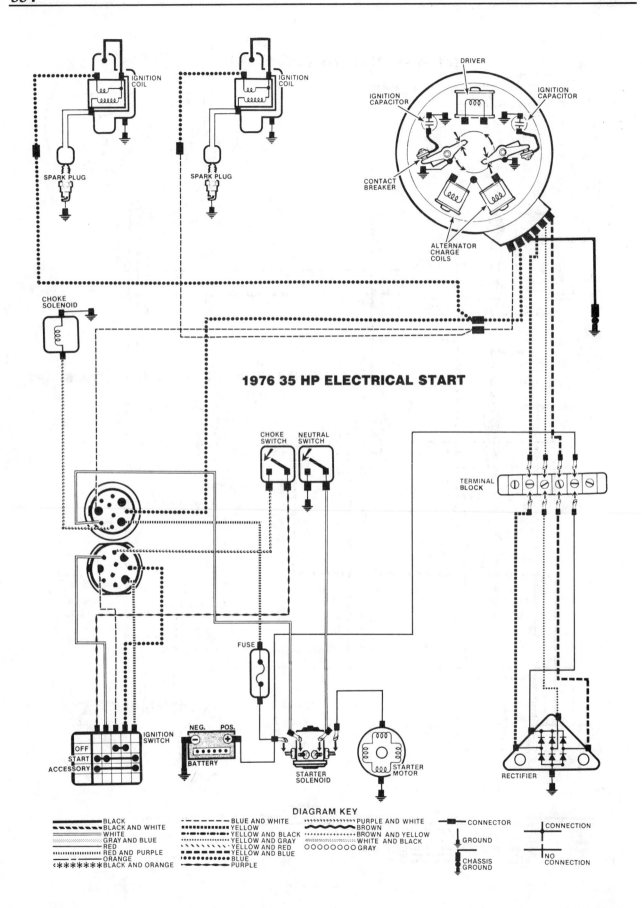

IGNITION COIL

SPARK PLUG

IGNITION COIL

SPARK PLUG

DRIVER

IGNITION CAPACITOR

IGNITION CAPACITOR

CONTACT BREAKER

ALTERNATOR CHARGE COILS

CHOKE SOLENOID

1976 35 HP ELECTRICAL START

CHOKE SWITCH

NEUTRAL SWITCH

TERMINAL BLOCK

IGNITION SWITCH

OFF
START
ACCESSORY

NEG. POS.

BATTERY

FUSE

STARTER SOLENOID

STARTER MOTOR

RECTIFIER

DIAGRAM KEY

BLACK
BLACK AND WHITE
WHITE
GRAY AND BLUE
RED
RED AND PURPLE
ORANGE
BLACK AND ORANGE

BLUE AND WHITE
YELLOW
YELLOW AND BLACK
YELLOW AND GRAY
YELLOW AND RED
YELLOW AND BLUE
BLUE
PURPLE

PURPLE AND WHITE
BROWN
BROWN AND YELLOW
WHITE AND BLACK
GRAY

CONNECTOR

GROUND

CHASSIS GROUND

CONNECTION

NO CONNECTION

1977-1981 25 HP MANUAL START

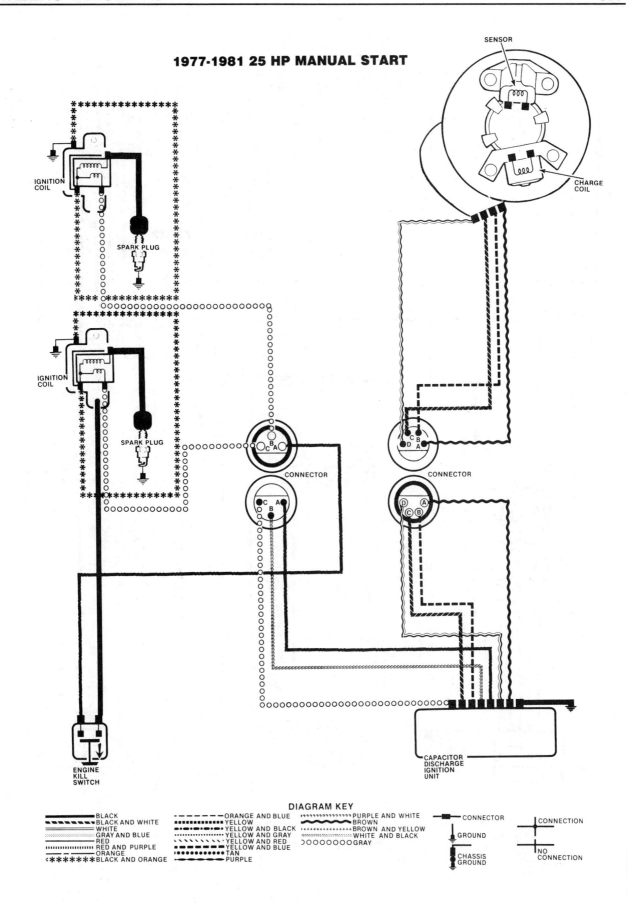

SENSOR

IGNITION COIL

SPARK PLUG

IGNITION COIL

SPARK PLUG

CHARGE COIL

CONNECTOR

CONNECTOR

CONNECTOR

CONNECTOR

ENGINE KILL SWITCH

CAPACITOR DISCHARGE IGNITION UNIT

DIAGRAM KEY

———— BLACK	– – – – – ORANGE AND BLUE	~~~~ PURPLE AND WHITE
▰▰▰▰ BLACK AND WHITE	▪▪▪▪▪▪ YELLOW	CONNECTOR
———— WHITE	▰▪▰▪▰ YELLOW AND BLACK	~~~~ BROWN
░░░░ GRAY AND BLUE	▰▰▰ YELLOW AND GRAY	++++++ BROWN AND YELLOW
———— RED	▰▰▰ YELLOW AND RED	░░░░ WHITE AND BLACK
▪▪▪▪▪ RED AND PURPLE	●●●● YELLOW AND BLUE	○○○○○○○ GRAY
———— ORANGE	●●●● TAN	
✶✶✶✶✶ BLACK AND ORANGE	———— PURPLE	

GROUND

CHASSIS GROUND

CONNECTION

NO CONNECTION

14

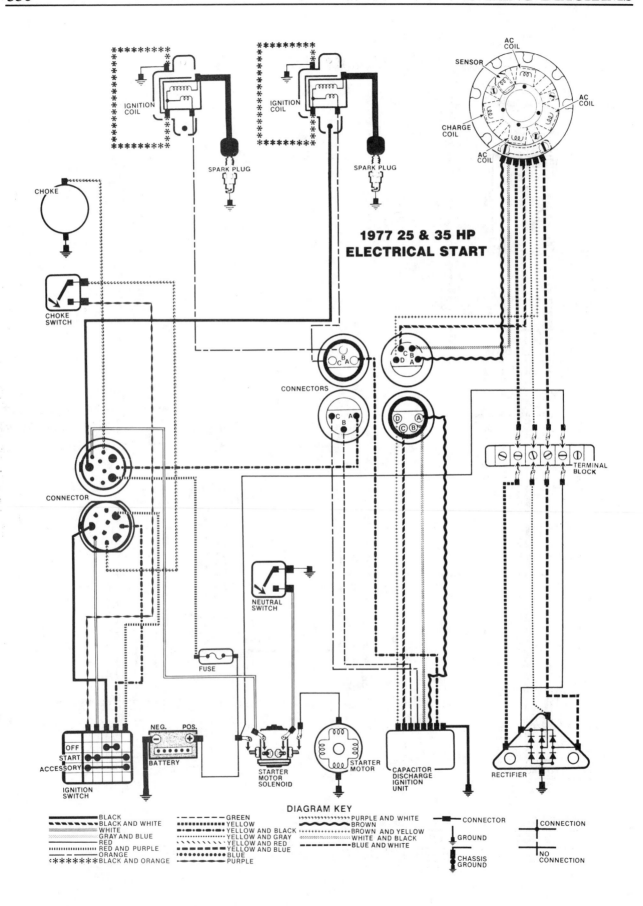

IGNITION COIL

IGNITION COIL

SPARK PLUG

SPARK PLUG

SENSOR

AC COIL

AC COIL

AC COIL

CHARGE COIL

1977 25 & 35 HP ELECTRICAL START

CHOKE

CHOKE SWITCH

CONNECTORS

CONNECTOR

TERMINAL BLOCK

NEUTRAL SWITCH

FUSE

NEG.   POS.

BATTERY

STARTER MOTOR SOLENOID

STARTER MOTOR

CAPACITOR DISCHARGE IGNITION UNIT

RECTIFIER

OFF
START
ACCESSORY

IGNITION SWITCH

DIAGRAM KEY

BLACK
BLACK AND WHITE
WHITE
GRAY AND BLUE
RED
RED AND PURPLE
ORANGE
BLACK AND ORANGE

GREEN
YELLOW
YELLOW AND BLACK
YELLOW AND GRAY
YELLOW AND RED
YELLOW AND BLUE
BLUE
PURPLE

PURPLE AND WHITE
BROWN
BROWN AND YELLOW
WHITE AND BLACK
BLUE AND WHITE

CONNECTOR

GROUND

CHASSIS GROUND

CONNECTION

NO CONNECTION

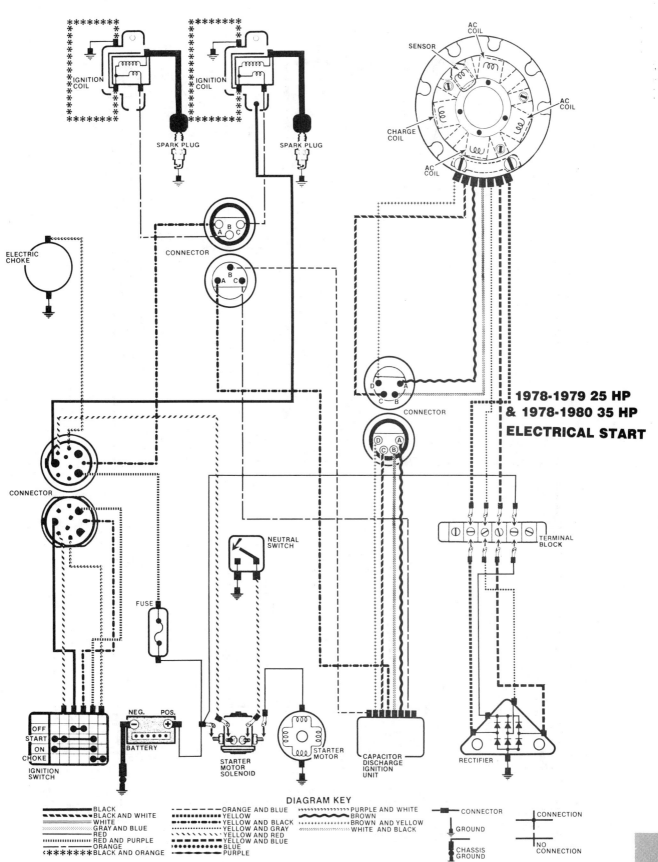

1978-1979 25 HP & 1978-1980 35 HP ELECTRICAL START

IGNITION COIL

SPARK PLUG

ELECTRIC CHOKE

CONNECTOR

CONNECTOR

NEUTRAL SWITCH

FUSE

IGNITION SWITCH

OFF
START
ON
CHOKE

NEG. POS.

BATTERY

STARTER MOTOR SOLENOID

STARTER MOTOR

CAPACITOR DISCHARGE IGNITION UNIT

RECTIFIER

TERMINAL BLOCK

AC COIL

SENSOR

CHARGE COIL

AC COIL

DIAGRAM KEY

BLACK	ORANGE AND BLUE
BLACK AND WHITE	YELLOW
WHITE	YELLOW AND BLACK
GRAY AND BLUE	YELLOW AND GRAY
RED	YELLOW AND RED
RED AND PURPLE	YELLOW AND BLUE
ORANGE	BLUE
BLACK AND ORANGE	PURPLE
PURPLE AND WHITE	CONNECTOR
BROWN	GROUND
BROWN AND YELLOW	CONNECTION
WHITE AND BLACK	CHASSIS GROUND
	NO CONNECTION

14

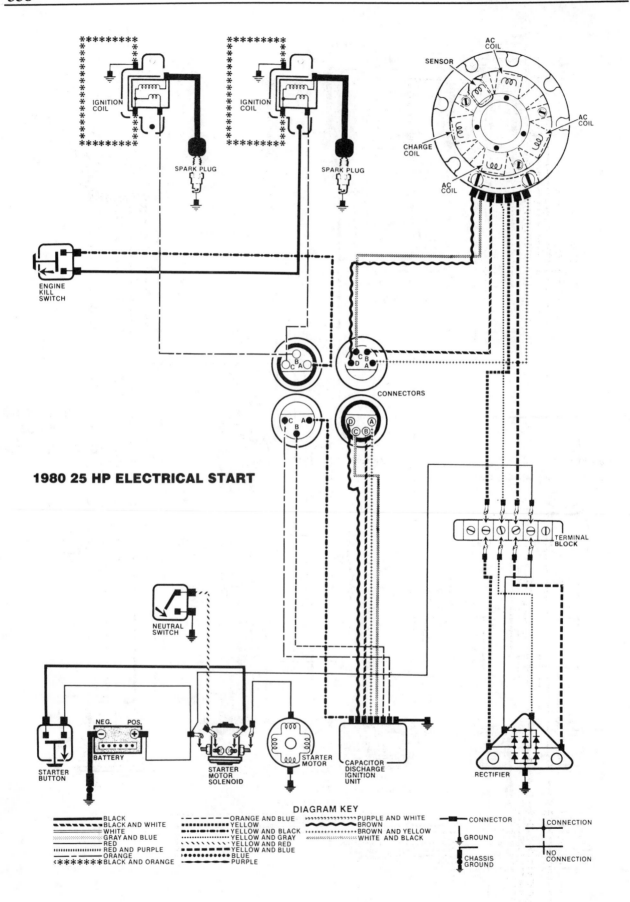

1980 25 HP ELECTRICAL START

CONNECTORS

IGNITION COIL

SPARK PLUG

ENGINE KILL SWITCH

NEUTRAL SWITCH

STARTER BUTTON

BATTERY

NEG.   POS.

STARTER MOTOR SOLENOID

STARTER MOTOR

CAPACITOR DISCHARGE IGNITION UNIT

RECTIFIER

TERMINAL BLOCK

SENSOR

AC COIL

CHARGE COIL

DIAGRAM KEY

BLACK	ORANGE AND BLUE
BLACK AND WHITE	YELLOW
WHITE	YELLOW AND BLACK
GRAY AND BLUE	YELLOW AND GRAY
RED	YELLOW AND RED
RED AND PURPLE	YELLOW AND BLUE
ORANGE	BLUE
BLACK AND ORANGE	PURPLE

PURPLE AND WHITE
BROWN
BROWN AND YELLOW
WHITE AND BLACK

CONNECTOR
GROUND
CHASSIS GROUND

CONNECTION
NO CONNECTION

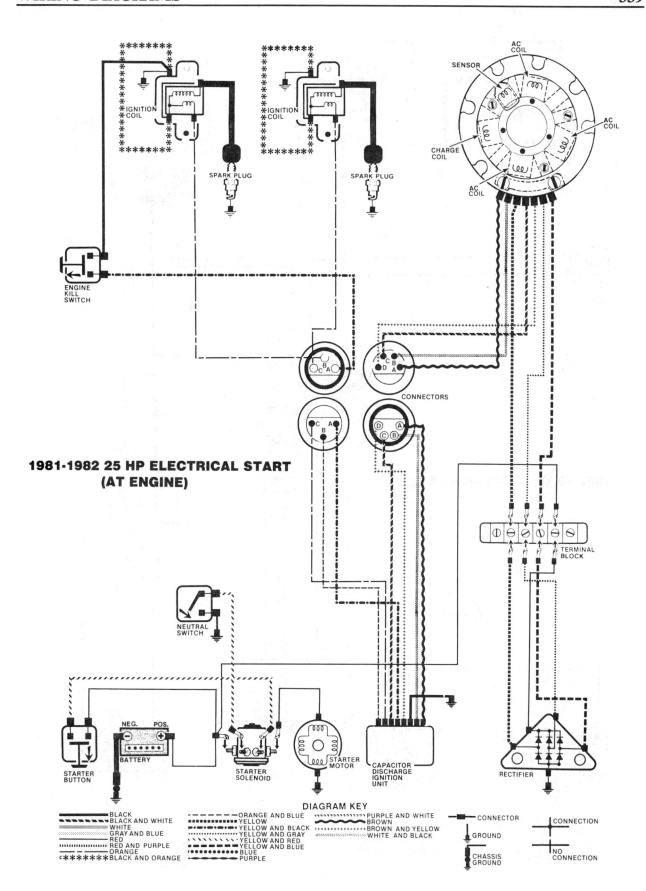

**1981-1982 25 HP ELECTRICAL START
(AT ENGINE)**

DIAGRAM KEY

340

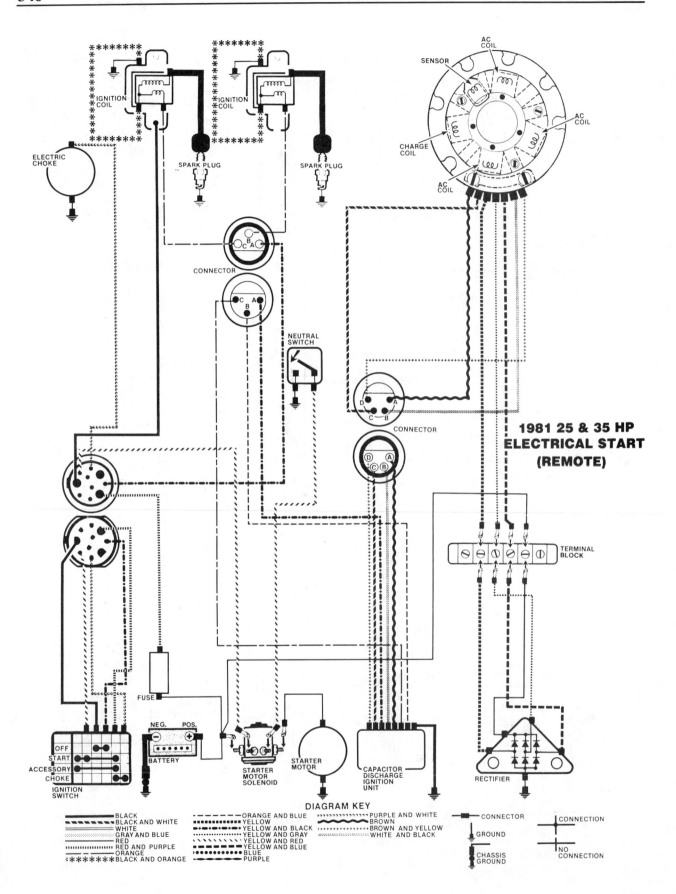

ELECTRIC CHOKE

IGNITION COIL

IGNITION COIL

SPARK PLUG

SPARK PLUG

SENSOR

AC COIL

AC COIL

CHARGE COIL

AC COIL

CONNECTOR

CONNECTOR

NEUTRAL SWITCH

CONNECTOR

**1981 25 & 35 HP
ELECTRICAL START
(REMOTE)**

TERMINAL BLOCK

FUSE

OFF
START
ACCESSORY
CHOKE
IGNITION SWITCH

NEG. POS.
BATTERY

STARTER MOTOR SOLENOID

STARTER MOTOR

CAPACITOR DISCHARGE IGNITION UNIT

RECTIFIER

DIAGRAM KEY

———————————— BLACK	— — — — — — ORANGE AND BLUE
＝＝＝＝＝＝ BLACK AND WHITE	■■■■■■■■■■ YELLOW
———————————— WHITE	—————— YELLOW AND BLACK
GRAY AND BLUE	•••••••••••••• YELLOW AND GRAY
RED	///////////// YELLOW AND RED
•••••••••••• RED AND PURPLE	YELLOW AND BLUE
— — — ORANGE	●●●●●●●●● BLUE
✱✱✱✱✱✱✱ BLACK AND ORANGE	—————— PURPLE

'''''''''''''' PURPLE AND WHITE	━■ CONNECTOR
～～～～～～ BROWN	
•••••••••••••• BROWN AND YELLOW	◆ GROUND
WHITE AND BLACK	

CONNECTION

CHASSIS GROUND

NO CONNECTION

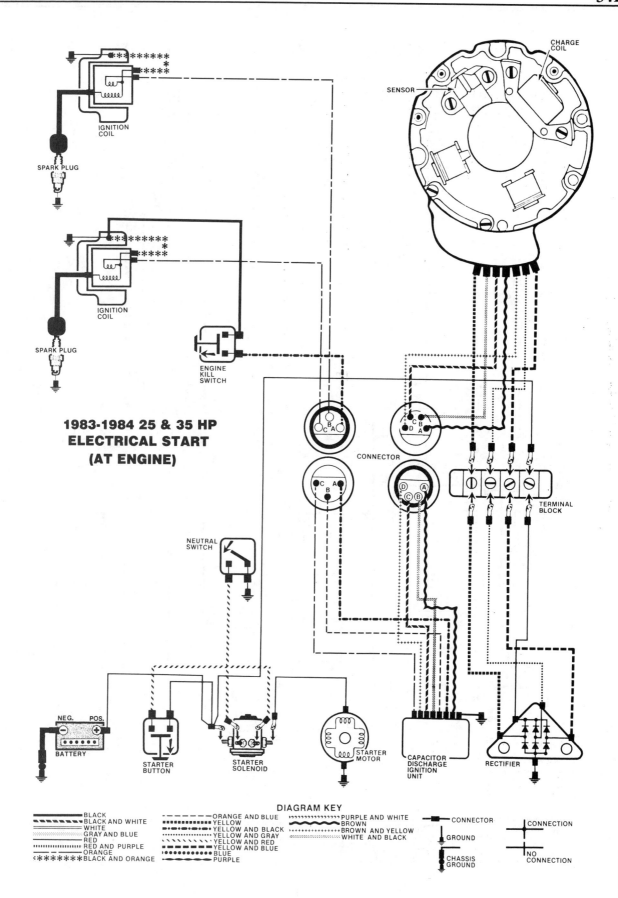

1983-1984 25 & 35 HP
ELECTRICAL START
(AT ENGINE)

SPARK PLUG

IGNITION COIL

SPARK PLUG

IGNITION COIL

ENGINE KILL SWITCH

CHARGE COIL

SENSOR

CONNECTOR

TERMINAL BLOCK

NEUTRAL SWITCH

NEG. POS.
BATTERY

STARTER BUTTON

STARTER SOLENOID

STARTER MOTOR

CAPACITOR DISCHARGE IGNITION UNIT

RECTIFIER

DIAGRAM KEY

BLACK	ORANGE AND BLUE	PURPLE AND WHITE
BLACK AND WHITE	YELLOW	BROWN
WHITE	YELLOW AND BLACK	BROWN AND YELLOW
GRAY AND BLUE	YELLOW AND GRAY	WHITE AND BLACK
RED	YELLOW AND RED	
RED AND PURPLE	YELLOW AND BLUE	
ORANGE	BLUE	
BLACK AND ORANGE	PURPLE	

CONNECTOR

GROUND

CHASSIS GROUND

CONNECTION

NO CONNECTION

14

1982-1984 20, 25 & 35 HP ELECTRICAL START (REMOTE)

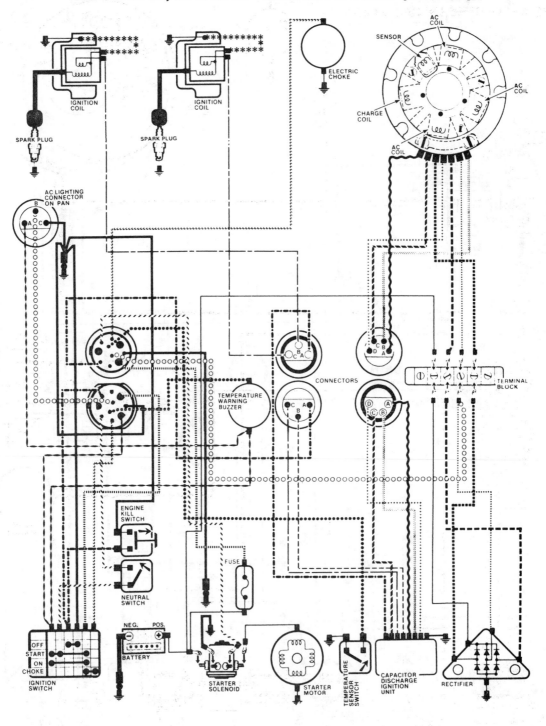

DIAGRAM KEY

——— BLACK	– – – ORANGE AND BLUE	›››››››› PURPLE AND WHITE
═══ BLACK AND WHITE	■■■■■■ YELLOW	~~~~~ BROWN
≡≡≡ WHITE	•••••• YELLOW AND BLACK	++++++ BROWN AND YELLOW
░░░ GRAY AND BLUE	\\\\\\ YELLOW AND GRAY	≈≈≈≈≈ WHITE AND BLACK
·····RED	////// YELLOW AND RED	⊃⊃⊃⊃⊃⊃ GRAY
·|·|·|· RED AND PURPLE	●●●●●● YELLOW AND BLUE	
– · – ORANGE	•••••• TAN	
✱✱✱✱✱ BLACK AND ORANGE	■■■■■ PURPLE	

─●─ CONNECTOR	─┼─ CONNECTION
⊥ GROUND	─┼─ NO CONNECTION
⊥ CHASSIS GROUND	

1973 40 HP ELECTRICAL START

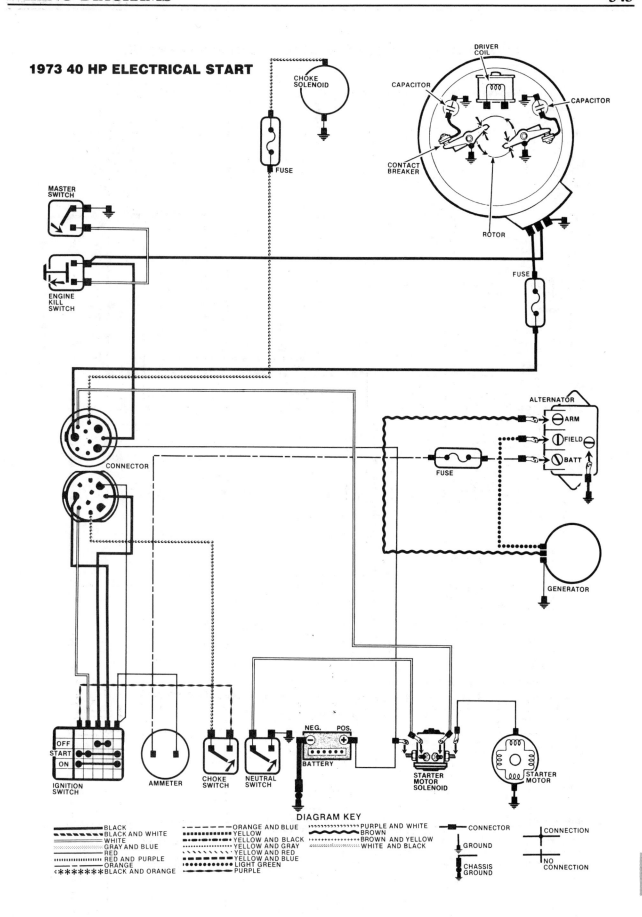

DIAGRAM KEY

BLACK
BLACK AND WHITE
WHITE
GRAY AND BLUE
RED
RED AND PURPLE
ORANGE
BLACK AND ORANGE

ORANGE AND BLUE
YELLOW
YELLOW AND BLACK
YELLOW AND GRAY
YELLOW AND RED
YELLOW AND BLUE
LIGHT GREEN
PURPLE

PURPLE AND WHITE
BROWN
BROWN AND YELLOW
WHITE AND BLACK

CONNECTOR

GROUND

CHASSIS
GROUND

CONNECTION

NO
CONNECTION

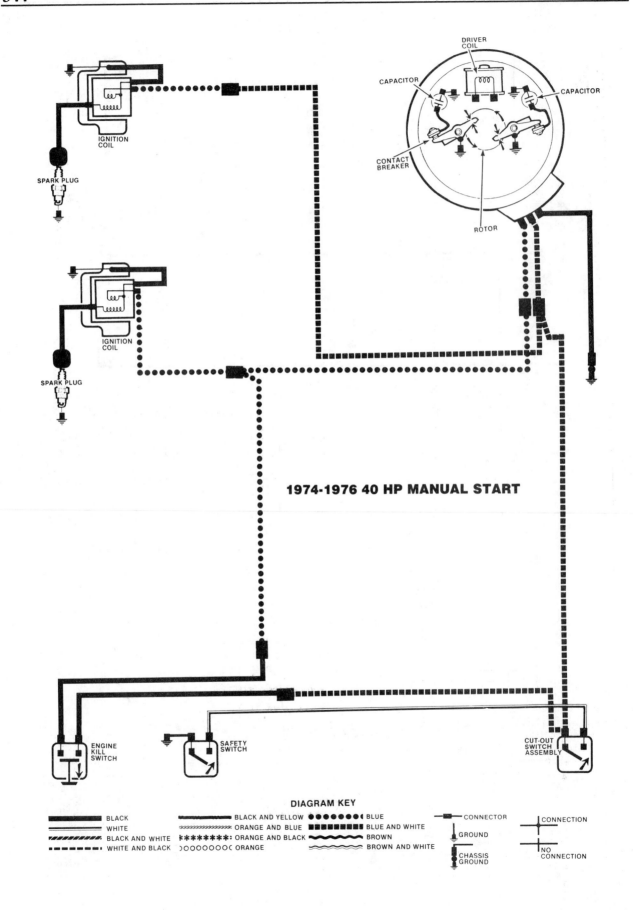

IGNITION COIL

SPARK PLUG

IGNITION COIL

SPARK PLUG

DRIVER COIL

CAPACITOR

CAPACITOR

CONTACT BREAKER

ROTOR

1974-1976 40 HP MANUAL START

ENGINE KILL SWITCH

SAFETY SWITCH

CUT-OUT SWITCH ASSEMBLY

DIAGRAM KEY

BLACK	BLACK AND YELLOW	BLUE
WHITE	ORANGE AND BLUE	BLUE AND WHITE
BLACK AND WHITE	ORANGE AND BLACK	BROWN
WHITE AND BLACK	ORANGE	BROWN AND WHITE

CONNECTOR

GROUND

CHASSIS GROUND

CONNECTION

NO CONNECTION

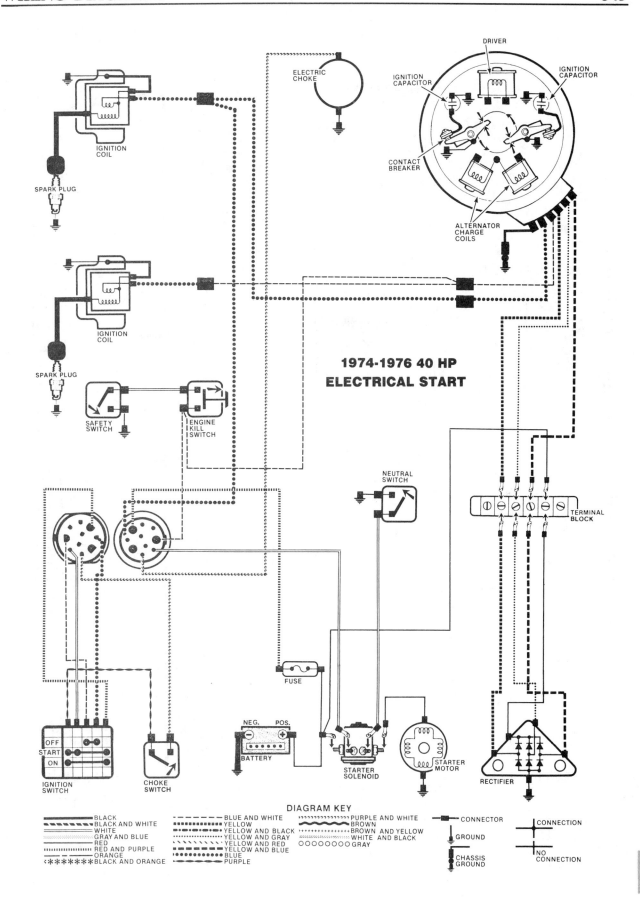

1974-1976 40 HP
ELECTRICAL START

14

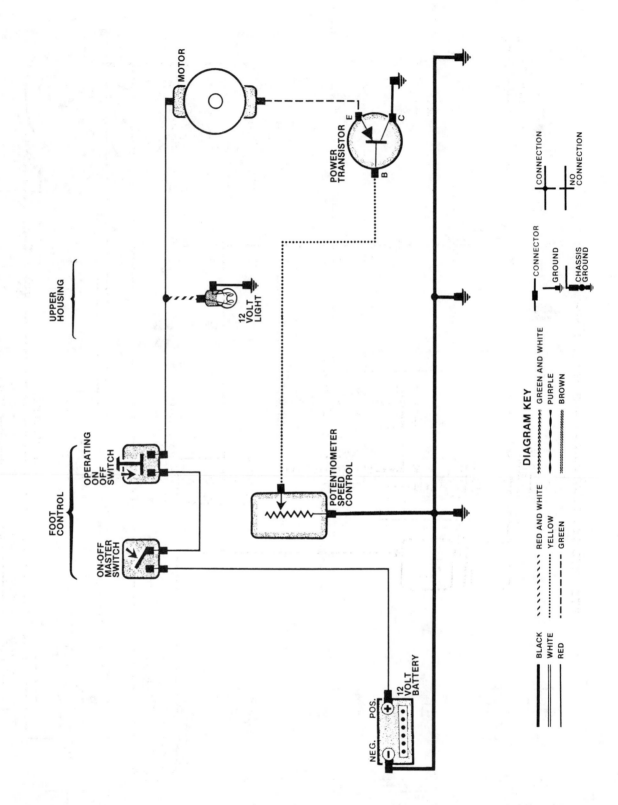

1975-1976 12V ELECTRICAL MOTOR (BOW-MOUNT)

MOTOR

UPPER HOUSING

POWER TRANSISTOR

E   C

B

12 VOLT LIGHT

FOOT CONTROL

OPERATING ON OFF SWITCH

ON-OFF MASTER SWITCH

POTENTIOMETER SPEED CONTROL

NEG.   POS.

12 VOLT BATTERY

DIAGRAM KEY

CONNECTION

NO CONNECTION

CONNECTOR

GROUND

CHASSIS GROUND

GREEN AND WHITE

PURPLE

BROWN

RED AND WHITE

YELLOW

GREEN

BLACK

WHITE

RED

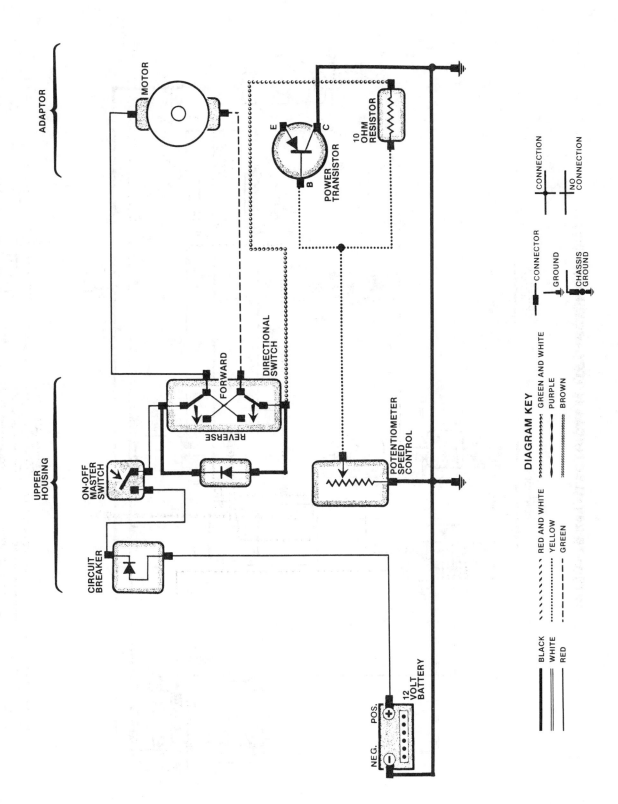

1975-1976 12V ELECTRICAL MOTOR (TRANSOM MOUNT)

1975-1976 24V ELECTRICAL MOTOR (BOW-MOUNT)

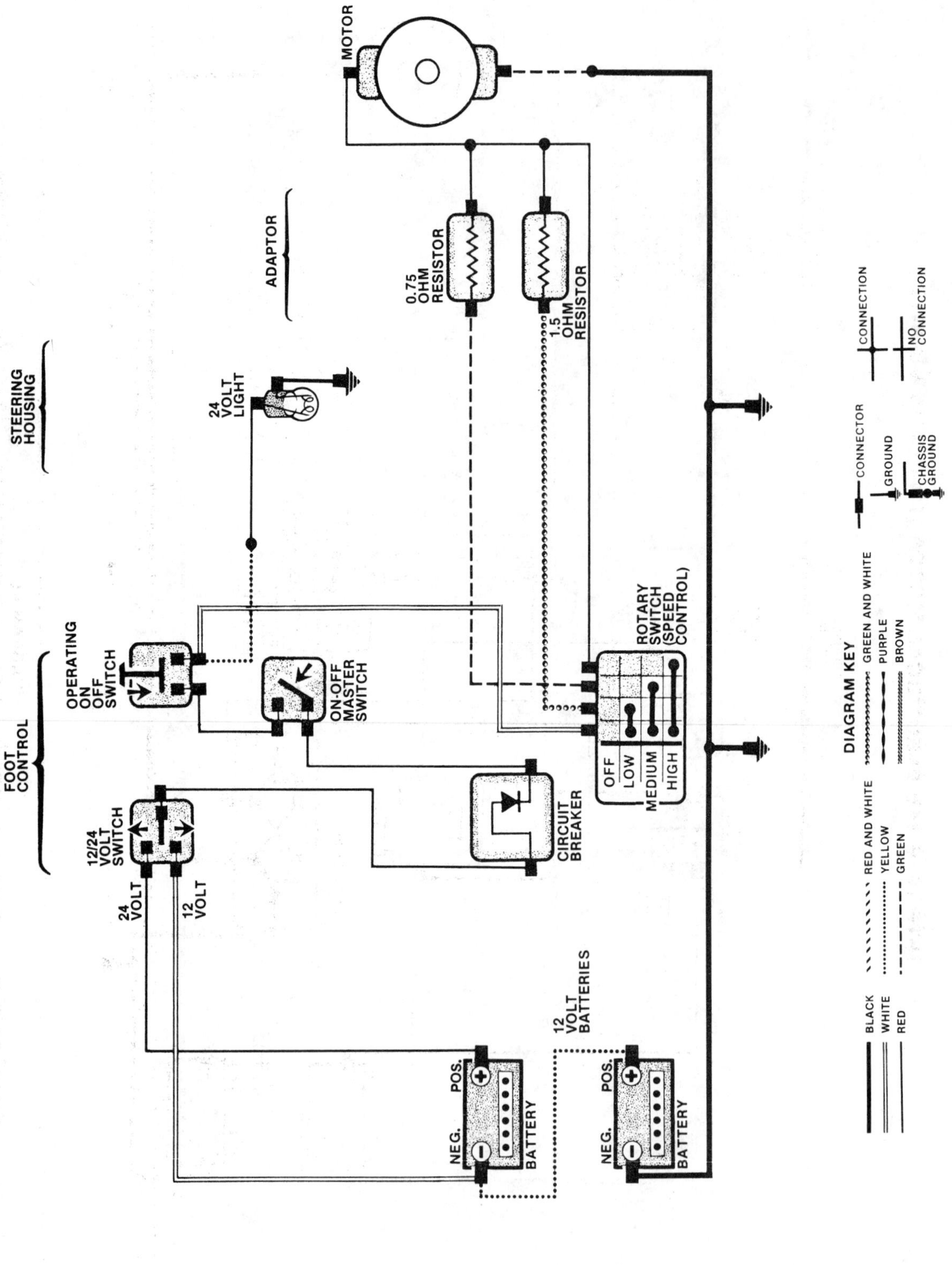

MOTOR

ADAPTOR

STEERING HOUSING

0.75 OHM RESISTOR

1.5 OHM RESISTOR

24 VOLT LIGHT

OPERATING ON OFF SWITCH

ON-OFF MASTER SWITCH

FOOT CONTROL

12/24 VOLT SWITCH

24 VOLT

12 VOLT

CIRCUIT BREAKER

ROTARY SWITCH (SPEED CONTROL)

OFF
LOW
MEDIUM
HIGH

12 VOLT BATTERIES

POS.
NEG.
BATTERY

POS.
NEG.
BATTERY

CONNECTION

NO CONNECTION

CONNECTOR

GROUND

CHASSIS GROUND

DIAGRAM KEY

BLACK

WHITE

RED

RED AND WHITE

YELLOW

GREEN

GREEN AND WHITE

PURPLE

BROWN

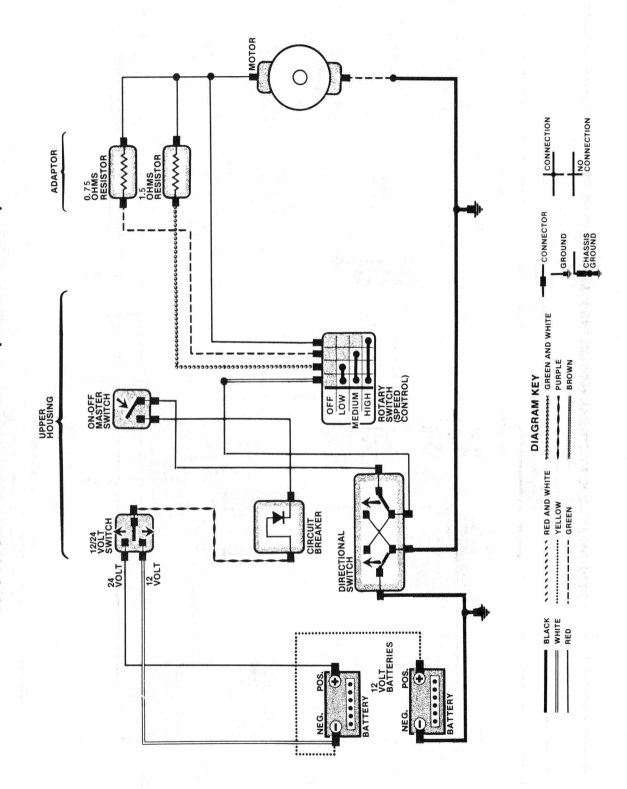

1975-1976 24V ELECTRICAL MOTOR (TRANSOM MOUNT)

MOTOR

ADAPTOR

0.75 OHMS RESISTOR

1.5 OHMS RESISTOR

UPPER HOUSING

ON-OFF MASTER SWITCH

ROTARY SWITCH (SPEED CONTROL)

OFF
LOW
MEDIUM
HIGH

12/24 VOLT SWITCH

24 VOLT

12 VOLT

CIRCUIT BREAKER

DIRECTIONAL SWITCH

12 VOLT BATTERIES

NEG. POS. BATTERY

NEG. POS. BATTERY

DIAGRAM KEY

BLACK
WHITE
RED
RED AND WHITE
YELLOW
GREEN
GREEN AND WHITE
PURPLE
BROWN

CONNECTION

NO CONNECTION

CONNECTOR

GROUND

CHASSIS GROUND

14

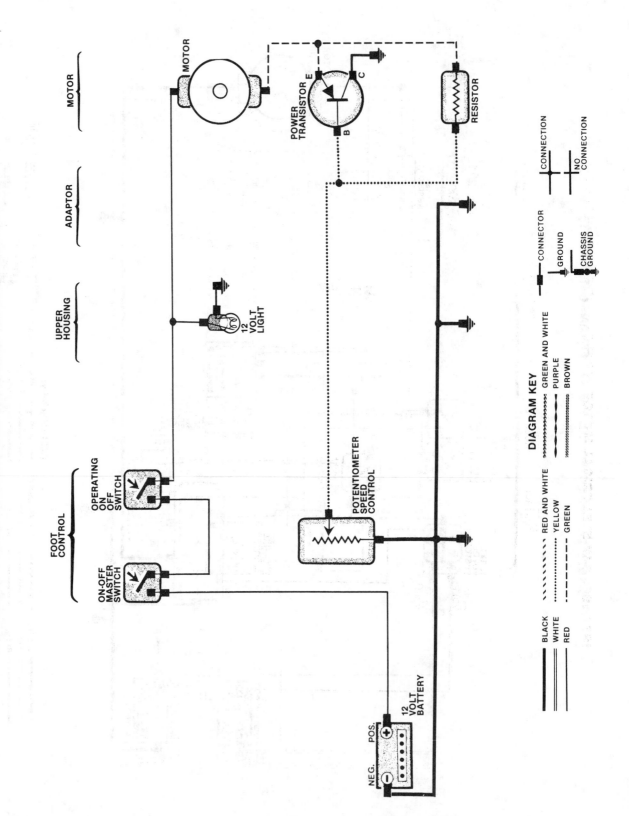

1977-1981 12V ELECTRICAL MOTOR (SPEED-FOOT CONTROLLED)

MOTOR

MOTOR

ADAPTOR

UPPER HOUSING

FOOT CONTROL

OPERATING ON OFF SWITCH

ON-OFF MASTER SWITCH

POWER TRANSISTOR

RESISTOR

12 VOLT LIGHT

POTENTIOMETER SPEED CONTROL

12 VOLT BATTERY

NEG. POS.

DIAGRAM KEY

CONNECTION

NO CONNECTION

CONNECTOR

GROUND

CHASSIS GROUND

BLACK

WHITE

RED

RED AND WHITE

YELLOW

GREEN

GREEN AND WHITE

PURPLE

BROWN

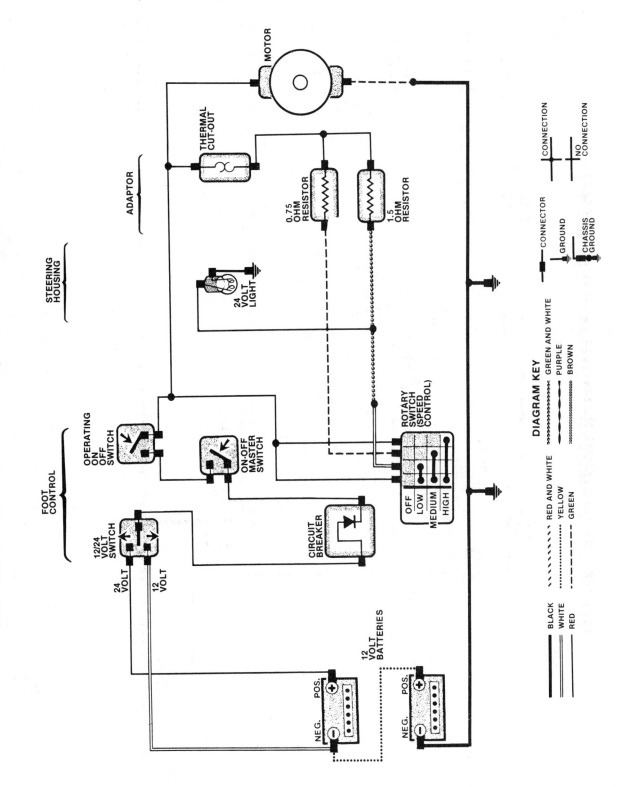

1977-1981 24V ELECTRICAL MOTOR (SPEED-FOOT CONTROLLED)

MOTOR

ADAPTOR

STEERING HOUSING

THERMAL CUT-OUT

0.75 OHM RESISTOR

1.5 OHM RESISTOR

24 VOLT LIGHT

FOOT CONTROL

OPERATING ON OFF SWITCH

ON-OFF MASTER SWITCH

ROTARY SWITCH (SPEED CONTROL)

OFF
LOW
MEDIUM
HIGH

12/24 VOLT SWITCH

24 VOLT

12 VOLT

CIRCUIT BREAKER

12 VOLT BATTERIES

NEG. POS.

NEG. POS.

DIAGRAM KEY

BLACK
WHITE
RED
RED AND WHITE
YELLOW
GREEN
GREEN AND WHITE
PURPLE
BROWN

CONNECTION

NO CONNECTION

CONNECTOR

GROUND

CHASSIS GROUND

14

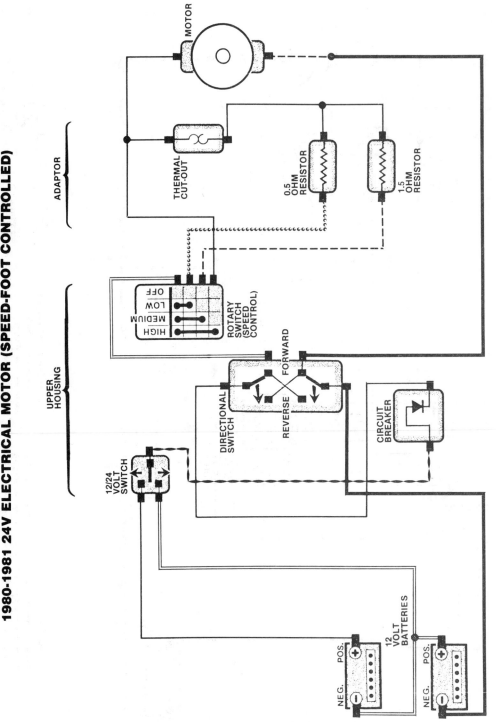

1980-1981 24V ELECTRICAL MOTOR (SPEED-FOOT CONTROLLED)

DIAGRAM KEY

1982-ON 12V ELECTRICAL MOTOR (SPEED-FOOT/HAND CONTROLLED)

MOTOR

ADAPTOR

THERMAL CUT-OUT

0.17 OHM RESISTOR

0.5 OHM RESISTOR

STEERING HOUSING

12 VOLT LIGHT

FOOT CONTROL

OPERATING ON OFF SWITCH

OFF
LOW
MEDIUM
HIGH

ROTARY SWITCH (SPEED CONTROL)

12 VOLT BATTERY

NEG.   POS.

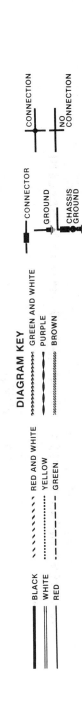

CONNECTION

NO CONNECTION

CONNECTOR

GROUND

CHASSIS GROUND

DIAGRAM KEY

GREEN AND WHITE

PURPLE

BROWN

BLACK

WHITE

RED

RED AND WHITE

YELLOW

GREEN

14

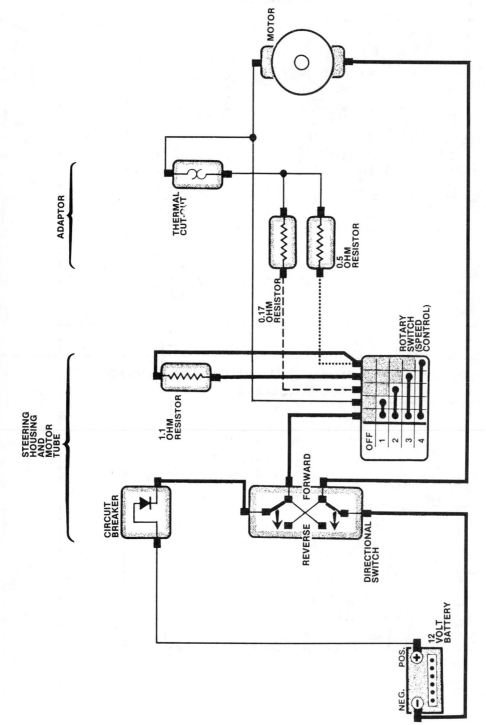

1982-ON 12V ELECTRICAL MOTOR (TRANSOM MOUNT)

DIAGRAM KEY

1982-ON 12/24V ELECTRICAL MOTOR (SPEED-FOOT CONTROLLED)

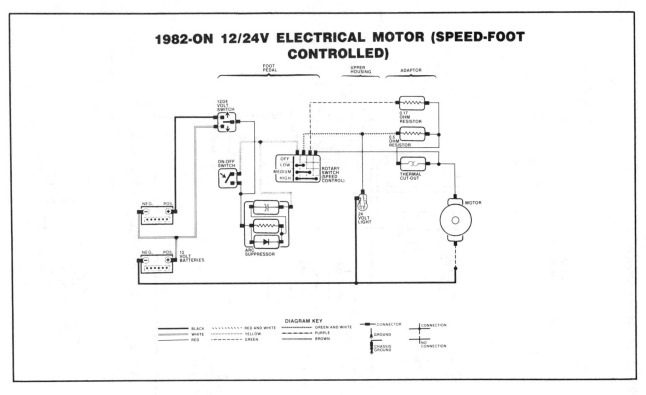

1982-ON 12/24V ELECTRICAL MOTOR (SPEED-HAND CONTROLLED)

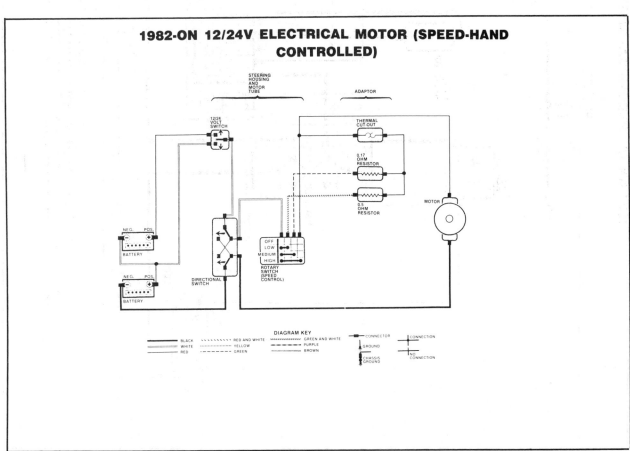

14

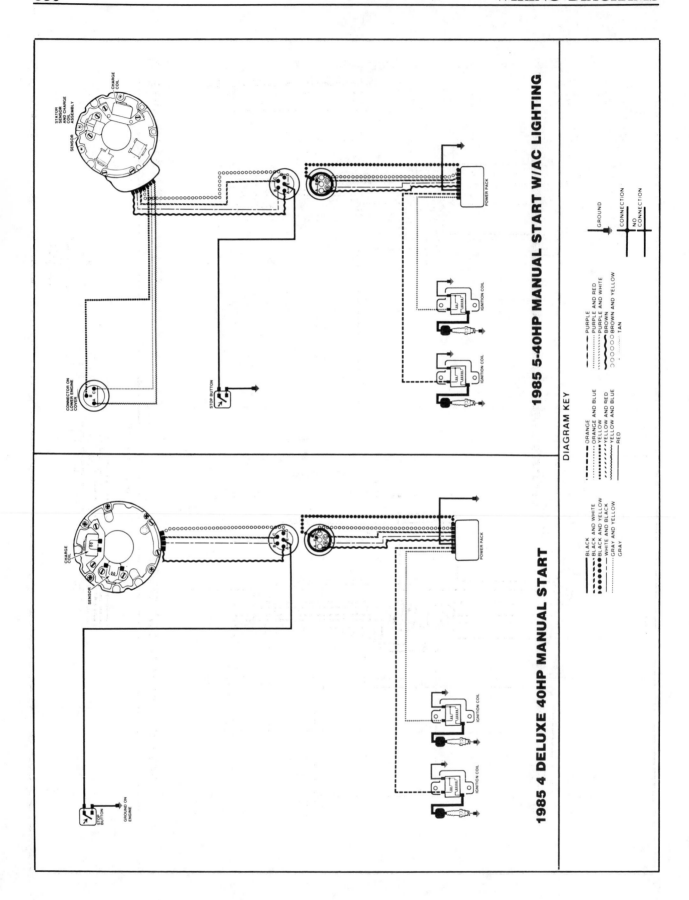

1985 5-40HP MANUAL START W/AC LIGHTING

STATOR SENSOR AND CHARGE COIL ASSEMBLY

CHARGE COIL

SENSOR

CONNECTOR ON LOWER ENGINE COVER

STOP BUTTON

POWER PACK

IGNITION COIL

IGNITION COIL

DIAGRAM KEY

———— BLACK
– – – – BLACK AND WHITE
●●●●● BLACK AND YELLOW
········· WHITE AND BLACK
·········· GRAY AND YELLOW
———— GRAY

———— ORANGE
·········· ORANGE AND BLUE
///// YELLOW
///// YELLOW AND RED
———— YELLOW AND BLUE
———— RED

– – – – PURPLE
·········· PURPLE AND RED
///// PURPLE AND WHITE
∿∿∿∿ BROWN
ooooo BROWN AND YELLOW
———— TAN

⏚ GROUND

╪ CONNECTION

┼ NO CONNECTION

1985 4 DELUXE 40HP MANUAL START

CHARGE COIL

SENSOR

POWER PACK

IGNITION COIL

IGNITION COIL

STOP BUTTON

GROUND ON ENGINE

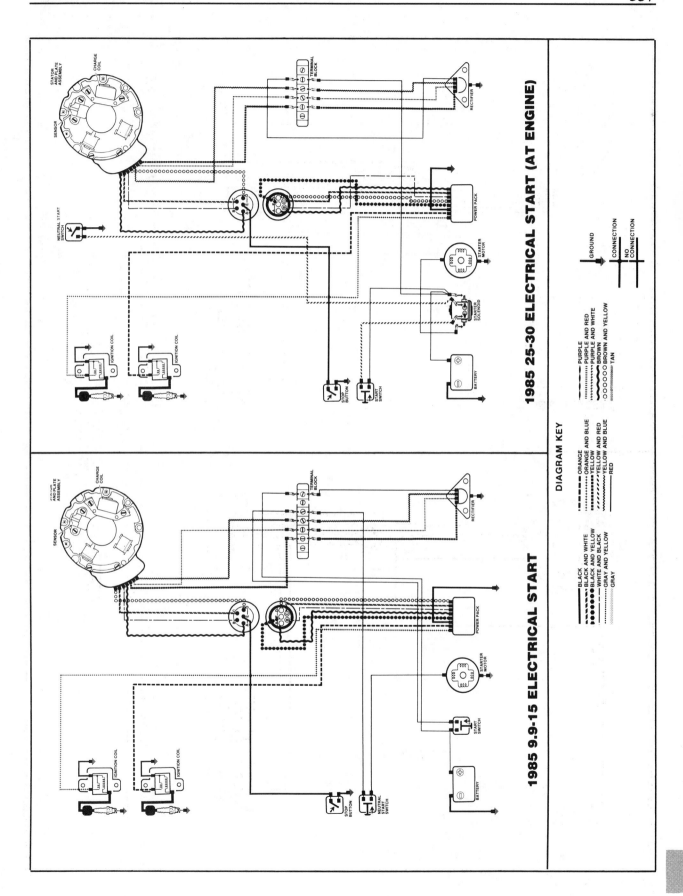

1985 25-30 ELECTRICAL START (AT ENGINE)

1985 9.9-15 ELECTRICAL START

DIAGRAM KEY

14

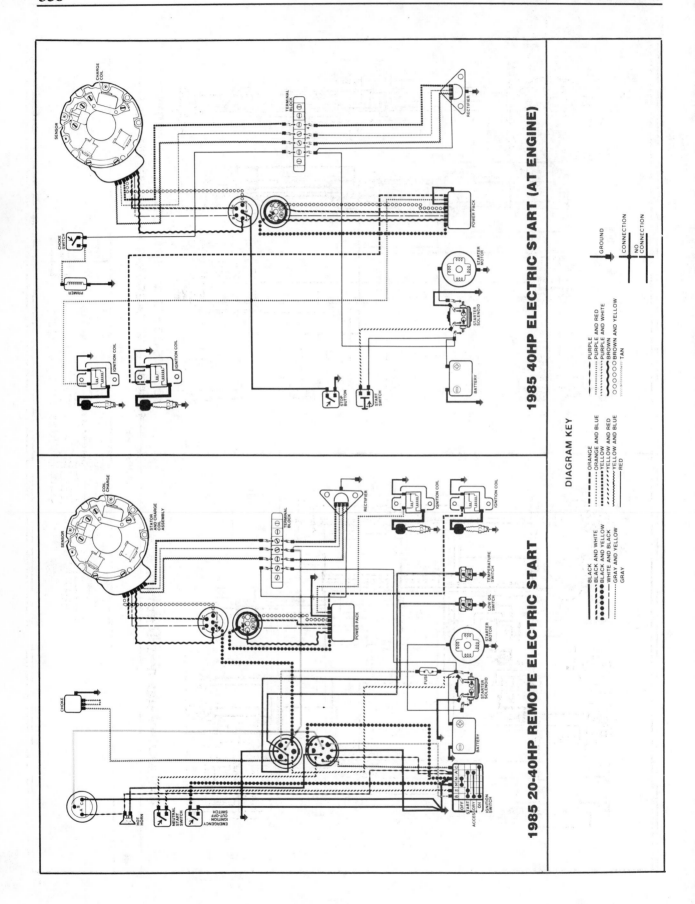

1985 40HP ELECTRIC START (AT ENGINE)

1985 20-40HP REMOTE ELECTRIC START

DIAGRAM KEY

GROUND

CONNECTION

NO CONNECTION

PURPLE
PURPLE AND RED
PURPLE AND WHITE
BROWN
BROWN AND YELLOW
TAN

ORANGE
ORANGE AND BLUE
YELLOW
YELLOW AND RED
YELLOW AND BLUE
RED

BLACK
BLACK AND WHITE
BLACK AND YELLOW
WHITE AND BLACK
GRAY AND YELLOW
GRAY

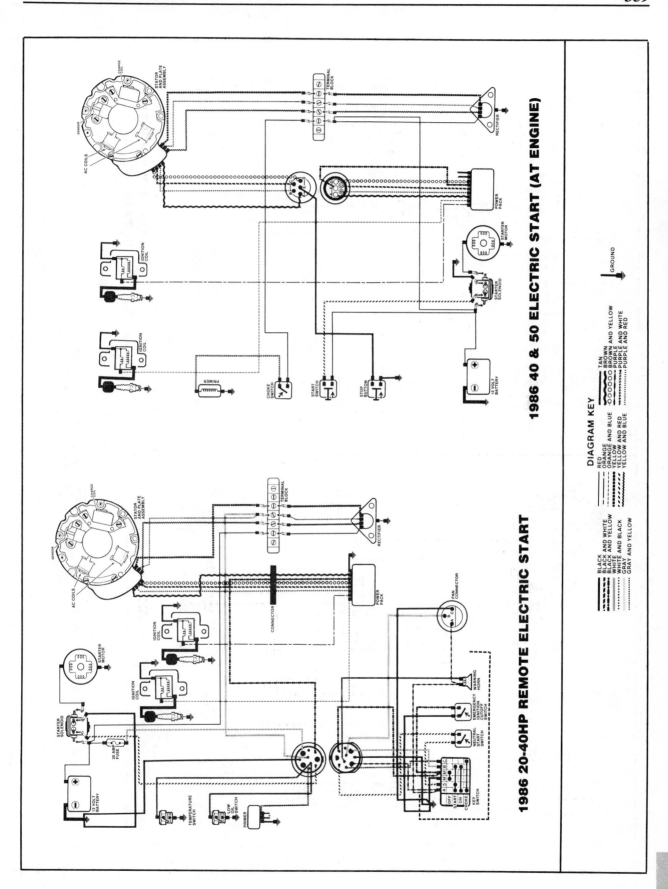

1986 40 & 50 ELECTRIC START (AT ENGINE)

1986 20-40HP REMOTE ELECTRIC START

DIAGRAM KEY

RED
ORANGE
ORANGE AND BLUE
YELLOW
YELLOW AND RED
YELLOW AND BLUE

TAN
BROWN
BROWN AND YELLOW
PURPLE AND WHITE
PURPLE AND RED

BLACK
BLACK AND WHITE
BLACK AND YELLOW
WHITE AND BLACK
GRAY
GRAY AND YELLOW

GROUND

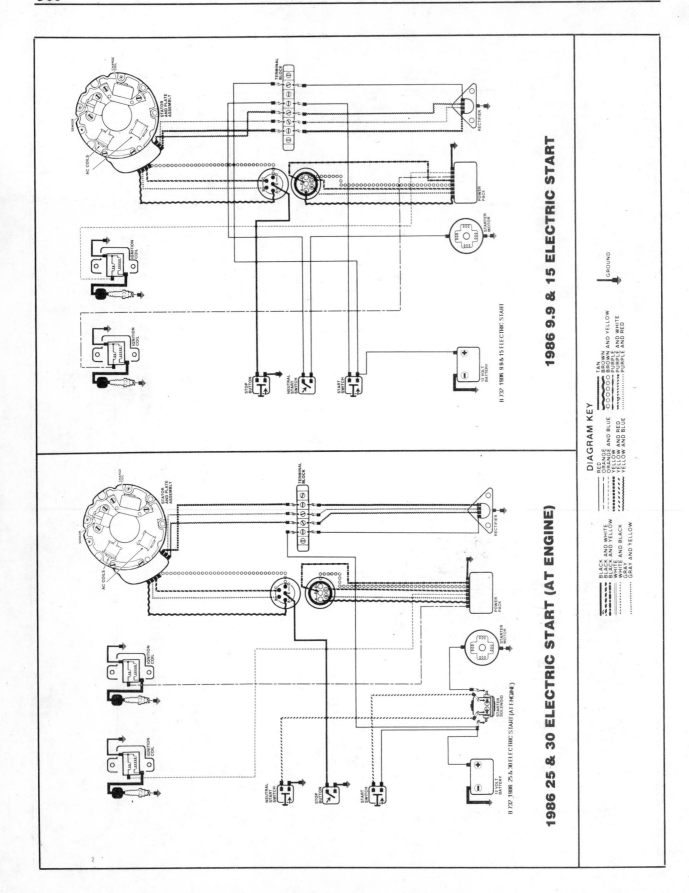

1986 9.9 & 15 ELECTRIC START

1986 25 & 30 ELECTRIC START (AT ENGINE)

DIAGRAM KEY